DATE DUE

Critical Essays on
REYNOLDS PRICE

CRITICAL ESSAYS
ON
AMERICAN LITERATURE

James Nagel, General Editor
University of Georgia, Athens

Critical Essays on
REYNOLDS PRICE

edited by

JAMES A. SCHIFF

G. K. Hall & Co.
An Imprint of Simon & Schuster Macmillan
New York

Prentice Hall International
London   Mexico City   New Delhi   Singapore   Sydney   Toronto

G. K. Hall & Co.
An Imprint of Simon & Schuster Macmillan
1633 Broadway
New York, NY 10019

Library of Congress Cataloging-in-Publication Data

Critical essays on Reynolds Price / edited by James A. Schiff.
    p.   cm. — (Critical essays on American literature)
   Includes bibliographical references and index.
   ISBN 0-7838-0074-6 (alk. paper)
   1. Price, Reynolds, 1933– —Criticism and interpretation.
 I. Schiff, James A., 1958– . II. Series.
 PS3566.R54Z62   1998
 813'.54—dc21   97-39394
                                        CIP

This paper meets the requirements of ANSI/NISO Z3948-1992 (Permanence of Paper).

10 9 8 7 6 5 4 3 2 1

Printed in the United States of America

For Hayden and Walker

Contents

ESSAYS

General Editor's Note

♦

This series seeks to anthologize the most important criticism on a wide variety of topics and writers in American literature. Our readers will find in various volumes not only a generous selection of reprinted articles and reviews but original essays, bibliographies, manuscript selections, and other materials brought to public attention for the first time. This volume, *Critical Essays on Reynolds Price,* is the most comprehensive gathering of essays ever published on one of the most important modern writers in the United States. It contains both a sizable gathering of early reviews and a broad selection of more modern scholarship. Among the authors of reprinted articles and reviews are Anne Tyler, Fred Chappell, Eudora Welty, Simone Vauthier, Robert Alter, Rosellen Brown, and Anthony Burgess. In addition to a substantial introduction by James A. Schiff, there are three original essays commissioned specifically for publication in this volume, new studies by Doris Betts, Michael Kreyling, and Allen Shepherd. There are also reminiscences published here for the first time by Toni Morrison, Stephen Spender, and James Taylor and Kathryn Walker, along with a tribute by James Dickey. We are confident that this book will make a permanent and significant contribution to the study of American literature.

JAMES NAGEL
University of Georgia

Publisher's Note

◆

Producing a volume that contains both newly commissioned and reprinted material presents the publisher with the challenge of balancing the desire to achieve stylistic consistency with the need to preserve the integrity of works first published elsewhere. In the Critical Essays series, essays commissioned especially for a particular volume are edited to be consistent with G. K. Hall's house style; reprinted essays appear in the style in which they were first published, with only typographical errors corrected. Consequently, shifts in style from one essay to another are the result of our efforts to be faithful to each text as it was originally published.

Acknowledgments

♦

I wish to thank Melissa Delbridge and the Special Collections Library at Duke University; the interlibrary loan staff at Langsam Library at the University of Cincinnati; Daniel L. Daily, William King, and the Duke University Archives. I am indebted to Charles Guggenheim and Guggenheim Productions for their assistance in my acquisition of transcripts of interviews from the Guggenheim film *Clear Pictures*. Additional thanks go to the Center for Documentary Studies at Duke University, the Lyndhurst Foundation, Toni Morrison, James Taylor, Kathryn Walker, Natasha Spender, Suzanne Marrs, Michael Kreyling, Allen Shepherd, Doris Betts, James Nagel, Beth Schiff, Robert and Adele Schiff, and Agnes Hiance. Finally, special thanks go to Reynolds Price, who answered questions, made telephone calls, and was always helpful and encouraging. In spite of such wonderful assistance from so many individuals, the responsibility for accuracy in the text is solely mine.

Introduction

James A. Schiff

Overview

Reynolds Price is probably the finest living southern novelist and, perhaps, the most significant southern man of letters of the latter half of the twentieth century. Since the 1962 publication of his award-winning first novel, *A Long and Happy Life,* which was translated into 14 languages and has never been out of print, Price has been a visible presence in American letters, and he has gone on to publish 28 more volumes, the majority of which have drawn great praise and respect. Though known primarily for his novels, Price is also a short-story writer, poet, playwright, essayist, translator, and memoirist, and unlike others who have tried their hand widely, Price has proven himself competent, sometimes even brilliant, in each genre to which he has turned. The accolades bestowed on his novels are, of course, well known: Michael Kreyling, for instance, has spoken of *The Surface of Earth* as "one of the more significant American novels of the twentieth century."[1] However, the interest in and high appreciation for his work in other areas—Price has been variously described as a significant figure in no less than a half-dozen genres[2]—has yet to be felt and acknowledged by the critical community. One who is knowledgeable about Price and his oeuvre, Stephen Spender, has compared Price to Hemingway and Joyce and has stated, "He ranks very high, with Eudora Welty and, I suppose, Faulkner."[3]

Though Price has often resisted, and rightfully so, the prejudices and narrow labeling that sometimes come with the tag "southern writer," he has nevertheless spent nearly his entire life in the South and set most of his fiction there. Born in the small rural Piedmont town of Macon, North Carolina, on 1 February 1933, Price spent his childhood in a variety of small North Carolina towns, living with his parents (and later a younger brother), with whom he developed an unusually close relationship. Though his artistic nature led to occasional isolation and torment from his peers, Price found a niche in the classroom, where he excelled—first at Broughton High School in Raleigh, then at nearby Duke University, where he was an Angier B. Duke scholar. Though he would go on to win a Rhodes scholarship and spend three years at Oxford University (England), Price would return to his Piedmont roots in 1958 to teach in the English department at Duke, where he has remained ever since. Teaching courses in writing, Milton, and more recently the Gospels as literature, Price has influenced a range of student writers, including Anne Tyler, Fred Chappell, Josephine Humphreys, David Guy, and Charlie Smith. Says Price of his decision to spend his life within 60 miles of the home in which he was born, "This part of North Carolina is where 95 percent of my emotional intensity has been grounded. My early childhood familial experiences, all my later intense emotional experiences have occurred here. . . . Also, from my point of view, I'm the world's authority on this place. It's the place about which I have perfect pitch."[4]

Despite his small-town background and rural lifestyle—Price lives surrounded by woods in Orange County, between Durham and Chapel Hill—there is conversely a cosmopolitanism and cultural intellectualism to his character. For instance, Price speaks knowingly of opera as well as of classical music and painting; he has written long essays on Rembrandt and Milton and has taught himself Koine Greek in order to translate the Gospels; he is an avid and knowledgeable traveler, familiar with the neighborhoods of New York City as well as Jerusalem. What is interesting about Price's work is that a reader of a novel like *A Long and Happy Life* or *Kate Vaiden* would have little sense that the novelist spent several years at Oxford writing a thesis on Milton's *Samson Agonistes,* or that he can quote from Italian and German operas. Though Price is knowledgeable on a range of issues, he does not necessarily broadcast this in his fiction, much of which covers the lives of untutored working-class secretaries, mechanics, and salesmen from central and eastern North Carolina. Because his intellectual sensibility is so versatile and far reaching, Price is able to write discerningly of southern family cooking as well as of the work of Henry James, depict homosexual love as well as heterosexual desire, and write convincingly from a woman's perspective as well as from a man's. In many respects Price is that rare writer who has bridged those gaps separating male and female, homo- and heterosexual, black and white, intellectual and commoner.

One of the reasons for Price's great success is his ability to modulate his voice. Sounding like no one else in contemporary American fiction, Price is capable of generating a range of memorable, highly charged voices, from the southern colloquial rhythms of *Kate Vaiden* and *Blue Calhoun* to the biblical, almost oracular tones found in *Permanent Errors* and *The Surface of Earth.* In a recent interview, John Updike, lamenting the decline of the oral tradition in America, states, "[I]n a writer like Reynolds Price you still have that yarning feeling. He's somebody who's trying to push words into your ear as much as trying to push images into your visual cortex."[5] The same can be said of Price's speaking voice, which strikes observers as his most distinct and arresting personal characteristic. Though he has been confined to a wheelchair since 1984 (the result of a battle with cancer of the spinal cord), what one tends to notice about Price is not so much his paraplegia but rather that same characteristic that is most distinctive in his fiction: his voice. Interviewers and journalists have continually made reference to Price's "rich baritone,"[6] which has made him popular on the lecture circuit, in the classroom, and in various forums of media (in recent years Price has been hired by National Public Radio to broadcast personal commentaries, and PBS as well as the Museum of Modern Art have commissioned him to narrate film and audiotape). Given Price's vocal abilities, one is not surprised to discover that his novels have been called psalmodic, melodic, and harmonious; that Price has written songs with singer/songwriter James Taylor;[7] that his trilogy of plays, *New Music,* has been described as literal music, "a score for voices";[8] that Price has had a long and deep interest in operatic soprano voices, particularly that of Leontyne Price; or that Price and Samuel Barber in the early 1960s discussed collaborating on an opera about the life of Pocahontas.

Literary Career and Reviews

Price's debut as a novelist was impressive. His first novel, *A Long and Happy Life,* which traces the troubled love of Rosacoke Mustian and Wesley Beavers, was published in its entirety in the April 1962 issue of *Harper's,* and in cloth by Atheneum in March of 1962. The novel received overwhelmingly positive reviews; it also won the William Faulkner Foundation and Sir Walter Raleigh Awards and went on to sell more than a million copies. It was an auspicious start to a literary career, catapulting Price almost overnight to the rank of significant American novelist; yet conversely the success created a difficult critical environment for his future work: expectations were now unusually high, and for some critics Price would spend the next two decades failing to match the artistic success of his first novel.

The original dust jacket for *A Long and Happy Life* contained extensive praise from Eudora Welty, Harper Lee, Lord David Cecil, and Spender; and Price, at the time relatively unpublished, was compared to major literary figures of the twentieth century and heralded for his "astonishing gifts" and "genius." Reviewers almost unanimously agreed with this prepublication chorus of distinguished British and southern writers. Granville Hicks in the *Saturday Review* called the novel "a love story, and one of the simplest and most poignant I have ever read."[9] Catharine Hughes in *Commonweal* wrote, "*A Long and Happy Life* is considerably beyond being merely a good first novel. . . . [I]t is a mature and beautifully flowing work."[10] And Dorothy Parker in *Esquire* wrote, "Meticulously observed, beautifully told, it strikes too deep to fuss around with analysis. You can say only of it that it is indeed a lasting novel . . . a lovely novel."[11] Price was praised for his rich colloquial prose style and his powers of observation, both of which enabled him to generate a real and fixed sense of place. Yet perhaps his finest achievement in *A Long and Happy Life* was to create the work's heroine, Rosacoke Mustian. In the words

of Hicks, one of the more important critics in promoting the early Price, "To
have created Rosacoke Mustian is an achievement that the most mature novelist might envy."[12]

Few negative reviews of the novel appeared. Those that did tended to
view the writing as overstylized and Price as simply a Faulkner imitator—criticisms that would hound Price for the subsequent two decades. As to the former charge, Spender, who read an early draft of the novel, explained 30 years
later, "[I]ts most striking quality was the extreme self-consciousness of the
writer"—a fact that tended to polarize readers. Though Spender was one of
the novel's great admirers, he stated how some early readers were appalled:
"*A Long and Happy Life* perhaps struck my colleagues as being almost artificial . . . and it aroused a very strong reaction, sometimes of antipathy. . . . I
happen to know that it was offered to Random House, and I think that Jason
Epstein said he'd resign from Random House sooner than publish this. So
anyhow this showed the tremendous force behind the personality of the writing."[13] As to the second charge, Whitney Balliett in the *New Yorker* referred
to the novel's long opening sentence as "garble," "written in imitation of
Faulkner—a wearisome and hopeless style."[14] Though winning the Faulkner
Award was an early boon for Price, it ironically added to the perception that
Faulkner was a significant influence. It would take critics years to see, largely
at Price's prompting, that the Bible, Milton, Tolstoy, and Eudora Welty were
his primary literary influences. And if one wished to locate, in Price's words,
"the truest list of a novelist's influences," it would be "a list not of other artists
however grand but of private names," mostly family members.[15]

Price's next two books—a collection of stories, *The Names and Faces of
Heroes* (1963), and a novel, *A Generous Man* (1966)—also received much critical praise, though the tone was slightly less enthusiastic than it had been for
A Long and Happy Life. Of the characters from *The Names and Faces of Heroes,*
William Barrett wrote, "Out of their simplicity [Price] is able to distill a wonder and awe at the most commonplace situations of life."[16] Barrett's remark
employed one of the two most commonly used terms to describe Price's story
collection (terms used pervasively also in reviews of *A Long and Happy Life*):
simple and *southern.* Paul Pickrel in *Harper's* called attention to Price's "simple
people"; Hicks referred to Price's "simplicity"; the reviewer in *TLS* wrote of
Price's "simple, earthy themes" in a review entitled "Southern Folk"; and
Barrett went on to cite Price's ability to "convey feeling so simply."[17] Though
the term *simple* was almost unanimously laudatory—critics were greatly
impressed with Price's ability to write so powerfully about seemingly unex-
traordinary events and people—Richard Gilman in the *New York Times Book
Review* offered a dissenting opinion, arguing that the stories "suffer from the
very ease of their conception and execution." Gilman used the term *southern*
no less than six times in his review, chiding Price for being "the typical
Southern writer" and for producing what "sounds to us like a parody of
Southern writing."[18] However, in perhaps the most interesting review of *The*

Names and Faces of Heroes, R. G. G. Price in *Punch* answered Gilman's charge by suggesting that Price's decision to write about rural southern life demonstrated not simply "dilute Faulkner, adrip with Southern charm" but rather "a mind sufficiently independent not to avoid material because other writers may have used it for banalities."[19]

With the publication of *A Generous Man* most of the comments about Price's "simplicity" ceased, largely because the novel employed the most complex plot found in any of his works. Described as a story of "exuberant good humor,"[20] *A Generous Man* received positive reviews, and Price's introduction of the mythical as well as the supernatural was mostly applauded. Those critical of *A Generous Man* again focused on how the novel seemed typically southern and how Price was derivative of Faulkner.

Price's first three books accounted for what some have called his "Mustian period," Mustian being the rural North Carolina family that dominated his fiction from the time he wrote "A Chain of Love" in 1955 to the publication of *A Generous Man* in 1966. Based on the rural farm children Price had encountered in his youth, the Mustians were popular with readers. In fact, more than 30 years later, Rosacoke Mustian is still the Price heroine many readers best remember and most often associate with the author. Though Price took a radical step away from the Mustians after 1966, he returned to them on two later occasions: in 1977 he published a dramatic version of *A Long and Happy Life,* entitled *Early Dark;* and in 1988 he published *Good Hearts,* a novel continuing the story of Rosacoke and Wesley.

The publication of Price's next two books—a novel, *Love and Work* (1968), and a collection of stories, *Permanent Errors* (1970)—marked a new phase in his writing and revealed a departure in character, tone, and style. Price's characters were no longer the rural farm children he had encountered in his youth; rather, his protagonist in these works was most often a well-educated and highly self-conscious writer. Unlike the earlier works, these two volumes gave the impression of being more closely autobiographical. In addition, they were darker and graver than the earlier writings. One wonders whether the wide acceptance of his earlier works, along with the appreciative and even occasionally saccharine reviews, pushed Price toward a darker and more personal fiction.[21] Finally, Price's style, particularly as he turned toward reading and translating biblical narrative during this period, became spare, dense, and severe. As Michael Kreyling later explained, "The style of the prose becomes almost hieroglyphic; image, symbol, scene, dialogue, are set flush against each other with a minimum of prosaic mortar and ornament."[22]

Because these two volumes were more peculiar and disturbing than Price's earlier works, they failed to elicit the same enthusiastic popular response. Geoffrey Wolff condemned *Love and Work* for its language, "grotesquely swollen and vainglorious," and asked, "What has gone so wrong with Reynolds Price?"[23] For many, *Love and Work* seemed literary, pretentious, controlled, overwritten, excessively spare, and gratuitously dark. Yet the reviews were still more favorable than not, and a small group of critics viewed the transformation in Price's work as a bold step forward. Francis King in the *London Telegraph* wrote, "Mr. Price has always struck me as a highly talented writer; but the skill with which he dovetails diary entries, childhood recollections, letters and even a poem to make an immaculate work of art suggests something brighter than talent."[24] Louis D. Rubin Jr., describing the novel in the *Washington Star* as "one of the most interesting explanations of the nature and relationship of art and love ever written," saw the transition from the Mustians to Thomas Eborn as a "confirmation" of Price's "considerable range and depth."[25]

Permanent Errors found a similar reception, strengthening the perception that Price was not, as *A Long and Happy Life* had suggested to some readers, simply an author of pastoral romances but instead an extraordinarily versatile writer, capable of producing, among other things, dark, private, highly enigmatic works. The difficulty of these stories—as John Hazard Wildman wrote in the *Southern Review*, "Price is not kind to readers. He puts them to work"[26]—arose from their intensely personal nature, their bleakness and anxiety, their laconic mysteriousness, and Price's heavily chiseled prose. Many reviewers praised Price's craftsmanship and courage (to confront such emotional pain), yet even some who applauded the collection regarded it as "an interim production," the end of "a long grueling phase in Price's career."[27] One of the more noteworthy remarks came from Guy Davenport, who wrote in the *New York Times Book Review*, "*Permanent Errors* must take its place as a pivotal book in our literary history, as one of the brave steps beyond the fiercely Calvinist pessimism of Southern writing in general."[28] Finally, Theodore Solotaroff's review in *Saturday Review* was important in demonstrating how Price had broken with, essentially outgrown, the southern pastoral tradition (and with it any ties to Faulkner).[29]

The culmination of Price's second phase of writing, which extended from 1967 to 1984, was the publication of the first two volumes of his Mayfield trilogy, entitled collectively *A Great Circle* and individually *The Surface of Earth* (1975), *The Source of Light* (1981), and *The Promise of Rest* (1995). Price had begun work on *The Surface of Earth* as early as 1961 but was "balked" in his attempt for more than a decade.[30] When the most ambitious of Price's novels finally appeared in 1975, the reviews were again polarized, from sublime praise to scathing rejection. On the positive side, Robert Ostermann viewed *The Surface of Earth* as "Homeric" and referred to it as the new "standard" for the family saga that thus "demonstrate[d] how these things should be done."[31] Fred Chappell wrote of the novel's "grand design" and "Homeric sense of time" and called it "the most ambitious American novel since the earlier works of James Jones and William Styron."[32] And Michael Brondoli wrote that the novel "reveals every authentic mark of a work that will stand for a good long while, one of our deepest plotted soundings of human grief."[33] A few years later several critics would rank *The Surface of Earth* as one of the more significant American novels of the century.[34]

Yet in a review that appeared on the front page of the *New York Times Book Review* (and that apparently played some role, both positive and negative, in many subsequent responses), Gilman attacked the novel for being "old-fashioned," referring to it as "a great lumbering archaic beast," "a mastodon sprung to life from beneath an ice-field."[35] Gilman's point, which stood as a culmination of the early sort of criticism denigrating Price for being a *southern* writer, was that a semirealistic novel dealing with family life and obsessive love in the South had already been written so often that it had become extinct. Gilman's review sparked response from several writers and critics, including Eudora Welty, who sent an angry letter to the editor of the *Times*. Other reviewers criticized the novel, for its length, its formal and artificial prose, its contrived grand scheme, and the similar-sounding voices of the characters. Though nearly all of these criticisms had some merit, Price, it would appear, had crafted a work that had more in common with the Bible and Milton, both of which might elicit similar criticism, than with contemporary postmodern fiction.

Like *The Surface of Earth, The Source of Light*, Price's next novel and the second installment of the Mayfield trilogy, received mixed reviews. Some critics were plainly losing interest in Price. For those who preferred the colloquial southern pastoral of *A Long and Happy Life*, Price had spent nearly 20 years failing to produce any work equal to his first success. Writing in the *Saturday Review*, Benjamin De Mott echoed an old cry by placing Price once again beneath "the spreading shade of the great Faulkner tree" and then concluding, "[W]hat's missing is the quality of freshness and surprise that makes novels novel."[36] For a small group of critics, however, Price continued to be a master craftsman who wrote serious, fashion-resistant literature. Joyce Carol Oates called *The Source of Light* "a somber, rather beautifully muted work," and Gail Godwin wrote, "Reynolds Price, in the magnificent accomplishment of these two novels, has fulfilled critic C. Hugh Holman's criteria for the outstanding Southern novels of past and present. He has sought a pattern in the past, evolved a meaning out of large sweeps of history, converted the pattern of events into myth, and somehow managed to unite the sense of tragic dignity with the irony of comedy."[37]

The Source of Light was followed by *Vital Provisions*, Price's first volume of poetry, which had taken several decades to surface. Though he had been writing poetry since high school and had been publishing in journals and in limited editions from small private presses, Price waited until 1982, when he was nearly 50, to assemble his verse in a volume. Though William H. Pritchard found the poems lacking in form, "flat . . . and too often bathed in the general aura of reverence," most critics offered qualified praise.[38] George Garrett called *Vital Provisions* "an impressive collection" and Price a "richly gifted

Southern poet," and Suzanne Juhasz wrote, "Price's poems are literate and clean, with, at their best, an astringent aftertaste."[39] Finally, John Hollander wrote, "Verse by novelists is sometimes jotted with the left hand, sometimes only a matter of juvenilia abandoned and later resurrected. Reynolds Price's poems are a different matter." He then added that *Vital Provisions* "has an interesting, problematic relation to the world of his novels."[40]

This second phase of Price's writing, extending from 1967 to 1984, has been called his "stoic" period,[41] though the term *self-reflective* may more accurately define these years. The central characters in Price's major works of fiction during this period—Thomas Eborn, Charles Tamplin, Hutch Mayfield—were rather introspective writers who, although not Price himself, bore a certain resemblance to the author. In addition to the works of fiction he produced during these years, Price fully established himself as a man of letters by publishing a volume of essays, *Things Themselves* (1972); a play, *Early Dark* (1977); a volume of biblical translations, *A Palpable God* (1978); the previously mentioned volume of poetry, *Vital Provisions* (1982); and a commissioned television play, *Private Contentment* (1984). Generally speaking, reviews of these other volumes were positive. For instance, *A Palpable God,* which displays Price's desire to draw closer to the more primitive urges at the heart of storytelling, drew praise from Anthony Burgess and Frank Kermode, and the volume went on to receive a National Book Award nomination for translation. Writing in the *New York Times Book Review,* Burgess stated that Price's introductory essay on the aims and origins of narrative "from now on must be required reading in creative writing courses."[42] Despite his many successful forays outside of fiction, however, Price at this point in his career was still regarded primarily as a novelist.

The next phase of Price's writing was signaled by the most dramatic change in his life. In the late spring of 1984, when he was approximately one-third finished with the manuscript of *Kate Vaiden,* Price began experiencing problems walking. After entering Duke Hospital for tests, he soon learned of a "pencil-thick and gray-colored" tumor, 10 inches long and cancerous, which was "intricately braided in the core of [his] spinal cord."[43] Following immediate surgery and heavy doses of radiation, Price became a paraplegic, confined to a wheelchair and dependent on multiple prescription drugs. It took two further radical surgeries in 1986, along with biofeedback and hypnosis to relieve the intense pain, before Price was able to return to a productive and "relatively" normal life of writing, teaching, and travel.

Initially the illness prevented Price from writing, but after receiving a commission in the fall of 1984 from Hendrix College in Arkansas to compose a play, he began a prolific burst that has yet to cease and that he attributes to three causes: decreased time spent performing life's chores, now that he has employed an assistant; sublimation of sexual energy into his work; and acquisition of a word processor. Though Price maintains that the imminence of his own mortality has not had much of an impact on his increased production, one surmises this may have been an additional factor.[44] In the subsequent 11 years (1986–1997), Price published 16 books: 5 novels, 2 volumes of memoir, 3 volumes of poetry, 2 collections of plays, 2 collections of stories, a collection of essays, and a volume of biblical translations and essays. By comparison, the "old Price," though never a slow worker, took 22 years (1962–1984) to publish his first 13 volumes.

In addition to writing faster, Price, in the eyes of many, was also writing better. *Kate Vaiden* (1986) won the National Book Critics Circle Award and became Price's most commercially and critically successful novel since *A Long and Happy Life*. The primary explanation for the novel's success was its voice; as Rosellen Brown wrote in her front-page review in the *New York Times Book Review*, "[T]he voice of Mr. Price's heroine blows like fresh air across the page."[45] With Kate, Price created an inviting, appealing, forgiving, and spirited voice—a vast departure from the omniscient narrators of his preceding three novels, each of which could sound at times austere, solemn, detached, and even oracular. In addition, with *Kate Vaiden* Price returned for the first time since *A Long and Happy Life* to a central female character—the female psyche and voice being, in the eyes of many critics, a particular strength of his. Michiko Kakutani in the *New York Times* wrote, "At once tender and frightening, lyrical and dramatic, [*Kate Vaiden*] is the product of a storyteller working at the full height of his artistic powers."[46] And across the Atlantic Ocean, Jonathan Keates wrote in the *Observer*, "Reynolds Price ought to be as well known and admired among us as Updike or Bellow. That he isn't may have something to do with the gentleness and detachment of his authorial voice."[47]

The triumph of *Kate Vaiden* was followed by a string of successful productions, and interestingly, of the 16 new Price volumes published between 1986 and 1997, only 5 were novels. During this period, Price established himself as one of contemporary America's most esteemed and versatile men of letters. Like John Updike and Joyce Carol Oates, Price turned to short fiction, poetry, drama, essay, and memoir (in addition, he tried his hand at translation), and for the most part he was praised for his work in these other genres.

The two volumes of poetry Price published during this time,[48] *The Laws of Ice* (1986) and *The Use of Fire* (1990), largely elicited the same mixed reception he first found as a poet with *Vital Provisions*. These volumes—which contain elegies, lyrics, sonnets, and dramatic monologues, as well as Price's verse diary ("Days and Nights") chronicling his battle with cancer—were viewed by some critics as "uneven," and Price was criticized for being "pedantic and uninvolving" and for writing poetry that, largely because of its narrative thrust, reads less like poetry than like "wonderful prose."[49] Yet Price received praise for his "narrative velocity," for his "clear and startling" images, and for his personal, autobiographical poems, particularly "A Heaven for Elizabeth Rodwell, My Mother."[50] Ashley Brown called *The Use of Fire* "one of the most attractive books of poetry to have been published in 1990."[51] Dan Brown saw the volume as "a commanding achievement" and wrote, "[H]ow about some increased critical recognition for the poetry of Reynolds Price? (No fair holding his novelizing against him.)"[52] Perhaps the gulf separating Price's admirers from his detractors was best articulated by Robert B. Shaw in his review of *The Laws of Ice* in *Poetry.* Viewing Price as an unusual poet of "strange works," Shaw wrote, "[I]t is no denigration to say that we don't read his poems in the way we read most poetry." Shaw believed Price was "exercising his skills as a novelist in verse": "we are caught up in the narrative velocity and the imposing scale of his conceptions" rather than in the "fine turns of phrase," he said, and he concluded, "[P]oets . . . could learn a lot from studying this gifted interloper."[53]

The dramatic works Price published (and saw produced) during this period likewise received mixed reviews, though again the positive outweighed the negative. *New Music* (1990), a "six-hour trilogy" of full-length plays that premiered at the Cleveland Play House in November 1989, was heralded by David Patrick Stearns in *USA Today* as "the most ambitious piece of theater by a U.S. writer in years." Stearns went on to say that Reynolds Price "must now be considered a major playwright."[54] Though Mel Gussow in the *New York Times* was not quite as enthusiastic, he offered solid praise: "[W]e come to recognize the characters as old friends and to feel the tautness of the bonds of blood, marriage, and acquaintanceship."[55] *Full Moon and Other Plays* (1993), a collection of previously published dramatic works as well as a new play, also received favorable reviews. Of the three plays in the volume, R. C. Fuller wrote, "Price's building tensions and evolving perspectives will fascinate readers and theater audiences alike."[56] However, several theater critics who viewed various productions of the volume's title play, *Full Moon,* were highly critical of Price. It would appear that certain aspects of a Price drama, such as its language, dialogue, and moments of supernatural occurrence, have fared better with book readers than with theater critics, the latter often expecting pure realism and nonpoetic language. For instance, reviewing the world premiere of *Full Moon* in Durham, Dan Neil criticized the play's improbabilities, "the indecorous appearance of not one but two ghosts," and also what he called its "studied Southernness": the "ham-handed" interracial sex theme, the "static, corn-syrupy dialogue."[57] Steven Winn was also critical; he described an American Conservatory Theater production of *Full Moon* in San Francisco as "static and self-consciously literary."[58]

During the most recent period of Price's career (from the mid-1980s to the present), there have been significant changes in his writing. Most notably, Price has become less demanding of his readers, more accessible. The Price of recent years would not begin a novel with a 192-word serpentine sentence, as he did in *A Long and Happy Life,* nor would he generate a novel as literarily self-conscious as, for example, *Love and Work.* The Price of recent years has become less astringent, more inviting. In addition, he has become particularly interested in creating in his narratives the sound of an actual human voice rather than the poetic speech of a narrator. Though splendid examples of first-person narrative abound in the many letters he included in four of his first five novels, Price spent the initial 25 years of his career writing almost exclusively in the third person. This has changed, however, in recent years, as the story-telling "I," the personal voice, has become dominant. Three of the four novels he published between 1986 and 1992—*Kate Vaiden, The Tongues of Angels, Blue Calhoun*—and sections of the fourth, *Good Hearts,* were written in the first person. Building perhaps on the success of *Kate Vaiden,* Price turned repeatedly to the first person, demonstrating his ability to capture and work the voices of middle-class, middle-aged southern men and women.

Written during the worst part of his cancer crisis, *Good Hearts* (1988), which alternates between the first and third person, returned Price to two of his earliest characters, Rosacoke Mustian and Wesley Beavers, who had now survived 28 years of marriage. Jefferson Humphries, an important Price critic, called the novel "the most compelling and sensitive book Price has written" and concluded, "I don't know of any writer who has more important things to say, more really indispensable comfort and advice to offer."[59] Sven Birkerts also praised the novel, though his evaluation was probably a more representative critical response: "an honorable, winning book—the slightly weaker panel of a powerful diptych."[60] *Good Hearts,* as Monroe Spears explained, also demonstrates how Price's writing evolved over the years: from the "pastoral isolation" and "long dreamy sentences" of *A Long and Happy Life* to the plainer style and greater cultural awareness of *Good Hearts.*[61] Those more critical of the novel took exception to the "goodness" of Price's characters and authorial sensibility—"Mr. Price carries good-heartedness about as far as it can go," said one critic—as well as to his depiction of rape and rapist: "Price's attempt to understand the inner life of Rosa's gentle rapist, and relate that boy's yearning to the universal quest for love, dissolves in fatuity."[62]

The Tongues of Angels (1990), a mystical work as well as a coming-of-age novel, likewise found an accepting readership, though it was viewed as less ambitious, less complex than the novels preceding and following it. George Garrett saw it as "a wise and wonderful novel," the finest he had read about camp life, and he praised Price for "celebrat[ing] the possibilities of healing when easy nihilism is all the literary rage."[63] Reginald Ollen also found much to admire, though he was more critical of Price's "anticlimactic story line and the dwindling intensity of Price's language as the novel progresses." For Ollen, "the confessional perspective Price adopts here doesn't quite burn hard."[64] Interestingly, readers were less captivated by the voice of Price's male narrator, Bridge Boatner, than they had been by the female voices of Kate Vaiden and Rosacoke Mustian in the two preceding novels.

With *Blue Calhoun* (1992) Price again turned to the voice of a first-person male narrator, though the resemblance in tone and structure was to *Kate Vaiden* rather than to *The Tongues of Angels.* Like *Kate Vaiden, Blue Calhoun* was a first-person, largely confessional, eponymous narrative, in which the speaker, a moral outlaw of sorts, offers an account of his or her life and how it went wrong. *Blue Calhoun* drew the same enthusiastic reviews as *Kate Vaiden* had and largely for the same reason: the fluidity and grace of Price's narrative voice. Reviewers called the novel "wonderfully lyrical," "near operatic," "rhythmic and exact, almost psalmodic."[65] Yet a small group of reviewers was highly critical of *Blue Calhoun* in regard to two matters, the same two, incidentally, for which many others praised the novel: the voice and credibility of Price's narrator, and Price's depiction and treatment of his women characters. Though reviewers Robert Towers and Susan Wood found the female characters to be idealized, weak, and doomed (by the author) to excessive suffering, others such as Irving Malin, Dale Neal, and Charles Sermon praised Price for his perceptive depiction of strong, interesting female characters.[66] As with *Kate Vaiden,* questions involving gender proved particularly interesting as well as critically polarizing.

In keeping with the increased use of the first person in his recent fiction, Price turned to more personal modes of narration in his nonfiction as well, composing during this period two volumes of memoir, numerous personal essays, and a personal gospel. With the four Price volumes of nonfictional prose (and translation) to appear during this period—*A Common Room, Clear Pictures, A Whole New Life, Three Gospels*—Price realized tremendous critical and popular success.

A Common Room (1987), Price's collected essays, was praised largely for its wide and diverse range (the volume includes essays on Milton, Faulkner, Hemingway, Cervantes, Rembrandt, Jimmy Carter, religion, Duke University, and southern cooking). Writing in the *Washington Post Book World,* George Core called Price's example as a contemporary man of letters "luminous," and he praised him for his "distinct voice" and "supple prose" as well as for "the penetration of his critical judgments." Core went on to call Price "one of our best critics of contemporary fiction."[67]

Clear Pictures (1989), Price's memoir of childhood and the individuals who influenced his early growth, also received a positive response. Jonathan Yardley wrote in the *Washington Post Book World* that "*Clear Pictures* is a dignified, admirably old-fashioned book, written by a man who treats the language with respect," and a brief unsigned review in the *New Yorker* called the memoir "at once unpretentious and magnificent."[68] The book was praised mostly for Price's gifts of memory and perception, his ability to depict a mid-twentieth-century rural South, and his portrayal of the complex and deep bonds of familial relationships. On the negative side, David McKain, writing in *Chicago Tribune Books,* criticized Price for failing to "div[e] down to explore what lies beneath the surface," and David Gates echoed this sentiment by stating that Price "sensed darker places in the past he wasn't ready to explore. So do we."[69]

Of Price's various efforts in nonfiction, *A Whole New Life* (1994), his memoir depicting his battle with and recovery from spinal cancer, received the most attention and acclaim. As William Henry stated in a *Time* magazine feature story, "Reviewers are being even more generous than usual, and TV talk masters . . . are beckoning." Henry went on to explain one of the reasons for the book's success: "Rarely if ever has a patient of Price's writerly gifts taken on the story of physical devastation."[70] Joanne Brannon Aldridge found Price's narrative "compelling and riveting"; Joseph Flora stated, "Few memoirs are at once so personal and so genuinely concerned for others"; and Geoffrey Wolff wrote, "You will like the teller of this tale, and learn from him."[71] The book's success demonstrated not only Price's courage in surviving a tremendously difficult illness but also his excellence with personal narrative.

Price's subsequent effort in nonfiction, *Three Gospels* (1996)—a miscellany containing translations, essays, and Price's own midrashic re-creation of a Gospel—continued his original journey as writer and storyteller. The book, which climbed to near the top of the religious best-sellers list, was praised widely, and reviewers took note of Price's multiple abilities as essayist, translator, and storyteller. Larry Woiwode in the *Washington Post Book World* called *Three Gospels* "a wonderfully engrossing book," and Robert Alter in the *New York Times Book Review* praised Price's translations for "captur[ing] the homey directness of the Gospel stories with a new freshness."[72] In his conclusion, Alter wrote, "The last words of the Apocryphal Gospel, after the cry of the disciples, 'Lord, come now!' are: 'In other lives their cry has lasted near 2,000 years.' As translator, commentator and reimaginer, Reynolds Price has adroitly managed to catch the reverberation of that cry."[73]

As for his work in short fiction, Price went nearly two decades (from 1970 until 1988) without publishing a single short story, then returned in the early 1990s with two volumes of stories, *The Foreseeable Future* (1991) and *The Collected Stories* (1993). As was evident in such early works as "A Chain of Love" and "The Names and Faces of Heroes," Price's expertise is in the long story, and in *The Foreseeable Future* he composed three stories of novella length. As Susan Dodd wrote in the *Washington Post Book World,* "The longer, more commodious story form seems to suit Reynolds Price and his characters to a tee." Dodd went on to say, "These stories glorify all creation. Above all, they resound with the implications of eternity and the promise of redemption."[74] Greg Johnson in the *Georgia Review* also praised Price—for his prose, his depiction of "sex in the context of genuine intimacy and healing," and his "thorough understanding" of his characters and their world. Johnson concluded that the prose of *The Foreseeable Future* demonstrates "why Price has become one of the South's most important and revered writers."[75] As for *The Collected Stories,* James Person in the *National Review* referred to "A Chain of Love" as "one of the most moving and best crafted American short stories of this century," and Ron Carlson in the *Southern Review* exclaimed, "I have become certain of one thing in the last half-year," which is that *The Collected Stories* "will exist somewhere as a thread in the fabric of twentieth-century

American literature."[76] Finally, Dennis Drabelle wrote in *USA Today*, "As much as any American writer since Walt Whitman, the Reynolds Price of these stories is a poet of the human body."[77]

Price's subsequent effort in fiction was *The Promise of Rest*, which, like the earlier two volumes of *A Great Circle*, was given a mixed reception. Bruce Bawer in the *Washington Post Book World* referred to it as "the disappointing last volume" of the trilogy, and he found Price's dialogue "pretentious" and his protagonist, Hutch Mayfield, "callous, smug, wishy-washy and generally less interesting than Price seems to realize."[78] Greg Johnson, writing in the *Atlanta Journal-Constitution*, also found fault with the novel, echoing the critics of the earlier two volumes of the trilogy: "*The Promise of Rest* remains an inert, slow-moving morass of big themes, preachy dialogue and contrived situations. All the characters . . . sound like Price at his most mannered and self-conscious."[79] Yet *The Promise of Rest* had its admirers. John Skow in *Time* viewed it as a "powerful, brooding novel," and Robert Gingher in the *Washington Times* wrote, "Here is a harrowingly honest fiction, unflinching 'sine cere' in its own design and promise."[80] A painful and harrowing novel, *The Promise of Rest*, according to R. C. Fuller in the *Southern Quarterly*, "helps create and conclude Price's own Adamic myth of modern America with rewarding patterns, connections, and secrets for the careful witness."[81]

Though *A Great Circle*, or the Mayfield saga, stands as Price's most ambitious effort to date, it has been published only in its individual volumes and thus has not been reviewed as a collected set. One is curious, however, to see how posterity will judge it, particularly since the individual novels of the trilogy, of all Price's works, have been the most critically polarizing. The only critics who have addressed the entire work, which was completed in 1995, are Michael Kreyling and myself, and we share a high regard for Price's accomplishment. In my recently published *Understanding Reynolds Price*, I devote nearly a third of the text to *A Great Circle* and refer to it as Price's "most significant achievement to date."[82] In his essay in this volume, Kreyling writes, "Over two decades and more than one thousand pages of prose fiction, Price sustains a human universe comparable to the one dreamed by his imagined giant. Trilogies produced by American novelists in this century can scarcely match *A Great Circle*'s sweep and finesse."[83]

As of 1997, Price has 29 books to his name, yet his literary career is hardly complete. His *Collected Poems* has just been published, and a new novel, *Roxanna Slade*, will appear early in 1998. Given that plans are under way for other projects, Price seems likely to continue his prolific output, and as Constance Rooke and I have stated elsewhere, one must continue to be vigilant concerning the new directions his work may take.[84]

In summary, Price's books have enjoyed a largely appreciative response from book journalists throughout America and England. The overwhelmingly positive reviews that greeted *A Long and Happy Life* have continued in recent years for *Kate Vaiden, Blue Calhoun, A Whole New Life,* and *Three Gospels.* And the largely mixed response that such novels as *Love and Work* and *The Surface of Earth* elicited has continued for such volumes as *The Laws of Ice* and *The Promise of Rest.* Perhaps the major distinction between early and more recent reviews of Price's work reflects his evolving stature. Having now earned his place as a distinguished American writer, Price is treated with increased admiration and respect. As for other changes, contemporary reviewers seldom speak anymore of the supposed Faulknerian influence, or of Price as a generic or derivative southern writer. His place as an original craftsman, even in the eyes of his detractors, seems confirmed. Finally, reviewers continue to focus on those themes that proved significant in Price's early work, such as love, family, and place; however, there is more interest now in his narrative voice and prose style, and more attention to issues involving gender, religion, and authorial compassion (toward his characters).

CRITICAL ESSAYS AND BOOKS

The first critical essay to appear on Price's writings was John Stevenson's "The Faces of Reynolds Price's Short Fiction" in 1966.[85] Since then, there have been approximately 40 essays and three books devoted to the study and interpretation of Price's works (excluding biographical pieces and essays written by the author about his own work). Interestingly, as far as critics are concerned, no single Price work has clearly emerged as his most famous or significant. Though his novels have drawn the most attention, interest has been divided rather equally between *A Long and Happy Life, Love and Work, A Great Circle,* and *Kate Vaiden.*[86] In addition, there have been essays and book chapters devoted to his plays, short fiction, memoirs, and biblical translations.

The graph reflecting the annual publication of essays on Price since 1966 does not, however, express the same consistency; instead, its fluctuations shadow the rise and fall, then rise once again of Price's popularity. Between 1966 and 1972 the young Price drew much attention—the equivalent of 10 essays or book chapters—nearly all of which concerned the Mustian novels. Between 1973 and 1987, however, a period more than twice as long, Price's work drew relatively little interest: six essays and one book. With his movement away from the Mustians, and with the evolution of his style, tone, and characters in such novels as *Love and Work* and *The Surface of Earth,* Price lost the attention of the academic critical community. Riding the wave of his success with *Kate Vaiden* in 1986, however, interest returned; and between 1988 and 1996 there was more critical interest in Price than ever—more than 20 essays and two books. Furthermore, in light of the widespread journalistic attention devoted to such recent works as *Blue Calhoun, A Whole New Life,* and

Three Gospels (all published between 1992 and 1996), and the publication of Price's collected essays (1987), stories (1993), and poems (1997), one would guess that the rising wave of critical attention will continue.

The early essays, which appeared between 1966 and 1972, dealt almost exclusively with Price's Mustian works. In his 1967 book, *The Art of Southern Fiction,* Frederick J. Hoffman examined Price's first three volumes (which led to his being "hailed as a special product of Southern writing") and argued, unlike most reviewers of the time, that "the point of resemblance [for Price] is not Faulkner, but (if at all) Miss Welty and Miss O'Connor."[87] Clayton Eichelberger's article "Reynolds Price: 'A Banner in Defeat' " also departed from reviewers in suggesting that Price's early work was more ironic and pessimistic than was typically perceived. Eichelberger demonstrated how characters such as Rosacoke and Milo Mustian are meant to frustrate reader expectation by "fall[ing] short of realizing their potential."[88] Daniel Barnes in "The Names and Faces of Reynolds Price" considered the manner in which Price explores the concept of identity in his fiction, and Stevenson in "The Faces of Reynolds Price's Short Fiction" addressed how concepts of love and giving figure in Price's first volume of stories.[89] Finally, Hicks, in a collection of his reviews, devoted an entire chapter to Price, placing him in company with such previously established figures as Bellow, O'Connor, Malamud, Nabokov, and Updike.[90]

The two most significant early critics of Price's work were Allen Shepherd and Simone Vauthier, who together published six articles on Price between 1970 and 1975. Both devoted the majority of their attention to *A Long and Happy Life,* which figures centrally in Vauthier's two essays and in three of the four pieces from Shepherd. In "Love (and Marriage) in *A Long and Happy Life,*" Shepherd considered how Price's epigraph offers a clue to Rosacoke's future, and he discussed the major tropes of the novel, such as the gesture of gift giving, the sucking/pulling imagery, and various references to the novel's title. In "Notes on Nature in the Fiction of Reynolds Price," Shepherd demonstrated how nature figures significantly in Price's work, though in a manner quite distinct from that of, say, Faulkner, Warren, or Dickey: Price "is not given to celebrating nature," but rather in his work there is "an engagement with nature" through which "characters receive or miss messengers, signs, emblems."[91] Simone Vauthier in "The 'Circle in the Forest': Fictional Space in Reynolds Price's *A Long and Happy Life*" also considered the role of nature in Price's first novel, demonstrating that it is "above all the gathering spot of happenings, experiences, feelings which are linked directly to Rosacoke's and the narrator's sense of life as something beautiful and yet awe-inspiring, whose very beauty is terrifying." Vauthier's essay, more theory driven than most on Price, focused on the author's creation of a dynamic fictional space, a "circle in the forest" where he "stages" his "games."[92]

In that falling-off period of Price criticism in the late 1970s and early 1980s, an appreciative overview of Price's work appeared in a chapter from

Paul Binding's 1979 book, *Separate Country.* Of *The Surface of Earth,* Binding wrote, "The novel in my view is a great one; indeed, I think it stands unsurpassed among fiction written in the English language since World War II."[93] Kreyling, who wrote two important essays on Price during this period, offered similar praise for *The Surface of Earth* in his chapter on Price, which appeared in *The History of Southern Literature.* In his brief chapter, which provides a brilliant critical overview, Kreyling described the "two planetary influences [that] shaped Southern writing in the latter days of the Southern Renascence": "How does this novel match Faulkner?" and "How does this theme advance or baffle the cause of social justice for the Negro in the South?"[94] Kreyling then went on to demonstrate how these factors have worked against the growth of Price's literary reputation. In an essay published in 1980, "Motion and Rest in the Novels of Reynolds Price," Kreyling provided a fine discussion of how *The Surface of Earth* engages in debate with Augustine's *Confessions,* and he examined how the tension between impulses of motion and rest figures in Price's first four novels.[95]

The first book devoted exclusively to Price, Constance Rooke's *Reynolds Price* (1983), written for Twayne's United States Authors Series, was quite good and offered thoughtful, accessible, and appreciative readings of Price's first five novels and first two collections of short stories. Rooke's most significant contribution was her general discussion of the novels, though she also provided excellent, albeit brief, analyses of Price's prose style and of his "single vision." In explaining the latter, Rooke wrote of how nothing in Price's work is "accidental or extraneous or mere decoration" and how each book "repeats and expands the knowledge of the last" so as to provide "the integrity of a single vision."[96]

Consideration of Price revived in the late 1980s and early to mid-1990s, during which four critics—Humphries, Gary M. Ciuba, Lynn Veach Sadler, and myself—published multiple pieces on his work. In addition to his collection of interviews, *Conversations with Reynolds Price,* Humphries published a significant review-essay of Price's writings of the mid- to late 1980s and an eloquent personal essay, "Taking Things Seriously: Reynolds Price as Teacher and Writer." In the latter he revealed in both Price's teaching and writing a generous but demanding seriousness, and he argued, "[I]n no other contemporary American writer is such a concerted opposition to the trivial . . . so apparent."[97]

Ciuba's two essays on Price, both of which appeared in 1991, were "Price's *Love and Work:* Discovering the 'Perfect Story' " and "The Discords and Harmonies of Love: Reynolds Price's *New Music.*"[98] The former, included in this collection, provided a close reading of one of Price's darker and more demanding novels and argued that Thomas Eborn is "a failed version of Price's *homo narrator*" and thus a storyteller out of touch with Price's sacred and crucial demands for narrative. The latter essay, the first to deal with Price as dramatist, demonstrated that Price's "imagination originates in and instinctively gravitates toward what is dramatic" and viewed the trilogy as literal music, "a score for voices."[99]

Sadler published three important essays in the late 1980s. The first and perhaps best, "Reynolds Price and Religion: The 'Almost Blindingly Lucid' Palpable World," considered the role of God, religion, biblical narrative, and mysticism in Price's life and work. Sadler demonstrated that Price's world is one "of common objects and ordinary people meaning more than they or we know, being 'almost blindingly lucid' with a meaning beyond themselves."[100] The second essay, "The 'Mystical Grotesque' in the Life and Works of Reynolds Price," covered some of the same territory and demonstrated how Price's mysticism has led to the label "southern gothic." Sadler then turned to *The Surface of Earth* and *The Source of Light* to discuss how the southern gothic and the grotesque figure in his writings.[101] In her third essay, " 'Small Calm Pleasures': The Mustians Revisited in Reynolds Price's *Good Hearts*," Sadler offered the first careful examination of *Good Hearts*. Paying close attention to character and language, Sadler demonstrated how Rosacoke and Wesley have evolved over time, and she suggested that the novel may draw "some concern from . . . women readers . . . because of the changes in Rosacoke and the attitudes of Rato and the rapist toward women."[102]

In addition to her own writings, Sadler edited with Sue Laslie Kimball the second book to appear on Price, *Reynolds Price: From "A Long and Happy Life" to "Good Hearts," with a Bibliography*.[103] A collection of essays first delivered as papers at the Seventh Annual Southern Writers' Symposium (held at Methodist College on 15–16 April 1988), the volume was most valuable for its biographical pieces and bibliography (see pages 21 and 22 in this introduction). Of its nine critical essays, two offered interpretations of *Love and Work*—Dan Daniel's "Amazing Crossroads in *Love and Work*" and Frances Roe Kestler's "*Love and Work:* Excursions into the Subconscious"—whereas two others were concerned with the Mayfield novels: William N. Claxon Jr.'s " 'With This Ring, I Thee Wed': The Mayfield Men" and Bes Spangler's " 'A Dry Rag to Suck': Old Maids in *The Surface of Earth*." Additional essays included Frank K. Shelton's "The Family in Reynolds Price's *Kate Vaiden*"; Kimball's "Reynolds Price, Biblical Scholar: 'Validation in the Narrative Bones' "; Jane Cherry's "Rosacoke Mustian as a Warren County Woman"; and reprints of Kreyling's "Reynolds Price" (from *The History of Southern Literature*) and Sadler's essay on *Good Hearts*. Finally, the volume contained a panel discussion concerning the "themes and characterizations" of Price's second play, *Private Contentment*, which was being staged in tandem with the conference.

My own work during this period included a book, *Understanding Reynolds Price*, and an essay, "Fathers and Sons in the Fiction of Reynolds Price: 'A Sense of Crucial Ambiguity,' " the latter of which has been revised and included here.[104] The book, a volume in the Understanding Contemporary American Literature series from the University of South Carolina Press, offered the second full-length critical analysis of Price's writings. Published in

1996, *Understanding Reynolds Price* covered the Price oeuvre from *A Long and Happy Life* to *The Promise of Rest* and provided readings of his first 10 novels as well as his 2 volumes of memoir. In addition, the volume provided a short biography, a critical overview, and a selected bibliography of primary and secondary works. Among other things, the volume demonstrated how literary trends have often run counter to Price's career and argued that Price has remained committed to a personal vision unlike that of any contemporary American writer. As for the essay, it considered the mysterious, charged eroticism between fathers and sons in Price's writing and revealed how the author works to maintain "a sense of crucial ambiguity" in his depiction of this eros.

Other essays of note published during the early 1990s included two on *Kate Vaiden:* Joseph Dewey's "A Time to Bolt: Suicide, Androgyny, and the Dislocation of the Self in Reynolds Price's *Kate Vaiden*" and Edith T. Hartin's "Reading as a Woman: Reynolds Price and Creative Androgyny in *Kate Vaiden.*"[105] Dewey's brilliant essay demonstrated how Kate Vaiden redefines herself through masculine stereotypes. Yet for Dewey, Kate ultimately defies gender—"the voice of Kate is no straining falsetto"—and he concluded, "Price disturbs the easy assumptions of gender to explore the possibility of shared rather than tensive gender."[106] In a largely feminist reading of *Kate Vaiden,* Hartin covered some of the same territory yet contended that Kate's voice and characterization are "completely the product of a masculine imagination, a masculine tradition," which "sounds more like a man's fantasy than a woman's experience." She concluded that although Price "can sing in a cool soprano, many readers remain aware that all he must do is clear his throat to resume a resounding baritone."[107] Interestingly, Price himself participated in this debate concerning gender and the reversed-gender novel, though his involvement preceded the essays of Dewey and Hartin by five years. In his provocative essay "A Vast Common Room," which was published in the *New York Times Book Review* a few months after the publication of *Kate Vaiden,* Price argued, among other things, that men and women share "total human sympathy" such that they are mutually capable of knowing and creating characters and voices of the opposite gender.[108] The essay disputed the sometimes feminist notion that a man cannot understand or write from the perspective of a woman and vice versa, and it encouraged writers to work across gender lines, as Price had with *Kate Vaiden.*

During the early to mid-1990s Gloria Jones and R. C. Fuller, both of whom wrote dissertations on Price, published essays on his work. Jones's "Reynolds Price's *A Long and Happy Life:* Style and the Dynamics of Power," which is included here, provided a detailed exploration of the relationship between language, gender, and power in Price's first novel.[109] Fuller's "Lunging in the Dark: Blindness and Vision, Disappointment and Aspiration in Reynolds Price's Trilogy," also included here, considered the vital role of audience as witness in *New Music* and examined the process by which Neal Avery transforms himself and realizes a vision of hope.[110]

Other essays or book chapters of note that have been published recently include Linda Orr's "The Duplicity of the Southern Story: Reflections on Reynolds Price's *The Surface of Earth* and Eudora Welty's 'The Wide Net' "; Robert O. Stephens's section on Price's Mayfield novels in his book *The Family Saga in the South;* Barbara Bennett's "Outrage and Delight: Southern Scatalogical Humor in Reynolds Price's *The Tongues of Angels*"; Monroe K. Spears's chapter, "Reynolds Price: Passion and Mystery in Fiction," in his *One Writer's Reality;* and Robert Hogan's "Man to Man: Homosocial Desire in Reynolds Price's Short Fiction."[111]

Appearing in print for the first time in this volume are three newly commissioned essays. Michael Kreyling's "Men without Women: Communities of Desire and Race in *A Great Circle*," a consideration of Price's Mustian trilogy in terms of gender and sexuality, demonstrates the centrality of male bonds of love while placing those bonds within a classical Greek framework. In a highly intelligent and eloquent essay that praises the trilogy, Kreyling nevertheless questions Price's attitude toward his female characters in a way that will likely spark further discussion. Allen Shepherd's essay *"The Collected Stories:* A Whole Living World" traces Price's evolution as a short-story writer and offers close readings of seven stories, from "A Chain of Love" to "An Early Christmas." Though Shepherd values Price's short fiction less than his novels, he nevertheless writes that "reading these stories is serious business, for they confront the reader with consequential choices of belief and behavior." Finally, Doris Betts's "From the Virgin Mary to Rosacoke" is an intelligent, thoughtful, and appreciative essay that considers Price as a religious writer and typological thinker. Using examples from Price's fiction, memoir, and biblical essays and translations, Betts demonstrates how Price believes history has a larger purpose and meaning through which "good will be brought out of evil."

Of course one of the best and most useful critics of Price's work has been Price himself, who has published numerous pieces on his own writing. As early as 1963, Price discussed the composition process of his story "The Warrior Princess Ozimba" in the *Duke Alumni Register,* and later he addressed his creation of such works as *A Long and Happy Life, A Generous Man, The Surface of Earth, Kate Vaiden,* "A Chain of Love," "Waiting at Dachau," and "The Annual Heron." In addition, Price has discussed in his essays a range of literary topics—the southern novel, the reversed-gender novel, the making of art, the aims and origins of narrative—which has shed light on his own work. Because most of Price's essays have been collected in *A Common Room,* I have opted not to include them here. The only writing of his I have reprinted is *"A Long and Happy Life:* Fragments of Groundwork," a series of diary entries extracted from the notebook Price kept while planning his first novel. Since 1955, Price has kept notebooks about his ongoing work, and he is currently preparing these voluminous notebooks for publication.

In summary, critical attention to Price's work has increased and diversified dramatically since 1988, so that there are now essays or book chapters devoted to each of his novels and to his efforts in other genres. Though still not as familiar in academic circles as John Updike, Toni Morrison, or Thomas Pynchon, Price has become a significant figure in contemporary American literature. In addition, whereas the early studies of his work focused on themes of love, family, and nature, as well as on Price's identity as a southern writer, more recent critical analyses, though still interested in these earlier themes, have expanded the dialogue, turning to issues involving gender, religion, and sexuality. Whereas writers in their later years often become less engaging to younger critics and generations, the opposite seems true with Price, whose writing falls naturally into contemporary critical conversations on sexual identity and polysexuality, gender issues and reversed-gender novels, mysticism and spiritualism, health issues and AIDS, race and interracial relationships.

INTERVIEWS AND BIOGRAPHICAL SOURCES

The best source for interviews has been the aforementioned collection from Humphries, *Conversations with Reynolds Price,* which contains significant, previously published interviews as well as a valuable new interview from Humphries himself. Three additional and more recent listings of note are Frederick Busch's *Paris Review* interview, Susan Ketchin's conversation with Price on the religious aspects of his writing and thinking, and Joseph Dumas's interview concerning race and the South.[112]

As for biographical sources, the first piece on Price appeared in the Raleigh *News and Observer* in July 1956. Subsequent sketches and essays about his life can be located in various bibliographies. In 1983 a small, privately published pamphlet entitled *For Reynolds Price* appeared, containing short tributes from James Dickey, Anne Tyler, Eudora Welty, and Chappell (the tribute from Dickey is included here).[113] During the late 1980s several significant biographical essays were published, all written by former Price students: Michael Ruhlman's "A Writer at His Best," Tyler's "Reynolds Price: Duke of Writers," Chappell's "Welcome to High Culture," and Humphries's "Taking Things Seriously: Reynolds Price as Teacher and Writer" (the pieces by Tyler and Chappell are included here). In addition, Kimball and Sadler's *Reynolds Price* offered valuable biographical material from William S. Price Jr., Price's brother; Wallace Kaufman, Price's former student and friend; and Daphne Athas, a friend and fellow writer. Finally, interviews about Price with former teachers, friends, and fellow writers can be found in Charles Guggenheim's 1994 film *Clear Pictures,* as well as in the transcripts of the outtakes from that film.[114] Included in this volume and published for the first time are excerpts from interviews with Toni Morrison, Stephen Spender, James Taylor, and Kathryn Walker (note that these remarks by and large do not appear in the final version of the film).

Though Price has made an effort to keep his personal life personal, a biographical image has formed through the various sketches and essays that Price and others have written. That image, interestingly, is contradictory and mysterious. For instance, though he has lived a largely solitary existence without a steady companion or spouse, Price is an extremely sociable person who has surrounded himself with a vast constellation of friends and intimacies. And though some of Price's writings and interviews suggest arrogance and intellectual detachment, he mostly displays unusual warmth and generosity. Finally, though Price has written openly of his battle with cancer and intimately of the problems and humiliations that come with paralysis and life in a wheelchair, he has kept his sexuality and sexual intimacies mostly private. No Gore Vidal is he. Perhaps, as Spender has said of some future Price biography, "people will become extremely interested in his personality, and they'll find that his personality is much more interesting than that of most writers who have great public reputations."[115]

BIBLIOGRAPHIES

Though several bibliographies and checklists of Price's work exist, an updated volume is needed to account for his prolificacy since the mid-1980s. The earliest bibliographical efforts, which have been superseded by subsequent volumes, were Clayton Owens's 1976 bibliography (a master's thesis) and Ray Roberts's 1981 checklist.[116]

The first published bibliography was *Reynolds Price: A Bibliography, 1949–1984,* compiled by Stuart Wright and James L. West III.[117] This volume, which today remains the best source for Price's primary works, offered a description of Price's known publications through 1984: books; contributions to books, periodicals, and newspapers; pamphlets; broadsides; limited signed editions; Christmas greetings; translations of his work into other languages; and juvenilia,[118] including poems, stories, editorials, and essays for the Broughton High School *Hi-Times* and the Duke University *Archive.*

A more recent bibliography was compiled by Kimball and Sadler and appeared at the back of their *Reynolds Price.*[119] This bibliography, indebted to the earlier work of Roberts, Wright, and West, updated Price's oeuvre to 1988. More important, however, it provided the most comprehensive listing of secondary materials: reviews, critical essays, profiles, and dissertations. One more recent effort was my own selected bibliography, which appeared at the back of *Understanding Reynolds Price.*[120] Though more limited in its scope, this bibliography provided an annotated listing of the significant essays and reviews of Price's work through 1995.

Finally, it should be noted that Price's papers—manuscripts, correspondence, notebooks, clippings, and miscellaneous items—are housed at the Special Collections Library at Duke University, Durham, North Carolina.

Notes

1. Michael Kreyling, "Reynolds Price," in *The History of Southern Literature,* ed. Louis D. Rubin Jr. et al. (Baton Rouge: Louisiana State University Press, 1985), 521.

2. As a translator Price has been a finalist for the National Book Award, and his biblical translations have won the praise of Anthony Burgess, Frank Kermode, Robert Coles, Frederick Buechner, and Robert Alter. In drama Price has been referred to as "a major playwright," and his plays have been produced on numerous stages across the country and on public television's *American Playhouse.* As a poet Price has received the Levinson, Blumenthal, and Tietjens Awards from *Poetry,* and his poems have been praised by John Hollander, Toni Morrison, George Garrett, and Stephen Spender. As a short-story writer Price has been compared to Chekhov, Hemingway, Joyce, Faulkner, and Welty; his stories have appeared in the annual editions of *The Best American Short Stories* and *The O. Henry Prize Stories;* and his *Collected Stories* was a finalist for the Pulitzer Prize in fiction. As a memoirist Price has drawn considerable media attention and great accolades. His first volume, which Spender called "a masterpiece of a very rare kind, reminding me of Thoreau's *Walden,*" inspired a documentary film about Price's life, and the second volume, a cancer memoir, was hailed as extraordinary. Finally, as a critic Price has written significant essays on Hemingway, Rembrandt, Milton, Welty, and others, and he has been described by George Core as "one of our best critics of contemporary fiction."

3. Cited in Michael Ruhlman, "A Writer at His Best," *New York Times Magazine,* 20 September 1987, 134.

4. Cited in Ruhlman, "A Writer at His Best," 133.

5. Sanford Pinsker, "A Conversation with John Updike," *Sewanee Review* 104.3 (Summer 1996): 424.

6. Ruhlman, "A Writer at His Best," 132.

7. The collaboration between Price and Taylor goes back to 1982, when Taylor wrote the score for a PBS television production of Price's play *Private Contentment* (Taylor's former wife, the actress Kathryn Walker, starred in the play). The first song Price and Taylor wrote together was "Hymn" in 1988. Taylor had wanted to write a song for the retirement of an old friend, Bishop Paul Moore, and Price suggested they write a hymn. He then wrote the lyrics to "Hymn," which can be found in *The Use of Fire* (1990), and Taylor added the music (it was recorded several years later under the name "New Hymn" on Taylor's *Live* CD). The other song, "Copperline," which they cowrote in 1991 while Price was staying with Taylor at his Connecticut home, can be found on Taylor's *New Moon Shine* CD as well as on his *Live* CD (Reynolds Price, interview with author, Durham, N.C., 26–28 August 1994).

8. Gary M. Ciuba, "The Discords and Harmonies of Love: Reynolds Price's *New Music,*" *Southern Quarterly* 29.2 (Winter 1991): 124.

9. Granville Hicks, "Country Girl Burdened with Love," *Saturday Review* 45 (10 March 1962): 17.

10. Catharine Hughes, "A Mature First Novel," *Commonweal* 76 (27 April 1962): 124.

11. Dorothy Parker, "Six Collections of Stories and a Lovely Novel," *Esquire* 57 (June 1962): 67.

12. Hicks, "Country Girl," 18.

13. Stephen Spender, interview with Charles Guggenheim, from outtakes to the film *Clear Pictures,* dir. Guggenheim (London: Direct Cinema Ltd., 16 August 1991), GPI no. 595 (Reel 2): 19, 20.

14. Whitney Balliett, "Substance and Shadow," *New Yorker* 38 (7 April 1962): 180.

15. Reynolds Price, "The Thing Itself," in Price, *A Common Room: Essays, 1954–1987* (New York: Atheneum, 1987), 13.

16. William Barrett, "Plain Folk," *Atlantic* 212 (July 1963): 130.

17. Paul Pickrel, "A Chain of Love," *Harper's* 227 (August 1963): 96; Michele Murray, "A Heavy Price," *Commonweal* 78 (20 September 1963): 568; Granville Hicks, "Two Kinds of Tears," *Saturday Review* 46 (29 June 1963): 36; "Southern Folk," *TLS,* 27 September 1963, 730; Barrett, "Plain Folk," 130.

18. Richard Gilman, "This Is the Way It Happened," *New York Times Book Review,* 30 June 1963, 4.

19. R. G. G. Price, "New Fiction," *Punch,* 16 October 1963, 578.

20. William McPherson, "The Exuberant Chore of Growing Up Generous," *Life* 60.14 (8 April 1966): 10.

21. Certainly a major explanation for the darkening in Price's work was the death of his mother in 1965. As he later wrote of her death, "[H]ome ended instantly"; and of the time following her death, he added, "I had a bona fide old-fashioned breakdown, like the ones in Chekhov. . . . The given and taken scars of that decade are charted, at an unsafe distance, in the novels, stories and poems of those years" (*Clear Pictures* [New York: Atheneum, 1989], 301, 302).

22. Kreyling, "Reynolds Price," 521.

23. Geoffrey Wolff, " 'Murder Your Darlings,' " *New Leader* (17 June 1968): 24, 25.

24. Francis King, "In the Last Resort," *London Telegraph,* 17 November 1968, 24.

25. Louis D. Rubin Jr., "Reynolds Price Novel on Art and Love," *Washington Star,* 2 June 1968, D2.

26. John Hazard Wildman, "Beyond Classification—Some Notes on Distinction," *Southern Review* 9.1 (Winter 1973): 234.

27. Patrick Cruttwell, "Fiction Chronicle," *Hudson Review* 24.1 (Spring 1971): 184; Theodore Solotaroff, "The Reynolds Price Who Outgrew the Southern Pastoral," *Saturday Review* 53 (26 September 1970): 46.

28. Guy Davenport, "Doomed, Damned—and Unaware: *Permanent Errors,*" *New York Times Book Review,* 11 October 1970, 4.

29. Solotaroff, "The Reynolds Price Who Outgrew the Southern Pastoral," 27–29, 46.

30. Reynolds Price, "Given Time: Beginning *The Surface of Earth,*" *Antaeus* 21/22 (Spring/Summer 1976): 57–58.

31. Robert Ostermann, "Price," *National Observer* 14 (2 August 1975): 19.

32. Fred Chappell, "*The Surface of Earth:* A Pavement of Good Intentions," *Archive* 88.1 (Fall 1975): 75, 82.

33. Michael Brondoli, "Landscape of Exiles; Two Families in the South," *Providence Journal,* 3 August 1975, H34.

34. Kreyling, "Reynolds Price," 521; Paul Binding, "Reynolds Price," in *Separate Country: A Literary Journey through the American South,* 2nd ed. (London: Paddington, 1979; Jackson: University Press of Mississippi, 1988), 167.

35. Richard Gilman, "A Mastodon of a Novel, by Reynolds Price," *New York Times Book Review,* 29 June 1975, 1–2.

36. Benjamin De Mott, "A Minor Faulkner," *Saturday Review* 8.4 (April 1981): 72.

37. Joyce Carol Oates, "Portrait of the Artist as Son, Lover, Elegist," *New York Times Book Review,* 26 April 1981, 3, 30; Gail Godwin, "A Southern Family Doomed by the Patterns of Its Past," *Chicago Tribune Books,* 26 April 1981, 1.

38.   William H. Pritchard, "Poetry Chronicle," *Poetry* 143 (January 1984): 229.

39.   George Garrett, "Reynolds Price Offers Fresh, Free Poetry," *Columbia (S.C.) State,* 30 January 1983, 10G; Suzanne Juhasz, *"Vital Provisions," Library Journal* 108 (1 January 1983): 54.

40.   John Hollander, "Poetry in Review," *Yale Review* 73.1 (August 1983): xxi.

41.   Jefferson Humphries, ed., introduction to *Conversations with Reynolds Price* (Jackson: University Press of Mississippi, 1991), viii.

42.   Anthony Burgess, "Good Books," *New York Times Book Review,* 12 March 1978, 22.

43.   Reynolds Price, *A Whole New Life* (New York: Atheneum, 1994), 28.

44.   Reynolds Price, interview with author, Durham, N.C., 26–28 August 1994.

45.   Rosellen Brown, "Travels with a Dangerous Woman," *New York Times Book Review,* 29 June 1986, 1.

46.   Michiko Kakutani, "Books of the Times," *New York Times,* 24 June 1986, C17.

47.   Jonathan Keates, "Southern Discomfort," *Observer,* 22 February 1987, 29.

48.   Though elsewhere I have stated that Price published three volumes of poetry during this period, *The Collected Poems* (1997) appeared just as this collection went to press, thus reviews were not yet available.

49.   Thomas Swiss, "Voices of Power and Conviction," *Chicago Tribune Books,* 25 January 1987, 6; Helen Buck Bartlett, *"The Laws of Ice* by Reynolds Price," *Los Angeles Times Book Review,* 17 May 1987, 13; J. D. McClatchy, "Amid the Groves, under the Shadowy Hill, the Generations Are Prepared," *Poetry* 158.5 (August 1991): 283.

50.   Robert B. Shaw, *"The Laws of Ice,* by Reynolds Price," *Poetry* 150 (July 1987): 233; Bartlett, *"The Laws of Ice,"* 13; Lawrence Rungren, *"The Laws of Ice,"* *Library Journal* 111 (December 1986): 116; Swiss, "Voices of Power," 6–7.

51.   Ashley Brown, "Reynolds Price: *The Use of Fire,"* *World Literature Today* 65 (Summer 1991): 490.

52.   Dan Brown, review of *The Use of Fire, Harvard Book Review* 19/20 (Spring 1991): 25.

53.   Shaw, *"The Laws of Ice,"* 233.

54.   David Patrick Stearns, " 'New Music' Rings with Promise," *USA Today,* 20 October 1989, 5D.

55.   Mel Gussow, "Love and Loss and the Salve of Time," *New York Times,* 4 November 1989, 16.

56.   R. C. Fuller, *"Full Moon and Other Plays,"* *Southern Quarterly* 32.2 (Winter 1994): 152.

57.   Dan Neil, "Moon for the Misbegotten," *Raleigh Spectator,* 3 November 1988, 18.

58.   Steven Winn, *"Full Moon* Slow Going until the Very End," *San Francisco Chronicle,* 4 March 1994, C1.

59.   Jefferson Humphries, " 'A Vast Common Room': Twenty-five Years of Essays and Fiction by Reynolds Price," *Southern Review* 24.3 (Summer 1988): 689, 695.

60.   Sven Birkerts, "Rape and Transfiguration," *Los Angeles Times Book Review,* 22 May 1988, 13.

61.   Monroe K. Spears, "Scenes from a Marriage," *Washington Post Book World,* 10 April 1988, 5.

62.   Lee Lescaze, "The Seductions of Routine," *Wall Street Journal,* 14 June 1988, 32; Vince Aletti, "A Song of Old Lovers," *Village Voice Literary Supplement,* June 1988, 13.

63.   George Garrett, "Portrait of an Artist," *World and I* 5 (August 1990): 433.

64.   Reginald Ollen, "Indian Summer," *Nation* 251 (30 July/6 August 1990): 140.

65.   Steve Brzezinski, *"Blue Calhoun* by Reynolds Price," *Antioch Review* 50 (Fall 1992): 771; Melinda Ruley, "Amazing Grace," *Durham (N.C.) Independent Weekly,* 20 May 1992, 24; Janet Byrne, "An Old-School Rake and His Teen Muse," *Wall Street Journal,* 26 June 1992, A9.

66.   Robert Towers, "June and January in Raleigh, N.C.," *New York Times Book Review,* 24 May 1992, 10; Susan Wood, "Blue Moon of Carolina," *Washington Post Book World,* 10 May

1992, 5; Irving Malin, "*Blue Calhoun,*" *Southern Quarterly* 31.3 (Spring 1993): 123; Dale Neal, "Reynolds Price Returns with Tale of Passion," *Asheville Citizen-Times,* 31 May 1992, 6L; Charles Sermon, "A Powerful Tug," *Columbia (S.C.) State,* 10 May 1992, 4F.

67.   George Core, "Reynolds Price: Teacher, Novelist and Man of Letters," *Washington Post Book World,* 14 February 1988, 6.

68.   Jonathan Yardley, "Reynolds Price: Snapshots from a Writer's Album," *Washington Post Book World,* 18 June 1989, 3; unsigned review of *Clear Pictures, New Yorker* 65 (14 August 1989): 91.

69.   David McKain, "In His Memoir, Reynolds Price Would Rather Not Recall Pain," *Chicago Tribune Books,* 11 June 1989, 6; David Gates, "Distant Images," *Newsweek* 114 (17 July 1989): 54.

70.   William A. Henry, "The Mind Roams Free," *Time* 143 (23 May 1994): 66.

71.   Joanne Brannon Aldridge, "Therefore, Choose Life: And Work at It," *Commonweal* 121 (17 June 1994): 24; Joseph M. Flora, "*A Whole New Life,*" *Carolina Quarterly* 47 (Fall 1994): 82; Geoffrey Wolff, " 'Though Much Is Taken, Much Abides,' " *Washington Post Book World,* 12 June 1994, 10.

72.   Larry Woiwode, "And the Word Was Made Fresh," *Washington Post Book World,* 5 May 1996, 5; Robert Alter, "The Greatest Story Ever, Retold," *New York Times Book Review,* 19 May 1996, 12.

73.   Alter, "The Greatest Story," 12.

74.   Susan Dodd, "In the Heart of North Carolina," *Washington Post Book World,* 21 June 1991, 1, 9.

75.   Greg Johnson, "Homecomings," *Georgia Review* 45 (Winter 1991): 778–80.

76.   James E. Person Jr., "*The Collected Stories,* by Reynolds Price," *National Review* 45 (7 June 1993): 68; Ron Carlson, "The Collected Stories of Reynolds Price," *Southern Review* 30.2 (April 1994): 371–78.

77.   Dennis Drabelle, "The World of Reynolds Price: Wry Humor, Earthy Humanity," *USA Today,* 18 June 1993, 4D.

78.   Bruce Bawer, "Dying Generations," *Washington Post Book World,* 16 July 1995, 16.

79.   Greg Johnson, " 'Promise' Not Quite Fulfilled," *Atlanta Journal-Constitution,* 28 May 1995, K10.

80.   John Skow, "Staring Down Loneliness," *Time* 145 (22 May 1995): 73–74; Robert Gingher, "The 'Promise' of Guilt and Redemption Is Explored," *Washington Times,* 23 July 1995, B8.

81.   R. C. Fuller, "*The Promise of Rest,*" *Southern Quarterly* 34.2 (Winter 1996): 153.

82.   James A. Schiff, *Understanding Reynolds Price,* (Columbia: University of South Carolina Press, 1996), 6.

83.   Michael Kreyling, "Men without Women: Communities of Desire and Race in *A Great Circle,*" in *Critical Essays on Reynolds Price,* ed. James A. Schiff (New York: G. K. Hall, 1998), 300.

84.   Constance Rooke, *Reynolds Price,* Twayne's United States Authors Series 450 (Boston: Twayne, 1984), 144–45; Schiff, *Understanding Reynolds Price,* 173, 178.

85.   John W. Stevenson, "The Faces of Reynolds Price's Short Fiction," *Studies in Short Fiction* 3.3 (Spring 1966): 300–306.

86.   Although interest has been divided equally, before the late 1980s *A Long and Happy Life* clearly elicited the most attention.

87.   Frederick J. Hoffman, *The Art of Southern Fiction* (Carbondale: Southern Illinois University Press, 1967), 143.

88.   Clayton L. Eichelberger, "Reynolds Price: 'A Banner in Defeat,' " *Journal of Popular Culture* 1.2 (1967): 410–17.

89.   Daniel Barnes, "The Names and Faces of Reynolds Price," *Kentucky Review* 2.2 (1968): 76–91; Stevenson, "The Faces of Reynolds Price's Short Fiction," 300–306.

90.   Granville Hicks, "Reynolds Price," in *Literary Horizons: A Quarter Century of American Fiction* (New York: New York University Press, 1970), 229–42.

91.   Allen Shepherd, "Notes on Nature in the Fiction of Reynolds Price," *Critique: Studies in Modern Fiction* 15.2 (1970): 83–94.

92.   Simone Vauthier, "The 'Circle in the Forest': Fictional Space in Reynolds Price's *A Long and Happy Life*," *Mississippi Quarterly* 28 (Spring 1975): 123–46.

93.   Binding, "Reynolds Price," 167.

94.   Kreyling, "Reynolds Price," 521.

95.   Michael Kreyling, "Motion and Rest in the Novels of Reynolds Price," *Southern Review* 16 (1980): 853–68.

96.   Rooke, *Reynolds Price*, 144.

97.   Jefferson Humphries, "Taking Things Seriously: Reynolds Price as Teacher and Writer," *Southwest Review* 74.1 (Winter 1989): 10–24.

98.   Gary M. Ciuba, "Price's *Love and Work*: Discovering the 'Perfect Story,' " *Renascence* 44.1 (Fall 1991): 45–60; Ciuba, "The Discords and Harmonies of Love: Reynolds Price's *New Music*," *Southern Quarterly* 29.2 (Winter 1991): 115–30.

99.   Ciuba, "The Discords and Harmony of Love," 115, 124.

100.   Lynn Veach Sadler, "Reynolds Price and Religion: The 'Almost Blindingly Lucid' Palpable World," *Southern Quarterly* 26.2 (1988): 1.

101.   Lynn Veach Sadler, "The 'Mystical Grotesque' in the Life and Works of Reynolds Price," *Southern Literary Journal* 21.2 (Spring 1989): 27–40.

102.   Lynn Veach Sadler, " 'Small Calm Pleasures': The Mustians Revisited in Reynolds Price's *Good Hearts*," *Southern Quarterly* 26.4 (1988): 5.

103.   Sue Laslie Kimball and Lynn Veach Sadler, eds., *Reynolds Price: From "A Long and Happy Life" to "Good Hearts," with a Bibliography* (Fayetteville, N.C.: Methodist College Press, 1989). I have opted not to reprint any of these essays, since they already exist in a collection.

104.   Schiff, *Understanding Reynolds Price;* James A. Schiff, "Fathers and Sons in the Fiction of Reynolds Price: A Sense of Crucial Ambiguity," *Southern Review* 29.1 (Winter 1993): 16–29.

105.   Joseph Dewey, "A Time to Bolt: Suicide, Androgyny, and the Dislocation of the Self in Reynolds Price's *Kate Vaiden*," *Mississippi Quarterly* 45.1 (Winter 1991–1992): 9–28; Edith T. Hartin, "Reading as a Woman: Reynolds Price and Creative Androgyny in *Kate Vaiden*," *Southern Quarterly* 29.3 (Spring 1991): 37–52.

106.   Dewey, "A Time to Bolt," 24, 28.

107.   Hartin, "Reading as a Woman," 48, 51.

108.   The version of the essay that appeared in the *New York Times Book Review* was called "Men, Creating Women" (9 November 1986, 1, 16ff.), a title Price did not choose and that he felt was a "combative flag to fly over an essay whose main intention is to tend the deeper wounds of gender warfare" (preface to Price, *A Common Room*, xii). A revised version of the essay, "A Vast Common Room," from which I have quoted, appears in Price, *A Common Room*, 375.

109.   Gloria G. Jones, "Reynolds Price's *A Long and Happy Life*: Style and the Dynamics of Power," *CEA Critic* 56.1 (Fall 1993): 77–85.

110.   R. C. Fuller, "Lunging in the Dark: Blindness and Vision, Disappointment and Aspiration in Reynolds Price's Trilogy," *Southern Quarterly* 33.2–3 (Winter–Spring 1995): 45–56.

111.   Linda Orr, "The Duplicity of the Southern Story: Reflections on Reynolds Price's *The Surface of Earth* and Eudora Welty's 'The Wide Net,' " *South Atlantic Quarterly* 91.1 (Winter 1992): 111–37; Robert O. Stephens, *The Family Saga in the South: Generations and Destinies* (Baton Rouge: Louisiana State University Press, 1995), 171–84, 204–11; Barbara Bennett, "Outrage and Delight: Southern Scatalogical Humor in Reynolds Price's *The Tongues of Angels*," *Thalia* 14.1–2 (1994): 30–39; Monroe K. Spears, "Reynolds Price: Passion and Mystery in Fiction," in Spears, *One Writer's Reality* (Columbia: University of Missouri Press, 1996); Robert

Hogan, "Man to Man: Homosocial Desire in Reynolds Price's Short Fiction," *South Atlantic Review* 62.2 (Spring 1997): 56–73.

112.   Frederick Busch, "Reynolds Price: The Art of Fiction CXXVII," *Paris Review* 33.121 (Winter 1991): 150–79; Susan Ketchin, "Reynolds Price: Interview," in Ketchin, *The Christ-Haunted Landscape: Faith and Doubt in Southern Fiction* (Jackson: University Press of Mississippi, 1994), 69–99; Joseph Dumas, " 'Largely Southern Realities': A Conversation with Reynolds Price," *Reckon* 1.3 (Fall 1995): 72–79.

113.   The pamphlet, with a print run of 150 copies, was published in celebration of Price's 50th birthday, in 1983.

114.   The transcripts are housed at the Center for Documentary Studies, Duke University.

115.   Spender, interview with Guggenheim, *Clear Pictures,* GPI no. 595 (Reel 3): 35.

116.   Clayton S. Owens, "Reynolds Price: A Bibliography" (master's thesis, University of North Carolina, 1976); Ray A. Roberts, "Reynolds Price: A Bibliographical Checklist," *American Book Collector* 2.3 (1981): 15–23.

117.   Stuart Wright and James L. West III, *Reynolds Price: A Bibliography, 1949–1984* (Charlottesville: University Press of Virginia, 1986).

118.   One other source of juvenilia is a privately printed volume of Price's entitled *A Start (Early Work)* (Palaemon Press, 1981), which contains a play written in eighth grade, 10 poems and three prose sketches from high school and college years, and a new preface.

119.   Kimball and Sadler, *Reynolds Price,* 120–54.

120.   Schiff, *Understanding Reynolds Price,* 194–202.

REMINISCENCES AND TRIBUTES
◆

Reynolds Price: Duke of Writers

Anne Tyler

He used to wear a long black cape with a scarlet lining. Or at least I always thought he did. Everybody thought so. Whenever we compared our freshman English instructors, someone was sure to say, "Reynolds Price? Isn't he the one with the cape?"

Turns out it wasn't a cape after all. It wasn't even black. It was a navy-blue coat that he wore tossed around his shoulders. That's what he tells me now, at any rate, and I suppose he knows best. But I prefer to have it my way: He wore a long black cape with a scarlet lining, and he dashed across the campus with his black curls bouncing on his forehead and his cape swirling out behind him. Ask any of the people who went to Duke in the fall of 1958; I bet they'll say I'm right.

He was twenty-five years old back then, he tells me now, but in 1958 he seemed older than God. (I was sixteen and a half.) Which made it all the more remarkable when he perched on his desk tailor-fashion to read us his newest story; or when he said, to a student analyzing a poem, "You're *good* at this, aren't you!" (He seemed genuinely pleased, and admitted straight out that he hadn't seen what she had seen. For me, that girl's face will always symbolize the moment I first understood that we students, too, had something to offer—that we weren't the blank slates we'd thought we were in high school.)

"Wouldn't it be something," he says now, "if we could locate a photograph taken of us together as children?" I'm puzzled. Together? As children? But then I realize that in fact he wasn't quite grown up himself when he started teaching—and that maybe, in the best sense, he never will be. And I remember a thought I had when I was a sophomore, listening to one of his funny, incisive discussions. *He must have been a very much loved child,* I thought. I believe that occurred to me because he seemed, sitting in our midst, a naturally happy man. Not to mention the fact that there was something childlike about his face, which was—and still is—round and serene and gravely trusting.

And the other thought that occurred to me—not then but years later, when I revisited Duke and found him gray-haired but otherwise unchanged,

Reprinted from *Vanity Fair* 49.7 (July 1986): 82–85, by permission of the author.

affectionately guiding a whole new generation of students—was that Reynolds has had the great good fortune to know his place, geographically speaking. More than any other writer I'm acquainted with, except perhaps for Eudora Welty, he has a feeling for the exact spot on earth that will properly contain him, and he has never let himself be lured away from it any longer than necessary.

As luck would have it, that spot is his family stomping grounds—semi-rural North Carolina, a country of scrubby woods and scrappy little towns. He was born in Macon, North Carolina, in 1933, the son of a door-to-door salesman and a woman who hadn't been educated past the eleven years of public schooling then available. The family moved from place to place within a narrow radius, incidentally exposing him to a nearly unbroken stream of those dedicated, selfless teachers who used to be so prevalent back when teaching was still recognized as a noble profession. ("They were mostly single women that seemed old and wise," says the heroine of *Kate Vaiden,* his latest novel, ". . . and the fact that I've made it this far upright is partly a tribute to their hard example that you get up each morning and *Take what comes.*")

It was his eighth-grade teacher in Warrenton who first encouraged his interest in writing and art—especially art. The two of them used to paint everything available; if they had nothing better to do, they'd decorate wine bottles and china dishes. Then in eleventh grade, at Broughton High School in Raleigh, Reynolds began to concentrate on writing under the direction of Phyllis Peacock, an English teacher whose name is legend to anyone who grew up in Raleigh during the fifties or sixties.

From Broughton he went on to Duke University, and there, during his senior year, he wrote his first two short stories, "Michael Egerton" and "A Chain of Love," for William Blackburn's creative-writing class. (Do you notice how his history—as told by Reynolds himself—is a progression from teacher to teacher? It may explain why he's so wholeheartedly poured his gifts back into his students.)

While he was at Duke, he met Eudora Welty, who came to give a lecture during his senior year and arranged for him to send his writing to her agent, Diarmuid Russell. Reynolds had heard she'd be arriving alone on a three A.M. train, so he showed up to escort her to her hotel. He wore a gray suit which Eudora, decades later, remembers as snow white. I don't know why everyone is so confused about Reynolds Price's wardrobe.

After graduating in 1955, he spent three years on a Rhodes Scholarship to Oxford, where he was encouraged by such people as Lord David Cecil, Stephen Spender, and W. H. Auden. But he felt he should settle near home—his father had died by then, leaving a widow and younger son—so he returned to Duke to teach and finish his first novel, *A Long and Happy Life.* And at Duke he has remained, except for one further year at Oxford and brief trips abroad. He is now James B. Duke Professor of English; he teaches one semester a year and writes during the other semester. Some of his students are the children of the students he taught when he first arrived.

What this stability has meant for his writing is that his fiction has roots—deep, tenacious roots to a part of the country that remains absolutely distinct from other parts. You may find shopping malls in North Carolina; you may come across those ubiquitous chocolate-chip-cookie boutiques and Olde English potpourri marts; but the people still have very much their own style of speaking, and Reynolds Price knows that style by heart. Any North Carolinian, reading one of his novels, must stop at least once per page to nod at the rightness of something a character says. It's not just the tone that's right; it's the startling, almost incongruous eloquence, for some of the state's least educated citizens can sling a metaphor pretty handily and know how to pack a punch into the homeliest remark. A bosomy girl in *A Long and Happy Life* has "God's own water wings inside her brassiere," according to one of the characters, while in *A Generous Man* a boy describes tobacco farming so vividly that the reader sags in sympathy: ". . . lose half my plants to frost and blue mold, then transplant the rest in early May and nurse it all summer like a millionaire's baby—losing half again to wet weather, dry weather, worms, blight."

It may be too that staying on home ground has helped Reynolds Price keep his fiction centered on the family he grew up in. He has remained intensely curious about his parents, alert to every story they passed on to him. *Kate Vaiden* began to take form after he wrote a poem, "A Heaven for Elizabeth Rodwell, My Mother" (*Poetry,* June 1984), in which he took the three hardest events his mother had to endure and gave them happy endings. Then he began remembering her tales of an orphaned childhood, and her stoicism when she faced death from an inoperable aneurysm. (She died in 1965.) Kate Vaiden is not literally Reynolds's mother, but she does have his mother's independence and strength of character. She's a bit more self-possessed, is all, Reynolds says; she was offered a bit more scope than Elizabeth Rodwell Price ever was.

In the summer of 1983 he started writing the novel, and he finished Part One at the end of May 1984. Then in June he learned that he had cancer of the spinal cord. He underwent immediate surgery, followed by an exhausting course of radiation and steroid therapy. The tumor was arrested, but he was no longer able to walk, and he entered a rehabilitation clinic to learn the practical strategies for life in a wheelchair. A mere three months after the original diagnosis (though it must have seemed an eternity), he was back at work—first not writing but drawing, as if retracing his career from childhood on; then two months later inching into the written word with a play, *August Snow,* commissioned by Hendrix College; and sailing off on an astonishing creative burst that produced two more plays, a volume of poetry, and a collection of essays. At that point he felt ready to continue with *Kate Vaiden.* He worried that the break might have altered his narrative voice, but he worried needlessly. Following his usual routine, working in longhand on legal pads, he picked up with Part Two and continued to the end of the book.

Kate Vaiden, too, develops cancer, and Reynolds says that that part of her story emerged from his recent experiences. But otherwise the novel remains untouched by his illness, and lacks any trace of bitterness. You could say the same for Reynolds himself. Whatever those first months must have cost him, he is now as high-spirited as ever. All that's new about him is a bigger set of biceps (he's changed shirt sizes since he started wheeling himself around) and a stock of funny stories about nurse's aides and wheelchair salesmen.

He lives where he has lived for the past twenty-eight years, next to a pond in the pines outside Durham; and when I visited him a younger writer, Daniel Voll, was sharing the house in order to help him navigate the stairs. (A single-floor addition that's now being built will soon allow him to be self-sufficient.) The rooms are stuffed with a mesmerizing collection of unrelated objects: fossils, cow skulls, death masks, and a personal letter from General Eisenhower dated 1943. Even the bathrooms are hung with photographs, and the kitchen windowsills are so densely lined with antique coins and pottery shards that for a moment I took an ordinary black metal window lock to be some kind of prehistoric artifact.

Around this labyrinth Reynolds wheels competently. He has returned to teaching after an eighteen-month sabbatical; even if he were a billionaire, he says, he would want to go on teaching. Teaching is his "serious hobby"; it keeps him in touch with the next generation. And he knows he has at least one thing of value to offer his students: practical, concrete advice for getting on with the job of writing. (I can bear witness to that, certainly; and so can at least a half-dozen other published writers he's taught, in addition to who knows how many more who will sooner or later hit print.) Really what he offers is *strategy,* he says. In fact he's a sort of rehab clinic. This notion makes him smile.

Dan Voll, who audited Reynolds's course during undergraduate days, tells how he spent his first session lurking apprehensively just outside the classroom doorway. Oh, Reynolds is thought to be pretty intimidating, if you ask the average Duke student. But that's only at the start, Reynolds argues. At the start he tells his class how he loves to root through Dempster Dumpsters in hopes of finding other people's mail to read, and then everybody relaxes. How can you be intimidated by someone who's confessed to that?

He smiles again. He does a little turn in his sporty tour-model wheelchair. The scarlet lining of his long black cape swirls out behind him.

Reynolds Price: A Tribute

JAMES DICKEY

I discovered Reynolds Price by a means I would normally distrust: by reading about him in the book section of a weekly newsmagazine. Though I can't remember who the effusive review of *A Long and Happy Life* was by, the reviewer had the wit to quote from the book, and Price's words cut through the attempt at journalistic praise like an acetylene torch through an empty beer can. *A Long and Happy Life* is one novel I did not wait to buy when it came out in paperback, and today, whenever I pass the paperback section of the bookstore or the turnaround rack in the drugstore, I always buy another copy, to give to some special friend—but mainly I keep 'em for myself: I have a whole row of editions of *A Long and Happy Life*.

From the beginning I was struck by Reynolds Price's extreme openness and honesty. This is not the honesty of the plodding, faithful, list-making, button-examining "naturalism" of someone like Zola or Dreiser, or James T. Farrell, but an honesty of very clear imaginative depth, and some other quality that makes me want to use the word "clean." Another reviewer for a national magazine, a much better one, said of Reynolds's second book, *A Generous Man,* that "everything in Price's story seems to happen under a bright golden spotlight so that the world he portrays casts a shadow larger than itself around it. Everything aims toward one ultimate moment when understanding and truth will break over reader and character alike." Seldom have I encountered a more exact or fitting characterization of an author than this reference to the golden glow in which the events and characters of Reynolds Price's fiction are set forth. These things happen, these people live, usually in small towns in the South, and Price's main themes have extraordinary rootedness and depth: the interrelations of people in a family and those connected with them, and love when it means something, and will lead to something: the difficulty of discovering the kind of love which also includes responsibility: the difficulty of discovering it and the difficulty of maintaining it and living up to it.

In dealing with these things, one cannot be unmoved by Price's utter sincerity and his caring imagination. As Peter Wolfe said, "Price makes you

Reprinted, with the permission of the author, from a private printing of *For Reynolds Price,* 1 February 1983.

feel that you are living through an experience, not reading a book." The author's sense of responsibility to his characters and his deep involvement with them is always apparent, and is the very lifeblood of the stories he tells. He has the kind of imagination that cannot be faked, and his depiction of character is utterly without the sense of scoring-off people or demonstrating the author's superiority to them.

If I were to tell you that Reynolds Price was born in Macon, North Carolina, in 1933, that he attended public schools there and elsewhere in North Carolina, graduated from Duke, then went on to Oxford as a Rhodes scholar, and that he returned to Duke in 1958 and teaches there now, you could believe me, for these things are all true. If I were to tell you, also, that in addition to *A Long and Happy Life,* which received the William Faulkner Foundation Award in 1962, that his second novel was the equally fine *A Generous Man,* and his third, *Love and Work,* that he has two collections of stories, *The Names and Faces of Heroes* and *Permanent Errors,* that a genuine epic of a novel, called *The Surface of Earth,* appeared around ten years ago and that a new one, equally epical, called *The Source of Light,* followed it, these things would also be true, and some of them you probably already know.

But what you might not know is that he is also one of our finest interpretive critics, and if you read his book *Things Themselves* you will quickly see what I mean. As a critic he is fiercely personal and extremely incisive, penetrating and releasing: he can open an author up to you more graciously and lastingly than anyone I know, and, at the same time, open you up to the author.

As if this were not enough, he is an extremely interesting and valuable translator, and (praise God!) has now turned his hand to poetry. Doubtless he knew all the time that he is a poet essentially, anyway: everything he writes is full of highly individual imagination, but it is interesting to note that he came into poetry first from his translations from the German, notably from Rilke, and from the Bible. He tells me that there will soon be a book of poems, and I look forward to *that,* I can tell you.

So . . . here is Reynolds Price, among us. He is of the South: the South made him and all its good qualities are in him, and none of the bad ones. He is not in the least chauvinistic or "regional" in any programmatic sense, but the deep golden glow that envelops his characters and their actions is essentially a Southern glow. His qualities are straightness and unwarped depth: sincerity and imagination, and caring, and, in his words, "a complicated sense of joy."

Welcome to High Culture

FRED CHAPPELL

When we think how many people it takes to produce one writer—how many tolerant relatives, gracious teachers, forbearing friends, and imposable strangers—it becomes obvious that the end product is not worth all the effort. But then, what is? It takes just as much warmly disinterested effort to turn out an athlete or a scientist or a responsible citizen. The State is going to spend the money anyway, those merry folk who have patience with young people are still going to be amenable; so that we may consider the appearance of a poet or fiction writer as an unexpected bonus, as the civilized world always has done.

Usually, though, the first serious encouragement that greets a writer is well-intentioned discouragement. "Writing," said my high school teachers, "is a good hobby, something you'll always be able to do. But don't expect to be successful at it. Most aspiring authors never get published." My parents saw the prospect in an even gloomier light, or darkness, than my teachers. Most of my friends thought I was certifiable for the mental wards, or was striving to become so.

It makes no difference. If a writer is going to write, he writes; if he does not write, then he is no writer. I didn't know what I was supposed to do with the first poems I wrote at ages twelve, thirteen, and fourteen. I buried many of them in the bottom cornfield, returning them to the soil I felt had given them birth. Others I placed on wood chips and, after setting them afire, floated them along the turgid currents of Duckett's Creek. I watched them drift out of sight, feeling jubilant and forlorn at the same time . . . Such grandiose self-pity neither helped nor harmed the feverish lines on the Blue Horse notebook paper.

But—thank you, Mrs. Kellett. Though you never lodged the fourth declension in my disordered head, you showed me that others besides myself could be excited by books. I haven't forgotten the story of your becoming so absorbed in Dickens by lamplight that the room filled with smoke and you never noticed.

Reprinted, with the permission of the author, from *An Apple for My Teacher*, ed. Louis Rubin Jr. (Chapel Hill: Algonquin Books, 1987), 14–28.

Thank you, Bill Anderson and Fuzz Fincher. It was good to have high school friends who thought that I was only immensely silly and not a raving lunatic.

Thank you, Tom Covington, wherever you are, whatever course of life you pursue. I never learned to write a proper science fiction story suitable for those magazines, but you did manage to teach me to write a straightforward sentence, a comprehensible paragraph. I can still recall my astonishment when you broke off our correspondence upon joining the Navy; I had pictured you as a wise old man, in his thirties *at least.*

Once having opened the Catalogue of Debt, writers, even the most regretful and bitter among us, could go on and on and on, like the tearful young ladies in the Academy Awards ceremonies, until our audience too would cry out, "Say, didn't you do *anything* yourself?"

And that question ought to be taken seriously. Writing is such an inescapable part of literate culture, such an ordinary part of communal aspiration, that a writer should not much pride himself on his precious volumes. Even if he is the most radical of thinkers, someone who desires to tear his culture down and build it again from the bottom up, society—American society, anyhow—can turn to him and say, "Yes, but the reason you were educated was to enable you to think precisely these thoughts." The radical writer in America is stuck with this anomaly, that his only audience is the literate Establishment, who are by and large a broadminded and tolerant bunch. This fact makes him fight the band that needs him.

Because one of the guildmark characteristics of a young writer is self-dramatization, it may be that many of the early slurs and snickerings he endures are partly imaginary. A writer seems to feel instinctively that it is necessary to have something to struggle against, and I have met no writer, even among best-selling novelists, who did not believe that this reviewer or that one was out to get him, that his publisher has not advertised him lavishly enough, that his agent is an economic simpleton. This attitude of aggrieved affront may be a holdover from the years when none of the heartbreakingly pretty cheerleaders sufficiently adored his sonnets. Or it may come down to the other fact that writing is an inevitable part of culture, that a writer owes too much to too many, that at last he does have little for which he can take personal credit, and all this makes him uneasy and defensive. For no matter how many Miltons, Chekhovs, and Prousts have appeared or shall appear, the writer in the end remains what he was in the year 6000 B.C.—the village scrivener, a clerk.

Perhaps the cruel world is aware of this fact, perhaps that is why it gives him such a hard time. The village vests a heavy responsibility in its scrivener, who is to draw its portrait, preserve its memories, and keep its accounts, both material and spiritual. Perhaps the world is careful to weed out those not nervy enough to do justice to the office. If the writer prefers to impute motives of heartless jealousy, that is only one more instance of his trying to make himself look good to himself.

But then he has to look good to himself, since to everyone else he looks merely odd.

College! I thought. If I can ever graduate from high school and get into college, I'll find kindred spirits, other people who will sympathize with my aspirations and respect my goals. I had heard of the legendary teacher of creative writing at Duke University, Dr. William Blackburn (though I thought his name was "Blackstone"), and I was confident that I was the student he had been praying to come along. I had given up science fiction and had recently written two heavily symbolic stories that were so mythically sophisticated I couldn't understand them. I was just hell on symbolism, and I felt certain that Dr. Blackstone would appreciate these superior endeavors.

I got into Duke all right, though it is not clear how I did—not on the strength of my high school grades, surely. There I found out that freshmen were not allowed into the writing class. I would have to get through my first year, making passing grades in my physics and logic classes, before I was eligible to be admitted to the sanctified novitiate. And then I would have to submit a manuscript that met favorably his iron scrutiny.

A year, that year, it seemed to me, would be ten eternities coupled together like boxcars. I would shrivel and die, scarab beetles would gnaw my dessicated bones tangled on the chair and writing desk of my dormitory room, before that year passed. What in the world was I to do in the meantime?

I drank a great deal of beer and whiskey, and I wasn't very expert at it.

And there was a literary magazine, *The Archive*, which was the oldest college literary magazine in the United States, and had, among my convivial unliterary buddies, the reputation of being the dullest publication the Lord ever suffered to plummet from the presses. "Dull, is it?" says I. "*Archive*, your nondescript days are past. Here comes Fred Genius with his stories and poems to set you zooming the glittery avenue to international acclaim."

Then another obstacle presented itself. *The Archive*, I found out, had an editor. If the editor liked your material, he published it; if he didn't publish it, he returned it with a note explaining why it was unspeakable garbage. This editor's name was Reynolds Price. He was a straight-A senior, and he was, by all accounts, nobody's fool. Other undergraduates spoke of him with contempt, of course—in the way they spoke of all the literary crowd—but with *awed* contempt.

The most interesting revelation was that he was a flesh-and-blood human being like anyone else one might run into on campus. My experience with editors was that they were sinister spectral entities who occasionally scribbled crabbed notes on little blue rejection slips: "Your exposition is silly"; "This is not how Martians talk to each other"; "The pace of this story is like a

Boy Scout hike—half trotting, half dawdling." But Reynolds Price was a student like myself . . . Well, no, he certainly wasn't that; but he did live in a room on the third floor of the Independent Dormitory. My first obvious step toward making *The Archive* a famous magazine would be to accost this man and flash my blinding credentials.

I got cold feet. What if I wasn't such hot stuff as I'd been telling my shaving mirror? What if I was an ignorant hayseed from a farm three miles outside of Canton, North Carolina? What if Reynolds Price decided to talk in French? What if—what if, after all—what, O God, if I wrote badly?

I had already made friends with the deeply pondering, slow-talking poet James Applewhite, and I confided my plan and my fears to him, delighted to discover that he had considered the same plan and had nursed the same fears. We decided to pool our courage and face the wizard together.

The pool of courage we resorted to was an unwise quantity of beer and cooking sherry. Our evening of destiny started early and got late quickly, but when we felt we had girded ourselves sufficiently, we returned to campus and stumbled up the narrow stairs. We pounded, lurching, on his door and Reynolds let us in.

Into, it seemed, an entirely different universe. Our rooms in the freshman dormitories suddenly seemed a thousand miles away, those rooms with the mimeograph-paper-green walls and bare, pocked linoleum tile floors and for decoration only the naked, inscrutable smiles of Hugh Hefner's pinup girls. Reynolds' room was another kind of place. It was agreeably lit with lamps, not with those bald overhead lights found in dormitories and police stations. There was a rug on the floor; it wasn't large or expensive-looking, but it meant that we didn't feel we were hiking a chopblock when we crossed the room. On the walls were *framed* reproductions of Botticelli and Blake and Matisse, on his desk a miniature of a classical torso. A record was playing— Elisabeth Schwarzkopf, I think—and there was an autographed photo of her on the wall.

"Hello, jerks. Welcome to High Culture," Reynolds said.

—No, he didn't. He couldn't say those words, or think them in an eon of trying. Yet I had the fleeting but certain conviction that he was entitled to say them.

In fact, he was polite and cordial, much more so than the situation warranted. Reynolds has almost always managed to maintain a smooth and pleasant demeanor to match his pleasing looks, and I hope that his easy manners have always worked as sturdily in his service as they did during that awkward evening. He treated us amiably, with a reserved humorous gravity, no doubt having sized up our unsober conditions. We sat—that is, we collapsed into chairs—and he sat, and we attempted conversation.

Reynolds talked then just as he does now: fluently, nonchalantly, knowingly, allusively, and always with a partly hidden humor. His manner was so assured that we began to question the impulses that had brought us here, and our defensiveness returned to bully us worse than before. Jim and I began to pretend to talk more to each other than to our host, dropping scraps of poetry and code names, *Pound, Eliot, Hart Crane, Rimbaud.* The friendship of young writers is usually marked by this cryptic patter; it is as if they feel themselves members of a spy ring. But Reynolds picked up our hints.

The horribly deflating thing was that he not only picked them up, he bandied them easily, as if these subjects which had cost Jim and me so much trouble to find out about were the common and legitimate coin of social intercourse. That was a blow. There are always writers or certain kinds of writing that other, especially young, writers feel proprietary about, and I have watched even famous poets and novelists turn mildly belligerent when some-one else in the room evinced knowledge of works which they have decided belong, godammit, only to them. But here was Reynolds Price, cheerfully, blithely, opining right and left in territory where Jim and I felt we had, if not first claim, then squatters' rights, at least. He made it worse by being invul-nerable; it was clear he had actually read the stuff he talked about.

That fact ought finally to have made us furious, but it didn't. Reynolds' insouciance began to work a calmness upon us, and we began to relax a little, to enjoy ourselves. We began to welcome the discovery that here was some-one else who was *one of us.* It got to be time, and long past time, for us to depart, and there was little pleasure in walking back through the mazy halls to the freshman dormitories. My position in life seemed grubbier to me than ever before, and I made stiff resolutions to change myself.

I could not change my life and it later brought me to minor disaster and major embarrassment. But that was not Reynolds' fault; he did the best he could with me, and it is astonishing to me now that a young man of twenty or twenty-one could have so much cheerful patience with a prickly adolescent only a few years his junior. There is a patience which is born of experience, but there must also be a patience born of innate wisdom, and it is this latter that Reynolds was graced with.

I began to bring him my work to read, long arcane poems and wild con-fused stories. I have mercifully forgotten this material by now, and almost all that I remember is Reynolds' good-natured meticulous attention as he went with a pinpoint-sharp pencil over line and line, word and word. His queries and objections on the page were delicate little breathings of graphite. This is how Rilke must have read through manuscripts, I would have thought—if I'd known who Rilke was. Sometimes he would use technical terms to criti-cize rhythms and tropes and I would never admit that I didn't know what those terms meant. "Ah yes," I said, nodding. "I see." Thinking, What in the name of seven sunken hells is an amphibrach?

He must have admired my persistence, at least. There was one longish, heavily Eliotic, tainted poem that I brought to him some dozens of times. Was it about a mystic nun? I can dimly recall only some image about a stained glass window. I must have written that poem forty times, following his intimations and encouragements. It never worked out. Finally I wrote an ugly parody of it, then gave up. And there were many other pieces to which we gave the same treatment. I spoke loudly and quarrelsomely in their favor; he argued gently and reasonably against certain passages. Little by little I would mollify and acquiesce at last.

He was never wrong. He wasn't always right; he was sometimes unable to diagnose the *exact* illness of a passage, and he would sometimes object to certain phrases and subject matter out of inevitable and necessary personal prejudice. But he was never wrong; his objections made logical, if not always artistic, good sense; or they appealed to some separate standard I'd never heard about or to some authority unknown to me. (Who, pray tell, was Herbert Read? Who was Geoffrey Scott?) It didn't matter whether he was right or not; it was too important that he was never wrong.

I learned a great deal, perhaps as much about literature as I ever learned from anyone. I trudged to the dictionary and looked up *amphibrach*, to the library and checked out Read and Scott. Mostly I picked up knowledge simply by contact, the way the cat in the weedy field picks up beggar's-lice and Spanish needles. I learned that even the pantheon contemporary writers were living sinful creatures like me and the postman. Reynolds possessed a kind of movie-fan worship of writers and loved to collect gossip about Auden, Faulkner, Welty, Hemingway, and he loved to pass it on. These tidbits must have been special fun to pass on to a wooly kid who would sit openmouthed to hear about William Empson's toping habits.

He published a couple of his own stories in *The Archive*. They were good stories, appearing later in his collection, *The Names and Faces of Heroes*. Strange that they did not influence my fiction, because I certainly admired their accomplishment. But maybe it was already clear to me that Reynolds and I were headed in different directions. There seemed to be a tacit agreement that I was to be intense and wild and experimental, while he was to be traditional, Olympian, and successful.

Everyone who knew him took his eventual success for granted, and "eventual" was assumed to be only a few short years off—as indeed it was. Reynolds took a Rhodes scholarship, as we all knew he would, and impressed the powerful literary figures at Oxford, just as we expected him to do. "A Chain of Love," the longish story he wrote for Dr. Blackburn's class, Stephen Spender published in *Encounter*. Reynolds then returned to Duke as a freshman composition instructor and wrote his first novel. *A Long and Happy Life* was published to lucky, but well-deserved, wide acclaim. Here was his picture in *Time* and on the cover of *Saturday Review*. His carefully planned career seemed to have flourished exactly on schedule, and this fact occasioned some inescapable natural resentment, even from me. Maybe especially from me.

There were some gruff times between us at this period, but in the end they didn't matter. My gratitude was larger than, though perhaps for a while not as fierce as, my jealousy. I never forgot what I owed to Reynolds, and if I ever do I shall have become someone the human race ought to cease speaking to. Sometimes I've wondered if others have remarked the Goethean qualities about the man, his steady adherence to the highest ideals, his immense easy knowledge of all the civilized arts, his cultivated ease. It is an index to his character that if he reads these present lines, he will not be embarrassed, however much he may disagree with what they say.

There were others besides Jim and me for whom he was mentor. There was the poet Wallace Kaufman and the novelist Anne Tyler, and there must be many others of whom I am unaware. Their memories of Reynolds will differ vastly from mine, and yet I can't help imagining that their essential experiences of him as friend and teacher must be like mine in general outline.

He was, you see, a genuinely cultured person, and there are precious few of them in any situation, even in the universities. If you happen to entertain the fantasy, as I once did, that these figures are to be met with only in novels or history books, then you will be pleasantly shocked to meet one as a friend. It marks us when we do; it refreshes our ambitions and reillumines our sensibilities; it warms, for a longer time than we expect, our cooling existences.

In order to conclude in proper fashion this excursion into heartfelt sentimental nostalgia, it has occurred to me that I ought to drink a glass of wine in honor of Reynolds Price. What is needed is a rich red, full-bodied wine, with an earthy but not harsh aftertaste, a rather soft finish. There is no drink like that in the house and I shall have to go to the wine shop, describe to the proprietor what I'm looking for, and ask his advice.

That is the difference between us, of course. Reynolds would know the correct vintage and the best year.

Speaking of Reynolds Price

The following statements by Toni Morrison, Stephen Spender, James Taylor, and Kathryn Walker are taken from interview outtakes from Clear Pictures, *Charles Guggenheim's 1994 documentary film about Reynolds Price.*

TONI MORRISON

I have never been with Reynolds when I didn't remember it. And that's saying a lot you know, after you reach sixty. I haven't seen him all that much, but every one of the occasions in which we were together I remember; nothing has ever gotten fuzzy. . . . There's a little bit of theater in our relationship. He laughs and he understands laughter the way I do. Which is more than mere amusement. It's controlling the reins of our imagination. And some of the things that break Reynolds up might not do the same for other people, but I will scream. He understands incredibly well a level of irony and outrage, the exaggerated moment that you cannot. But he'll also cry. I remember very clearly sitting with him in this theater, and I think we were in California for the literature panel of the National Endowment for the Arts, and we were looking at a film and I sat next to him and the film was about Native Americans. I don't remember whether it was a terribly good film, but it tried to talk about the necessity for encouraging art among young Native Americans. As a matter of fact, my distinct impression is that it wasn't a very good film, but on the screen a young boy appeared, fairly unattractive . . . and not at all appealing, just young and Native American. And he began to talk about what he thought his future might be. And it was interesting but not particularly eloquent; you know, the kind of thing you'd expect. And I felt this tremor next to me. And I looked to my right at Reynolds—tears were running unashamedly down his face. He was simply looking at that boy and knowing on some level that probably none of that would ever happen, and why it would never happen, and who knows what else. Now this was in a theater full of other writers, critics, scholars, et cetera, and he was overwhelmed in the nicest way and he was fearless and it was more than compassion. It was

Published with the permission of Charles Guggenheim, Toni Morrison, Natasha Spender, James Taylor, and Kathryn Walker.

a kind of physically intelligent response that he made in a public sphere. And I don't know many men like that. . . .

I know a lot of his work and mostly his poetry, which is so powerful and well crafted. I don't know what his reputation is among poets. They tend to be very cliquish. But I cannot imagine his not having the strongest following and reputation among poets. His poetry is extraordinary to me. . . .

When he was recuperating in some fashion—not completely but he was able to work and move about—everything began to pour out of him. And not just volume but quality, just incredible, beautiful things, and I thought, Well, maybe it's the up-against-the-wall syndrome. The magnificent work that can somehow come out of unbelievable pressure. You think of the wonderful work that was done in the 40s under Hitler in occupied France. I mean sometimes with the proximity of the end you strip away all of the weighty, vain, comfortable things that we yearn for, but can delay and distract a writer or a painter. Maybe that's it. I know I didn't begin to write young, the way Reynolds did. I was over thirty, and when I did begin to write it was because I was in a very hard place and there was nothing else to do. And it may be the same for him. I'm only speculating, but it's just amazing and delightful. He's so productive and so good at it.

Reynolds, for me, has this extraordinary combination of recklessness and discipline in some combination that is astonishing. So I see the discipline in the pedagogy and the recklessness in other aspects of his life, and in his humor and in his insight. What he sees in nature, in animals, in people is both inventive and reckless, but he reveals it with a masterful discipline of the language and the responsibilities of the language. . . .

Charles Guggenheim {director and interviewer}: One of the criticisms of Reynolds is that he puts rather eloquent, insightful dialogue in the mouths of some of his characters who are really quite simple, rather middle-class people. Some people find that hard to accept. I was curious what your reaction to that is.

Toni Morrison: I guess I know the nature of the complaint because there is the assumption—it's a funny kind of elitism—that lower- or middle-class people are functionally illiterate and don't have complicated thoughts and complicated language and complicated images. I find it just hopeless to try to persuade anybody differently, and probably one of the reasons that Reynolds and I have always loved one another is because in this area of black-white relations, having to do with the language of black people and the language of poor people who are black and white, he never patronizes his characters, you never pity those people—neither one of us does, in the text I mean. And their language is powerfully articulated, whether or not the grammar is the grammar of standard English. . . . I think it's an illegitimate complaint on the part of the critics. I thought Ibsen solved all that. Or James Joyce. I mean, you can really have tragedy that belongs to people who are not in the so-called aristocracy or the upper class. It's amazing that anybody would still level that kind of charge at his work.

Charles Guggenheim: You've been and lived in a number of places. Other writers that you know have lived around and had adventures, been in wars and wrote movies, come back home, and then left. Reynolds never left. Do you know anyone who has stayed in one place as long as he has and still been interesting?

Toni Morrison: Well, there are people who have stayed in one place and become interesting writers, but I'm not so sure they were as interesting as people as he is. But it's a source of great delight to me to know that he has chosen, even before he became ill, to stay in that place, because his is a long-distance mind and that's what's important. It's like saying Emily Dickinson never went anywhere—so what? Or some of the nineteenth-century novelists. Some people really need adventure and odd encounters in order to ignite their imagination, or they need to bump up against some curious anecdote in the newspaper or in a history to ignite their imagination, but Reynolds is an autodidact in that regard. He has always been his own ignition. He always had the seed and the blossom. And knew that the nurturing and the water and the soil was already there. . . .

He's a quintessential American writer. He understands so much about the bravery and the dreams and the failures of men and women who live in these small towns—people who go to big towns and come back or don't go where most of the people in the world live; people who have managed to get through a devastating history in some way that is fascinating and enlightening to read about. I get more of a sense of American people from his work than I do from some of the grander themes in other people's work. He knows the jewelry of them. He knows the intricate clockwork, and he knows not just the sinews but also the way the whole thing works when they make these terrific mistakes or manage certain kinds of reconciliations.

[Interview conducted by Charles Guggenheim in Princeton, New Jersey, on 14 May 1992.]

STEPHEN SPENDER

When Reynolds was at Oxford, when I first knew him, the fact that he was a southerner stuck out a mile and he played up to this in a delightful way. I mean he acted the southerner and there were the southern stories, and also just the way he talked. He was half doing a parody of himself from North Carolina. With this accent and these turns of phrase. That's part of what was delightful about him. . . .

His writing seems to come out of the idea that the South, or anyhow Raleigh and Durham, is one big family. And I think it does actually all come out of his family background. So I don't think that in his writing he is fash-

ioning this. He is accepting his position as a member of the family. . . .
There's a peculiar kind of Reynolds' way, when he's describing his southern
characters or making them funny, which is really the attitude of someone who
is both an insider and an outsider looking on at the same time, which is one of
the things that makes his writing, which is often tragic, actually a kind of
comedy. It's a sort of comedy of manners. And this, I think, can be irritating;
I often find if I'm reading a novel by Reynolds that in the first twenty pages I
feel rather irritated by this. But when he gets into it, he changes as it were
and becomes hypnotic, and you get fascinated and hypnotized by it and
you're no longer outside. He's sort of drawn you into the center of it. But he
is a very mannered writer, I think. And I don't know whether he's aware of
that. I don't know whether he'd think of himself exactly as a kind of manner-
ist. Partly perhaps as a result of his having traveled and having these two
years in England, he has that quality. . . .

I think that his whole situation in life is that of a loner. And there's
something perhaps slightly deceptive about Reynolds because he is so capable
of intimacy and so gifted for friendship, but there must have been quite a few
people who thought, I'll spend the rest of my life with Reynolds, but I don't
think Reynolds really wants to be twenty-four hours a day, weeks on end,
with anyone. And I think this comes out of his childhood. . . . He was forced
at a very early age . . . to be head of the family, and I think this gave him a
great sense of responsibility and probably forced his development so that
when I met him, and he was about twenty-two, he was really quite beyond
his age. Very mature in certain ways. A very developed kind of person. But it
also means that he's at once open to other people, and at the same time
there's something very inaccessible and lonely about him. . . .

Reynolds would resent very much being docketed, earmarked as a
southern writer. And he's not. He is a master of English or American, whatever you want to call our common language. . . . He seems to be universal in
the same way as, say, Thomas Hardy is universal, and very much like that
because he is really dealing with universal themes of love and death and
human relationships. . . . And just as much as if you read, say, a Greek
tragedy, you're dealing with a universal situation which happens to be situ-
ated in a particular time and place. Reynolds is very much that sort of
writer. . . .

He sent me this very long story, *A Long and Happy Life,* and I was fascinated by it. Its most striking quality was the extreme self-consciousness of the
writer, this very young writer, of what he was doing. He has a way of writing
which incidentally is the way that Iris Murdoch writes, and that is that he
writes the main body of his text on the right-hand side of the notebook or
page, and on the left-hand side he'd keep notes about what he was writing,
and he'd carry a kind of running criticism of what he was writing while he
was actually writing it. Well, I think there's something of this in his early
writing. Something of this extreme kind of self-awareness, self-consciousness,

does get into the writing. And so I think *A Long and Happy Life* perhaps struck my colleagues as being almost artificial because of this, and it aroused a very strong reaction, sometimes of antipathy. At that time Dwight McDonald was helping us edit *Encounter*. And he was absolutely horrified by this story, and I happen to know that it was offered to Random House, and I think that Jason Epstein said he'd resign from Random House sooner than publish this. So anyhow this showed the tremendous force behind the personality of the writing. Although I would think of this extreme self-consciousness as, rather surprisingly, perhaps an American characteristic. I think it was Henry James who said that the Americans are the most self-conscious people in the world. . . .

[*A Long and Happy Life*] must have hit some very deep nerve, it must have hit some kind of repression in themselves which I really can't account for. . . .

In Reynolds' later work, [the self-consciousness] hasn't gone out, but I think that he is so much more in his material that one accepts it. . . . In his later work he's plunged so very deeply, with all his sympathies, into the lives of the people whom he's describing that one forgets this, or one admires it. One thinks, Well, this is what makes it, this story or novel or whatever it is. That's such a work of art. . . .

I did feel that Reynolds had the capacity to become a kind of modern Henry James, really a sort of writer who covered the whole English area of experience. He was so amusing about Oxford and the people he met there. . . . He seemed at that time to be the kind of writer who travels a great deal. I suppose rather like Gore. I mean not a sort of writer like Gore Vidal, but rather like Gore in his ability to spread over a whole continent. . . .

He knows North Carolina as he knows his own family. And one always has the sense in his novels that he is writing about a family. Southerners. . . .

I certainly think he's one of the more important [writers in America today], but I do think that there's something about Reynolds which I can see that might limit his public. And that is that he is a very private person. Somehow he's a very private person even in his writing. And I think there's a kind of feeling amongst readers today that they want the writer to be a public person and to belong to a public world in a way that they recognize. But when you read Reynolds Price, you are immediately entering into a private world created and minted by a private person, but it takes a very long time for a general public to catch up with this. I should say that Reynolds would be a writer whose fame would increase as the years go on. And I suppose when he dies, which I hope won't be for a long time, I suppose that someone will write his biography and people will become extremely interested in his personality, and they'll find that his personality is much more interesting than that of most writers who have great public reputations. And also they'll find out things about all his work—not just his novels but his essays and his poems. His poems are very peculiar. But very, very interesting—anyway as revealing his personality. I think he is one of those writers whose relationship between his personal life and his writing is truly interesting and will be more and more discussed.

[Interview conducted by Charles Guggenheim in London, England, on 16 August 1991.]

At the request of Natasha Spender, the following excerpt from a 1987 interview of Stephen Spender, conducted by Michael Ruhlman, has been appended. Said Spender of Price:

> He is unique, really. He ranks very high, with Eudora Welty and, I suppose, Faulkner. Reynolds's writing is a kind of writing that is actually poetry. The dialogue is like real dialogue, but it's been elevated into a special language which he carries through with great consistency. Reynolds persuades one that his characters not only speak in character, but also that they talk out of a whole culture. I was always hoping he'd become an English writer [meaning that he hoped Price would stay in England]. (Michael Ruhlman, "A Writer at His Best," *New York Times Magazine* [20 September 1987]: 134)

JAMES TAYLOR AND KATHRYN WALKER

James Taylor: For me there's a very strong sense of landscape [to North Carolina]. A very geologic kind, with a sense of the climate and the character of the light and how time passes, and with the trees and the fields and the weeds that grow there, and things that stick to your trousers as you walk through the brush. It's just a strong sense that I have, a very physical sense of the place, and Reynolds clearly is on that wavelength too. I can almost taste it or smell it when I read about the Mustians or any of his stuff that's set down there. . . .

[M]y experience of working with Reynolds has been that there is never any feeling of obligation or pressure, or of the difficulty of trying to include and make a consensus of two different wills; it's just that he simply will not have that be a problem. . . .

It's always difficult to describe exactly who does what and how, but he was just involved from the very beginning [with the composition of "Copperline"], and that song is, as I have said before, about North Carolina. It is very much that sense of landscape and the physical sense of growing up down there and what it was like, and Reynolds and I share that. . . .

The song "Hymn"? Well, I had taken some things down to North Carolina and showed them to Reynolds and recorded them on a tape for him, some musical ideas, and I asked him also to just send me, without music, some lyrical things, and he sent two things up, one of which was this poem, "Hymn," and I sat with it for a while and came up with the music to it.

Kathryn Walker: I think he's a profoundly spiritual person, but he certainly isn't conventionally religious. I mean one doesn't feel in the presence of someone who has a tenacious orthodoxy. He's antic and irreverent often and very funny. He seems to me Eastern in his religion—like a sort of bodhisattva or an adept, someone who's reached another plane. He has great calm and focus. I would say that the essential quality of experiencing Reynolds' being is that he is profoundly compassionate and wishes well to all creatures, so in that way, as well as the antic spirit, he seems more Eastern than Western to me. Even though, of course, he's done those translations on the New Testament. He seems to understand quite a lot about suffering, mercy and grace. He's interested in that. What that actually means in people's lives. . . .

About his language . . . the language [in the television play *Private Contentment*] is, in fact, not at all the way people talk. It's extremely literary, it's very poetic, very dense. It doesn't exactly have the sound of spontaneous language, but it is poetic in the true sense in that it sounds as if it comes out of someone's soul. It's like the voice of someone's deepest mind reflecting, rather than the way someone actually speaks to other people. . . . [As an actress] I adored it, I loved it. It was like doing—I don't want to sound excessive—but it was like doing poetry as drama, like doing Shakespeare or the Greeks. Large themes, rich language.

James Taylor: [A]s lyrics go, the lyric to "Hymn" is unusually dense and, as Kathryn says, kind of developed. It's distilled. But it also has a strong sense of cadence and there is a rhythm to it. It's just hard to find. And it's not a light piece of work, it's an intense and profound thing to say, and it's dark, you know. A lot of it is really dark.

Kathryn Walker: It's compressed but it's not constructed. I mean, it has the cadence of human speech—that's what makes it possible to use that sort of higher language, even in what's meant to be a naturalistic film [*Private Contentment*], and have it sound as if these southern people might actually speak that way.

James Taylor: I was going to say that the tolerance and delight and acceptance and goodwill that you feel Reynolds bringing into his life in general he also brings to his own work, and if there are things about it that might be considered stylized or might be criticized from one point or another, that's OK. The main quality to knowing him is that he really just allows for everything to exist. You asked before about religion. Religion for him is not something that closes him down, and so often when you think of religion you think of rigidity and of a sort of self-limitation; people use religion to stave off and hold off existence. But you don't feel that Reynolds does very much of that. He just doesn't. You really get a contagious feeling from him that everything's OK.

[Interview conducted by Charles Guggenheim in New York City on 9 December 1991.]

REVIEWS

Country Girl Burdened with Love

Granville Hicks

Reynolds Price is one young writer—he was born in 1933—who cannot complain that his first novel has been neglected. In advance of publication *A Long and Happy Life* (Atheneum, $3.95) has been heartily praised by Eudora Welty, Stephen Spender, and Lord David Cecil, among others, and *Harper's* magazine plans to publish the entire novel in a special supplement. Happily, the book deserves the attention it is being given.

It is a love story, and one of the simplest and most poignant I have ever read. Rosacoke Mustian has been in love with Wesley Beavers for six years, and she has never known, and does not know when the novel opens, what he feels about her or whether he feels anything. On the surface they are just ordinary young people: she lives on a farm in North Carolina and works in the local telephone exchange; he, recently discharged from the Navy, is selling motorcycles in Roanoke.

The novel begins with a dazzling passage:

> Just with his body and from inside like a snake, leaning that black motorcy-cle from side to side, cutting in and out of the slow line of cars to get there first, staring due-north through goggles towards Mount Moriah and switching coon tails in everybody's face was Wesley Beavers, and laid against his back, like sleep, spraddle-legged on the sheepskin seat behind him was Rosacoke Mustian who was maybe his girl and who had given up looking into the wind and trying to nod at every sad car in the line, and when he even speeded up and passed the truck (lent for the afternoon by Mr. Isaac Alston and driven by Sammy his man, hauling one pine box and one black boy dressed in all he could borrow, set up in a ladder-back chair with flowers banked round him and a foot on the box to steady it)—when he even passed that, Rosacoke said once into his back "Don't" and rested in humiliation, not thinking but with her hands on his hips for dear life and her white blouse blown out behind her like a banner in defeat.

When one first reads the paragraph, it seems excessive, almost flashy, but then one realizes how much Price has done, how much he has told us

Review of *A Long and Happy Life*. From *The Saturday Review* (10 March 1962): 17–18. Reprinted by permission of *The Saturday Review* 1962, SR Publications, Ltd.

about Wesley and Rosacoke, how well he has suggested the setting of his tale, how beautifully adapted his style is to the movement he is describing. As one reads on, he proves to be a stylist of great resourcefulness. He effectively uses not only the vocabulary but also the syntax of common speech: "Everybody was bowed, including Baby Sister who took prayer serious to be so young." Yet he can range as far and as high as he sees fit.

The novel begins with Rosacoke at the funeral of a Negro girl, Mildred, a friend of hers who has died while bearing a fatherless child. From this touching scene, observed with the greatest precision, we move rapidly to a boisterous picnic and then there is an inconclusive conversation between Rosacoke and Wesley. By this time we know both of them well. Wesley is headstrong, wayward, self-centered, and aloof, but we suspect, as Rosacoke does, that there may be more to him than is immediately apparent. As for Rosa, she is just a country girl, bright enough in her way but remarkable in only one respect—her bottomless capacity for love. She demands little of Wesley, but she would like to know where she stands.

This, of course, is what she cannot know, and, as the story develops, we feel her agony. At last she gives in to Wesley's sexual importunity, hoping that in this way she can come to terms with him, but she finds in the end that they are further apart than ever, and she is left with nothing but pride and despair. When she discovers that she is pregnant, she cannot bring herself to let Wesley know but resolves to bear the burden alone. That her friend Mildred has died in childbirth, that her sister-in-law has borne a dead child, these are not thoughts to comfort her, but fear for herself is nothing in comparison with her loneliness.

The novel comes to its climax with the Christmas pageant in Delight Baptist Church. Although he has scarcely seemed to try, Price has made us acquainted with the little community: paralyzed Mr. Isaac with his faithful colored servant and his horehound candy, the multitudinous Guptons, the members of Rosacoke's family, and all the others.

The pageant is like a thousand other pageants that take place in small towns every Christmas in every part of the country, and Price records it with tenderness and exactitude: the songs, the extemporized costumes, the cheap jewel box and the butter dish in which the Wise Men carry their gifts.

Because Willie Duke Aycock has run away to get married, Rosacoke has to take the part of Mary, watching over one of the Gupton progeny while the angels and the shepherds and the Wise Men make their appearances and sing their songs. As she sits there, Price takes us inside her mind, so that we feel with her as we rarely feel with a character in fiction. "All this time," she thinks, "I have lived on the hope he would change some day before it was too late and come home and calm down and learn how to talk to me and maybe even listen, and we would have a long life together—him and me—and be happy sometimes and get us children that would look like him and have his name and answer when we called. I just hoped that."

The ending is ambiguous, but the epigraph, which is from Dante, permits us to believe that the briar may blossom, that Rosacoke may realize some part of her dream. But that doesn't really matter. We have shared in Rosa's great ordeal, and it is an experience not soon to be forgotten.

Although he writes of simple matters, Price can make use of sophisticated literary devices. There are certain motifs that recur: the deer, Mr. Isaac's spring, the pecan tree, Rosacoke's father's sunken grave. The hawk Rosacoke sees and the white heron she doesn't see are both significant. When she says she has hoped that she and Wesley "would have a long life together . . . and be happy sometimes," she is unconsciously and ironically echoing something she said about Mildred at the funeral service: "There I was just wanting to give her a pair of stockings and wish her a long and happy life and she was already gone." Indeed, the last scene, the scene of the pageant, is full of echoes, and one realizes how carefully conceived this apparently artless narrative is. All the author's skills, however, are tools in the service of this insight, which is phenomenal. To have created Rosacoke Mustian is an achievement that the most mature novelist might envy.

Mantle of Faulkner?

John Wain

Mr. Price's new novel is highly elaborate, complex in plot, mannered in style, booming with symbolic overtones; to use an old-fashioned expression, it "smells of the lamp." Literary fashion certainly has come round in a circle. Forty years ago it was the thing for novelists to cut down the narrative element in their work and make the action limited and static, or even nonexistent, while they got on with psychological exploration. Critics used to shake their heads over the disappearance of plot or, worse still, its abandonment to thriller-writers who could only vulgarize it. They need not have worried. Much fine plotting still went on.

Hemingway's mastery alone would have kept it alive through the doldrums; and in England there were Graham Greene and Evelyn Waugh, both good constructors of plot. But with Mr. Price we circle back to a conception of plot that would have seemed conventional to Wilkie Collins or Dickens: enormous coincidences, an uncanny resemblance between uncle and nephew, a large sum of money hidden among the rotting boards of a hut in the woods, the unexplained reappearance of a character long assumed to be dead, etc., etc.

Dickens would also have felt at home with the large recurrent symbols. A man who has seduced a woman and left her with their child, hopelessly dependent on such scraps of affection as he tosses to her on his infrequent casual visits, goes to see her for the last time and gives her a snake for a present. She becomes sufficiently attached to the reptile to add other snakes to it and join a traveling fair with her own snake-show. She brings up her lover's child and the snake together: finally, both girl and snake are responsible for a dramatic involvement with the Mustian family, whose acquaintance we made in Mr. Price's first novel, *A Long and Happy Life*.

Here we are in the presence of one of those large symbols like the dustheaps of *Our Mutual Friend* or the prisons of *Little Dorrit*, though what it symbolizes is less clear. The ramifications of the plot are just as mystifying, especially since the story is told sideways rather than from beginning to end. There are two long flashbacks, each narrated by a woman character; one goes

Review of *A Generous Man*. From *The New Republic* 154 (14 May 1966): 31–33. Reprinted by permission of *The New Republic,* © 1966, The New Republic, Inc.

on for seventeen pages and the other for twelve; each reveals crucial plot material at a rapid pace, in the manner of those crude nuggets of exposition that one learns to forgive in Victorian novels. In addition, there are little excursions, loops from the main line of the story, which describe, in detail, characters and events whose relation to the rest of the novel is illustrative and perhaps symbolic. (A broken-down veterinary surgeon who declares a mad dog incurable and thus unwittingly sets the plot in motion: a Negro child guarding an illicit still in the woods.) To find all this in a novel of less than three hundred pages will at any rate confirm us in our impression that Mr. Price is a writer who works hard and expects his reader to work hard also. But what else? What does it add up to?

As the dream of the Great American Novel fades further and further from memory, the literary map of the USA comes to resemble a cozy plot of crazy paving, with everyone sitting comfortably on his own little stone. There must be many people who know more about current American fiction than I do, but nobody seems to be able to tell me of a writer who still tries to capture the American experience in anything like its entirety. Perhaps the time has gone by when it could be captured. John O'Hara's Pennsylvania WASPs just don't have the same American experience as Kerouac's Beats, Philip Roth's big-city Jews or the Catholic fathers of J. F. Powers. Everybody has chosen to "cultivate his garden." The result is that European readers simply cannot settle down to read "an American book" as they might have done in the days of Mark Twain or even of Sinclair Lewis or even of Hemingway. In fact the last-named is a good example because, however cosmopolitan his settings, he saw himself as the spokesman for a particularly American set of values; when he asserted that all American fiction came out of one book, *Huckleberry Finn,* Hemingway was standing up to be counted; the statement was his way of placing himself firmly in the tradition of Mark Twain, who, whatever he wrote about, was always understood by the whole world to be speaking for "America." (The extent to which both men cultivated their personal appearance and staged their public personalities is a clue to the roles they felt themselves to be playing. And on the whole it has to be said that they both played their roles creditably, and deserved well of their country.)

This has now entirely disappeared as a novelistic ambition; in fact, the very idea of it has disappeared. The Jewish school of novelists who dominate American fiction at the moment are obviously altogether free of any illusion that they speak for "America." So are the very active Negro novelists. The middle-class world we enter with Cheever, or Updike, or (in a more loaded way) with Salinger, has no national flavor; it is simply part of that vast Western suburban middle class that lives anywhere between the Pacific Coast and the Berlin Wall: wearing the same suits, occupying the same houses, reading the same magazines, watching the same programs on TV, as their counterparts in France or England, Canada or Norway. What these writers explore is a general social situation. Whereas the Great American Novel, in the days when it was projected and dreamed about, was to have explored a situation unique in its geography, its history, its emotional inheritance, as well as its sociology.

Possibly we have now to face the fact that the great American novel, if it is to come, will have to be written in depth and not in breadth: that some writer who accepts his regional boundaries as finally as Proust or Ibsen accepted the limited societies about which they wrote, will nevertheless lay bare the American heart. The reception given to Mr. Price's *A Long and Happy Life* made one think that perhaps this possibility was in sight. Like many others, I rushed to read it. And I must bluntly record a disappointment. Ably done, vivid, as the book is, it confirms me in two beliefs I would willingly not be confirmed in: namely, that the two deadly enemies of the American novel are (1) a too willing acquiescence in the conventions of realism, (2) Creative Writing courses in the universities.

A Long and Happy Life is "Southern" in the sense in which we, the rest of the world, have long since come to understand the term. It deals with simple characters; it describes a rural setting and rather consciously old-fashioned ways. It is also written in a prose that we may call stylized, if we wish to be kind, or affected, if we feel it necessary to be astringent; it has the *faux-naïf* quality that seems to hang round Southern writing. The action is described through the eyes of the adolescent girl Rosacoke Mustian, and the language of the book is a lumpy mixture of Rosacoke's idiom and Mr. Price's. The result is that nothing comes across quite clearly: as with Faulkner, we have to peer at the action through a clouded window of half-dramatization. William Faulkner was a major imaginative writer who deserved his Nobel Prize, but that is not the same thing as being a good influence on other writers, and I felt a vague disquiet at the book's closeness to Faulkner, whose irritating mannerisms are so much more imitable than his moral and imaginative largeness: a disquiet that was intensified when I read that it had been given the Award of the William Faulkner Foundation, whatever that may be.

As to the Creative Writing programs, it is my impression that they do vastly more harm than good, and the syllabus time that is lavished on them ought to be spent on learning something solid. I don't, of course, know whether Mr. Price ever followed one of these courses, and it is irrelevant, because the whole case against them is that they foster a certain kind of approach to fiction-writing which then becomes common among people who have never been near a Creative Writing hothouse, simply because it gets into the air: an approach with too much head in it, too much symbol-sowing, too much of the sort of thing that is calculated to please critics by giving them something to extract and discuss. Creative Writing courses are run by critics (an imaginative writer who gets tempted into them gives up being an imaginative writer until he gets out again and becomes, for that period, a critic), and when a literature is written (consciously or unconsciously) to please critics, to attract their attention and give them some discussion-fodder, that literature is not in a healthy state. *A Long and Happy Life* pivots too easily on its symbolism; the wild deer which the little girls see in the woods, in Rosacoke's reminiscence near the beginning, comes back too patly as the harbinger of her seduction by Wesley Beavers; it seems a conventional sign, like a key-signature in music. Again, the final scene of the book is loaded with a factitious symbolism that is exactly the kind of thing encouraged by Creative Writing professors. And, for that matter, by William Faulkner: not the great Faulkner of the twenties and thirties, but the old gasbag Faulkner of the campus years, the Faulkner of *A Fable*.

So to open *A Generous Man* and find that it deals with the Mustian family again, at an earlier point in their history, is a disagreeable experience. This sort of "Southern" writing, easily taking over the pretentiousness of Faulkner but rarely able to rival his flashes of genius, is too easy, too predictable. The rural life of the South, twenty or thirty years ago, is tempting to the novelist because of its picturesque qualities. It offers a ready-made source of color and character; in American writing, it occupies exactly the same place as books about Ireland occupy in English writing. The Irishman is rural, fanciful, possessed by strange religious emotions, sometimes driven to outbreaks of violence. So, to the English writer who happens to know the background—or to the Irish writer with his eye on the international market—he is a natural subject. But the more serious writer will keep away from such stereotypes: not from the subject, necessarily, but from the subject in its stereotyped aspects. One doesn't wish to apply the parallel too patly to Mr. Price: but he is a writer of obvious gifts, powers and ambitions; and perhaps it is not too late to remind him that Faulkner's books have already been written, and that, whichever way you look at it, one Yoknapatawpha County is enough.

[Review of *Love and Work*]

Marston LaFrance

Mr. Price's third novel may seem slight in poundage, but it is extremely well-done: soundly conceived, carefully constructed, well-written. If there is a cracked timber anywhere in the framework, it is probably the scene in which, by coincidence, the protagonist happens upon an automobile wreck; but whatever fissure exists Mr. Price has painted into a pleasant appearance with a prose style that has been noted by others. I do not happen to admire Mr. Price's overworking the dash, or the somewhat disjointed rhythm he favors, the result of dashes and semi-colons laced into comparatively short sentences, but the author of such a novel as this has earned the right to indulge his own stylistic preferences.

Thomas Eborn, the protagonist—thirty-four, childless although seven years married, writer, English professor—is a psychological basket-case who would be tolerated in the worlds of Richardson, James, Proust, Hartley, Cozzens, but would be drop-kicked forthwith from the more knockabout preserves of Fielding, Melville, Crane, or Hemingway. Nor would Eborn be at home in Yoknapatawpha County, because he is neither burdened by any discernible weight of history, personally gifted with either irony or humor, nor morally strong enough to qualify even as water-boy at the sidelines of a tragic encounter, even though his professions make him heir to the wealth of Western literature. Some characters seem larger than life; Eborn, if only he could be pried out of the context of this novel, would seem smaller than life. An implicit measure of the author's ability lies in the fact that he is able to make this John Marcher of a protagonist not only vivid and alive, but also interesting, even sympathetic.

Eborn, an emotional remora ready to attach himself to anyone or anything capable of yielding him sustenance, occupies the center of the stage from first page to last. There is no attempt to move beyond him and his own problems—which certainly are sufficient—and thus there are no symbolic images that reverberate from any sounding-board other than his own shivering psyche. His function as a vehicle for truth develops from two great reservoirs of significance into which he channels his energies, and thus masks his

Reprinted, with permission, from *Studies in Short Fiction* 8 (1971): 345–46. Copyright 1971 by Newberry College.

own emptiness: love and work. Through the way in which he uses these two realities in a futile attempt to sustain his bankrupt personality, Thomas Eborn becomes a recognizable North American Tom Everyman, and the context that he brings to focus illustrates how even such noble pursuits as love and work can be turned to ashes.

Eborn is selfish. Worse, his selfishness derives from his immense vanity which, like that of a child, is quite innocent. Hence, he continually takes, from both love and work, and gives as little of himself as possible in return. In teaching his classes he says "the things he had said for eight years past." His creative writing group works "not to learn to write but to make a beginning." And the best work he is able to produce himself is judged correctly by his wife as "easy lies."

His approach to love ends in the same cul-de-sac as his pursuit of work because he is as incapable of the one as he is of the other. He merely uses his friends and sincerely suffers from the delusion that his dreams may affect their lives. Most of all, he uses his wife as cook, servant, buffer to the world, general lackey-in-residence, and she is "dead-tired, bone-tired, from slouching out here, slinking round your stoop while you fling out the scraps to slick fat strangers."

Work and love unite to reveal Eborn's monumental ego when he begins to create in fiction what he believes to be the unlived lives of his dead parents, to rescue them from having lived lives of insignificance. Given the examination of love and work through the personality of a conspicuous failure at both, the prose is freighted with a quiet irony that continues to unfold within one's mind long after one has read the book.

The only salvation for Eborn and his kind lies in an honest confrontation with the self. This encounter with truth implicitly occurs at the climax of the novel—the penultimate sentence—that aware readers will find at once obvious, ironic, and wonderfully ambiguous. Mr. Price's work, the opposite of Eborn's, is neither easy nor lies, and this novel is a worthy addition to his canon.

The Reynolds Price Who Outgrew the Southern Pastoral

Theodore Solotaroff

Eight years ago Reynolds Price, then twenty-nine years old, published a first novel called *A Long and Happy Life,* which immediately established him as the legitimate heir of the great Southern writers of the past generations. The book is about a sweet, firm, country-wise girl named Rosacoke Mustian, who works for the phone company in a hamlet in the Piedmont region and waits for a boy named Wesley Beavers to stop running around and settle down.

Rosacoke's name is but the first of the indignities of her life that she bears with a natural and virtually unremitting grace, and Wesley's name is only the beginning of his intent, elusive, and horny nature. Otherwise, Price didn't have much to work with. But from these banalities, enclosed in a world where little happens except births, deaths, and Christmas, Price constructed a novel with what Mark Twain once called "the calm confidence of a Christian with four aces," one so full of feeling that it reverberates in every sentence. Here is the opening one:

> Just with his body and from inside like a snake, leaning that black motorcycle side to side, cutting in and out of the slow line of cars to get there first, staring due-north through goggles towards Mount Moriah and switching coon tails in everybody's face was Wesley Beavers, and laid against his back like sleep, spraddle-legged on the sheepskin seat behind him was Rosacoke Mustian who was maybe his girl and who had given up looking into the wind and trying to nod at every sad car in the line, and when he even speeded up and passed the truck (lent for the afternoon by Mr. Isaac Alston and driven by Sammy his man, hauling one pine box and one black boy dressed in all he could borrow, set up in a ladder-back chair with flowers banked round him and a foot on the box to steady it)—when he even passed that, Rosacoke said once into his back "Don't" and rested in humiliation, not thinking but with her hands on his hips for dear life and her white blouse blown out behind her like a banner in defeat.

Review of *Permanent Errors.* From *The Saturday Review* (26 September 1970): 27–29, 46. Reprinted by permission of *The Saturday Review,* © 1970, SR Publications, Ltd.

Some beginning—of a book, of a career. Its sheer virtuosity is like that of a quarterback who on the first play of his first professional game throws a sixty-yard pass on the run, hitting the receiver exactly at the instant he breaks into the clear: a tremendous assertion of agility, power, timing, and accuracy. I won't try to give this sentence the English 31 treatment; I shall merely point out that detail by detail, image by image, Price has built up a complete synoptic view of the novel to come: its movement, figures, ground, issues, tonality, meaning. It is a sentence made up of charged essences—bits of imaginative uranium that radiate implications. It is also a sentence whose unfolding, suspenseful syntax marks the born storyteller. Finally, it is a sentence that could only have been written by someone in perfect touch with his material. The experience of connection with a society is behind every word, simile, cadence—a live experience caught at the point of overflow and then bodied forth as art.

I have paused too long over this one sentence, but no matter. I write of Price out of a sense of appreciation that I want you to share, and so I have to be specific. Also, the sentence marks a starting point in what has become a complex career. In his second novel, *A Generous Man,* Price returned to the Mustian family, this time focusing on Milo, Rosacoke's older brother, in his three days of passage into manhood and his one brimming moment of glory as the prince of his erotic desires and all they surveyed. Already moving on from *A Long and Happy Life* and from *The Names and Faces of Heroes* (a first collection of stories as sure in their realism as Chekhov's), Price turned Milo's story into something very different.

A Generous Man is a romance in form: the elegiac note of Milo's adventure rising and falling through melodrama, farce, and even literary burlesque. Partly the farce is there to convey the leveling and coarsening that awaited Milo and would turn him into the bitter buffoon who appears six years later in Rosacoke's story. But it is also there as a kind of distance that Price was opening up between himself and the tradition of Southern pastoral in which he had begun so securely. Much of Rosacoke's world, though no less coarse, had been composed as a kind of vibrant emptiness of woods, fields, and lonely roads; Milo's was filled in by a community of misfits and clowns. It was as though Price had now brought together Faulkner and Erskine Caldwell: the theme of *The Bear* turned into a desultory, silly hunt for a carnival snake named Death; the motifs of rootedness—to place, family, folkways, etc.— undercut by a chronicle of displaced kin wandering into weird reunion attended even by a murderous family ghost. There is a lot of playfulness in Milo's story, but it is finally a bitterer one than Rosacoke's.

When the impotent sheriff, a kind of backwoods Montaigne, says to Milo, "Don't think it's morning when it's late afternoon," the burden of the novel which follows is that Milo's golden energy is not only his own valedictory but also that of a way of life, youth being the one glowing coal in these ashes. Among the losses, catalogued as well as foreseen, in *A Generous Man* is, I think, the loss of Price's early, full, harmonious relationship with the inhabitants of Mustian Corners, or whatever it's called, and possibly with the place itself.

In any case, his fiction since then has steered clear of it. His last novel, *Love and Work,* and this new collection of stories, *Permanent Errors,* are obviously intended to bring his writing level with his later experience and temperament. If he had grown up partly with people like the Mustians, he was also a boy from the Southern middle class who had gone to Duke and to Oxford University in England, and had returned to Duke as a teacher and writer-in-residence. Indeed, the last is mainly what these two recent books are about: a writer in residence in himself. They are also the work of a man who is further along in his life. The precocious brilliance and composure of his first novel no longer seem of much interest to Price; the artistry is still there but it is case-hardened, mainly by his own experience and the issues that relate to it. The sense of loss that still works through his themes like yeast in bread is now for a girl one has loved for years, or a mother, or a wife. Instead of the losses of life cresting, there are those of life already dwindling. By the time a writer is well into his thirties, the bonus of energy he has received from his ambitions and enthusiasms begins to run out, and other things—sacrificed, ignored, misunderstood—catch up with him. The thirties are a time to pay up and to try to start anew.

Love and Work is a virtually complete portrait of a writer who has placed working before living, who expected his art to strengthen and redeem his life when the practice of it was chilling his already cool nature down to the freezing point. "The perfection of the life or of the work?" Yeats's choice isn't that simple, not if one lives with others, not if one is still attached to them by the chains (in both senses) of love. Thomas Eborn, a writer in his early thirties, has kept his hostages to fortune down to two: his mother, who has an inoperable aneurysm, and his wife, who dutifully helps support both of them but is becoming skeptical.

While Eborn is writing an essay on the blessing of work (". . . free through the exercise of my proud and growing skill from other human beings, free even from those people I love, especially them . . . free from ourselves, our final enemy . . ."), his mother tries to reach him. But he has a deadline, can't be disturbed, and before he gets back to her the "time-bomb" in her forehead has gone off. His dreams tell him that he has been secretly willing it. A second death soon follows: a boy whom he has helped pull from a wrecked car.

Eborn feels himself to be the victim of some black destiny. When will it end, he asks. "When I let it. When I've stripped all attachments from myself; stand clear of my family, friends, hindering strangers; stand alone, my own." But then his work begins to come through for him. Partly as reparation, he starts a novel about his dead parents' courtship, writing some thirty pages that have a genuine authority of detail and feeling (it most reminds me of Reynolds Price's early fiction). He coaxes a reaction from his wife; when it comes, it is devastating: "Easy lies," she says. Other revelations follow, the final one being a blinding vision of his parents' actual love for each other, which in his willed self-isolation he can now no more write about than share.

That's a superficial reading. In its deeper reaches, *Love and Work* is a novel about the unconscious and its circuits of love, fear, and punishment—what used to be called God. There is more than a hint of the spiritual in Price, rather like that in E. M. Forster or Rilke, which takes a psychological rather than a theological form: a powerful sense of dark unseen forces and influences that are only partly explained by the description of emotions and that require not just attention but supplication. This preoccupation comes increasingly into the foreground of *Permanent Errors,* a collection of stories and other pieces that, written over a period of seven years, lead up to and away from the issues of *Love and Work.*

In a brief, rather cryptic introduction Price tells us that the pieces are joined by a common intention: "the attempt to isolate in a number of lives the central error of act, will, understanding which, once made, has been permanent, incurable, but whose diagnosis and palliation are the hopes of continuance." Most of the errors in the book are committed by writers, who share Eborn's view that a writer needs solitude and detachment as a fish needs water (which happens to be true), but who use this need as a cover for vanity, timidity, selfishness, blindness, and other modes of withdrawal and assault.

There are two, possibly three, main examples. The first is Charles Tamplin, a young American writer living in England, who is involved in four pieces collectively titled "Fool's Education." Tamplin is something of an esthete and a prig who tends to view his experience from a self-protective literary attitude and to take his knowledge of life from the happiness and the scars of others. But he is not merely foolish: he has a quick, relevant understanding of what he sees, and though it comes too late to profit him in his life, it can, once recognized, accepted, and grieved over, perhaps help to strengthen him in his vocation. His situation is beautifully rendered in the first story, which deals with the last day of his long-standing affair with a girl from home, a Rosacoke who has been to Vassar. To Tamplin, it is a day to get through, to kill gracefully and lightly, like the affair itself, and round it to a close. From their failure "to meet, to serve one another, to delight in the work" he will now gain his freedom to make art from it. They visit a favorite church near Oxford and end up trading, rather bitterly, the epitaphs on the tombs. His is an elegy by Ben Jonson for a friend who died young, in which the poet finds consolation in the very brevity of the life:

> In small proportions, we just beauty
>   see;
> And in short measures, life may
>   perfect be.

Sara's inscription is from a family tomb and speaks of the ties of love under the aspect of death:

> And they that lived and loved either
> Should die and lie and sleep together.
> Go reader. Whether go or stay,
> Thou must not hence be long away.

"It's a truer poem," she says. "It could change whole lives." Tamplin is unimpressed. A short while later their car almost collides with a flock of sheep. A young shepherd follows them, apparently just awakened, refreshes himself with a last patch of snow, and calmly says, "Sorry." It is enough to light up Sara, who smiles and waves him pardon. A few small images of life's transience, but enough to make Tamplin realize that Sara will recover in ways he won't—or only enough to write truly about the burden of this day.

Tamplin's pitfalls and recognitions deepen as his chronicle moves along. He is a young man in flight, one foot out the door of any entangling relationship, ready to pull the door of his privacy shut at any sign of invasion. He closes it on a desperate woman who wants to use his bed to steal a few moments of love, but he ends up worshiping the bitter mysteries of her love-scarred life. For there is a stern beneficence operating in his fate that drives him out of his shell, turns his timidity to a certain kind of strength, leads him, some years later, to abandon his stiff-necked pride and ask forgiveness for not forgiving Sara's rightful distrust of him.

This difficult movement from grievance to grief surges powerfully through the last two stories in the book, which deal with an older writer, not unlike Tamplin, whose wife first attempts and then commits suicide. "Good and Bad Dreams" is an extraordinary tracing of the borderland of the conscious and the unconscious that lies between a husband and a wife who have reached a terrible ultimate stage, in which her life hangs in the balance of their love/hate, but who can only communicate in their sleep.

"Walking Lessons," a long story, picks up the husband's legacy of rage after her death and takes him to an Indian reservation and to certain ordeals that his wife's act has reserved for him. The theme of an intolerable but seemingly unbreakable connection is doubled by the situation of the friend he visits there, a lapsed medical student who has a hopeless job as a VISTA worker and a more hopeless relationship with an Indian girl with multiple sclerosis. To Dora and the other Indians, the writer is a new affliction, the husband of a suicide, whose ghost, according to their lore, will follow him by night. To his friend, Blix, he is an unfeeling monster, "the killing kind." I won't try to trace the complex movement of this story or its mystical undertow, by which the writer is dragged to the admission of his responsibility, then to his atonement for it. I suspect that "Walking Lessons" brings to an end a long, grueling phase in Price's career, deeply though not congruently related to his own moral accounting, and bearing in its searching, potent artistry the healed scars of his own suffering.

A Mastodon of a Novel, by Reynolds Price

Richard Gilman

Although their number is dwindling, essays and books continue to be written about Southern fiction, as though it were an ongoing cultural reality, inimitable and important. Yet the time is long past when Southern writers were either at the center of American literature or powerful influences on the flanks. However much fiction goes on being produced below the Mason-Dixon Line, whatever the density of its local, florid experience, such writing has only the most marginal place in general consciousness now. That there is no present Southern literary art of any distinctiveness, any special energy or élan, is part of the larger truth that there's no weighty, alluring regional literature (in the best sense of the term, beyond hymns to prairies or apostrophes to elk) being created anywhere in the United States today.

The mystique of place is of course one form of a mystique of time, which is why so much Southern fiction took the shape of invented family history and of inherited moral dilemma and quest. But such themes or dispositions have largely succumbed to the pressure of a radical leveling contemporaneity conceived of as universal, traditionless fate. For some time now we've been under the sway of the more or less detached, ironic, cool and essentially unlocalized American literary intelligence and vision: Thomas Pynchon, John Barth, John Hawkes, Donald Barthelme, even Saul Bellow, Joseph Heller and John Updike, whose sense of place is real but incidental, a ground for their wit and passion but not an instigation or a sustenance. We are all displaced persons to such imaginations; "home" is wherever the sensibility can defend itself, where humanness can begin to rediscover its outlines against a backdrop of ruins.

It's only with such a perspective as this that I can begin to account for the strangeness of Reynolds Price's new novel. As "Southern" in most ways as any regionalist could desire, as steadfastly devoted to local weathers and indigenous happenings, to downhome storytelling, as any work of Faulkner or Eudora Welty or Flannery O'Connor (to my mind the last Southern writer of genius, who died in 1964), *The Surface of Earth* comes to us like a great lumbering archaic beast, taking its place among our literary fauna with the

Review of *The Surface of Earth*. From *The New York Times Book Review* (29 June 1975): 1–2. Copyright © 1975 by The New York Times Company. Reprinted by permission.

stiff queer presence of the representative of a species thought to be extinct. A mastodon sprung to life from beneath an ice-field, it smells at first of time stopped, evolution arrested.

Who could have imagined that any novelist presumably sensitive to the prevailing winds of consciousness—Price's previous fiction has moved between competent conventional storytelling and a mild and somewhat brittle thrust into fantasy—could have written a relentless family saga at a time when most of us feel self-generated, inheritors of obliterated pasts? The only writers of stature I know of who have employed the genre recently are Gabriel García Márquez and Günter Grass, but in the former case it was for the purpose of a literary myth about history as a creation (*One Hundred Years of Solitude*) and in the latter for the sake of a perspective on grotesque politics (*The Tin Drum*). Price is moved by no such strategic considerations; his story is perfectly straightforward, entirely without allegorical or symbolic dimension.

The book's setting is rural North Carolina and Virginia, its time-span is 1903 to 1944, and in this space and period, into which penetrate only the barest hints of a surrounding world, are traced the lives of three or four generations of the Mayfields and the Kendals, families intertwined through marriage. I say their "lives," but this may suggest a large, spacious family epic such as *Buddenbrooks* or Faulkner's Snopes stories. The fact is that *The Surface of Earth* is a narrative of astonishingly fierce, parochial single-mindedness, whose narrow thematic range and indifference to nearly everything but its central obsession leave it largely bereft of dramatic incident, intellectual complication or any sense of full destiny.

The obsession is with love, its difficulty and rarity, the expense of giving and gaining it, above all the necessity of recognizing its basic simplicity. For against the hugely dominant literary tradition of love as mystery, revelation, disaster or derangement—in any case something extreme, fateful—Price sets a vision of it as "simple peace and continuance," as "kindness," "help," "generosity," "welcome," "promise," "pardon" and "gift," all words that recur again and again in the text. Love is a "house" or "home" which is "lasting," "useful," "safe," "harmless." It is "God's main gift, once he's given blood and breath." It is "faces [one] could honor . . . could need." It is "permanent thanks."

Price's characters seem invented only to seek and mostly fail to attain these unremarkable qualities and states. Love may be sexual for them (although curiously chaste and euphemistically rendered; penises are "horns" or "instruments," vaginas are "gates," intercourse is an "easing") but is much more crucially familial. The book's chief action is a painful questing dance of parents and children round one another, of siblings, relatives of every kind and even of those who are simply "nearby," servants, for example, with ties to the family which as in one Southern literary convention, are as close as those of blood.

The narrative begins with the elopement of 16-year-old Eva Kendal and her 32-year-old Latin teacher, Forrest Mayfield, and ends when their only grandchild, Hutch, is on the edge of manhood. Shortly after the elopement Eva's mother commits suicide (an event reported, not described), leaving a note for Eva which says "I do not want to live in a world that will harbor and succor a heart like yours." The anathema hangs over every subsequent development. Pregnant, Eva returned to her family. After nearly dying in childbirth, and in a fit of revulsion from the hastiness of her marriage and of penitence for having "deserted" her parents, she decides not to go back to Forrest, who for his own rather opaque reasons cannot take any step to reclaim her. The separation of the mother and son from the father lengthens into years.

The main body of the story concerns Rob, the son, who grows into a charming, easy-going man, oddly debilitated however by the family history (the taint seems less psychic than existential, a matter of fate). After a Telemachus-like search he finds his father and establishes a fragile friendship with him. Later he marries a girl recently recovered from a strange "illness," a hallucinatory hope of love and motherhood. "He saw, as a picture, the enduring future of this small choice—years of days with a poor child he knew he was bound to harm, as he had been harmed by his own mother's choice, so soon regretted. A future to which he was bound now by honor, natural courtesy, because this thin girl stretched here beside him, stroking his face, had asked for his life; no one else had."

The "harm" he does her is her death in childbirth (obstetrical reality is dark indeed in this novel). Rob and the child live on with Eva, her invalid father to whose care she has devoted herself, her brother and spinster sister Rena, who adores Rob as her own, and various other members of the "family," including a black servant named Sylvia, also exceedingly attached to Rob, and, intermittently, a black handyman called Grainger. Grainger is at some point revealed to be the bastard son of Rob's grandfather and turns up periodically to serve and protect both Forrest and Rob rather like the mysterious guardian brother in *Dr. Zhivago,* at the same time engaging in his own struggle for communion with a woman.

"Nobody in this house," Rena tells Rob once, "nobody that ever slept one night here, has ever got the thing they wanted from life." What they've wanted, as I've said, is love, and they go to extraordinary lengths, almost all of them verbal, to try to wrest it. They fall upon each other like characters in the most Russian, the most Dostoevskyan of novels, talking all the time (or writing long letters when separated), loading each other down with speech, baring their hearts in a continual urgency of self-revelation (or condemnation). One effect of this is to turn the novel away from any sort of conventional naturalism, even though the book's structure remains realistic throughout. Before one is a quarter-way through, the sense arises of being in the presence of a vast, awkward, overwhelming poem, a portentous lyric of such intransigent fixity of purpose, such deep melancholy *honorableness* as to ride over all demurrers.

Ride over them, not sweep them away. As I read on I was continually assailed by an awareness of everything that isn't present, all the wit and humor we have been accustomed to in recent fiction, for example, the pure verbal play or desperate jest stemming from a sense of the embattled relations between writing itself and life. What is missing here, too, is any element of terror at seeing the face of the times, any of that acute contemporary insight into the chasms that accompany changing moral systems and that lie in fact behind all values at any time.

The Surface of Earth takes its title from one of Rob's ruminations, a passage in which one can discover the novel's major theme or impulse as well as clear indications of its dominant style: ". . . his own old need—to ride such a deep and to probe its dark, its constant promise that the skin of a body, of maybe the earth, was only the veil of a better place where the soul would be borne. A sheltered bay."

To which I add another passage for the sake of making my ambivalent reaction to the book a degree firmer: ". . . the face with its calm breadths on which you could lay your whole flat hand if the skin itself didn't threaten to burn with a fierce life flickering out from the eyes which could watch you as steady as a picture of Jesus, as full as Jesus of the promise to speak and stay at hand till all wounds healed, perfect peace arrived."

It seems to me that writing such as this in these two representative passages—the sonorous abstractions, the quasi-mystical energies, the undramatic final ambition—can only succeed cumulatively, wearing us down, so to speak, with its commitment, its prophetic timbre, above all and precisely its strange anachronistic voice speaking insistently of what we may have overlooked or been too clever to acknowledge. Ionesco once spoke of the surreal as that which lies at our very feet; the whole long quest in our literature for reality as the extreme, the astonishing and incomparable is what this homely, ingenuous novel opposes. I can't imagine our fiction being greatly influenced by it, writers plundering it for secrets of style or morale, but for the rest of us it's there; stubborn, dreamlike, old-fashioned, incorruptible and hermetic.

Letters to the Editor

EUDORA WELTY, RICHARD GILMAN

To the Editor:

Your reviewer Richard Gilman protests (June 29) any sort of attention still being paid to the South, "as though it were an ongoing cultural reality," arguing that it has "only the most marginal place in general consciousness now." And Southern literature—all of which he is able to write off in a block ("downhome storytelling")—was finished, such as it was, in the year 1964; that was when Flannery O'Connor died. He had felt confident of hearing no more out of the place.

A column-load of such remarks were due his readers, Mr. Gilman explains, in order to provide a "perspective" down which he can look at *The Surface of Earth,* by Reynolds Price of North Carolina, just out. Mr. Gilman, let him tell you, has never caught sight of such an antediluvian monster—"a mastodon, sprung to life from beneath an ice field"—as this: a Southern novel, a regional novel, a novel that is written about a family—two families! Don't ask him how many generations.

"Who could have imagined that any novelist presumably sensitive to the prevailing winds of consciousness . . . could have written a relentless family saga at a time when most of us feel self-generated inheritors of obliterated pasts?" he asks.

This affording us a return-perspective on Mr. Gilman, we are not much surprised when he reacts blankly to the vocabulary of Reynolds Price. He is rather shocked by the terms Mr. Price uses to describe and express love. (Love is, to use Mr. Gilman's own term, Reynolds Price's "obsession.") "For against the hugely dominant literary tradition of love as mystery, revelation, disaster or derangement . . . Price sets a vision of it as 'simple peace and continuance,' as 'kindness,' 'help,' 'generosity,' 'welcome,' 'promise,' 'pardon' and 'gift'. . . . It is 'permanent thanks.' " As if these were terms too daring and altogether not fit, or safe, for him to handle, Mr. Gilman looks about for *some* password

From *The New York Times Book Review* (20 July 1975): 24–25. Reprinted by permission of the authors, with Russell and Volkening as agents for Eudora Welty. Copyright © 1975 by Eudora Welty.

the author might be familiar with: what about "penis"? No, the author gives it as "horn." He's not one of "us."

Instead of discussing the novel in terms of its fictional aims and achievements, which are considerable, Mr. Gilman is all the while elaborately tiptoeing away from its subject. A novel about family belongs with "apostrophes to elk," unfit for "all displaced persons" who are only "looking for their outlines against the backdrop of ruins."

I don't, myself, see *how* any novelist, applying himself to any subject at all—and I thought choice of subject, like choice of home address, was free— could benefit by cutting off any source of wisdom that he was heir to, or that he knew of at all—or why he should. Yet his reviewer, proclaiming himself thus crippled in feeling and cut off from some primary sources of understanding, is here swearing it's better that way. So did the Fox Without a Tail offer his suggestion to improve the rest of his tribe.

But if Mr. Gilman, self-generating up there in the prevailing winds, thought he was here delivering the body of the Southern novel a *coup de grace,* he has plain missed—by not knowing the nature of its vitality. He has kept himself meticulously removed from the *life* of this book and so has escaped the discovery that its territory is interior to a greater extent than it is exterior. He sees it, from far off, as "largely bereft of dramatic incident, intellectual complication, or any sense of full destiny." But seen in its own terms, this long, complicated, evolving novel has embraced a theme no less than the continuity of human experience.

I can't help suspecting that Mr. Gilman's trouble might have been that some deep nerve was touched. He says at the last that he came to find the novel wearing him down. With all of its being "archaic," it seemed to possess, and to wield, some strange power. But he's plainly not ready yet to recognize this power for what it is, the passionate working of a gifted and highly individual imagination.

When the catchwords it's secured by are taken away and the review is deflated of its nonsense, it remains a pretty shabby article, I think, to fly in the face of such a novel. I hope its hostile gyrations will not distract more investigative readers from finding out for themselves what an experience— rich and earthy, and also quite sufficiently mysterious (Gilman's report that the novel is "entirely without symbolic dimension" is to my mind perverse)— is waiting for them in *The Surface of Earth.* It is a novel for all readers to whom human relationships are of first importance and lasting significance, readers who are able to accept the reality of other people, living or dead, who have spoken and acted and dreamed out of their own lifetimes, to ask for and to give and to receive and to generate, as they can, affirmation and love.

EUDORA WELTY
Jackson, Miss.

Richard Gilman replies:

Eudora Welty has of course every right to take issue with my review of Reynolds Price's novel but not to misread it so thoroughly and perversely as she has.

I was not "shocked" by Mr. Price's vocabulary in regard to love, I didn't find it too "daring." Quite the contrary; my point was that Price's notion of love as "simple peace," "kindness," "welcome," etc. is extraordinarily soft and lacking in the kind of dramatic tension, the turbulence and sense of extremity that has almost universally characterized the treatment of the theme in serious fiction. I didn't say that Price had to share this approach, only that in not sharing it he risked the danger of being bland and simplistic. And I pointed out the degree to which I thought he had fallen into these things and escaped them, as well as the value of his unfashionable way of seeing love.

I didn't mention Price's euphemisms, such as "horn" for penis, in order to establish some sort of *au courant* superiority ("penis" a with-it term!) but because, they seemed to me an aspect of the novel's archaic cast.

I didn't say that a novel about families belongs with apostrophes to elk. Just the opposite; I was making a mild joke about the sort of silly regional fiction from which I carefully distinguished what I called Price's "honorable" effort.

I most certainly didn't "protest any sort of attention being paid to the South." I merely observed that "Southern fiction" as a distinctive presence in our literary consciousness is past its great period, a fact in which, needless to say, I take no pleasure.

It's easy enough to answer such gross instances of misreading. But how do I deal with Miss Welty's cultural paranoia and vision of me as some sort of big-city literary slicker, soulless, deficient in feeling, scuttling rat-like away from any revelation of the human heart?

Well, of course I can't prove my soulfulness, not in this reply anyway. One thing I can do, though, is call attention to Miss Welty's rhetoric of praise for the novel, which I find much more pompous, more flaccid and emptier than the worst moments of the book itself. "Rich, earthy"—the jargon is that of the blurb-writer. "A novel for readers to whom human relationships are of first importance and lasting significance . . . who are able to accept the reality of other people living or dead." What nonsense! Or rather what sententiousness.

Must I affirm that I don't consider animal or vegetable relationships of first importance and that I truly do think other people real? Not to accept the kinds of things Miss Welty says Price's novel is about may indeed be the mark of a monster. But to apostrophize them is to applaud the abysmally self-evident. Price's book is really better than that.

The Surface of Earth

ALLAN GURGANUS

Any undergraduate can characterize the Southern novel. In it, generations choke on crimes of their ancestors; the races wrestle, headlocked in incestuous combat; humidity stokes the malaise, misery and general sloth; the chivalric tradition, by now hopelessly depraved, doffs its tattered hat; and the ravaged remains of the wilderness serve as garnishing (the novelistic equivalent of parsley on a side dish). All these ingredients are then left to steep in crucial issues like blood-ties and original sin, and eventually the whole brew is sprinkled generously with an Old Testament itch for apocalypse. Surely any form this readily (and, of course, cheaply) spoofed must, by now, be as unreplenishable as played-out sharecroppers' topsoil.

But here is Reynolds Price, an exception, a writer of exceptional books. His fourth novel, *The Surface of Earth,* takes on exactly that South, with its usual dark brood of concerns. And, almost impossibly, in Price's hands the form shows why it lived long enough to *become* a form; it again springs to life.

The book is exactly as roomy and peripatetic as its name suggests. Beginning in the years 1903–05, the account leapfrogs into the '20s then on to June of 1944. Set in North Carolina and Virginia, it is a novel about families, but one purged of the usual tedium: dates for their own sakes, and the genealogist's passion for bloodline shoptalk (Noah begat Seth who begat . . . etc.). One is never at a loss to know who is great-aunt to whom, and on what side of the clan. The book commences without a preface, a sketched family tree, or a rustic map of the homeplace. Like the Book of Genesis, it simply starts, pure action, abristle with verbs. And like that other book, *The Surface of Earth* remains simultaneously a very specific family history and a generic one. Implicit in the fates of its numerous characters—their collective stumbling from innocence to experience—we see America's own "progress" and descent, from the pastoral reclusiveness of 1903 to the martial preeminence of 1944.

Again like Genesis, the book's first volitional act is a couple's fall from grace. Here, their exit involves elopement, a flight from family blessings and, by implication, from the claustrophobic security of the 19th century itself.

From *The Washington Post Book World* (13 July 1975): 1–2. © 1975, Washington Post Book World Service/Washington Post Writers Group. Reprinted with permission.

Our own century is seen as that thorny territory beyond the gates, Eden's antithesis.

Forrest Mayfield, a skinny 32-year-old Latin teacher, runs off with his prize pupil, Eva Kendal, 16, high-school class of 1903. Mayfield has "worked—drilling uses for the Dative of Reference, the Subjunctive of Purpose, into wall-eyed children who would spend short lives selling harness leather or lard or plowing, or spreading lean thighs every year on the wet head of one more baby." Despite his sylvan name, he is cursed with an advanced sense of 20th-century displacement. As an intellectual, a veritable orphan alone in a village of families, he is drawn to the sullen natural Eva. With all the odds against their happiness, the two secretly run away together, certain only of what they leave behind.

What follows, 41 full years of it, is as random and full of unexpected repetitions as experience itself. Cocteau wrote, "Life is a horizontal fall." This novel offers—on a human lateral chronological plane—a complicated version of that first theological fall.

Though of greater size and range, the new work is closely related thematically to Price's first three novels. *A Long and Happy Life* and *A Generous Man* both concerned the same rural Carolina family. In the first book, a young girl comes to understand the nature of love, its great demands, its absolute necessity. In the second, her brother is the central character forced to action when the problem of evil itself slithers allegorically into his community and, in turn, into his moral consciousness. The third novel, *Love and Work*, involves a writer who, in straining to re-create fictionally his dead parents, comes too close to the frontier between life and art. All four books concern transitional shifts between family generations, that painful moment when roles tilt and the growing children become, or choose not to become, morally responsible for their waning parents: the moment when protective parents and their sheltered children exchange parts. In the new book, as in earlier works. Price investigates what parents do for—and to—their offspring.

Many of the inhabitants of *The Surface of Earth* seem cut off from their origins. The book is filled with persons seeking lost relatives, real and imagined. There is a fierce need to feel that one has precedents in the world, and these characters, in searching, even questing, for some survivor literally akin to themselves hope to find a moral source or cipher, an inspirational model, or—at the very least—someone who is duty-bound, by blood, to listen, or counsel or assist. One old man who deserted his family years before justifies himself by complaining of his own childhood, "All I read was the Bible—all we had to read except medicine labels—and nobody gets along in the Bible. Not one happy pair, not one that lasts long enough to watch and learn *how* from. So I gave up reading and took to holding onto people."

There is, in our country, a continuing democratic suspicion (itself, ironically, something of a tradition) of that which can be passed on from generation to generation. While we, as a race, boast of our national heritage, we are bereft of a deep sense of personal continuous tradition, the sense of ourselves as the products of families, the genetic heirs to our parents' and grandparents' quirks and merits. Within a regional context, Price explores this national aversion and the needs it creates. It is a cycle that requires, generation to generation, a severence of family ties, requires that everyone "start from scratch," that every adolescent male become "his own man." The mystery of one's own paternity, the quest for a helpful knowledge of one's own birthright to a familial past, Price examines such questions with a subtle intelligence. He is sensitive—and on the necessary largest scale—to what makes the book's characters not only Southern, but, peculiarly, marvelously and, at times, hopelessly American.

When, on the novel's last pages, a few trivial heirlooms (a five-dollar gold piece, a ring) are passed, hand to hand, from one age of family survivors to the next, we are certain that these objects and their vast significance—which we, the readers, have understood for hundreds of pages—will be misconstrued or, if appreciated at all, for the wrong reasons. But that, finally, doesn't matter. What counts is the gesture itself, this handling on of continuity's symbols, this economic and natural circularity. As an ending, the act resounds back through the work, back to the disastrous elopement that began it all. We know that experience's central questions have not been resolved but, rather, refined, and passed on to the consideration of a more energetic age.

In a quick cataloguing of the novel's pleasures, a few more things should be mentioned. Price's ear for speech, its nuances and short-cuts, the telling exaggeration or reticence, is profound and thorough. Also, his understanding of the way time moves, alternately in lurches and slow motion. In the early pages of the book (and in turn, the century), there is never the sense, as in some other writing about a "period," that we are traveling in the amber, exquisite atmosphere of mellow tintypes. The year 1903 has its own ferocious, unsentimentalized integrity, and rawness. Unlike others who might suggest the era by forcing some character to mention former President Cleveland, or sport a straw boater, Price creates the period from the inside out, that is, from the vantage, the indigenous historical texture, of consciousness itself. He perceives that peculiar enlarged sense of personal consequence and autonomy that, in 1903, made a man's view of the world and his place in it very different from today's conception of self.

Another great bonus: Reynolds Price is one of the few living American novelists who can write naturally about Nature itself. Many practitioners get totally bullied by Hemingway's error: the confusion of equipment and lore with the force itself. In Price's writing, the natural world is not just a machismo testing ground or obstacle course, nor is it merely that rough-hewn terrain crying out for symbolical surveying. Rather, it begins and remains—first and always—a fact. His relation to nature is immediate, unselfconscious; the difference between Price and some other current novelists writing about the same woods is exactly the difference between a tourist photographing and conscientiously remembering a "colorful" place and a native's view of that same spot.

In all Price's fiction, there is a governing lucidity, a virtuosity judiciously restrained. In an age of arid stingy minimalism, his writing is haplessly generous, ready to do anything—everything. His earlier novels might be related to this new work as brilliant preliminary easel paintings compared to a heroic fresco. *The Surface of Earth* is a continuous organic work about organic continuity.

The Surface of Earth:
A Pavement of Good Intentions

FRED CHAPPELL

I

Simply by listing the titles of Reynolds Price's works in more or less chrono-logical order we can discern a pattern of intent. These are "A Chain of Love," *A Long and Happy Life, The Names and Faces of Heroes, A Generous Man, Love and Work, Permanent Errors, Things Themselves,* and now, *The Surface of Earth.* It piv-ots in 1968 upon the addition of that abrupt ugly-sounding word, *Work,* to the soft and mostly misused word, *Love.* Here is an ongoing *reduction of terms;* no more "generous" or "heroes" or "happy," but instead an insistence upon hard objects and perplexities. Was it Goethe who said that the serious writer is always striving to become truly objective?—Anyhow, this goal is what is partly at stake here.

But if there were not a paradox in the pattern it would draw no atten-tion. While the terms were being reduced, the ambitions for particular works have grown larger. These ambitions culminate in Price's last huge novel, *The Surface of Earth.* This book is in fact probably the most ambitious American novel since the earlier works of James Jones and William Styron. (I discount Pynchon, Vonnegut, and Berger, because their work has always been to some degree parodic, and therefore deliberately self-limiting.) Price's title tells us at least this much: that here is an attempt to trace, within the reasonable boundaries of intelligent writing, the shapes that a few lives make upon the circumscribed areas of their durations. What is not shown about them can be known, and what cannot be finally known, may be guessed; because there is a community of destiny in most American lives. One of the characters tells us as much, saying, "We are very plain people. We're the history of the world; nothing one bit unusual in any of our lives. You are just one of us; you have not been singled out for special mistreatment. Let me tell you my life; I can tell it in a minute, and it's sadder than yours."—This statement coming to Rob Mayfield at what he regards as an especially perilous moment.

That's the way it is, and that's one of the ways the author expects us to read his novel: always holding in mind the fact that two doors down the street other lives of equally intense shame, joy, and misery are taking place.

Reprinted from *The Archive* 88.1 (Fall 1975): 75–82, by permission of the author.

This is an intoxicating knowledge, and it lends to *The Surface of Earth* a breadth which is independent of its own length and scope, and which few other novels afford.

(For no really good reason I am reminded of the opening shot of Hitchcock's *Psycho*. It is a very high crane shot, traveling the skyline of a city. Finally the camera picks out one hotel, tracks toward it, and travels along rows of windows, hesitating now and then, as if deliberating which story to choose to tell. I don't know if Hitchcock means to generalize—the way Price is generalizing—with this shot. If he does, he's more a pessimist than anyone has dreamed.)

This contingent awareness of other lives is thrilling, but there is a paradox here too, for the writer must then always make us believe—even though he has caused us to know better—that the lives we are following are of special interest and importance. Not that others are of less interest, but that of the cases known this one is particularly urgent and illustrative. In other words, the author has now introduced his own method and manner as necessary elements of the work.

Is not this willful and artificial? Will not this intrusion (though in fact it is not all that intrusive) destroy the naturalistic illusion necessary to the sustaining of a reader's interest in quotidian lives? I think that in a work of lesser scope and poorer ambition, so much presence of the author's voice might indeed prove cumbrous, an embarrassment of riches; that it might call the reader away from the characters or place an elegantly pointed screen of style between him and them.

But really there is no other way to manage it. Once we have known that the novelist has deliberately chosen the story at hand, his presence is with us. After this moment, it is the author's *absence* which would be artificial and to some inevitable degree coy. The task for him to accomplish then is to give a feeling of presence, of control, of care, without becoming strident, or self-advertising, or overbearing.

And the only way to bring all these necessities to effect is by means of prose style.

II

Reynolds Price's prose style has always been remarkable. His sentence arrangements are rarely elaborate, and yet a reader receives an impression of elaboration. There is occasional ornament, and even ornament for its own sake, but it does not appear stuck-on or in any way superfluous. There is a great deal of metaphor, but often as not his metaphor lodges in his verbs and becomes indistinguishable syntactically from the literal import of his sentences. And there are other turns which identify Price's own manner: the use of parentheses, generally for qualification, but also quite often for additional information, and now and then—surprise!—parentheses used to attach a whole new perspective to a series of statements; the use of the colloquial, where the language the author writes and the language his characters speak is virtually identical—this not only in the interests of homogeneity, but also for precision of sensibility (the author not only approves of his characters' feelings; he sees them as the only possible genuine feelings in the circumstances); and the use of ellipsis. If I had to choose one single hallmark of Price's style I would take ellipsis.

Here is an example. Rob Mayfield is talking to his son Hutch, a young adolescent. Since Hutch was born they have helplessly been strangers to one another and are now trying desperately to patch something together between them.

> Hutch said, "What was the promise?—just to change your life?" They had passed all lights now and walked in pure darkness, guided by waves and the faint earthlight. . . .
>
> "To stop harming people in the ways I had, by not touching one human body again (not for my old reasons), by not drinking liquor; I had drunk a lot of that since I was your age."
>
> "Why?"
>
> "A form of ether, deadens the pain."
>
> Hutch said, "But you promised that *if* we two lived, Rachel *and* I. You got just half."
>
> "That was why I asked you; you were all that was left. I thought you should say. I thought you might be taken if I broke it."
>
> "And I told you Yes?"
>
> "In your sleep, age three."
>
> "Did you listen?" Hutch said.
>
> "Obey, you mean?" Rob stopped in his tracks.

Until Hutch's sentence, "You got just half," this fragment of dialogue could have occurred in anyone's novel; it is simple statement and rejoinder. After that point the conversation of the two men is overtaken by the blue mysteries of their separate but interpenetrant lives. They begin to speak inchoate love lyrics, to talk in highly charged tropes, and to reveal secrets not even the reader has known till now. They understand each other perfectly; they share a deep emotional knowledge which the reader—no matter how much he knows by now *about* them—has to piece out, by sympathy and intuition.

Not an impossible job. Rob and Hutch are two wise men talking together, but they are wise about precisely the same matters we readers are: the stresses and crises of human brotherhood. Nor is it only fathers and sons—every character in this novel talks in this same way to every other character. And why not? They too share deeply, have been sharing for a long time.

I am not going to present myself such a fool as to try to pretend that this is the way people actually do talk in ordinary life. If I accosted my Uncle Fudd with the question. "And then you loved me enough to—?" I should be privileged to witness his transformation into a species of green slime and to watch him ooze through the cracks in the floor. Price's dialogue is not naturalistic, but it is *realistic,* in that the things which the book is about are taken as legitimate matter for discourse. This manner of speech is merely one of the premises of the book, and if it is not a naturalistic premise, so what? No one ever *really* thought the way Bloom and Daedalus think; no one ever traveled centuries forward in time; foxes and storks never spoke Greek—but we allow these authors their premises, and we ought to allow Price his. For after all, these are the things we should like openly to speak of, if only we could. It is just that in *The Surface of Earth* there are no stammerers, no dodgers, no emotional illiterates, no savages.

I'm nakedly guessing now, but it has occurred to me that if there is in the background any sort of literature which partly served Price as model for *Earth,* it is a classical work. Perhaps a history like those of Livy or Tacitus, perhaps a biography, maybe even a late epic poem like the *Thebaid.* I make this conjecture on the basis of the rigorous formalism of the modes of speech in the book. There are, I believe, three. We have seen some of the question-and-answer dialogue, which is at bottom catechistic in nature. We have also the peroration, in which one character presents to another at great length a thesis or a piece of history. (A particularly fine example of this mode begins on page 70: "You want to know everything. . . .") And we have the frequent—and frequently long—letters the characters exchange; the language is mainly the same language as the dialogue, but in the letters there is more selection, more point, and often a heightened formality.

These modes of speech are carefully differentiated in the novel, as they would be in a Ciceronian biography. We know factually that the great generals never made those eve-of-battle speeches Tacitus and Livy wrote; but those speeches are history, because they are what the generals *would* have said.

III

I have probably made Price's prose appear too formidable.

We undoubtedly have among us the company of the impatient who will ask, "Why? All this jive, what for? If Mickey Spillane can write a slam-bang good story in plain goddammit English, why can't your precious Reynolds Price?"

The easiest response is: "Well, if you think to say, *Juno was a man,* is actually to *say* something, then love it and keep happy."

There is however a serious question underneath: When is there a necessity for a novelist's style to be equipollent with the other elements of his work, with structure, characterization, detail, and so forth?—That's a hard question, made harder by the fact that the novelists whom people think of primarily as stylists are not always those in whose work style is equally important with other elements. Faulkner is a magnificent stylist, yes; but even his boatload of baroque is secondary to structure and characterization. We think correctly of Conrad as a great stylist, but you could blow away his lovely velvet fog and still have a sense of ironic destinies and of the enormous pity of politics. Among the French you find the *necessary* stylists. Take style from Voltaire, Flaubert, and Colette and you have nothing, not even theme. Among Americans some *necessary* stylists are Twain, Poe, Lardner, and Nathanael West. We are accustomed to regarding as an artistic necessity congruence of style, subject matter, and theme. But we are surprised when we find works in which style and theme are not merely congruent but completely identical.

The condition requisite for this need for identity is that the author has decided to eschew indirection and is determined to come at his theme head-on, to talk about it as squarely as possible. For this purpose the author has to invent a language different from other kinds of language; he has put himself in the position of a philosopher and he must come up with *terms*. If Poe's language, or West's, or Price's look at first glance artificial, it is because these languages have been new-minted to deal with sensibly perceived problems. If Twain's language, or Colette's, or Lardner's, do not seem artificial, it is because we are usually only half-aware of what they are saying. A hard look at almost any random paragraph of *Life on the Mississippi* will show how much it is a newly invented language.

IV

The theme of *The Surface of Earth* is love, familial and romantic.

I have been dreading to write that sentence, because putting the matter so baldly makes it sound at the same time mawkish and defiant. Is not love also the single theme of Theodore Sturgeon, and of Erich Segal, and of Rod McKuen? Well . . . no. Those writers write about their own responses to the *idea* of love, and ideas have no teeth.

Price's love is a darker element; it is an omnipresent force, independent of the affairs of men and moving powerfully among them. It is the *Venus genetrix* of Lucretius, and her energy will prevail, no matter if the creatures she chooses to tenant are flawed and not strong enough to receive her. This power *will obtain,* and if it leaves some dozens of human lives a charred and smoldering wreckage, that will be pitiable but natural and inevitable. Only two other forces are so powerful in individual lives; these are space and time, and their powers are usually discernible only to a few poets and perspicuous biologists.

Price's view of love is not merely unsentimental, it is Schopenhauerean, angrily despairing, anguished. He sees love as Aeschylus saw Helen: destroyer of men, destroyer of families. It was a terrible mistake for Thad Watson to marry Katherine Epps (an action the primordial beginning of the novel), a mistake for Forrest Mayfield to marry Eva Kendal, a mistake for Rob to marry Rachel. Equally bad mistakes are made when, under the force of the Venus, these white men are thrust willessly into the bodies of black women. The family becomes an unstable atom, the particles hotly bound but fiercely striving apart. And there is no help for it; this is the way this universe works, and the novelist must observe and—final twist of the knife—must approvingly participate.

The family is love too, but family love is powerless; the family in this novel is like a child's play-fortress, easily taken and broken again and again by a larger and more genuine force. The family ought to be able to harbor its members safe but it cannot, because the universe which contains it is indifferently malevolent. The same force—the Venus—which creates the family is already at work in the moment of creation to destroy it.

While I was reading *The Surface of Earth* (it takes a time) word came that the New York *Times Book Review* had run an unfavorable article on the novel. Long ago I quit reading the *TBR,* natural roosting-place of small-bore minds and big-bore egos, and I wasn't surprised. Finally someone sent me a xerox, and I was even less surprised to find that the review was written by that witless butcher Richard Gilman. Gilman's contentions, so far as I can remember them (I threw away the piece in disgust), were that this novel couldn't be any good because 1) Flannery O'Connor is dead, 2) *Earth* is regional, and 3) the family is a dead letter north of the Mason-Dixon and so not fit subject for favorable treatment.

Only 1) is correct, alas.

The dust-jacket copy (one of my favorite kinds of prose poem) for this novel speaks of "the intensely evoked American of the first half of our century," and of the "destructive and healing power of place." I'd rather be dumped into the middle of an Arctic ice-field, compassless and clockless, than to have to depend upon *Earth* for a sense of place or time. The chapter headings are dates (so many notches in a stick) and a number of place names are dropped and now and again there is a peculiarly Southern detail (bird, food, weed), but mostly the drive is toward generalization. Nothing happens in this novel (which stops in 1944) which could not happen—*is happening*—right this moment every place in America. In California people dress more sportily and chew more gum, and instead of writing letters they run up telephone bills for calls to their parents in North Dakota and their siblings in North

Carolina, but they too are roiled along under the force of the Venus and importuned by the straining, breaking ties of family.

(Perhaps it is worth pointing out that Wright Morris, who—in the 1950's!—perfected, with *Love among the Cannibals,* the tieless, familyless novel which Gilman seems to want, has long since returned to writing about the bonds and consequences of familial love and responsibility.)

It is not worth anyone's serious time to bother with Gilman, but I bring him up because I think that his mistakes are those likely to be made by habitual novel readers who will come to the book expecting to read a traditional family saga. There is a family in the book, right enough, but in many ways it is an anti-family, a heap of rubble. Looming shadowily behind every page is a brightly obscure vision of what the family *might have been, if only. . . .* And it is the vision which in great part accounts for the distress of the characters, for the half-wild impulsive actions of the women and for the overpoweringly enervated sense of failure among the men.

In short, *The Surface of Earth* is not your expectable saga of a Southern family. It pushes counter to that genre with a fervor almost polemic.

V

Earth is fittingly prefaced by a quotation from St. Augustine, so perhaps it will not be amiss to take from him a hint for a last attempt at description. Augustine (mistakenly) derives the word *religion* from the verb *relegere:* to read and read again. It is in this sense, I believe, that *The Surface of Earth* is intended as a religious, as a sacred book. It is absolutely crammed with meanings about the theme of love. Actually to understand it rightly, we should have to read it as Tertullian teaches us to read scripture:

> I adore the plenitude of the scriptures in which every letter is a word, and every word is a verse, and every verse is a chapter, and every chapter is a book, and every book is a Bible; in which every twig is a branch, and every branch is a tree, and every tree is a forest; in which every drop is a rivulet, and every rivulet is a river, and every river a bay, and every bay an ocean, and every ocean all waters.

Is it not true that any book which tries to deal exhaustively with love partakes to some degree of the scriptural? In *Earth* the suggestions of holy qualities are reinforced, not only with the epigraph from St. Augustine, but with repeated quotations and parallels from Virgil and Milton. It will naturally put readers off to claim too much for the book, but I personally believe that part of its purpose is to justify God's ways to man. And the juxtaposition of Virgil and Milton makes simple good sense if we—momentarily, crudely—identify erotic love with paganism and family love with Christian duty.

That notion is a violation of the novel, but let us say that the two principal male characters have much in common with *pius Aeneas*. They have made themselves (usually cheerfully) subservient to Venus, the lovely mother. Because of this devotion each has been driven from his home place and forced to found—however shakily—a new beginning. The alien place they have been driven to is mostly their own interior beings, and no other wilderness is so darkly trackless. With the coming of the family, however, a new order is established, demanding responsibility, duty, stability—the Christian virtues, or some of them. Forrest and Rob Mayfield are not able to hold up under the necessities of this new order. Forrest flees, Rob drinks. But within these failing lives knowledge is being gained and accumulated. It is not enough, has not enough power, to lay safe foundations; knowledge is powerless when allied to a damaged will. Actually to found a solid base for the future of this family requires an act of grace. The grace that is given them is the birth of Hutch. Hutch will be, in some part, their savior.

This conjecture will seem to many readers about as plausible as a Flash Gordon serial. It will seem a ruthless dragging-in of celestial mechanics upon a book which if it is not relentlessly quotidian is nothing. But I'm not certain it wouldn't give *Earth* a harder disservice to describe it as a book about three generations of the dailiness of life. It is this sense of the grand design of the heavens which gives *The Surface of Earth* its two most paradoxically powerful qualities: its orderly clarity and its profound mysteriousness. Lacking either of these qualities, the novel would be an immense failure, and not even an interesting failure; but it possesses them in plenty.

Along with "sincere," "symbolic," "suggestive," "immediate," and some scores of others, I distrust the word "epical" as a descriptive term. Usually when people use the word "sincere" in describing a piece of writing, they mean *autobiographical*. By "symbolic" they mean *incomprehensible*, by "suggestive" *unfinished*, by "immediate" *importunate*, and by "epical" they merely mean *long*. I do not think *Gone with the Wind* is an epical novel; nor *Oblomov;* nor *Bouvard et Pecuchet;* not *Buddenbrooks*. But I am willing to defend "epical" as applicable to *The Surface of Earth*.

It has *intensity of design*. Design, grand design, it is which finally informs every dialogue, every detail, every characterization (here it may indeed be a bit intrusive, as in the Charon-like Bankey and the Delphic Luna Wall). And this novel has the Homeric sense of time; time is precisely marked off, but it doesn't count; the action really takes place in some corner of eternity.

Relegere, imperative infinitive. Read and read again.

He couldn't be a novelist, if there were someone so naive as to believe that he would have more than a few, a very few, readers who would actually try to appreciate what he was attempting to get down on every page, in every sentence. Even before he writes the first *The* of a projected book, a novelist counts on his most perspicacious critic as finding maybe 20° of what his book shall accomplish. The miracle is that he goes ahead and writes it anyway. We live in a time and place where in most matters, in politics, for example, we get what we deserve, or worse. But from the artists we always get more than we deserve, or have any right to expect.

Another act of grace.

Good Books

ANTHONY BURGESS

Reynolds Price is a considerable prose writer. *A Palpable God* must be taken as a serious testimony to a virtue rare among contemporary producers of fiction—the compulsion to examine at intervals the rationale of his craft. All we novelists forget too often that our job is not to spin words to the greater glory of the complex, book-drenched, allusion-loving, ambiguity-adoring civilized sensibility, but to tell tales. The telling of a plain tale is, however, as hard for the contemporary writer as plowing with a plank and a nail would be to the contemporary agricultural operative. Sometimes we have to get back to see how the ancients did it, and Mr. Price's mode of self-refreshment has been to examine the Bible. Unlike Mr. Rosenberg, he has schooled himself in the Hebrew of the Old Testament as well as the demotic Greek of the New. Here, in 30 stories out of the Bible, he seeks to recapture the physicality—palpability, or feelability, is the right word—of the ancient narratives. Neither the King James version nor the later, more scholarly renderings of Holy Writ have, in his view, caught the essential tones. Here is the opening of his "The Good News According to Mark":

"... John wore camel's hair and a leather belt round his hips, ate grasshoppers and wild honey and proclaimed saying 'He's coming who is stronger than I—after me—of whom I'm unfit stooping to loosen the strap of his sandals. I baptized you in water but he'll baptize you in Holy Spirit.' "

This is both English and not English. Where the tonalities of our tongue are strained, we divine that we are not far from the original Greek. The linking *kai* (or *et* of the vulgate), invariably rendered as "and" in the King James version (providing one of the traditional flavors of biblical English, as in Bunyan) he does not find it necessary always to translate; to the Greeks *kai* was not invariably "and." But the physical force of "unfit stooping" goes back literally to *non dignus procumbons* in the vulgate, which is a straight rendering of the Greek.

And the contractions "he's," "I'm," "he'll," though they seem at first inept in the formal declaration of the Baptist or "Baptizer," do catch the swift informality of the koine, which was not the Attic Greek of Sophocles.

Review of *A Palpable God*. From *The New York Times Book Review* (12 March 1978): 14, 22. Copyright © 1978 by The New York Times Company. Reprinted by permission.

There is the same plain force in his version of, say, the tale of Joseph and Potiphar's wife:

> . . . And it happened that though she spoke to Joseph day by day he did not listen to her—to lie by her and be with her. Then it happened about this time—he came into the house to do his work and there was no house servant there in the house.
> She seized him by his coat saying, "Lie with me."
> He left his coat in her hand—and fled outside.

The 19th-century Roman poet Giuseppe Belli, in the translation I have, put it like this:

> One morning, bringing the hot
> water to her,
> He found her naked, the sweet
> buxom slut,
> So damped her with the contents
> of the ewer.
> She grabbed him by his single
> garment but
> He left it with her, naked but
> still pure.

And ran away, the bloody idiot. Belli, refreshing the dialect of the Roman streets through contact with the Bible, was, in his own way, on a quest that is perennial among writers. We have to get back to the beginning again, startle the dullness of our everyday language with a swipe from the exotic, and remember that "a need to tell and hear stories is essential to the species *Homo sapiens*—second in necessity apparently after nourishment and before love and shelter." That comes from Mr. Price's long introductory essay, which from now on must be required reading in creative-writing courses.

Portrait of the Artist As Son, Lover, Elegist

Joyce Carol Oates

Portraits of artists are most adroitly approached aslant. One thinks of Joyce showing us Stephen Dedalus lost in a romantic reverie, then awakening to squash a louse on his neck; or of Oscar Wilde's Basil Hallward, the artist in *The Portrait of Dorian Gray* who is not only murdered by his subject, but dissolved in nitric acid. By contrast, is there anyone more insufferable, and more improbable as an "artist," than Virginia Woolf's tiresome Lily Briscoe, who is only shown painting and who seems to have taken a lifetime to paint one canvas?

The Source of Light, Reynolds Price's 10th book, is a portrait of the artist as son, as lover, as elegist; a romantic egoist who loves solitude, yet who reports on nearly every waking, and dreaming, hour of his life; a mourner who suspects that he must convert his private domestic suffering into something more substantial, into art, if he is to redeem it—and himself.

Hutchins Mayfield is a 25-year-old poet who thinks of himself as "an aging boy," who feels he must leave his North Carolina home, and his deep attachment to his father, in order to discover whether he is a genuine poet or a fraud. He goes to Oxford to read for a Bachelor of Letters degree, to write a thesis on "the love and nature of Andrew Marvell" and to work on his poetry in virtual solitude. Hutch is touchingly frank in the letters he writes home almost every day: "I've been huffing and puffing to cheer myself up in this odd high leap I find myself taking. What we didn't discuss . . . were the things I am scared of. The main thing is me—that once I've paid for and found this famous stillness around me, filled my fountain pen, and faced the window, then there'll be no work: not a thing I know that'll prove big enough to hold any human eye but mine and no words to say even small things in."

Hutch Mayfield believes he has successfully cast off the hobbles that restrain him—his father Rob, who is devoted to him; his recollections of Mayfield-Kendal family history; his confused and painful thoughts about his mother, who died giving birth to him. But his father's unanticipated death

Review of *The Source of Light.* Reprinted from *The New York Times Book Review* (26 April 1981): 3, 30, by permission of the author. Copyright, *The Ontario Review,* Inc., 1981.

calls him home and makes him realize that his subject will be his family, after all. In one of his final letters Hutch's father tells him, in essence, that he must be the means by which the various generations of their family are "made into a figure"—"a diagram"—"a writing in lines." "That's the hope, Son," his father writes, "that we make some figure. If we do you'd be the one to know (though it may take awhile to know you know)."

This richly detailed and intensely romantic novel, which covers approximately a year in Hutchins Mayfield's life, is not a sequel but a continuation of Mr. Price's *The Surface of Earth,* which was published in 1975. (That novel, which began with the disastrous elopement of Hutch's grandmother, then 16 years old, in 1903, moved with luxuriant slowness through some four decades, ending a few years after Hutch's birth.) Both novels are lyric, brooding, meditative, obsessive and possess, at their most powerful moments, the histrionic clarity of a vast tapestry in which action is necessarily arrested and individual figures exist only in their relationship to one another and the larger design.

Where *The Surface of Earth* had the structure of an old-fashioned family saga, *The Source of Light* is far narrower in scope, more centrally focused. If the "source" of light is Hutch's Mayfield-Kendal background, in all its melodramatic complexity, the "light" itself is Hutch—who, for good reason, is tormented by the possibility that he cannot be equal to it. Thus the mood of the novel is edgy, self-absorbed, questioning and uncertain. And, finally, it is elegiac, for Hutch, though capable of making his bold "high leap" to England, cannot escape obsessive thoughts of the deaths of his parents. (The depiction of Rob's death contains some of the most beautifully sustained passages in all of Reynolds Price's work.) Nor can he decide whether he loves a young woman well enough to marry her. Near the end of the novel, he learns, after the fact, that his girl has had an abortion to free herself of a baby that was probably, though not certainly, his.

As one might imagine, there are difficulties in assessing a writer in vigorous mid-career like Reynolds Price, and these difficulties are, in the present case, compounded by the fact that the novel under review is a continuation of an earlier work and gives every indication of leading to yet another Hutch Mayfield novel. It seems unfair to judge Hutchins Mayfield at this point and irrelevant to question whether he will ever be a poet, for that is not the concern of this novel. Mr. Price seems to be lightly satirizing Hutch, who believes that his self-obsessed letters home allow him to avoid "the rapt mirror-gazing that diaries invite"; then again, he indulges him at length, in long unedited letters that contain dreams recounted in full. One can see why Hutch's girl Ann becomes so impatient with him—he is romantically indulgent about himself and yet his manner with her is cautious and ironic, and he always seems to draw back from any forthright declaration of love. (Ann does not know, but perhaps can sense, that Hutch is attracted to other men—that, indeed, he has homosexual relations.)

Because he is so central to the novel, dominating virtually every page, it is disconcerting that Hutch remains so blurred to us and that Ann too lacks definition. We wonder whether she is as pallid as she appears or whether her passivity is part of her strategy to win Hutch for a husband? She takes pride, for instance, in confessing to a total lack of interest in a profession or in what might be called the world: "I'm a woman as old-style as anything painted on the walls of caves. . . . What I want is to work inside at home, making life easy (or easier) for two-to-four people in whom I'm involved and who want me to be." (The chilling complacency of the 1950's!—no wonder Hutch eludes her even as he insists he loves her.)

In this novel, as in Reynolds Price's previous work, the most appealing characters are garrulous storytellers, who are often peripheral to the central concern of a novel, but irresistible nonetheless, for it is through them that we experience the texture of life in a given place and time. Since the publication in 1962 of his justly acclaimed first novel, *A Long and Happy Life*, Reynolds Price has been superb at capturing voices, and so it is not surprising that the older, talky women of *The Source of Light* (one of them Hutch's grandmother Eva, the mother of Rob) are marvelous, as are Hutch's male friends—Lew, a Welshman whom he meets on the ocean liner, and Straw, a "nineteen-year-old reformed alcoholic" who had been Hutch's student at a rural Episcopal boys' school in Virginia. The women are warm, bemused, funny and wise, without necessarily being intelligent, and certainly without being self-conscious; the male lovers are uncommonly intriguing, in ways poor Ann, locked into her claustrophobic "feminine" role, can never be. (Indeed, it is one of the puzzling aspects of the novel that Hutch doesn't seem to grasp what the reader so quickly grasps—that his homosexual liaisons are much more meaningful to him, because more interesting, than his laconic courtship of Ann.)

In all, *The Source of Light* is a somber, rather beautifully muted work, in which the melodrama of earlier generations has receded, leaving a hero who is, in his very uncertainty, absolutely convincing. It is a measure of Reynolds Price's integrity, that he ends this novel on so restrained, and so unresolved, a note: Hutch back at Oxford, Ann at home, the Atlantic between them as well as the death of an unborn child, and a sense of great injury. Perhaps suffering will deepen Hutch, perhaps it will make him into the poet his father has required him to be.

Price's New Volume of 50
Earns Him His Poet's Spurs

Henry Taylor

Over the past 20 years, Reynolds Price has produced a remarkably distinguished body of fiction, characterized by a respect for tradition and the skill and patience to extend and enrich tradition. From time to time he has also published poems, in respectable journals and in exquisite limited editions like those produced by Stuart Wright's Palaemon Press. Fifty of his poems are now presented in *Vital Provisions*.

Thanks to writers like Robert Penn Warren and George Garrett, we are emerging from an annoying period of specialism, during which a book like this would have been called "a novelist's poems," much as Eugene McCarthy's poems were called "a senator's poems." Price's poems are often narrative but in judging them we need not allow him a novelist's handicap.

This is not to say that all 50 of these poems are successful. A few of the more personal recollections of erotic encounters are slightly embarrassing, not merely because of their subject matter, but because the experiences recounted have not had lavished upon them the full resources of the poetic art; they seem too much like private notes, with too little attention paid to the overhearers. The bulk of the book, however, made up of longer poems recounting dreams, tense episodes in friendships, and even the life of Christ, are compelling and unobtrusively skillful.

In the first of the book's three sections, for example, we come soon to "The Dream of Lee," a four-page narrative based on an extravagant premise: Price, in the late 1970s, drives north from Durham, N.C., to Lexington, Va., to collect Robert E. Lee, who will spend two days at Duke University visiting classes and presenting a formal lecture. The poem is balanced precariously between solemnity and hilarity, Price's shyness and Lee's greatness combine to make a strained drive back, punctuated by Lee's guesses at Price's life. Lee is brilliant in the classrooms, and at the end of the poem, as Lee approaches the podium for the lecture, the story takes a delicious turn:

Review of *Vital Provisions*. Reprinted, with permission, from *The Washington Times* (1 February 1983): 3D, 16D.

When oceanic welcome subsides,
The General rises, steps to the lectern,
Slowly unties a black leather case,
Then looks back to me and says "I regret
Not telling you. I hope my changed
Plan will cause you no pain." I smile.
He doesn't. He faces his crowd and says
"I shall read from my poems tonight."

It is a wonderful moment, brilliantly resolved in the 13 lines which follow these. To refuse to spoil the ending may be a concession to narrative's power over poetic technique, but I won't give it away, beyond saying that it contains the revelation that makes reporting this dream more than a mere oddity. It is a fine poem.

The second section of this book consists entirely of a sequence called "Nine Mysteries," narratives and monologues based on episodes in the life of Christ. Each is preceded by an epigraph from the Gospels or the Acts, in Price's own versions, which are sometimes distracting. But the poems themselves are often moving and evocative of the human and divine forces at work in the narratives. The encounter between Jesus and His mother at Ascension is remarkable for the conviction with which Price has assigned the speaker's role to Jesus, and for the delicate balance it maintains between believable speech and the remoteness of the event itself.

The sequence contains one lapse: "Instruction," a monologue of Judas, compares unfavorably with James Wright's briefer "Saint Judas," and seems self-conscious in its use of low-life slang: "I'd got out of town by Friday / Dawn to miss the dustup I launched / In the garden." But on the whole, "Nine Mysteries" is a strong reaffirmation of the power inherent in the story, and of Christian faith as humanly desirable.

The third section of the book is the most miscellaneous; it has not been arranged to the advantage of several poems which seem trivial in comparison to their immediate neighbors. But the section does contain "The Annual Heron," the best poem in the book.

The story line of this six-page poem is in itself fraught with risks of portentousness or sentimentality, both of which are avoided. In the ninth year of his annual return to the speaker's pond, a heron finds it frozen, its fish unattainable. The speaker thaws a trout, delivers it and discovers the next day a few feathers which suggest that local dogs have eaten both the trout and the heron. But the next year, the heron, identifiable by a tumor on his leg, is back. What to think?

Endurance is fed: here, in time.
Therefore endure. . . .
You hope in vain. The heat is fed

> *Only where I go when I leave you here.*
> *Follow me.*

The poem's splendor arises from a deft and energetic use of the tensions a skillful poet may draw between sentences and lines, and from the storyteller's keen perception of the right details.

Several of Price's previous publications of poetry have seemed, in their exquisite limited editions, declarations of his amateur status as a poet. With this collection he renounces that status.

Travels with a Dangerous Woman

ROSELLEN BROWN

"*I*'*d caused their deaths.*" Every writer who has produced a large body of work has themes that play as relentlessly as a ground bass beneath the changing melody of plot and character; every book could yield up a single sentence from the center of the author's obsession. Reynolds Price has shaped many of his novels around the lives of children whose mothers have died giving birth to them, or whose conception is in some other way clouded—children, that is, who feel or are treated as if they are guilty from their first breath.

Kate Vaiden, which teems with orphans and murderous and suicidal generations—all the expected passions of a Price book—is nonetheless different from the North Carolina novelist's other work. It is a forgiving, immensely readable story, set mainly in the early 1940's, almost light in feeling (although its tale of early death and frustrated passions is hardly frivolous). But the voice of Mr. Price's heroine blows like fresh air across the page. *Kate Vaiden* even *looks* different from its eloquent but frequently ponderous predecessors, typographically dense from margin to margin.

Only a few of Mr. Price's stories have been told in the first person, notably the richly textured title story of *The Names and Faces of Heroes.* Therefore the full weight of narrative authority has often borne down heavily on his prose; the ominous burden of his concerns shows in the seemingly endless recurrence of certain favorite words: loss, waste, blame, guilt, choice. Lives are unequivocally "stopped" or "saved," characters "know" in an instant whom to trust or flee, and they follow those intuitions more loyally than reason can guarantee. But this time we hear a brand-new narrative voice trying those words, that of Kate Vaiden herself, and she is a candid but rarely portentous guide through the secrets and imperatives of her life. Kate, like most of Mr. Price's creations, has to struggle under a doom not of her making, but she describes and then contrives a hedged escape from it with wit and resolution. She is feisty and full of self-knowledge, "a real middle-sized white woman that has kept on going with strong eyes and teeth for fifty-seven years. You can touch me; I answer." Already the rhythm of the prose promises an author in uncharacteristically good spirits, more exuberant than solemn.

Review of *Kate Vaiden.* From *The New York Times Book Review* (29 June 1986): 1, 40–41. Copyright © 1986 by The New York Times Company. Reprinted by permission.

Kate tells us before the first two pages are finished that she abruptly abandoned a baby 40 years ago "while he was down for a nap," and that when she was a child her father killed her mother and then himself. This puts us instantly in Reynolds Price country, but Kate, unlike the characters whose cursed lives not only haunt future generations but even at times carry over from book to book, has clearly, after all this time, made a kind of peace with these events. Her story, told in patient retrospect, puts us in the midst of death, shock upon shock, but the very fact that she is recollecting in relative tranquillity separates *Kate Vaiden* from the minute-by-minute discoveries, the constructions of Oedipal angst, of *The Surface of Earth, The Source of Light* or *Love and Work.*

Having had an invulnerably happy early childhood, Kate remembers her young parents as attractive, fiercely devoted, her mother depressive, her father jealous of what he takes to be his wife's special relationship to her family; Kate's mother, for her part, had been abandoned by a mother who succumbed to the dangers of childbirth (which endlessly shadow Mr. Price's pages). Kate recalls the mysterious circumstances in which her father, Dan, shot his wife, Frances, and then himself, and her own safekeeping by her aunt and uncle. At the age of 11 she seems less scarred by their deaths than one might expect—less than might even be realistic—but the lesson that passion is profoundly dangerous and that she herself might be the unwitting carrier of some of that danger is waiting, like a cancer, to assert itself when she is older and ready for commitment.

Thinking of lovers as well as family, Kate too comes round in time to the old ground bass: "*I'd caused their deaths.*" Abandoned in a flash of gunfire by father and mother and in an equally inexplicable flash of a different kind of gunfire by her sweet early love, she takes to a life of desperate lurches and disappearances. After the age of 16, the most predictable behavior Kate can manage seems to be unplanned periodic flight and reappearance on the doorstep of anyone who promises comfort, then flight again whenever the threat of permanence begins to suffocate her like a Southern summer day. (She does linger long enough to conceive a child by an enigmatic lover with a parentless background to match her own.) She is "led or carried," as she puts it, apparently active in her choices but actually passive in muddled self-defense against being unvalued, unloved; 40 years later she wonders if she was "carried by anything but my selfish hope and steady fear—*Leave people before they can plan to leave you.*"

Thus the old curse of family recurs, and the understandable suspicion that she is tainted: she is, she fears, "a thing people took up and then put down," and her response is to blow across her own life and the lives of others like a leaf, searching for permanence but fleeing when it threatens. She crosses the landscape of North Carolina, from her small town of Macon to Raleigh, up to Norfolk, Va., to Greensboro and back again, getting on and off trains on a whim or a premonition, showing up at the houses of relatives she barely knows, casting her lot with strangers. Kate has the personality to command affection and respect, a mysteriously fed, good-natured charm that engages people in her struggle to find the home she thinks she wants.

She is helped more than she wants to acknowledge by an assortment of lively characters who sustain her and ask little in return—a saintly aunt and an alcoholic but silently loving uncle; their young black cook, who gives her sharp advice, hard and edgy with wit; a taxi driver almost too old to dare to love her. Gritty and sure of herself at an early age, still she is deeply, invisibly damaged. She and the orphaned father of her son are similar, for example: "Not good enough magnets to hold even *parents.*" Given her conviction that she spreads contagion, Kate's desire to be needed—"used," she says, as a necessity, not as a mere opportunity for warmth, sexual or otherwise—does not seem to express quite seriously enough, uniquely enough, the real terror at her core that prevents her from settling into satisfaction. This would be a believable quest for most women, to be loved for who they are. But Kate's history, she assures us, and shows us the scars to prove it, has separated her from the ordinary: she does not sound like a woman eager to be recognized, for what she *is* is dangerous.

One of the beguiling things about *Kate Vaiden,* though, is that Mr. Price allows some real ambiguity into Kate's story. Of all the unthinkable actions for a woman whose life has been formed and deformed by her parents' sudden disappearance, Kate walks out on her own child, Lee, presumably because she believes he will have a better chance to grow up healthy in the care of someone less suspect than she. But of course the paradox—and are we to judge her for it?—is that she must perpetuate the curse of abandonment in order to save him. Is that, we are allowed to wonder, her real intention or is she merely self-serving? ("Lee Vaiden's been lucky not to grow next to me. When they made me, they left out the mothering part," "the tending rearing permanent patience and the willingness to take such slim reward as most mothers get. . . . Many times I've regretted it as my worst failing.")

There are moments when it feels as if we are seeing the ultimate wages of Kate's neglect, her incapacity to commit herself to anyone, adult or child; and other times when the author's mind seems to have wandered from his central preoccupation and to have let Kate off her own psychological hook rather casually. Mr. Price's characters have always been obsessives, and Kate until that point has been no exception. Her behavior is that of a woman possessed by her own history and capable of making searching comments about it. So it seems alternately a relief from an epic self-absorption and a too easy resolution to have her walk out on her own child and then wonder about him precious little through the next four decades. Her delayed search for him is like an undone duty, undertaken only when the shadow of death has fallen across her. Thus the ending, not so much happy as unburdened by regret, feels borrowed from someone else's book. Mr. Price is more convincing at retribution.

But until those final somewhat facile pages, Kate is superbly in control of her own tale. The informality of her voice, with its Southern storyteller's love of vivid metaphor, takes precedence over the depressing facts she has to relate, and her tendency toward conciseness and irreverence let her render the tragic with the poise of distance. Just before she tells us about her father's awful departure from her life she says: "Why did I think I was part of a thing that weighed enough in his mind and heart to gentle him now? All my life I've run like a shot dog to similar conclusions. I live on hope the way most humans do on air and coffee. He did have the finest neck on earth, and it was the last I saw of him alive till more red dust roared up and took him."

This tone gives Kate one thing that has often been conspicuously absent from Mr. Price's novels: a particularized personality (not to mention a sense of humor). Rosacoke Mustian and Wesley Beavers in his first published novel, *A Long and Happy Life,* have their idiosyncrasies, viewed affectionately through a distancing lens. They are country people and their dignity, a matter of innate but surprising superiority over their surroundings, gives them the charm of the exotic, a carefully observed specificity. The father in "The Names and Faces of Heroes," apparently modeled closely on Mr. Price's own, also possesses a uniquely inflected personality. But a great many of Mr. Price's other characters, though their creator is hugely articulate on their behalf, often seem to sink under the weight of their blood-soaked histories and passions. The more resonant the prose, the more an abstract quality prevails, in which their generic relation to each other—*son, wife, mother*—keeps them from full individuality.

But *Kate Vaiden,* intense and powerful though it is, is never so absorbed in the elevation of circumstance to myth that it becomes unsympathetic. Kate herself gives us a language in which to feel a recognizable life move forward. Mr. Price's successful creation of a female voice may be a tour de force, but it never feels like a showy ventriloquial act. Instead, Kate is a wholly convincing girl and a not improbable woman, her growing up before and during World War II informed by a mass of unselfconscious detail, and the town of Macon made visible under dust and midday quiet. (The only implausibility enters when the author continues the habit of his other novels and overgenerously makes some of the speech and all the written communications of his characters oddly similar in style and eloquent beyond any English teacher's proudest dreams. He also tends to idealize his black characters, who seem to borrow their wisdom from Faulkner—they are clever, earthy and bold.)

I can think of no novelist whose effect on readers is more polarizing than Reynolds Price; his work seems to some darkly poetic, a welcome alternative to the flat, cool, uncompelling shaggy dog stories of "minimalist" fiction, and to others pompous and inflated, a fierce agon composed of shards of memoir obsessively reordered. *Kate Vaiden* should please readers of both persuasions. Mr. Price has found a narrator of great charm whose sad story, from which she manages to set herself free, sounds (as Kate might say) new as morning.

[Review of *The Laws of Ice*]

ROBERT B. SHAW

This is Reynolds Price's second book of poems; like Raymond Carver, he is best known for his fiction, which in his case includes novels as well as short stories. As with Carver's, autobiography is much in evidence in Price's poems. But differences outweigh similarities. Price is a lusher, denser stylist, and in his central sequence, "Days and Nights," he has a continuous, progressively unfolding story to tell, offering what amounts to a verse diary covering the months before and during which he was diagnosed and treated for spinal cancer. (The disease, still under treatment, has confined him to a wheelchair.) The miscellaneous poems in other sections, too, usually approach narrative more expansively than Carver's ascetic fragments do: they reach without embarrassment for amplitude and layered symbolism.

Although I was impressed by the emotional sweep of the "Days and Nights" sequence, moving as it does from foreboding through stoicism to a tentative, renewed hopefulness, I was even more struck by some of the other long pieces. The three poems grouped as "Three Visits" make use of classical archetypes in ways that are at once funny and intense, as the poet details his encounters with Dionysos, Aphrodite, and Hermes. The tone in these pieces is highly complex, able to move from wicked wit to genuine awe. "Dionysos" begins chattily, "A god stopped in at the house last night, / Claiming to be a Jehovah's Witness / Peddling tracts. . . ." But when the visiting missionary dozes off in an armchair, his metamorphosis lifts the poem to a shocking theophanic vision:

> Then slowly still his essence gathered;
> Limbs, trunk, head throbbed, coalesced—
>
> . . . .
>
> The glare consumed his peddler's mask
> Till he sat up near my face, then rose—
> Himself revealed, incendiary core,
> A megatonnage unforeseen

From *Poetry* 150 (July 1987): 232–33. Copyright 1987 by The Modern Poetry Association; reprinted by permission of the editor of *Poetry*.

> By any computer or institute:
> Precisely the grandest male I'd found,
> Exhaling from every pore of a skin
> Dusted with a pelt of slant tan hair
> The constant ground-bass of majesty.

In their energetic blend of the archetypal with the everyday, these poems may put us in mind of such a work as Eudora Welty's *The Golden Apples*. Price is, after all, a Southern writer, and he shares the propensity of his culture for reinvigorating the old myths. Mythmaking even more elaborate occurs in the long poem "House Snake." In its portrait of an intrusive black snake as a demigod, this piece catches a bit of the animistic power Faulkner drew upon in "The Bear" and his other wilderness stories. These are strange works, and even stranger are the poems commemorating the author's father and mother—gothic contrivances driven and contorted by painful honesty. Neither poem is easy to forget, although for bizarre inventiveness "A Tomb for Will Price" takes the prize. It is an extended fantasy in which the poet turns his memories of his father into a monument-*cum*-museum around which he can guide the visitor, pointing out artifacts ("the fossilized bones of a fried-chicken dinner / His mother cooked him to eat on the train toward National Guard / Camp in Morehead City") and finally, with a nightmarish but oddly tender clarity, the man himself:

> The man before you
> In the overstuffed chair is no real man but a risen body.
>
> . . . .
>
> Note the eyeglasses, apparent bifocals, thin gold frames—
> The eyes behind them, clear steel-gray; the speckled hands
> Mottled with age. Note the wide lips, parted to speak,
> Moist with yearning to call your name. No words come;
> He's lost your language, knows only the nine chief angel tongues
> Unknown on earth. Even I'm unable to hear his message.

It is no denigration of Price to say that we don't read his poems in the way we read most poetry. The minutiae, however cunningly deployed, are overshadowed by his broader gestures, and we don't pause over fine turns of phrase (though there are those) because we are caught up in the narrative velocity and the imposing scale of his conceptions. To put it simply, he is exercising his skills as a novelist in verse. Poets, even if they have no intention of poaching on the estate of fiction in return, could learn a lot from studying this gifted interloper.

Reynolds Price's Words Ring Sure and True

JOSEPHINE HUMPHREYS

With the simultaneous publication of two books by Reynolds Price (*A Common Room: Essays 1954–1987* and *A Long and Happy Life*, republished in celebration of its 25th anniversary), I am transported, both with pleasure and in memory.

I first saw Reynolds Price in the spring of 1963, when I was a high school senior visiting the Duke campus. Invited to sit in on a class, I chose his sophomore lit, English 56, which happened to be meeting that day. Price's first novel, *A Long and Happy Life*, had been published the year before, and I had read it with the same charged emotion with which friends of mine were listening to rock 'n' roll. Elvis Presley had never made his way into my heart; but when I read the first sentence of *A Long and Happy Life*, I knew I was hearing a voice that could not only reach my heart but would stay there a long time:

> Just with his body and from inside like a snake, leaning that motorcycle side to side, cutting in and out of the slow line of cars to get there first, staring due-north through goggles towards Mount Moriah and switching coon tails in everybody's face was Wesley Beavers. . . .

It was a voice that sang to me as no other had. It wasted nothing and loaded each word with value. A writer's "style," I now know, is more than a simple accident of vocabulary and rhythm acquired from external sources; it is an accurate reflection of his understanding of the world, of human life. And even as a 17-year-old, I could sense—if not fully explain—a vision behind this language of the world as a meaningful place.

And after reading the novel, I knew two things: I wanted to be a writer (to work a similar magic, make worlds out of words); and I wanted to know this man. In one of the magazines I regularly borrowed from friends (I'd never have subscribed), *Glamour* or *Seventeen* or *Mademoiselle*, I found an article titled "Young and Promising," about people on the rise in various fields of endeavor. Listed there was Reynolds Price, who had recently returned to Duke University to teach. I applied to Duke immediately.

Review of *A Common Room: Essays 1954–1987* and *A Long and Happy Life* (25th-anniversary edition). Reprinted from *The Atlanta Journal-Constitution* (7 February 1988): J8, by permission of the author.

English 56 met on the second floor of Carr Building on the Duke campus, with the windows open to leafy trees inches away and all the spring sounds. In blue seersucker, Price was sitting on the desk at the front of the room, reading aloud Keats' "The Eve of St. Agnes." I was won, yet again, to the voice—deep, rich, full of humor and wisdom. I'd have been won even if he'd been reading a different poem, but that sensuous tale of lovers had an added effect. And the man himself was as darkly handsome as Elvis Presley. I could tell that the students were in his thrall, as I would be for the next four years.

I took every course he taught, including creative writing my freshman year and a course in the novel my senior year. When I think back on my Duke education, I believe it was Reynolds Price who most guided my thoughts and feelings: His voice giving what great teachers must give freely but sometimes painfully—lessons. The intensity of my bond to him was all interior; in actuality there was a distance and a formality between us. But I loved him, and so I learned from him; I believe that's how most true learning occurs. When I left Duke, I felt it a great loss that I would not hear him again.

And so it was with delight that I took up this new volume, *A Common Room,* a gathering of Price's essays of the past 33 years. Of course, during the last two decades, I have been reading his prodigious output of novels and poems and plays with as much dazzled enjoyment as readers ever hope for; but, suddenly, in these essays, I hear him once more talking to *me.* That is, of course, the charm of the essay form, it's wizardry: It reads like private communication, the writer saying *from me to you, these messages.*

But I have the added pleasure of hearing him say things he said to us 20 years ago, the lessons he gave then, still as strong as ever. They are, I guess, his obsessions: the nature of fiction, its roots in family and home, its function in what is still patently a meaningful world.

And though the subjects seem miscellaneous—Hemingway, the Southern novel, Jimmy Carter, sex in narrative, biblical translation—the essays give the impression of centering always on those few obsessions, one wise man's questions and answers delivered to us for consideration. He frequently uses a literal question-and-answer form, making his way toward whatever truths can be known. Life, he seems to say, is not simply meaningful; it is also mystery or meaning kept secret. The secret life of Jesus, the mysteries of our parents' lives apart from us, the puzzle of one's own history and development—these are subjects worth study; worth, in fact, a lifetime of hard work, which is what Price has given them.

I especially like his study of Ernest Hemingway and, for personal reasons, the essay "Finding Work," which he wrote at my request for the Duke University Yearbook my senior year and which I found immensely disturbing at the time. Only in work, he wrote, "could I free myself from the crippling emotional dependence upon other human beings which infects and afflicts any man who has nothing in his life upon which he can rely, nothing more permanent than other people." I was horrified then that he could choose work over love, but in rereading this essay, I find that now, 20 years later, I agree with his choice: It is not precisely a choice of work over love, but of work as a protection from love's hurt.

But my favorite of the essays must be the "Letter to a Young Writer," five pages of advice to someone just embarking upon that lifetime of hard work. His first admonition is, "If you can stop, you probably should." He knows, though, that the hunger to write is an addiction and cannot be easily stopped:

> To end then—it's a hard life. At least as hard as being a good parent and likely to last longer than parenting, harder than all the jobs which permit themselves to be switched off at the end of eight hours; maybe a little easier than being a good doctor or nurse, an earnest religious. But such gauging is absurd, in your case. You are not out for ease. You're out, I trust, for goodness—the perfection of your own peculiar compulsion, as a means of serving, maybe even augmenting the huge and permanent beauty of the visible world, the unseen piers on which the world rides.

A great writer is not automatically a great teacher. But these two books show Reynolds Price to be both. He is also a brave man, out for goodness, certainly augmenting the beauty of the world. Writers and serious readers need to own these books. I'm as grateful for them as for food after long hunger.

"A Vast Common Room":
Twenty-five Years of Essays and Fiction
by Reynolds Price

JEFFERSON HUMPHRIES

Reynolds Price published his first novel, *A Long and Happy Life*, in 1962. It received extraordinary critical accolades (after having been rejected by Jason Epstein at Random House) and won the William Faulkner Award for a notable first novel. Since then, in the course of twenty-five years, Price has published five novels, two books of poetry, two collections of short stories, two essay collections, two plays, and a book of translations from the Bible. None of those quite received the kind of unanimous ovation that had greeted the writer's first book until the appearance of *Kate Vaiden* in 1986. *Kate Vaiden* was also the first since 1962 to win a major national award (the National Book Critics Circle Award). It seems appropriate that Atheneum, which has published all of Price's books—beautifully printed and bound—should bring out a twenty-fifth anniversary edition of *A Long and Happy Life* now.

The two books not only represent milestones of critical recognition in the writer's career, but also are the only ones in which the chief protagonist is female (*Good Hearts* is not counted as a third because in it Rosacoke really shares equal billing with Wesley Beavers). *Kate Vaiden* is narrated in the first person by a woman, and the earlier book contains long letters written by Rosacoke Mustian, even though the whole story is not told by her. Why should these two, of all Price's very impressive body of work, have won such untempered praise? Could the fact of female point of view have anything to do with this?

A Long and Happy Life is in one sense a love story, a simple southern pastoral. Rosacoke Mustian, an unusually bright and sensitive country girl, loves Wesley Beavers, motorcycle salesman and youthful womanizer. Wesley may or may not love Rosacoke; it's hard to tell. He probably doesn't love anyone

Review of *A Long and Happy Life* (25th-anniversary edition), *Good Hearts*, *Kate Vaiden*, *The Laws of Ice*, and *A Common Room: Essays 1954–1987*. Reprinted from *Southern Review* 24.3 (Summer 1988): 686–95, by permission of the author.

the way Rosacoke loves him. Nothing could be simpler or more timeless: unrequited love and its consequences. Rosacoke and Wesley do wind up tied together in marriage. Many readers were aware of a chilling irony in the novel's title, and those who have followed Price's career will know how strongly he has denied identification with Rosacoke and defended Wesley: what Price says in many interviews is that Wesley is just a good old boy who enjoys his freedom, to which Rosacoke puts an untimely end. If this describes the affinities of Price, it does not correspond to those of the novel's narrative voice, however. In any case, the novel's ironic, doom-charged title—like an inscrutable peal of distant thunder when the sky is blue—is emblematic of the book. The more disturbing possibilities—that life with Wesley may be far from happy though long, or neither long nor happy, and that similar romances and marriages may be similarly chilly corridors past childbearing and rearing towards the grave—are easy to ignore for the reader who would rather not see them. I would guess that most of *A Long and Happy Life*'s readers have chosen to ignore its darker side, and that would include the critics who objected to subsequent books like *Permanent Errors,* whose title and content are far less ambiguously pessimistic. Their lesson is one which Price says he got from reading Hemingway: "The lessons of one master, diffidently but desperately offered—*Prepare, strip, divest for life that awaits you; learn solitude and work; see how little is lovely but love that.*"

Good Hearts, which has just appeared, gives us a look at Rosacoke and Wesley in middle age, still married, but facing now the chasm of mutual strangeness that has separated them from the start, and which has rubbed both of them fairly raw without their knowing it. Rosacoke is a secretary for a college department office, and Wesley works as a mechanic. They live in Raleigh, North Carolina, and have had only the one child with which Rosa was pregnant at the end of *A Long and Happy Life.* He is an adult now, married and living a few hours away. Wesley, a few days before Christmas, goes off to work and does not return home. He has, we are told, left for as much as four days on more than one occasion before, sometimes leaving notes hidden in his sock drawer. This time there is no note, and the absence stretches on far beyond his prior record. How and why Wesley turns away from Rosacoke will evoke pangs of recognition from most people over thirty. She tells it herself:

> I know this much at least, that you'd turned away from me slowly but more and more. You were always courteous about it—but the fact is, you turned. It hasn't been all that hard for me to bear. I've been able to think it was a natural movement of time, working in both of us. But I can't help seeing all those old couples on t.v. saying they've never been happier with their bodies than now, when their children are grown and gone, and they can be alone in the house together. Not that you and I are old, but we turned out not to know what to do alone together. That was one fault at least, and I bear at least fifty percent of the blame.

Rosa reacts, just as a reader of *A Long and Happy Life* would expect her to, by beginning a diary. Just as she spoke for herself in the earlier novel, not always but often—in first-person narration, letters, or out loud, to other characters—so she does now, twenty-eight years later. Her introspectiveness, her facility with words, which together make for a verbal compulsion to *make sense out of things*—things which usually don't make much sense—has not been good for the both of them, as it usually isn't when only one member of a couple has it:

> Wesley, you were always so slow to speak up for yourself that it took me long years to realize how I mowed you down time after time with all my orations and epistles. Of course I *didn't* mow you down. I never really won. You'd just tuck your square chin, nod, walk on off, and do your will in your own sweet time. But I wish I'd had the fairness to see years sooner how I shut you out of my own calculations and thought I was Miss Country Genius and Judge.

Is it too late now? To change, or make amends? As in the earlier novel, Rosa's eloquent candor makes her the star of *Good Hearts:* We love her because she has chosen us to confide in.

The more taciturn Wesley is shown to us in the third person, but we are made to understand here, as perhaps we were not in *A Long and Happy Life,* that Wesley is a genuinely *good* person, every bit as worthy of sympathy as Rosacoke. Price seems more concerned to tell Wesley's side of the story now than twenty-eight years ago, probably because of the one-sided view of the relation taken by so many readers of *A Long and Happy Life.*

The failure of both Rosacoke and Wesley to understand, to reach one another, to do whatever is necessary to keep their union living and vital, is in Price's vision an essential evil, as supernaturally *and* physically real as evil could possibly be. The lack of bad intention, of any will to harm on Rosacoke's part or Wesley's, does not make this evil any less what it is. Even though both Wesley and Rosa are essentially good and well-meaning people, a lack of vigilance is all it takes for them—for Rosacoke and their home—to become exposed: during Wesley's absence, Rosa must face Christmas alone, without Wesley or their son, and on New Year's Eve, she is attacked in their bed and raped. It is Wesley's abandonment of Rosa, and the accumulated wrong of their mutual estrangement, each taking for granted the other, that has left Rosa and their home open to such dark violence. This evil, though elemental, takes a firmly human form, as evil usually does. It does not have horns and breathe fire, or appear and disappear in a puff of smoke, but comes in the utterly ordinary shape of a deluded and disturbed though sane man—a rapist—who would never admit the evil, or even the wrong of his desires and acts, and who appears to be perfectly likable when under public scrutiny, completely unrecognizable—to all but Rosacoke—for what he is. He is also, like all real evil, finally ludicrous and pathetic. Price's depiction of this man is one of the most penetrating, believable, *true* portraits of evil I have ever seen or read, and is enough in itself to make this book extraordinary. In this case, and for the time being, evil does not prevail. This case, one feels, is given to us by the author as exemplary, one to emulate, not as a reflection of what usually happens in human relationships.

Good Hearts shows us two decent, kind people in deep, deep trouble as a couple. Facing the decision whether to let that trouble, stewing for so long, separate them, or try to face each other and reach over it (can any two people hope to reach *that* far?) is what this book is about. It is the most compelling and sensitive book Price has written. There cannot be a subject on which Americans of all ages living in 1988 more desperately need and crave (whether they know it or not) instruction: Can two good people live together for long without suffering or doing subtle, maybe invisible but nonetheless real, harm to themselves and each other—without "pecking each other bald," like two chickens nailed inside a single crate? If so, how?

This book is even more compelling in its subject matter than *Kate Vaiden,* I think, and the writing has the same quality as *Kate Vaiden.* In both of these books, there can be no mistake that we are in the hands of a master who has attained perfect ease in his art. You have the same feeling that the late Laurence Olivier could evoke on the stage: everything is effortlessly perfect. Do not worry, do not even think about how the artifice is accomplished. The perfection is so intense that it erases all trace of itself, and becomes apparently natural ease. One wonders why Price, who has always been one of America's great writers, should suddenly now transcend himself. The real wonder is that any artist, however great, manages to do so at all, ever. There is no answer to the question why. However and whyever, Price shows an ease with himself and with his readers that is the rarest quality in art. For example, in the opening page of *Good Hearts,* there is an aside by the narrator to the reader, like a parabasis in classical Greek drama—a moment in which the chorus of a play would remove their masks and step forward to speak directly in the author's name. The narration has been describing Rosa and Wesley in bed, about to fall asleep. Suddenly, there is this sentence: "You though, if you'd been transparent there, would have seen an apparently young married couple." Rosacoke is not the only one choosing to confide in us; the narrator is, too.

That Price should have returned, after so long, to his first and most popular characters is a surprise, perhaps to him as well as to readers who have followed his career closely. For many years he has replied to questions about what Rosacoke and Wesley might be doing now by saying that he had said all about them he knew in *A Long and Happy Life.* (Price has also just completed the manuscript of a memoir, something else which, he admits, he thought for years he would not or could not ever write.) But most surprising of all is how perfectly the Rosa and Wesley of *Good Hearts* dovetail with the depiction of their younger selves in *A Long and Happy Life.* One never doubts for an instant that these are the very same people. This is exactly and perfectly how they would have evolved. It could not have turned out any differently. On almost every occasion I know where a novelist has written a sequel to an earlier book, especially one in which the same characters are seen years later or earlier, the seams are too visible—there is a nagging discrepancy, beyond changes always wrought by time and events, between two characters which are supposed to be the same one. Here, that is not the case. I know of only one other modern writer who has accomplished this so well: Marcel Proust, who of course did so on a rather grander scale in *A la recherche du temps perdu*.

Kate Vaiden is the intermediate step between Price's previous work and *Good Hearts*. *Kate Vaiden* frames the typically, and unambiguously, astringent vision of Price's mature work (*The Surface of Earth*, for instance) in first-person narration rather than the somewhat lofty omniscience of the writer's other novels, stories, and poems since *A Long and Happy Life*. It ties that vision to the circumstances of a narrating persona with whom anyone can sympathize or identify. This makes it more palatable to more readers and critics, I suspect, than *The Surface of Earth* and most of Price's other, earlier work. *Kate Vaiden* grew out of what Price has described as the impulse to write a fictional autobiography. He says that "as I advanced on into 1982–83, the impulse began to change in mind to a woman's voice. I can only begin to understand the reason for that when I remember that at the same time I was beginning to do a great deal of thinking about my own mother." Kate's story is written by her late in life, when she knows that a cancer of the cervix will—perhaps?—soon kill her. This aspect of the story must have a great deal to do with Price's own recent bout with a cancerous spinal tumor, which interrupted work on *Kate Vaiden*. She tells the story of her life for a son abandoned when she was seventeen.

> Cervical cancer, no possible doubt. Seventy-two hours in near-solitary in a hospital room with radium seeds planted deep inside me, bombarding the guest. Except for nurses dashing in with my meals (which, since I couldn't raise my head, I couldn't eat), the only other human I saw was a man in a long pink smock who swore he was chaplain. I thanked him but said I dealt with God alone. A fool thing to say, but the pink smock threw me. I was dealing with death.

> I'd watched death at close range several times before but in other people's bodies. Like the average human, I'd assumed I'd escape. The absolute last invader I'd suspected was cancer *there*. But lying alone for two full days, with radium in me, I of course came round to the next deduction. I was punished at last in the place where I'd failed, the scene of the crime. Can you believe me if I say my first response was amusement? It seemed like a big tidy joke.

Kate Vaiden would be Rosacoke Mustian's polar opposite, at least in the way her desire expresses itself, without any of Rosacoke's fierce loyalty, determined bonding to one object of desire (Wesley) and unswerving commitment to see that bond through to the grave. Kate Vaiden is, as one reviewer put it, "a well-meaning betrayer." When Kate is a child, her father kills Kate's mother and himself after discovering that his wife has not been faithful to him. Kate loves many men, but is unable to commit herself to any of them. The very first, Gaston Stegall, might have been the exception if he had not been killed in training for World War II, or so Kate thinks. Of course, it's cheap to think so with the possibility firmly out of reach, and thinking so makes it easier to say no to others. As soon as anyone confesses his need of her, she takes the first opportunity to leave, usually without a word. This is not for lack of good will. Kate does not entirely excuse herself for being so simultaneously fickle and headstrong (though some readers will agree with Noony, Kate's black friend, mentor, and stern judge, that she comes too close), but she does not see, in retrospect, how she could have done any differently. She cannot contemplate spending the rest of her life, or even any large or indefinite portion of it, with any one other person. She abandons everyone who has ever loved or needed her, including her own illegitimate son. She believes, and may be right in believing, that she could not have lived any other way but alone. Still, she has damaged many lives by insisting on having things entirely her way—engaging in intimate relations while refusing the responsibility involved, never really accepting any responsibility for her own desire. When she begs Noony's pardon for her many sins toward the end of the book, Noony replies, "Too late." And many readers will agree. Nevertheless, to the end, Kate remains compellingly likable, even to Noony.

Kate's story, like Rosacoke's and all of Price's work, reflects a preoccupation with the difficult vagaries of desire between two, and sometimes more than two humans, the by turns healing and catastrophically rending force of love, all the more powerful and treacherous when it is sexual. I think Constance Rooke, in her excellent book on Price in the Twayne series, was right when she said that Price's work is haunted by a double bind: the impossibility of living alone without desiring others, and the impossibility of being with others without sacrificing a large part of the self's autonomy, without mourning a (perhaps illusory) freedom. This would appear to be *the* moral dilemma which must confront every adult wishing to be responsible in her/his dealings with others, and I know of no writer who has plumbed it as deeply or thoroughly as Price. Kate's story, like Rosacoke's, is absolutely compelling because it could be anyone's, man or woman. And it is told in a prose which is both starkly simple and beautiful.

I don't know of any other writer who can come close to the piercing, lyrical clarity of Price's language. Many critics in the sixties and seventies called Price's style "overwrought," "artificial." It has taken us this long to appreciate it for what it has always been: meticulously, carefully crafted. His voice, or maybe I should say his voices, have been shaped by many things, early study of Milton, the translation of Biblical Greek, the rhythms of southern speech, and have been for a while so perfectly achieved that they completely transcend time and space, the modern upper South (North Carolina and Virginia) in which Price's characters usually move.

Nowhere is this style more visible or purer (distilled down to an even denser, more white-hot version of itself) than in the poetry which Price has been publishing since the early sixties. Two volumes of his poetry have appeared, the first, *Vital Provisions,* in 1982, the second, *The Laws of Ice,* in 1986. *The Laws of Ice* contains work dealing, as the title indicates, with mortality and its consequences, the natural and supernatural dialectic of life and death. Many of these are poems dealing with Price's bout in 1984 with an astrocytoma, a malignant tumor on his spinal cord, which has left him confined to a wheelchair. The central section of the book, "Days and Nights: A Journal," comprises a poetic record of the days immediately before and after the discovery of that tumor. In one of those poems, Price meets in dream an avatar of death:

> I know he will make his thrust any moment;
> I cannot guess what aim it will take.
> Then as—appalled—I watch him quiver,
> He says "Now you must learn the bat dance."
> I know he has struck. It is why I came.
> In one long silent step, I refuse and turn toward home.
>
> I will walk all night. I will not die of cancer.
> Nothing will make me dance in that dark.

Other poems narrate natural encounters, either with animals (a snake, for instance) or other humans, both of which seem to have supernatural import. The healing power of contact with human flesh, the mysterious balm of sex, is a recurring preoccupation. Dreams—always in Price's work potential messages from the sphere of the divine—and narratives expanded from Bible verses have both become leitmotifs of Price's poetry by now. Nowhere is it clearer that Price has somehow, miraculously, emerged from his maiming brush with premature death without any bitterness, without any diminution of his gifts as a person or a writer—on the contrary. *"I'm simply | The one happy man I know, | Assured of witness and judgement entirely / Beyond my power to guess or change."*

The same style, and the same preoccupations, are evident in *A Common Room, Essays 1954–1987.* Having written novels, stories, poetry, plays, and essays, Price is one of the only true "men of letters" in our culture. The essays are about everything from Milton's *Lycidas* to Jimmy Carter to southern cooking, and in them the vision reflected in the novels and poetry comes through as *credo:* "A line scored in the earth beneath this much at least of a career grounded in the beliefs described. Credos are dangerous coats to wear; they may alienate readers to whom the beliefs look absurd or excluding." That credo is the Apostles' Creed, an ancient and elegant affirmation of Christian faith—simpler, shorter, and less doctrinaire than the Nicene—well-known to Catholics and Anglicans. Price has always defined his vision as essentially Christian.

> The final help I can offer the proof-hungry is a reminder that virtually identical beliefs powered perhaps a majority of the supreme creative minds of our civilization—Augustine, Dante, Chaucer, Michelangelo, Dürer, Milton, Rembrandt, Pascal, Racine, Bach, Handel, Newton, Haydn, Mozart, Wordsworth, Beethoven, Kierkegaard, Dickens, Tolstoy, Hopkins, Bruckner, Tennyson, Stravinsky, Eliot, Barth, Poulenc, Auden, O'Connor (to begin a long roll that includes only the dead). Pressed by their unanimous testimony to a dazzling but benign light at the heart of space, what sane human will step up to say "Lovely, no doubt, but your eyes deceive you"? Not I, not now or any day soon.

One of the best essays is the one for which the collection is named, "A Vast Common Room," in which Price proposes a radical approach to the failure of understanding between men and women which may be worse today than it has ever been—ironically so, at a moment when both men and women are freer than ever before to criticize and change the culture's definition of "masculine" and "feminine." That freedom seems too often to have led women to answer traditional male misogyny with a mirror image, an excoriation of maleness, and men defensively to fear and scorn women all the more. Price's solution may be best illustrated by the three novels, *Kate Vaiden, Good Hearts,* and *A Long and Happy Life,* and may answer in some degree the question I left unanswered at the beginning of this essay: why female point of view has produced the writer's most acclaimed fiction.

> Can we change? And should we? My own answer is an obvious Yes. Men should excavate and explore, however painfully, their memories of early intimacy with women, and attempt again to produce novels as whole as those of their mammoth and healing predecessors. More women should step through a door that is now wide ajar—a backward step, also painful but short, into the room of their oldest knowledge: total human sympathy.

What could be more obvious or more humane, but what other writer has said it?

Price, like Don DeLillo (unlike Price an urban and abstract novelist), is a writer working against the age. His realism, like DeLillo's, is in the service of a profoundly coherent and unique and *troubled,* though fervently hopeful vision of what it is to be human, and this means that it is a realism which does not defer to matter, does not stop at the material surface of things the way more popular writing does. While he has not been neglected, Price has not gotten the critical attention that more gaudily experimental novelists have, nor has he been very palatable to connoisseurs of a purely mimetic and material realism. But I don't know of any writer who has more important things to say, more really indispensable comfort and advice to offer, to a reader living in the second half of the twentieth century, or indeed in any time or place.

The Price of Grace

JAY TOLSON

Any male Southern writer worth his grits must bear up under a certain amount of unfair and generally pointless comparison with William Faulkner. It comes with the territory, as they say. But Reynolds Price has had to tolerate more than his share, and for reasons largely irrelevant to his work. It began with a coincidence. Price's first novel, *A Long and Happy Life*, came out the same year Faulkner died, in 1962, a symbolic torch-passing for those inclined to see it as such. If that were not enough to give influence-hounds the scent, the same novel went on to win that year's William Faulkner Foundation Award.

For lazier reviewers, it was hardly necessary to read the novel: this was a Faulkner epigone, clear and simple. Those who bothered would have thought their suspicions confirmed by the novel's first sentence. A serpentine creature of almost 200 words, it looks as though it crawled straight out of Yoknapatawpha County. But the sentence deceives. It is the only one quite like it in the book. The prose that bodies forth the tale of Rosacoke Mustian and her barely requited love for Wesley Beavers is, for the most part, closely pruned, quite unlike Faulkner's sprawling verbal undergrowth.

Absent as well are other hallmarks of the Faulkner style—the incantatory iterations, the neologisms, the poetic inflation. Price, in fact, favored a more clinched-in rhetoric, a rhetoric of understatement that owed more to Hemingway (an influence he acknowledges in one of the more self-revealing essays in *A Common Room*) than to Faulkner. Still, since Price was Southern, wrote about country people, and sometimes used dialect, the critics persisted. Over the years, Price complains, "It has been all but mandatory in discussions of my fiction to claim—and regret if not lament—the influence of William Faulkner."

Misleading as all this is, it is hardly necessary to rally to Price's defense. The 57 essays assembled in *A Common Room* do a more than adequate job on their own. Dating from 1954 to 1987 and spanning Price's productive career as a novelist, poet, playwright, and professor of English, they show how different Price's ambitions are—narrower, in a sense, but also more tightly har-

Review of *A Common Room: Essays 1954–1987* and *Good Hearts*. From *The New Republic* 198 (4 July 1988): 34–39. Reprinted by permission of *The New Republic,* © 1988, The New Republic, Inc.

nessed to considerations of craft. The essays, variously personal, critical, and hortatory, also make for an illuminating *autobiographia literaria,* as revealing about Price's life and background as they are about his literary tastes and designs.

Price, one quickly learns, is a writer firmly rooted in "one dear perpetual place," that place being the gently rolling tobacco and cotton country of east-central North Carolina. To those who know it, it's pleasant enough country at the right season and the right time of day, but it can also turn dry, dusty, and red-clay mean during the long hot bake of summer. Hard country, in other words: it's the sort of place that doesn't leave people too much leeway, and for which, as a result, folks develop a wary, grudging love. Not surprisingly, it tends to lose many of its talented young to more hospitable climes.

What kept Price at home, or at least within a very short drive of his native Macon, was people, kith and kin. Among the former are the South's two extremes: overworked and underpaid blacks and the fading remnants of the old planter aristocracy. Both types serve as secondary characters in Price's novels, though not merely as thickeners of the social soup: they are always vivid presences, strongly individualized. Still, the people Price knows, and the ones who figure centrally in his fiction, are the white upper yeomanry. Small farmers (or former sharecroppers), skilled mechanics, shopkeepers, salesmen, and clerks—they are the people Jefferson idealized and, to a large extent, the people who still keep the South running.

Raised with modest social ambitions—the more driven or fortunate rise into the solid middle or upper middle classes, but even to them the yuppie creed of ever-upward is anathema—they live by the Protestant virtues of work and faith. If their lives often turn out to be bitterly hard and disappointing, they are not the kind to blame others or the system. They're far more likely to blame themselves, their moral failings; and if faith can't save them from guilt, they may turn in desperation to the bottle or to some other crutch to help them go silently to their graves. All is not a Vale of Tears, though. It sounds corny, but they live for family, even though the bonds of kinship as often strangle as sustain. Most also live with hope of grace, which more than anything else can make the hard life seem worth living.

Price has paid close attention to these people, his family early on becoming a source of fascination and mystery. There was, for one, an alcoholic father, an insurance salesman who struggled through the Great Depression and who, the night Reynolds was born, swore to give up the bottle if his wife made it through a particularly difficult labor. Price came to wonder what he owed this troubled but deeply loving man for keeping that difficult pledge. And, in one sense, Price's fiction is the answer: it is both a long meditation on sacrifice and indebtedness and an expression of gratitude.

Price owes perhaps an even greater debt to the women of his family (and also to a number of outstanding women teachers who quite literally changed his life). Of one particularly cherished aunt who, during all his childhood years of moving around North Carolina, remained a fixed point in Macon, the embodiment of rootedness and home, he recalls that she served "all the functions of an ideal grandmother—unquestioned love and generosity, without the riptides of parental love." The ties with his mother, like those with his father, were more complicated. In "A Vast Common Room," an essay that explores the hermaphroditic nature of the artist, Price relates how his curiosity about his mother—"noted for youthful rebellion but then for impeccable loyalty to my father"—drove him one day "to write in a female voice, one whose atmosphere chimed in my ears with the timbre of my mother's lost voice, which I no longer remember." The book that issued from this compulsion was *Kate Vaiden,* to my mind Price's best novel to date, and powerful precisely because of the steady force of the protagonist's voice. As Price explains:

> However far my Kate ventured in rebellion and independence, she achieved in her voice and in all her acts a credible expression of my mother's own spiritual potential—a life whose courage and headlong drive I might have awarded my mother had I been able and were it not a life with even more pain than hers.

How we learn to handle the complicated "rip-tides" of love, and not just parental love, is Price's great theme, present from his first novel to his most recent. His constant attention to this question, and his quiet handling of its complex domestic ramifications, make him, finally, a very different writer from Faulkner. Faulkner's sights were set on something more grand, or grandiose: the creation of a mythic world in which a series of tragic destinies play themselves out. Price, more like Eudora Welty or E. M. Forster (two authors who are paid deep homage in *A Common Room*), is concerned with the problem of connecting.

What is more, as a number of these essays suggest, Price has found his own answer. It is work—steady, habitual attention to one's given trade. Work alone, he writes, "has freed me for the attempt to understand, if not control, disorder in myself and in those I love. It has even freed me at times to participate in the richest, most dangerous mystery of all—the love of what otherwise I should have feared and fled, a few human beings." In urging his solution on his readers and, no doubt, on his many fortunate students, Price sounds ever so much like the person I suspect his parents intended—the good, if unchurched, Protestant. (And it is not irrelevant that Price's longtime academic specialty is the Puritan poet par excellence, Milton.)

Price's hard-earned Protestant wisdom is an admirable guide to self-sufficiency, and to much else as well. But as a foundation on which to build fictions, it poses problems. A vision too strongly imposed upon the various world and its even more various inhabitants can lead to formula, a danger that threatens even Price's greatest gift, his powers of characterization. Price's characters, with occasional exceptions (notably the highly autobiographical protagonist of *Love and Work*), are shrewd rustics, blunt, funny, and honest folk who talk about themselves and their plights with the same sort of light irony one finds in the better country music songs—the "work your fingers to the bone, what do you get? Bony fingers!" variety. But it's not the countriness that troubles. Price's populism is never condescending. The problem is that Price knows his characters almost too well. Lacking an inner opacity, they sometimes seem too dependent on their creator and the vision they were created to serve.

Yet for all that, Price makes us want to know his people. We want to, because they come across as attractive and nearly as wise as Price himself. Nearly, I emphasize, because they almost all have great difficulty connecting, a problem that stems from excessive expectations—theirs of others, others' of them. We find these characters and the familiar blocked situations once again in Price's most recent novel, *Good Hearts*, which takes up the lives of Rosacoke and Wesley Beavers some 30 years after their rocky courtship in *A Long and Happy Life*.

The problem raised in that first novel was how a young woman of unusually subtle intelligence could resolve her unhappy love for a man who, while attractive and good-hearted, seems her intellectual and spiritual lesser. A standard variation on the classic small-town romance, in other words, but Price worked the familiar clay in quite marvelous ways, showing how a deep mutual attraction plays havoc with Rosacoke and Wesley's more obvious incompatibilities. The plot complicates when a tussle in the field leaves Rosacoke pregnant, and Wesley, an ex-Navy man and avid motorcyclist, unable to stay put in rural Afton, North Carolina, returns to the bigger lights of Norfolk, Virginia, unaware of what their lovemaking has produced. Even when he learns of Rosacoke's pregnancy and returns home to do the honorable thing, he cannot find the right words to satisfy Rosacoke. All seems doomed until both take part in a Christmas pageant at the Baptist church and Rosacoke is drawn by the laden symbolism of the occasion to see and accept Wesley for what he is. Marriage seems inevitable by novel's end.

To those readers who favor down-to-earth solutions, the conclusion of *A Long and Happy Life* may have seemed somewhat contrived: Was grace doing forced duty here? I, for one, felt that the resolution served as a fitting close to the book's larger theme: the mixed blessings of generation (there are other complicated births in the novel, both leading to deaths) and the mysterious claims and transformations involved in the engendering act. It also worked because Price convinced me that Rosacoke's perceptions and understanding were attuned to something more liminal than hard common sense. And furthermore, it was not, by any stretch, a snugly happy ending.

The novel left readers wondering about what might happen after this attractive though unevenly matched couple made it to the altar. *Good Hearts* tells us. Rosacoke (now Rosa) and Wesley have made their way from Afton to

Raleigh, raised a son, and seen him settle into his own career and marriage. Rosa and Wesley both have respectable jobs—she as a secretary in a university English department, he as a car mechanic—and though both stand out at what they do, neither views work as the royal road to self-fulfillment. They don't even live vicariously through their son, who, though loving, is a bit on the dull side. "Horace turned out as satisfactorily as we have any reason to expect, and I'd write him a good job reference tomorrow, but till I get a lot older than now, I won't be needing many days of his time," writes Rosa with her usual candor. Worse yet, Horace is married to an upwardly mobile schemer who plots her life with dining and decoration tips from *Family Circle* and *Southern Living*.

Despite life's small disappointments, Rosa and Wesley seem to have found contentment. They appear easy with each other, comfortable with their routines. But then one day in late December of what seems a recent year, after a night of troubled dreaming, Wesley decides to leave Rosa without warning or explanation. The dream is of failure, and Wesley's journey westward, ending in Nashville (where so many songs of dashed hopes are made), is his last effort to fan some spark of significance before giving up on his life. Wesley, we learn, suffers from what at first seems absurdly monstrous vanity, a ludicrous (though not altogether unjustified) feeling that he is God's gift to women, and that, in his marriage with Rosa, he has wasted his specialness. Worse yet, he thinks, Rosa has insufficiently valued his gift—or never even needed it.

Wesley easily could seem a pathetic, even contemptible character, but Price's achievement is to make the wayward quest of this failed Golden Boy seem neither trivial nor vapid. Wesley comes across as at least as complex and dignified a character as, for instance, Rabbit Angstrom, Updike's *homme moyen sensuel*. Wesley's imagination is obsessively, almost demonically erotic, but we are shown that the ways of eros can lead to a kind of knowledge. Even more, Wesley recognizes the limits of his knowledge, and does so precisely because of what he has learned in his marriage with Rosa. Long exposure to her patient if sometimes scouring intelligence has left him with an ironic perspective on his fantasies. He knows that what he wants is crazy, but he is at war with himself, and the struggle is precisely what makes for his complexity.

Rosa doesn't feel the same urge as Wesley to set off on a journey of self-discovery and renewal; she has always been far ahead of him. At the same time, she knows that she has lived too much for Wesley's love, even while being unable to love him in the way that would make him happy. (This, obviously, is neither a character nor a predicament to send shivers of delight through militant feminists' hearts.) She yearns for Wesley's return but doesn't really believe that some fundamental change in herself is possible. Nor, after searching her heart, does she believe that one is called for.

The agency of resolution, here as in *A Long and Happy Life*, is the mysterious power of Providence. We are asked to accept a high, purposive design behind seemingly unrelated events (Wesley's departure and the attack of a rapist) as well as preternatural forms of communication (Rato Mustian, Rosa's extremely eccentric brother, has a dream hinting at his sister's violation). The usual laws of cause and effect collapse in the novel because the author, like his characters, is convinced that there is a divine purpose behind mortal affairs. There is even a theological premise at work in Price's novel—that we sin in order to be upbraided, and that by experiencing God's will in this way we draw closer not only to God but also to what he intends us to be. Price, again, is a very serious Reformed Christian.

And his novels, I would argue, are variations on a Christian pastoral theme. They evoke Arcadias peopled by fallen creatures who struggle to regain a lost happiness, and sometimes, through grace, succeed. Even though *Good Hearts* is set largely in cities (with occasional dashes to the country), the atmosphere—the moral atmosphere, one might say—is decidedly rural. The novel, in fact, offers a quiet comment on the tensions between rusticity and urbanity. The rural ethos of the characters, their countrified ways of seeing and saying things, is at odds with the surrounding urban world and the lost souls who occupy it. But one wishes Price did far more with this conflict. Instead, he leaves it in the background, focused, for example, in the tense relations between Rosa and her daughter-in-law.

Price's failure to address this tension more directly in *Good Hearts* is no small weakness. For one thing, it leaves the novel, despite its many strengths, with too little to do. The heavily psychological examination of Rosa and Wesley's troubles grows attenuated—indeed, the last part of the book labors 36 pages beyond what could have been the novel's more satisfying conclusion. Yet as closely scrutinized as the rupture and reconciliation are, Price never gives any strong indication that the larger culture (television, jobs, the nature of life in Raleigh) plays a part in the Beavers' crisis. Those elements of the larger world are present, but they have no power. As a result, Wesley and Rosa live in something close to a historical void.

In his essay "Country Mouse, City Mouse," Price makes a very persuasive case for the importance of an "early and passionate relation between a writer and nature." Paraphrasing Wordsworth, he argues that it is only "permanent or permanently recurring objects which provide a sufficient reserve of imagery, an adequate sounding board for any but the most claustrophobic novel." He contends, moreover, that a number of otherwise excellent writers, including Baudelaire, Poe, and James, "maimed their work (or some portion of it)" by relying too narrowly on the imagery of city life. But Price's essay does not simply advocate rusticity for rusticity's sake. An intimate connection with rural life has provided the fullest writers, such as Dickens and Tolstoy, with the equipment to take on the larger world, the city as well as the country. Yet in Price's view (a view he might have revised since 1964), there have been since Forster no writers possessed of "the great whole rural-urban vision."

True or not, Price's remarks point to a shortcoming in his own work. Few contemporary writers of such consummate literary skill possess so enviably rich a grounding in the permanent world as Price. Yet he has insufficiently pressed his advantage. So far we have had sallies on the wider world, but no full-scale invasion. In *Kate Vaiden,* for example, the Great Depression and World War II swell into something more than background; they become palpable forces. Finally, though, Price seems to back away from a full exploration of their power over people and events. Doing so, he allows them to subside into devices of nostalgia, and we are left with a merely sentimental evocation of the past. This is the danger of a pastoral novel that lacks a firm historical vision. The novels that Price most admires chart not only the progress of the individual soul but also the progress of the age—and, indeed, the impingements of the latter upon the former. But using the still powerful idiom of the rural South, Price has brilliantly inscribed the story of the modern-day pilgrim's progress. He is our age's Bunyan.

Portrait of an Artist

George Garrett

As Bridge Boatner of Winston-Salem, North Carolina, tells it, this story is mainly an accounting of the summer when Boatner, now fifty-four, was twenty-one. *The Tongues of Angels,* like *Kate Vaiden,* Reynolds Price's highly regarded novel that won the National Book Critics fiction award in 1986, is a consistent first-person narration.

First-Person Stories

Any first-person story, at whatever angle and distance from the events depicted, is, in fact, a tale of here and now and essentially amounts to the time of its telling. The primary dramatic action of a first-person story is not to be found in the events themselves but in the telling of the tale. In any first-person story, the telling is the main thing that happens. Past and present are always here and now and are equal for as long as the telling lasts. In such a context there is an almost absolute freedom in time and space, to be exercised or inhibited as the teller (and, behind the teller, the artist) wills. There is freedom to react to events, to comment on events even as they are presented, and, when it pleases, to digress from the mainstream of action. In fact, there can be no such thing as digression in a well-executed first-person story.

Creating a special tension within this form, *The Tongues of Angels* is, nevertheless, a novel of precisely split time, of a then and a now, of highly significant past events being reviewed by a man mature and experienced enough to be skeptical of his own earned wisdom, and more than a little surprised at his earlier state of innocence. In our time—as distinct from the old-fashioned first-person story where a "discovered" manuscript (*The Turn of the Screw*) or a spoken voice later recalled (*Heart of Darkness*) provides a framework—first-person stories are usually assumed to be told somehow out of thin air, tilting between the extremes of the simply spoken and the purely written. In this slender book, we learn fairly late that the narrative of Bridge Boatner is, in

Review of *The Tongues of Angels*. Reprinted with permission from *The World & I* 5.8 (August 1990), 428. *The World & I* is a publication of *The Washington Times Corporation,* copyright © 1990.

fact, a written one (which we are reading over his shoulder, as it were), being addressed to a specific person, his younger son Rustum Boatner.

And, a little later, we learn that Bridge now intends to share it all with some of his friends. "Maybe these words will also last," he writes, though "not till the sun burns out of fuel, begins to swell and then ends Earthly life . . . . I mean also to give this to friends. More than most people I've watched through the years, I've had miraculous luck with friends, more friends in fact than I can maintain."

In a sense, this late revelation of the actual frame of the narrative is wonderfully apt, for it appropriately explains and justifies the range of prose styles, which includes elements of high style as well as the adroit recapitulation of the living vernacular. It also makes clear and meaningful the use of occasional self-reflexive elements in a context that is firmly opposed to the familiar tropes of fashionable metafiction—as, for example, when Bridge pauses briefly to explain his difficulty in describing the process of creating a painting:

> Again I'm up against a serious problem here. The thing is, I need to describe my difficulties in painting a particular canvas without a boring amount of technical discussion or art-critic hot air and without reproductions of the picture in its various stages. The only writer I can think of who comes even close to managing the task is Virginia Woolf.

GIFTED PAINTER

The Bridge Boatner who tells this tale is a gifted and quite successful painter, a representational painter, as it happens, who (rather like his own creator) has managed at once to be faithful to his own gifts and ideals and yet to survive the prevailing and antithetical fashions in the art world. The summer of 1954, the time Boatner is describing, was the time when Bridge managed to create his first important painting, "the first really decent accomplishment in all my work"—*The Smoky Mountains As the Meaning of Things.*

As Bridge writes, "Whatever else I did wrong that summer—and it was plenty—I managed to paint one sizeable picture, thirty-six by twenty." He did this while working as a counselor at a classic boys' camp of the period, Camp Juniper, where he also began to grow beyond the grief of his father's death the winter before. There he was wakened to much in himself and in the world as a result of an intense relationship with a young camper, Raphael Patrick Noren, a gifted dancer and a beautiful young man whose Indian name, Kinyan, aptly means "airborne." (During the summer Bridge himself formally earned the name Wachinton, or "wise." Like so many things in *The Tongues of Angels* this is more double-edged in implication than it is merely ironic or ambiguous.)

Raphael, called Rafe, named for the great artist but functioning in this story like his angelic original, is possessed of a secret and tragic past and comes to a sad end, an ending for which Bridge is at least vaguely responsible. There is guilt involved (nobody is blameless or guiltless in a Price novel; we are sinners in need of grace, healing, and salvation), but not quite in the conventional and secular sense of it.

"Rafe Noren marked me," Bridge writes.

> Not a wound or a scar but a deep live line, like the velvet burr in the darkest shadows of Rembrandt etchings, the ones I've mentioned where demons lurk. Let this be clear—never have I let myself for one instant think that Rafe died so that I might work with his rich fertilizing life behind me.

A little later he allows, "All I meant was, Rafe Noren's life enabled me. And now I've lived to say so."

This complex story stands at the center of the novel, forming an elegy for all lost innocence and youth. "No young person known to me, now or past, has thrown a stronger light than Rafe Noren or farmed more corners of the world than he touched with serious laughter. Young as he was, it was laughter launched with open eyes in full sight and knowledge of the final jaws."

Anyone familiar with the fiction of Reynolds Price knows that there is always a serpent in the garden. In the fable of *A Generous Man* (1966) there was a python named "Death." But there is also light in abundance, and the garden, the place where his people live their lives, is richly evoked and realized. So are the Smoky Mountains here. And there is an irrepressible, essential sense of humor, partly a matter of sly and sometimes elegant wit, a turn of phrase that comes out gently smiling, but there is also the belly cheer of deep rural American laughter, unabashedly vulgar and funny:

> I silently reminded my upstaged self that body wind in its two main forms, belches and farts, is half the foundation of boyish humor. I rightly suspected I'd hardly begun to experience their virtuosity in ways to smuggle farts like anarchist bombs into the highest and most sacred scenes of camp life.

FERVENT FIFTIES

Nostalgia reigns supreme. If there is a better book about camp life, in general and in detail, I don't know of it. Price makes as much of time, those much misunderstood 1950s, as he does of place. The power of first-person storytelling to digress without loss of purpose allows Bridge Boatner to comment on the times. Here, for instance, moving from a picture, half-amused and half in awe, of Albert "Chief" Jenkins, "youth leader and founder-owner of old Camp Juniper," Bridge says something, with a typically witty turn at the end of it, about the true history of those times:

> The time of my boyhood was a far more fervent time than many now believe. Today anybody whose eyes glint fire, and who sees himself as a gift to the world, is likely to be a flimflam man or an out-of-state strangler, maybe both. But don't forget, we boys born in the early 1930s had watched our parents body-surf the Depression and in some cases wipe out. We'd been too young to fight in the Second World War but just old enough to hear the news and understand what an all-time evil genius had brought on the conflict. And we got a thrilling dose of patriotism and high moral expectation from our participation in scrap metal drives, old bacon grease drives (to grease shell casings), paper drives, war bonds.

An important historical observation, that the generation of the 1950s was the children of Depression and the Second World War. Bridge has also been, "as an artistjournalist," to the later war in Vietnam.

The particular triumph of *The Tongues of Angels* is that so much is accomplished, and so gracefully, no sweat and no strain showing, in such a brief, lean novel. A lesser artist than Price would sink under the weight of events and the undeniable, if well-disguised, complexity of the story. A lesser artist than Price could not have introduced and kept alive such an extensive crew of distinctive characters.

Price is at a peak of artistic skill and maturity, able to challenge some strong literary fashions and daring enough to take great risks to achieve his goals. *The Tongues of Angels* proves that it is possible to be as witty as can be without being clever or smart-aleck. It also demonstrates that a complicated love story, subtly homoerotic but much more than that, can still be told and celebrated. Raphael Noren, angel/messenger/muse, is a richly dimensional ambiguous character. More to the point, he is entirely credible.

Daring? Well, at a time when most American writers are cultivating the ways and means of cynicism, Price continues to write stories of great sweetness. He can do this—and never better than here—without being silly or sentimental. He plays at the edges of the sentimental like a child at the beach, running just ahead of the waves, never getting wet. His stories, none more so than this one, are about forms of healing. He celebrates the possibilities of healing when easy nihilism is all the literary rage.

COMFORTABLE WINNER

Are there no flaws, no reservations or qualifications? Well, a few. The choices a true artist makes are more or less political. There are always trade-offs, losses, and gains. The calm and serenity achieved by Price are sometimes at the expense of pure energy. This carries over to the characters. For example, compared to the great Gulley Jimson in Joyce Cary's *The Horse's Mouth*—and sooner or later every modern book about an artist has to come to terms with Gulley—Bridge Boatner is about half-asleep. Cary's basic subject, the creator learning to live and work in a world characterized chiefly by injustice, does not enter into the professional life of Bridge Boatner.

Price's portrait of the artist, an artist of his own age and sharing much with the novelist, does not seriously imagine possibilities of failure. Perhaps—who knows?—this is because Reynolds Price, though sometimes subjected to unfair and unjust criticism, has not experienced failure. His first book, *A Long and Happy Life* (1962), won the Faulkner Foundation Award for first novels, and he has, as writer, remained in the comfortable winner's circle ever since. Nothing wrong with that. He earned his way. But there is something missing, an edge of anxiety and simple suspense, in the story of any artist whose only serious artistic problem is being, from time to time, out of fashion.

No matter. *The Tongues of Angels* is a wise and wonderful novel, a gift from an artist who understands as well as his central character "The Smoky Mountains As the Meaning of Things."

Love and Loss and the Salve of Time

Mel Gussow

Cleveland — In the final play of Reynolds Price's trilogy, *New Music*, a father reveals a closely guarded family secret to his son. The moment is both intimate and wryly amusing—and it is followed by other personal intimations. After almost six hours in the company of an extended family in a small North Carolina town, we come to recognize the characters as old friends and to feel the tautness of the bonds of blood, marriage and acquaintanceship.

The audience at the Cleveland Play House is asked to enter this world as if it were one of the author's novels. Like the fine writer he is, Mr. Price is not interested in manipulating theatergoers. As a novelist, he has been compared with Faulkner. As a dramatist, he is related to Horton Foote and Romulus Linney. All these writers, rooted in specific rural environments, share a gift for revealing character through atmosphere, and vice versa, and they have a natural love for the intricacies and the lyricism of local language. In the plays, as in his fiction, Mr. Price deals with stressful families whose energies are marshaled by strong, individualistic women.

The trilogy is leisurely in its unfolding. Each of the three connected plays takes place at a pivotal point in the lives of the Averys—in 1937, as Neal and his wife, Taw, face their first marital crisis; in 1945, as they and other townspeople try to overcome the effects of World War II; and finally in 1975, with the death of Neal's mother and with war in Vietnam as an additional shadow over the Avery household.

The first play, *August Snow*, is slight and anecdotal; in the second, *Night Dance*, the story becomes more dramatic and diverges from naturalism. The third, *Better Days*, is the most fully realized. It could stand on its own, but it is nurtured by our knowledge of earlier events. Seeing the play by itself, one would not know about the Huck-and-Tom skylarking days of Neal and his best friend, Porter Farwell; or about the hurtful truthtelling of Neal's embittered mother. These are two issues of increasing importance in understanding all of the characters. In true trilogy fashion, the plays work best when seen in sequence, as at one of the Cleveland Play House's regularly scheduled Sunday marathons.

Review of *New Music*. From *The New York Times* (4 November, 1989): 16. Copyright © 1989 by The New York Times Company. Reprinted by permission.

We hear about wars and domestic violence in harrowing—and sometimes black comic—detail. Men are killed in battle and in flagrante. There are few sad songs in *New Music,* but rather a rejuvenating sense that things will improve, that succeeding generations will dance to new emotional rhythms. Mr. Price is even-handed about apportioning responsibility. Even the most overtly unsympathetic of the characters—Neal's mother—is admired after her death for her loyalty and her common sense. Loyalty is the overweening attribute in the play, and the most difficult to maintain.

The principal themes are love and loss and the salving effects of time. This is not idealism but a kind of pragmatic acceptance of the fact that the weather will eventually change, if only the characters are not overwhelmed by their thoughts of suicide.

Even as one is warmed at Mr. Price's imaginative hearth, he maintains a novelist's quiescence, as if to say that dialogue and action will take care of themselves. It is not so much the literary quality of the dialogue—although as a stylist he can use three figures of speech in a row when one would be ample. The difficulty is in the avoidance of confrontations, so that it seems as if characters are traveling on separate tracks. They are revealed less in collision than in contrasting soliloquies, especially so in the case of Neal and his wife, who habitually sidestep showdowns.

Neal is meant to be the golden boy of this small town, the object of everyone's love and admiration. But there is little in the writing and even less in Kelly Gwin's performance to justify such a supposition. Perhaps that is the author's point, that Neal does not really stand out, except in the eyes of his beholders. But it is in these areas that one wishes Mr. Price had been more forthcoming as a playwright. In the third play, we finally receive a more complex picture of Neal, as played in middle age by Bill Raymond. His telling portrait is that of a man approaching the other side of the hill, and, to his astonishment, maturing into an optimist.

Until that final play, Neal and Taw are upstaged by minor characters— their flirtatious young landlady (Kathleen Mahony-Bennett), the landlady's crusty father-in-law (John Carpenter) and Neal's best friend (John Hickey). Each of these three is artfully delineated both in the writing and in the performance. In the case of Mr. Carpenter, he is so colorful he may deserve a subsidiary play of his own, so he could tell us more about his reprobate days and nights and about his singing dog Dave, who could only manage to get through the first verse of "The Star Spangled Banner" before breaking down in sobs.

A strength of the plays is in their shaggy humor and tall, tangential ruminations, but the trilogy has a sense of dramatic momentum, culminating in a poignant moment of honesty as survivors make their peace and try to face their inextricably linked future.

This trilogy would be a daunting prospect for any theater. Josephine R. Abady and David Esbjornson, as co-directors, have undertaken the assignment with resourcefulness, though the plays would be improved with sharper casting and a more inventive scenic design (and some further definition by the author). In common with Mr. Price's novels, *New Music* is indigenous to its time, place and characters, seemingly ordinary country people who rise, in what Anne Tyler has accurately called "startling, almost incongruous eloquence."

What He Did, Why He Did It

Elizabeth Beverly

Imagine this: You are a fifteen-year-old girl, holding in your hands an enormous document, 364 pages long, written to you by your sixty-five-year-old grandfather. During the past year your mother, his daughter, has died one kind of agonizing death. Your father has died another. You blame your grandfather for your father's death, and the document you hold is your grandfather's means of asking for your mercy. Within his long story, covering a span of pain for thirty years, lie stores of great tenderness, honesty, and remarkable beauty. His suffering has been tremendous. He tells you things.

He tells you that when he was thirty-five he fell in love with a girl only slightly older than you are now, despite the fact that his thirteen-year-old daughter, your own dead mother, was devastated by the betrayal she intuited. She and her mother already knew what it was like to lose him to drink. Your grandfather admits that he shouldn't tell you certain things, except that he wants your mercy: so he tells you anyway. These "facts" concern his body, its wild longing for Luna, the girl he loved. He is not coarse, nor is his account detailed, but there is a moment during the telling in which he slips and, although throughout the text he has always said "you" when he means you alone, his excitement compels him to write this: "You could tell (Luna) barely knew what next, but just when you were about to lead her—or pull back short of something you'd craved for thirty years—she'd flow right on to that perfect place, just before you, and make it pay you triple the gain you'd gambled on." No matter what pain or experience has prepared you to hear these words, what can such words do to a girl's heart?

Imagine this: You are sixty-five-year-old Bluford August Calhoun, and the day of reckoning is at hand. You believe that you have scorched all the decent women in your life, and you believe that you alone can explain to your granddaughter Lyn the reason that her own short life seems to lie in ruins around her. You can even assign a date to the beginning of this end: April 28, 1956, the day Luna strolled into your store behind her mother, in search of an auto-harp. If you are Blue Calhoun, you want to be loved, and everything will become a song-like story in your mouth, even this confession: you will find

Review of *Blue Calhoun*. Reprinted with permission from *Commonweal* (22 May 1992): 17–18. Copyright © Commonweal Foundation 1992.

the words of longing and shame crooning out of you, evoking landscapes and heads of lettuce and even your own dead mother, Miss Ashlyn. When you speak of April 28, you will say, ". . . that one day fell down on me from a clear spring sky, no word of warning. It tore the ground from under my feet, and everything around me shook the way a mad dog shakes a howling child." Nice. Powerful. Not quite accurate. Because you'll know, even as you write these words, that the Day didn't do everything by itself. You were the one who unzipped your pants.

There are moments in this long flow of language where your own honesty startles even you: ". . . Every drunk I've ever known—me included . . .—has one secret he'll fight like a rabid pit bull to keep. *If the truth be told . . . we don't give a pickled goddamn on Earth for the harm we do. Any pain you feel in the wake of me is your tough luck. You likely deserve every tear you shed. Sit there and eat it. . . .* Those 'you's' don't mean you at all, my darling: but they did apply, years back, to your mother." If you are Blue Calhoun, you must wonder, as you write this, why anyone should trust you.

Now imagine this: You are simply a caring reader, in search of a good book. You understand that Reynolds Price has a new novel, and since Price tends to take the world seriously and finds that fiction can provide the ground for moral inquiry, you are eager to read *Blue Calhoun*. The frame is simple, a letter addressed to a grandchild; the novel itself promises to clear up the mysteries resident in the opening pages. Suspense is assured. Soon you find yourself in the presence of a storyteller who seems to have forgotten nothing over the course of thirty years, a man who, if he overwrites, may be forgiven on the grounds of passion. He seems to be a man who desires to take full responsibility for the misdeeds of his past. He's willing to bear with uncommon humility whatever sins and accusations he can heap upon himself. As you read you grow to like him. He is immensely likable. Occasionally he reminds you that he is not really speaking to you, but to his granddaughter. Then you recollect the narrative frame and recall that this novel is at once an explanation and a plea for mercy.

At moments it occurs to you, as it occurs to Blue, that perhaps it is inappropriate to heap such a confession on a child. Priests, therapists—*they* are trained to withstand the onslaught of truth. Why a child? You know that this is a novel about literal corruption, something breaking, about the lost innocence of children, about "good enough" men like Blue who cannot seem to remember that certain violations are violations even if, especially if, a child craves and awaits love.

Reading this novel confuses you, *because* you should be able to close a novel and place it on the shelf after you are satisfied that it expresses laudable intentions and acts of love. Everything about Blue's confession compels you to forgive him now. He has so bravely told the story of his failures, and in telling it, has faced them. A novel like this may be about redemption. It seems that even the publisher believes it is.

But imagine this: You decide to take Reynolds Price as seriously as he deserves. And then you know that what you have been reading is not a novel, but a letter intended for someone else. Blue is not asking for your forgiveness—he is asking for Lyn's—and the very extravagance of his effusive missive, regardless of the particular pain she has suffered, because of the particular pain she has suffered, is an onslaught on her soul. Reynolds Price has asked nothing less of you than to witness, in the most helpless fashion possible, a great and eruptive act that would violate a beloved child in the name of love. By the time you see the nature of the violation, the body of unasked-for knowledge pressing against a child's consciousness in the same way that an adult body can press open a child's waiting flesh, you too have grown to love Blue. You want the best for him, despite the voluptuous narcissism of an old sinner who believes in sin, a man who goes to AA to save his life but remains doggedly pure of the taint of late twentieth-century therapeutic rhetoric. You may understand that his wife Myra is codependent, but you want to believe along with Blue that she'll never be other than saintly.

If with Price's help, this novel becomes a letter which has accidentally fallen into your hands, you will recognize young Luna's plea and warning for what it is. Buried in the heart of the text, these are the words she speaks to Blue after waking from a deep sleep: ". . . Everything I do is known to God. He's yet to claim I've gone astray, my conscience says I'm moving right, but don't you fail to go back home and read the verse where Jesus says, 'Don't harm a child or you'll be wishing some kind soul would hang a millstone round your neck and throw you out in the midnight sea.' "

How many children have been harmed, and continue to be harmed, by men who love as fiercely and protectively, as ineptly and selfishly as Blue? How many children are harmed because the body of their innocence cannot be left alone by those who claim to cherish them? Why do so many of us refuse to love our children, to know our children, the way God loves and would know us all? Blue is not an evil man; he's better than many of us will ever be. Braver. More hopeful. Full of faith. But perhaps to be "good enough" is not to be good at all. Or perhaps within the final paragraph resides the salvation that will allow Blue to find a way to be truly good at last.

Naturally this novel is flawed in the ways that such a letter must always be flawed, in the way that Blue's particular brand of self-indulgence requires. Characterizations are more or less successful. The plot could tighten in places, surge forward in others. The final section is particularly troubling in its failure to bring Lyn to life as a person, not a destination. But through its insistence to be every bit as anguishing and baffling and disheartening as a good life, *Blue Calhoun* becomes a great novel. It enraged me. It broke my heart.

The Collected Stories of Reynolds Price

RON CARLSON

I have become certain of one thing in the last half-year: the rich collection of stories in *The Collected Stories* of Reynolds Price—the galley copy of which I have absolutely torn apart, used up, wrecked—will exist somewhere as a thread in the fabric of twentieth-century American literature. The fifty stories here were written over the span of almost forty years (though Price notes in his introduction that he wrote exclusively in other forms between 1970 and 1990), and half of them come from his earlier collections, *The Names and Faces of Heroes* (1963) and *Permanent Errors* (1970). Price has been known as a "Southern Writer," and these stories for the most part would confirm that in their locale, in the situation of the characters (picking ticks, chewing snuff, eating hominy), and in that thing most often evoked by the name of Faulkner, that is a sense of familial mystery and loss—told in a form which many times overtly addresses its own identity as story. That last is exactly the kind of sentence which tries to bale fifty stories with one piece of wire, and it will not work. That ancient sins and secrets are hot for the characters in these stories, that the characters have a keen sense of regret which roils and simmers within them, an urgent need to testify, a fear of being damned and a stoic wonder for the ways they are redeemed—these may start to make this the book of a southern writer, but there is as much Sherwood Anderson here as Faulkner, and there's another thing throughout the stories, the thing most appreciated perhaps, and that is Reynolds Price's ability to infuse his stories with candor, a simple but powerful sense transcendent fiction has that confronts, invades the reader with the knowledge that if one sits at the table long enough with this writer he's going to show all his cards, unexpected as they may be, and in a beautiful way make something true.

The old word "duty" appears frequently in the stories, family duty—to take in an aging aunt, to be a good father, to pay a visit to a relative, to find the missing inner strength. In fact, there are several stories in which a young man calls on an old woman who used to work for his family. In "The Warrior Princess Ozimba" and "Two Useful Visits," secrets are hinted at, revealed. The latter opens, "Back then your kin could lean down on you with the weight of the world and still not quite say, 'Get yourself up here to see Mary Greet;

Reprinted from *Southern Review* 30.2 (April 1994): 371–78, by permission of the author.

she's dying fast, and it's your plain duty.' " Both "visit" stories offer the men glimpses of the lost world of the South, and both men are suffused with a kind of gratitude for the care and trust the women have bestowed. These are short stories, the visits almost vignettes, yet news is exchanged and the young men are affected. Throughout the stories, which range in length from two to almost one hundred pages, Price is able to work very well in a small space. Part of this is because of his profound understanding of the scenes he creates and the depth of human potential in each, and part is his ability to marry language and the moment. There are a few stories with the pure lyric reach of prose poems and, of course, there are sections of others which brim with a diction so fluent and apt as to be arresting in themselves. In the last paragraph of "Bess Waters," a story in eight short sections which spans one hundred years, 1863–1963, in the life of the former slave, the title character tries to answer the request of a young visitor (he is named Reynolds Price) to tell her story:

> And honest to God, Bess tries to tell it. Her dry lips work and her mind sends words—she only recalls these scattered hours—but what comes out is dark shine and power from her banked old heart and the quick of her bones, dark but hot as a furnace blast with a high blue roar. It burns the boy first. Bess sees him blown back and starting to scorch; then it whips round and folds her into the light till both of them sit in a grate of embers, purified by the tale itself, the visible trace of one long life too hard to tell.

The longest story in the book, "Walking Lessons," is set, surprisingly, in the desert Southwest and begins with one of Price's stunning openers: "My wife killed herself two weeks ago, her twenty-sixth birthday. . . ." In Price's stories, most often people *start* in trouble, and things get worse. The twenty-eight-year-old writer and college teacher who, deep in fresh grief, flies to see his college friend Blix Cunningham where he works on the Navajo reservation in Arizona, meets a world so dark, troubled, and squalid as to be the physical manifestation of his sorrow. Blix lives in a hovel with an Indian woman, Dora Badonie, whose own maladies rival anybody's. "Walking Lessons" follows the three through a rough mission of mercy, a trek really, that becomes—in its magnitude, calamity, and poor weather—life-threatening. There are, the narrator discovers, no easy answers to the quandaries in which any of them are lost. And with convincing realism of scene and of voice, Price is just that tough-minded as he moves toward the resolution of the story. Redemption isn't something found suddenly on the ground like a coin, but something that breaks imperceptibly into a life like the gradient degrees of dawn. Here, as in many of the stories, the protagonist is a writer, and Price is unafraid of talking like one, breaking frame to be a storyteller and to address the reader. Here, after the travelers are first stranded, their walking lessons begin:

I'm capable of spelling it out for you, in every increasingly pressurized moment—finding stripped howling language to compel your company every step of my way toward agony, physical and mental desperation; but you've read Jack London, you've seen Yukon movies (Preston Foster, Bruce Cabot—eyelashes frosted). May I leave it to you? You have all the elements; build it around me—the night, the struggle.

Elsewhere in the book (frequently, it seems), Price speaks as a storyteller long past the pivotal events, using the accrued gravity of time to add weight and substance to happenings, as in one of my favorites, "The Company of the Dead," a story about two teenage boys who become "setters," those hired to sit up with corpses to keep watch and offer company all the long night before the funeral. Near the start, the narrator says, "By the time Simp and I had our truly wild night—the one I must tell before too late—we were good sized boys, fifteen years old." There is a "must-tell" quality about many of the stories in this collection, as if they were insistent testimonies burning their ways out of a storyteller's heart. "The Company of the Dead" ends with this: "I'm ninety-two years old, writing this line, a man at peace with what he's done and what comes next. I leave this story, in both its parts, as my best gift to a world I've liked and thank, here now, but have never pressed for the black heart's blood of actual love." Parallel passages resound in the stories, "all these many years since" and "Thirteen years on, I tell whoever reads these lines," and this swift, poignant coda which closes "A Full Day":

> *In four months Buck will die from a growth that reached decisive weight in his body this full afternoon and threw him down.*
> *His elder son has made this unreal gift for his father on the eighty-ninth passing of Buck's birthday, though he died these thirty-five years ago.*

The effect of this narrative strategy is clear: in a world of such scope, the dead affect the living (one character says about his life that it's like the Bible: there're more ghosts than good women), and the powerful sweep of time in these stories is as real as the weather. Price, in his form and narrative traits, demonstrates the long reach.

Three short pieces lodged a hundred pages apart in the collection are couched as letters from fathers to sons. Each is an emotional tour de force, as the men try to say in writing those essential things that can't be said aloud. "The Last News" is a graphic confession by an alcoholic father of personal crimes he committed long ago. He's not exactly looking for forgiveness, but for something deeper—the paying of a debt. "If you want to kill me once I'm out of here, be my guest," he says, and means it. And listen to the last line, the last word a knife-thrust: "I'm waiting to know your answer, sir." "Breath" is similar, being a brief, brutal history, a request for pardon by a father caught in an ongoing cycle of abuse, and it contains the slight hope that father and son might reconcile, "breathe in the same room." What is remarkable in these stories is how urgent the messages feel, how heartwrenching, how guileless. These are broken men speaking from the depths, and they are what gives so much of Price's fiction an edge that cuts. "A Final Account" shows us a third father, this one writing a letter of gratitude and explanation moments after meeting with his grown son twenty-four years after walking away from his wife and baby. The father is dying of AIDS, alone among strangers, and he says, "Son, you count the most to me of anybody left alive. I knew if I said that straight to your face, blind as I am, I'd just seize up." Writing is the deeper way, these stories show us. The other note that sounds so clearly in this work, in these letters, is that as irremediable as the crimes and as permanent as the regret and as late as the hour may seem, there is still a shred of something to be salvaged.

Sometimes it is a bit of mercy. In "An Evening Meal" Sam Traynor, after five years fighting stomach cancer, has won the battle, and he celebrates his cure by going to dinner at a café. Years before he met and had a brief, intense affair with one of the waiters, who, startlingly, is still there. But the surprise of the story comes after the meal when, as he leaves, Sam sees the desiccated shell of one of his first loves, Richard Boileau. The young man hunched in the booth is obviously late in his struggle with AIDS. And the tableau Price leaves us with could have been painted by Hopper: it's dark, and the world is empty, but isn't that a light in the window? This broad summary is a disservice to a delicate story, one of the finest in the collection.

The motif of betrayal figures prominently in the stories of Reynolds Price. "Truth and Lies" is an intense confrontation between Sarah Wilson and her former student Ella Scott, who is sleeping with Sarah's husband, Nathan. The women spend all but two pages of the 5,000-word story closed in Sarah's car. The interview came about because of a note Sarah found in her drunken husband's pocket: "I have got something to tell you and will be on the tracks tonight at eight o'clock." Sarah meets Ella instead and comments, "Well, your writing's improved." From there the interview works through the layers of the Wilsons' marital history and through the pride and hopes of young Ella Scott. Both women come away changed in ways they could not have imagined—and with more resolve. In "Nine Hours Alone," it's the teacher who bears the guilt and the consequences of betrayal. Here Price uses her goodbye letters to tell her secrets. Secrets—regardless of how deep they are buried—will out in Price's world, and once out, they demand reckoning. Once alerted to betrayal, we find the truly human character in the heady and powerful "Serious Need," a fitting title for thirty-six-year-old Jock Pittman's unabashed tale of the way he conducted himself with an old classmate's sixteen-year-old daughter. In that story there is an epiphany (or what I'll call one) in a cemetery that I'm going to teach from here on in, but don't let that diminish your energies toward this story.

There is one Civil War story in this collection. "Endless Mountains" starts with the wound that is the source of every sentence for the thirty pages—and some months—of the story: "The shot went through the white inside of my right thigh on Wednesday near noon." The scavenger who stands over the wounded man a while later rifling his wallet says, "Well, Trump, it's your goddamned birthday." Trump experiences a tormented, half-waking dream brought on by fear of amputation and then by fever. He then flees—such as he can—not sure he isn't dead. The writing here is close and convincing in its delirium and pain as Trump stumbles across a ridge into the mountains. It's really a quest he's on, though he's not sure for what besides survival. The story grows into the metaphoric parallel to "Walking Lessons"; Trump is the damaged soul here, and his descent into pain is intended to cauterize him from the harm war and regret can bring. His "cure" includes one long night wrestling with a naked angel who takes the fever away, a beautiful, frightening scene which is magnified by Trump's stunned and desperate state of mind. His recovery is laden with memory of his own family, and Price describes Trump's courtship in a scene that gets as much out of snow and memory as Joyce. Finally, like the writer-narrator of "Walking Lessons," Trump sees he will go on, must go on, "done with war." These two long stories form a kind of spine for this book; they are poetic and stark examinations of how one might proceed when all is lost.

My favorite stories in the book, however, are those where Price engages early manhood and adolescence. His talent for seeing into the secret heart of men and women is magnificent, but the way he portrays the hot cusp of manhood is unnerving. "The Enormous Door" would be a good story to read first, as it offers a sense of the expectations many of Price's male characters bring to their world. The month the narrator turns twelve, his family moves into a small hotel. "From the word go," he says, "I loved the air of mystery in the building." And there are mysteries, many in his own head. "What are grown men like, truly, in secret?" he wonders. The narrator's desire for a model of manhood (and some quirks in the hotel itself) lead him into a delirious career as a voyeur, spying on his neighbor, a teacher named Simon Fentriss whose magnetism overpowers the boy. Oh, it's a charged time all around, and add to it a purloined copy of *Sacred Joy: The Marital Beacon,* a four-inch-thick reference book, orange in color, with chapters covering the "beauty" of sexual congress and "The Oral Tradition" and you've got a twelve-year-old in a stew. Then Price, again, turns his story toward a greater place when the things the boy sees in his peeping become genuinely magical, astounding (if that were still an effective word), and lead to the kind of realization Price approaches again and again in his fiction, that is, one not easily captured in a phrase or a moment, but applied instead to the span of life ("As I write this tale, I'm sixty years old . . ."), a larger understanding of love and flesh that wants to elude language forever.

Two other boy/men stories require mention. One is the homage to father-son love, "The Names and Faces of Heroes," which is tender and vast—and encompassed in one long automobile ride home at night. The narrator is nine years old and lies with his head on his driving father's lap. "The short cut to being a man," a minister said to the boy the summer before, "is finding your hero, somebody who is what you are not but need to be." Swimming in the boy's mind are appropriate models: Helen Keller, Abraham Lincoln, Enos Slaughter. But the lessons of the night will go beyond conventional notions into that region of conscience nine-year-olds own: the terrible responsibility of knowing who will die (this is illustrated again, beautifully, in "A New Stretch of Woods"). "The Names and Faces of Heroes" is one of the best stories of its kind, truly required reading. It does not claim more than it earns.

"Troubled Sleep" is also narrated by a nine-year-old, Edward Rodwell, who spends a hard evening in the secret glen he shares with his unreliable and flashy cousin Falcon Rodwell. Their talk about travel and death is more comic than any we've seen in Price's stories, colored as it is by Falcon's imagination, reminiscent of scenes from Twain. This poignant story explores the thin line between innocence and romance; for Falcon, things are play, but the narrator drinks it all deep:

> When we played cowboys, everybody else who had to die died of bullets or arrows, but Falc never died of anything but blood poison or brain fever or milk leg and even then only after he had called me over to where he lay and whispered his Last Will and Testament, leaving me his radio . . . and making me give my oath to bury him in a copper casket and go to Sunday School and church weekly and turn into a great scientist and destroy germs. I would cry and offer to go with him . . . thinking to myself, "No radio on earth will ever be what Falcon Rodwell was to me."

Thumbing through this big red book again to type some of the above has further harmed the volume, and soon pages will be loose. There are dozens of stories I have not mentioned which another reviewer might, stories which carry a reader through different doorways of the fine big house I have tried to describe. I have become certain of one thing about these collected stories over the past five months, and that is that I'd rather meet them on my own terms. I wish I'd encountered Price's stories one by one like the many little seasons of a life, but I didn't, and getting them now at once, in such a way that ruined the physical book, well, there's something real about that, believe me. Reynolds Price has assembled a moving book of stories, not an unambitious paragraph in over seven hundred pages. His accomplishment lives. I'm glad to have this book, which will have a rubber band around it for a while, and I plan to do more than this review to share my luck at having had such a noble companion.

The last story in the collection, "An Early Christmas," is a journey by a painter on Christmas Eve into the dark and dangerous labyrinth of modern-day Bethlehem. He finds—by all the evidence—the very place of Christ's birth and emerges to have his life and art changed. The last paragraph of this story, indeed the book, came to me as what Price has been up to in his story writing, a kind of artist's credo. The painter claims "the driving will to show this world its visible likeness, front and back, crown to toe from where I've stood, in the clean new mirrors of honest pictures that mean to be guide lights usably placed in the frequent, sometimes permanent, dark."

[Review of *A Whole New Life*]

ROBERT COLES

Grave illness (with its consequences) is a natural subject for a writer of fiction—a chance to explore dramatically, psychologically, and morally a situation that will escape no one and therefore will potentially appeal to everyone. Reynolds Price, one of our most distinguished contemporary novelists (he is also a poet, short-story writer, playwright, and essayist), has chosen to tell us of illness not through the relatively detached strategy of storytelling, but by resort to autobiographical narration.

A decade ago, in April 1984, Price began to notice difficulty walking. A long-time professor of English at Duke University, which he attended, he was soon enough in that university's hospital, where he became an object of intense medical scrutiny. His doctors discovered a spinal cord tumor that he describes as "pencil-thick and gray-colored, ten inches long from my neck-hair downward." The growth itself was deemed to be ineradicable, but a neurosurgeon operated on him to relieve pressure on the cord, and he was given a course of radiation—and later, with the advent of laser technology, more surgery. The result: a patient whose prospects seemed grim indeed has survived to this day and now lets us know not only what happened to him in the course of a life-threatening illness, but how that experience has enabled him, in the words he chooses for his book's title, to build "a whole new life".

One important defining aspect of that new life is the paraplegia that has confined to a wheelchair a writer who formerly took great pleasure in travel and who had friends in many places, even other continents. Moreover, the new life brought constant, excruciating pain. Much of this book tells of suffering, of progressive loss of physical strength and loss of the lower limbs as useful parts of the body. We learn in great detail of that decline, that "devastation," the author calls it.

Because Price is such an engaging, even enchanting narrator, we are drawn to his story by the strength, the authority, the lovely charm of his "companionable voice," a phrase he uses at one point to describe his authorial ambition. The more time we spend with him, turning these pages as we have turned the thousands of pages that make up his fictional triumphs, the more

Reprinted by permission of the author from *The New England Journal of Medicine* 330 (23 June 1994): 1834–35.

we learn not only of his ordeal, but also of his eventual capacity to turn hurt and vulnerability and extreme jeopardy into quite something else: one literary triumph after another, to the point that readers the world over stand in awe before a breathtaking spell of fine literary productivity. It is almost as if the author's mind has flung away his wheelchair, raced confidently to many destinations, and returned to acquaint us with what was heard and seen.

A good novelist is a careful observer and listener who knows how to work the seen and the heard into a story that rings true for the reader, and that is what this book offers: an account of how affliction actually became a spur to further success rather than a sentence to jail with no hope of parole. A critical moment in this astonishing turn of events will surely interest many of the author's fans: his mind's encounter with Jesus, which he terms "an actual happening"; he relates it with no apparent fear of 20th-century skepticism, including the excesses of reductionism that occasionally accompany efforts by psychiatrists to understand the mind's workings. Jesus came to the author bringing assurance and concern, a kind of companionship badly needed, a big boost to a victim's mind, heart, and soul.

I suppose those of us who call on medical materialism for explanations of human subjectivity will scratch our heads as we are told of this "normal human event," in which the author describes himself as seeing Jesus, conversing with him. Nor does the narrator talk of the miraculous, though he does remind us that he has lived a life "rich in fantasy and longing." Ultimately, he settles for a "gift"—a moment in his life that had great, sustaining meaning to him and helped a distraught mind touch base with its lifelong moral and spiritual assumptions and thereby resume its travels through time toward its various destinations. One of those destinations turns out to be this candid, compelling book, which will surely teach us doctors much we need to learn.

Again and again Reynolds Price gives us glimpses of physicians who are kind and thoughtful, physicians who are callous, smug, and self-absorbed. He brings us close to the bodily agony of illness and, as well, to the terrible bouts of apprehension and hopelessness that can accompany such a time in one's life. He tells us of the way hypnosis has helped him contend with pain. He grants us access to his intimate daily struggles to compensate for his various disabilities—for example, the self-catheterization he now routinely performs. But he also tells us vividly of the redemptive side of illness, of adversity: our sometime capacity to find great strength amidst great trials and thereby affirm a certain earthly transcendence—in this instance, of a kind (the writer's) that can be shared with the rest of us.

End of the Line

JILL MCCORKLE

Many writers lead their characters to the last page and bid them farewell, with no plans of ever returning to them, their lives beyond that point more or less lost. But Reynolds Price is not such an author, and over the years, his families of characters have grown and continued to inhabit his native North Carolina setting, where they have a rich extended past and, better yet, a future. In his new novel, the final in a trilogy titled *A Great Circle*, Price returns to the Mayfield family where the last generational line, Wade Mayfield, has left New York City and come home to his estranged parents to die of AIDS. Though *The Promise of Rest* stands firmly on its own merits, both as a finely crafted novel and as a brilliant commentary on contemporary society, it also fits into the larger frame of the trilogy as if Price had never stepped aside to write the 16 books (including *Kate Vaiden*, which won the National Book Critics Circle Award in 1986) that have come in between.

Price began his trilogy 20 years ago with *The Surface of Earth*, where he introduced the Mayfield family, and then resumed their story in 1981 in *The Source of Light*. In the opening of the second novel, Hutchins Mayfield is 25 and just beginning his adult life. Now, in *The Promise of Rest*, he is 62 and once again living alone (his wife, Ann, having recently left him), and the son who *should* be living out his young adulthood is dying.

Hutch is a poet and a teacher of poetry, and the novel opens in the setting of his class, where students are discussing the sincerity of grief expressed in Milton's "Lycidas," a poem that Hutch claims "means more to me than all but a few of the humans I've known." He stands at the center of his class as a great source of wisdom, and yet, when asked by one student for marital advice, his response is: "My record on love is dismal. . . . I'm alone as a dead tree."

The one real romance in Hutch's life (a romance dealt with in *The Source of Light*) was his former student and dear friend, Strawson Stuart, who now (with his wife) helps care for Grainger Walters, Hutch's 101-year-old, biracial cousin who, aside from being a spellbinding storyteller, has for many decades stood in the center of this family. Despite the years and their

Review of *The Promise of Rest*. Reprinted by permission of the author from *The Boston Globe* (21 May 1995): 77, 80.

marriages, Hutch remains close to Straw: "Hutch saw him even more clearly again, remembered each atom of his face at its best; and not for the first time, he grieved at the choice he'd made against the boy Straw was. Even if the softer man here in the night burned slower and asked for far less worship, Straw was nonetheless a welcome presence—a tangible gift to any close watcher."

While the two are driving to New York to bring Wade home, Hutch turns the conversation to what he and Straw could not have done together: They could not have produced a child. The irony here is that Wade is the end of the Mayfield line, and that he, though dying of AIDS, does not regret his choices in life, including his lover, Wyatt Bondurant, who committed suicide after learning he had passed the disease to Wade.

The Promise of Rest is a novel as rich in history as it is in language. As in the previous works in the trilogy, Price incorporates family myths and historians, old letters and objects that get handed down through the generations. It is a huge world that he creates, tackling such issues as AIDS and racial tensions, in ways that are so unique and personal to the individual that they immediately translate to the universal screen with all emotional attachment in check. Price's omniscient eye never misses the opportunity to bring new conflict or reason to light. There is a constant mixing of blood—black and white, gay and straight, old and young—such that it begins to seem that a new race has been created. At times the omniscient eye glances away for a second, fixing on an individual who is not relevant to the heart of the novel, and yet it is not a distraction; rather, the attentive presence makes the reader feel that anything can happen at any time. There is a richness in this complex grand scheme that makes the isolated events ring flawlessly true.

Throughout the novel there are references to slavery and racial tensions, residue of a lengthy Southern heritage. In the present, the people who come closest to offering salvation to this family are black. The purest soul of them all, perhaps, is Jimmy Boat, who nursed Wade in New York and who comes to North Carolina to see him through; Jimmy is concerned about religion, about an afterlife, only to be reassured by Hutch that if anyone is in heaven, he'll get there. Then there's Ivory Bondurant, Wade's lover's sister, who at the novel's end offers a hope to Ann and Hutch that had never before existed.

The conversations among characters range from serious religious discussion to such Garden of Eden jokes as, "Why did God make queers? . . . Because he looked down at the Earth one day, well after that dustup in the Garden of Eden; and he said to himself 'they're just getting nowhere at *all* with the arts.' " In one of his final conversations, Wade is talking to a young gay man, a student of Hutch's who is assisting with Wade's care, when the topic turns to children. Whereas Hutch has instructed the young man to protect himself, to live cautiously, Wade's advice from his deathbed (aside from telling the man to use and enjoy his body) is "Someway. Have children. One child anyhow."

There is the need within this family, from one generation to the next, to hand something down: a child, a story, a poem. During Wade's illness, Hutch is haunted by what he refers to as "the waiting poem," which begins with the line: "This child knows the last riddle and answer." And Wade *does* know more than he has told, family secrets yet to be revealed.

The notion of giving life, sustaining and resurrecting life, is constant in this novel and those before it. Reynolds Price is a master of such creations and he is a benevolent creator, calling his fictional children back into the world again and again. Despite its sad commentary on a generation faced with a plague, following a generation that remained sexually closeted, this novel is spiritually uplifting, leaving the reader with great respect for this vivid world and for the man who flung it into motion.

The Greatest Story Ever, Retold

ROBERT ALTER

How are we to bridge the gap between an ancient foundational text and our own cultural moment without diminishing the power of the original through arid academicism or vulgar modernization? For his bold experiment in rendering the immediacy of the Gospels as story and vision, Reynolds Price, the fiction writer, essayist, poet and playwright, who has published translations from the Scriptures before, deploys all three of the generally available means—translation, commentary and midrashic re-creation.

Of the four canonical Gospels, Mr. Price has chosen to translate the two that seem to him to express the strongest differing yet complementary perceptions of the life of Jesus—Mark and John. To these he has appended a third text, roughly the same length as each of the other two, which he calls "An Honest Account of a Memorable Life: An Apocryphal Gospel." This modern midrash on the canonical Gospels is a kind of spare novelistic synthesis of all four, drawing as well on other ancient sources, some of them only recently rediscovered, on the life of Jesus. The three narratives are amplified by a general preface, mainly devoted to the problems of translating New Testament Greek, and by prefatory interpretive essays for Mark and John and an explanatory introduction to the modern Apocryphal Gospel.

Mr. Price, though striking a note of sharp dissatisfaction with what the sundry Christian churches through the ages have done with the original message of the Gospel, writes out of a deep personal conviction of their spiritual urgency, stressing their status as stories that "not only press directly on the present life of the reader, in whatever time and place he or she exists, but may very well confront the reader with choices of belief and behavior that will decide the reader's fate throughout eternity."

Mark exerts a particular magnetism on Mr. Price because, like the writers of the Hebrew Bible whom Mark kept in mind, he conveys his urgency not through exhortation or theological argumentation but through the terse telling of the tale, manifesting "the ancient trust of all those who bet their entire hand on *story,* whether oral or written: the thin compelling thread of an action that is worth our attention."

Review of *Three Gospels.* From *The New York Times Book Review* (19 May 1996): 12. Copyright © 1996 by The New York Times Company. Reprinted by permission.

What sort of English style might answer to the taut, story-driven, spiritually imperative nature of these texts? The King James Version (1611), the great bench mark for all English translations of the Bible, is justly famous for its eloquence, but it is too often grandly eloquent where the original texts are plain-spoken, and it levels all the biblical books to a single King James English; there are important stylistic differences not only between the Hebrew Bible and the Greek but between individual books in either, and (especially in the Hebrew) even between different elements in the same book.

The two Testaments, as a matter of fact, require somewhat different strategies of translation. The Hebrew writers appear to have used a stylized literary language—in all likelihood distinct from the ancient vernacular— that paradoxically combined lofty literary dignity with homespun directness. The New Testament writers, on the other hand, were denizens of a remote Roman province working not in an indigenous literary language but in koine—the international colloquial Greek current in late antiquity.

Mr. Price characterizes Mark's version of koine as "extremely plain, abrupt, often unidiomatic and dogged." John, by contrast, he sees as "a hugely skilled and intelligent expatriate . . . able to express himself readily and powerfully on most of the difficult matters he encounters but in a homemade and eccentric patois." Though I lack the competence to confirm the validity of these perceptions, they sound persuasively right, at least to someone reading the New Testament in English against the background of the Old.

The trick of translation, then, is to convey the Gospels in an English that is rough-hewn, even a little awkward, and yet can serve as a sturdy vehicle of arresting narrative. For readers raised on the King James Version, the ruggedness of Mr. Price's diction may take some getting used to, but I think most will find that it captures the homey directness of the Gospel stories with a new freshness. The cure of the deaf and stammering man in Mark is reported in the following concrete language: "The block on his tongue was loosed and he spoke right." In the previous scene, Jesus walks on the surface of the Sea of Galilee in the sight of his disciples:

But seeing him walking on the sea they thought it was a ghost and cried out—all him and were frightened.
But at once he spoke with them and said "Courage. I am. No fear." And he went up to them into the boat and the wind dropped.

The difference, perhaps understandably, between John's homemade eccentricity and Mark's abruptness is not always clear-cut in Mr. Price's versions. Nevertheless, he does give us an English John who repeatedly puts an odd and effective spin on the language of his tale, expressing (I would say) Hellenistic philosophic notions in a vernacular Greek influenced by a Hebrew mind-set: "So the Word became flesh and tented among us. We watched his glory, glory like that of a father's one son full of grace and truth."

The same brusqueness and compactness of language are evident when Jesus speaks: "Amen amen I tell you the one who trusts me has eternal life—I'm the bread of life."

In general, this new version pitches the story toward understatement and colloquial immediacy, without, however, turning it, as so many recent translators have done, into a prosaically flattened version of middling modern English. Thus, the moment of death on the Cross: "When he'd taken the wine Jesus said 'It's done' and bowing his head handed over his spirit."

After these translations, Mr. Price's Apocryphal Gospel must perform a delicate balancing act. On the one hand, he needs to preserve the stylistic starkness that he has achieved in his versions of Mark and John so that his own Gospel will not seem to violate the spirit of the canonical ones. On the other hand, as a novelist addressing an audience whose reading habits are largely formed by novels, he wants to visualize the details of the story's world, an aim of no evident interest to the ancient writers. Sometimes he does this with a terse comment, such as this one on the background of the sky during the Passion: "The blank sky gave no sign whatever of angels on clouds proclaiming the reign." Sometimes he provides a literal fleshing-out of the Gospel story, as in this description of the demoniac who is to be healed by Jesus, where the clenched concision of narrative report and the concreteness of diction counteract any tendency toward effusive elaboration:

> The man was naked and foul with wild hair. His hands and legs were locked in shackles, but he'd broken the chains.
> A boy on the strand said the man had been crazy all the boy's life, that he lived in the graves, cut at himself with flints and shells and ate raw fish which he caught by hand.

The last words of the Apocryphal Gospel, after the cry of the disciples, "Lord, come now!," are: "In other lives their cry has lasted near 2,000 years." As translator, commentator and reimaginer, Reynolds Price has adroitly managed to catch the reverberation of that cry. His own enterprise is actuated by faith, but beyond considerations of belief, it is an exemplary instance of how old and sustaining stories can spring to life again when the stylistic integrity of the tale is finely respected by its modern expositor.

ESSAYS

◆

A Long and Happy Life:
Fragments of Groundwork

REYNOLDS PRICE

In January, 1957, when I was a student at Oxford University—in my second year away from home—I began to make elaborate notes around a sudden idea for a story which, as I thought then, would be perhaps a hundred pages long. I kept the notebook throughout that year and into the next, as I completed my studies at Oxford. Then I returned to North Carolina and in the fall of 1958 began to write the story for which I had planned so long. The story ended two years later and, in iron obedience to Price's Second Law (Everything takes twice as long and *is* twice as long as you had anticipated), ended as a novel—*A Long and Happy Life.*

I offer these scattered excerpts from those notes (with some internal omission of irrelevant and personal detail), not as the Significant Scaffolding of an Eminent Author but as a fragmentary demonstration of the ways in which one writer attempted to comprehend—and prepare to transmit—one story, one knot of people who arrived, unsummoned but welcome, in his mind, his life.

Oxford, 14 January 1957

I had been thinking very vaguely—for a week maybe—of a story about a girl who has an illegitimate child, but it was only this afternoon while I was reading the letters to Santa Claus in the Warren Record that I saw how to do it (how to end it, at least). To begin with, it *has* to be a Rosacoke story. I know I've argued against that, but this girl is Rosacoke and it would be silly to rename her and fake in a new family just for the sake of novelty. If I finish the story and it's fine, then when I have a whole book I can put "Chain" as the first story and this one as the last.

Wesley gets her pregnant. Maybe just before he goes off to Norfolk to work (or maybe—yes—on a visit home). She writes him a series of letters, asking him to come home but not mentioning the baby (maybe she doesn't know yet). He just doesn't come, and finally she says, "Wesley, please come

Reprinted, with permission, from *Virginia Quarterly Review* 41.2 (1965): 236–47.

here. There's this thing I have got to tell you." But he doesn't (Why?) So Rosacoke meditates on all the possibilities, including abortion. And then decides to go to Norfolk too—to join a friend and work as a telephone operator until her time. But it's getting near Christmas and before she leaves, Mama wants her to be Mary in the church pageant. And Rc. agrees. Rehearsal goes all right because they use a doll but at first she doesn't think she can get through the actual performance because she has to hold Ethel Smiley's eight-months old baby. But she just holds on the baby and things get better, so good she wants to tell somebody, but who was there? So while they were all singing she told Ethel's baby, lying in her arms asleep, in something similar to swaddling clothes but smiling with what seemed like joy of fresh new love or birth.

Somewhere quote a poem she wrote for Wesley.

What is the conflict: abortion vs birth? home vs away? marriage vs bastardy? Can't it be a little "better" than that?

15 Jan. Opening?? It wasn't like it was something new. Hadn't she slept with her Cousin *** until he was old enough to get his driver's license . . . (expand and explain, of course).

Maybe the story would be effective in 3–4 blocks, each one a kind of set piece:

1. The night before Wesley leaves. They go somewhere (funny). He tries, unsuccessfully.
   —Maybe each section followed by letters: Rc to Wes, Wes to Rc.
2. His first visit home. Changed and faraway. She tries to hold him the only way left to her.
   —Letters
3. Her realization and self-conflict. Then the resolution to leave (ought she really to leave?). The pageant and the end.

Isn't the story really going to be—or can't it be—a kind of story about Vermeer's "Young Woman Reading a Letter"?

London, 20 Jan. But look, isn't this story in danger of ending with a kind of cheat, that is with no resolution? What *is* the end going to imply?: simply that she leaves home for Norfolk or wherever? Maybe Wes. had better make some kind of gesture, however small.

The pageant is on Xmas eve. Is Wesley there? They (or she) will leave in 2–3 days.

There's got to be a sort of showdown scene between Rc. and Wesley in which Rc. talks at great length, presenting all the real themes of the story. And Wes. sits silent the whole time, not even speaking when she asks those begging questions—though at the end of the scene, he does say one brief thing—something which is, for Rc., joyful *and* tragic.

In so many ways, I would have wanted a happier life for Rc., but surely this tragedy was implied in her at the start of "Chain"—her greatness as a woman, a person, was her desire, her obligation, always to make the kind gesture, the touch, the thing which seemed to her clearly, if not always desirably, *right,* and right because she thought it would make somebody else happy.

Oxford, 26 January 1957

It's reasoning after the fact, to be sure, but I don't think that makes the reasoning any less valid: in a way, this second Rosacoke story had to be written, for the reason that I suggested in the paragraph just above and to be true to the few things that I myself have discovered. "A Chain of Love" does have an ethic at the heart of it, the ethic of the freely given gesture. And that I would still stand by, as passionately as ever. But there is something to be said after I have said that: which is that when we give these gestures—especially when we give them for some kind of personal reason (Rc's desire to hold Wesley)—we might as well be prepared to have them lash back upon us, sometimes. The important thing is knowing what to do then, knowing how to complete them, to "connect."

Should any of the actual speeches of the pageant be given? I might write a sort of Address to the Babe of Bethlehem which Baby Sister or somebody else could give (in fact, Rc. herself might write it), but the difficulty there would be to prevent its sounding too "symbolic," too ironic. That's going to be a problem with the whole pageant ending, in fact: it could cause offense, I suppose, to some readers to visualize an illicitly pregnant girl impersonating the Virgin. But with care I can manage that, I think.

Oxford, 9 Feb 57

Almost every character in "A Chain of Love" is what EM Forster would call a "flat" character, everyone perhaps except Rosacoke (and maybe Papa, yes I think Papa). That isn't really a criticism of the story: it is and was meant to be and *ought* to be a story about Rosacoke, a story in which she can stand up straight and move freely. No one must take the story out of her hands—except death, and in her own way she conquers that—and even when Mama or Rato or anybody else takes the stage for awhile, they take it to teach us something about Rosacoke. (And to call them all "flat" is not to call them lifeless. They are intensely real, one might meet them anytime. No, they are flat, "humorous" characters because the story can only afford to see them from one side.)

But I'm saying all this to ask if the new story oughtn't to be different, if I mustn't bring more of them to life?—Wesley surely, and Mama, maybe even Baby Sister. For Rosacoke is older now and therefore infinitely more dependent on other people (nothing on earth is as independent as a child), more entangled—to the point, finally, of suffocation. Perhaps the meaning of that last pageant scene with the baby is that Rc. suddenly realizes the tragedy of growing up: involvement and responsibility. But the peace, the really terrifying peace, and the beauty (beauty because it promises decay) of this baby must flow through the end like love, when it's new.

Oxford, 25 Feb 57

Isn't this really a kind of temptation–sin–redemption story? The great question being, then: what kind of redemption? The Christmas pageant ending might suggest a religious solution, but that is not—at least not now—what I think I mean at all. I said before (on 26 Jan) that the important thing (the solution?) is knowing what to do when one's initial gestures fail. And I'm still not sure of that—except that one must go on making gestures, only trying even harder now to make the right ones. I'm sure, at least, that Rc. must keep the story in hand right to the end—or in the end. If she wavers or thinks of suicide or abortion or anything like that, then it is *she* who must save herself. Oh, the others can help, but always indirectly. Although, even in writing that, I'm not sure that the possibility of Wesley's having to return and save Rc. by love isn't the strongest idea and maybe the truest. Well, this is awfully confused.

The actual technical problem which interests me most about the story is the presentation of the sexual incident. I've said that the end of "Daphnis and Chloe" is the only successful description of the act that I know of. The point about that, though, is that it is a perfectly clear, purely poetic—though absolutely no-nonsense—presentation of a sexual *ideal:* free of guilt and given over to pleasure. So can it have any relevance to my story? Probably only an ironic relevance: that is, I might describe the actual union in those Greek terms to show the pure joy of the thing, once Rc. had made up her mind to it—but it would only show, in the end, the failure of the act and the tragic result of Rc's illusions about it: the illusion that it is her great, final means of holding Wesley *and*—once caught up in the passion—that it is a means of communication between them.

Oxford, 3 March 57

Before there can be profound tragedy, there must surely be a certain self-knowledge or, at least, self-perspective. So Rc. must do a great deal of thinking about her mistake and her situation. The problem is how to do that naturally. Some of it can come in her poems, but I'm not a poet after all, and I can't manage but so much of that. There will be the one big scene with Wesley in which she tries to explain. But I'll have to create other opportunities for her to think—but *not* in great long chunks of introspection: she's not that sort, nor am I. She thinks in bits and pieces—jarred into thought a thousand times each day by a face or a voice or a picture or a bird-song.

I wondered last night why Rc. loves Wesley? The problem is to make Wesley—for all his insensitivity and callous hunger—somehow a person whom Rc. can, believably, love. The scene when she sees him playing his harmonica will do a good deal to solve the problem. (And should he be playing a harmonica? Maybe a guitar: that way she could see all of his face.)

Of course, one of her great troubles is that she hasn't fully admitted how much her love for Wesley is based in desire.

Hadn't the story better begin with Rc. riding home from work? (Whoever she's riding with—Milo?—can say that he's heard about Wesley coming home for the weekend. So she goes on home, then goes to pay her respects to Mildred's family (taking some of Baby Sister's old clothes for the baby), and she plans to stop by Wesley's on the way home: the harmonica scene. This way I can compress the actual time, but Wes' first seduction attempt will have to be recalled somehow. If I do begin it this way, can I sufficiently suggest Rc's growing panic at the thought of losing him? Maybe not.

Rato was in the Army. Had been for going on five years and was still a messenger boy. When they asked him what he wanted to be in, he said "The Calvary." They told him there hadn't been any cavalry for nearly ———— years, and how about him being a messenger?

Oxford, 6 March 57

Is Rosacoke at all religious? That is, is her plight a religious as well as a personal one? Does she feel convicted of sin *against God* or simply of error and selfishness? Remember that in "Chain" her whole vision was a religious one. She wouldn't have changed, would she?

I wonder if I ought not to explore in this story the possibilities of treating the characters in a kind of Hardy manner—though all I've read is *Tess* and that years ago. What I really mean is: wouldn't it be possible here to go beyond the purely realistic treatment in "Chain," to transcend the limits of the speech that the Mustians really would use—to transcend it in Rosacoke's case only, I suppose. This is terrifyingly dangerous, of course, and I think it's precisely where Faulkner fails so often: he thinks he is giving his Negroes and his tenant farmers and his aristocrats a kind of "higher reality"—whereas, it seems to me that, in the end, they often have no reality at all. But his failures seem to arise usually from selecting such *extreme* characters and from his love of Southern court house rhetoric.

In "Chain" I attempted to create a style which—as I've said here somewhere—could swell from the purely stenographic to a more rapt, ecstatic poetry without a rough, noisy change of gear. I'm inclined to think "Chain" succeeds too, and it succeeds, surely, because Rosacoke seems, for all her rustic native qualities, a large, a spacious person. So perhaps my problem is already solved by simply having Rosacoke on the scene, a little older and finer-grained and a good deal more fluent. (Still, I'll read *Tess* and maybe some of the other Hardy novels and Lord David's [Lord David Cecil] *Hardy*.)

The point is that nothing must happen—as to purely external incident—that could not happen in Rc's world.

Lord David is always emphasizing the necessity of an author's realizing the "limits of his vision." I surely don't know the upper limits of mine, but there are some things that I'm quite sure I can't deal with, and violence is one of them. For instance, if the brief violence at the end of "Michael Egerton" is real, then it is real because it is seen through the rather dazed eyes of the narrator, who describes it very briefly. Surely, that is the best answer to the people who have asked me why the story wasn't fuller and more detailed: if I had made it fuller, I would probably have failed miserably to write a big torture scene.

Perhaps, after all, it's meaningless to talk of one's limitations. One simply trusts to his "vision"—whatever that is—to perceive the things that one *can* do: all on a more or less unconscious level. Perhaps, too, it's why I've never begun a novel or even sketched one out: I'm rather afraid of having to do things I can't do.

This is all a good deal too timorous, and I may not mean any of it.

Oxford, 16 March 57

It's obvious that, when the actual seduction, the actual union, takes place, a good deal of it must be described from Wesley's point of view. That is, there must be a strong sense of Wesley as the active force at the same time as it's being made obvious that Rosacoke is quite consciously and willingly yielding—for a definite purpose. Otherwise, it will all be much too uncomfortable and embarrassing, for a good many reasons. In fact, the whole business must be handled with the most extreme delicacy—to suggest the essential animality and to differentiate between the crude, pure animality of Wesley and the unacknowledged, veiled animality of Rosacoke: maybe it's impossible to do, but I'll have to attempt it.

How can I show Rc's growing sense of isolation throughout the story? She's almost like Juliet in that the outer world with which she can communicate—always small enough—grows smaller and narrower from the moment her trouble begins. The point and the poignancy of the whole last scene is that this baby—not even her own, someone else's—is the only person on earth to whom she can talk, and speak of her tragic joy.

Oxford, 7 April 57

Pictures—paintings or photographs, anything—seem to have a great importance for me when I think of writing and while I'm in the act of writing. It was, for instance, the combination of that mourning picture at Cherry Hill with the sight of Miss C———A———walking in the yard in June of 55 which set me off on "The Anniversary." And it was certainly that faded little photograph of that young man which Annie Belle gave to my father which formed the essentials of Pretty Billy's character. But in no story yet have I felt acted *upon* by so many pictures as I have in planning this one now. There is a whole gallery in my mind: Vermeer's "Young Woman in Blue Reading a Letter" (which bears very obviously on Rc's state), the Cartier-Bresson photograph in "Les Européens" of the boy playing the mandolin (from which—I hope—the really crucial scene of the whole story may arise), the Botticelli Portrait of a Young Man from the National Gallery, London (because it somehow suggests Wesley: I know he combined this same sort of electric but unselfconscious animality with a hint of brutality in the mouth and the chin), there is that photograph of the little boys which I found by the road, and the photograph of my father in the National Guard, and surely there will be others.

Perhaps—if I ever get good enough for anybody to care, *so* good that it won't just seem pompous foolishness—I might publish these notes with a long essay on the evolution of this story, and it might help to reproduce all the pictures—everything—that bore directly or indirectly on the story at any stage.

This really worries me—though it's hopeless to worry until I've really begun the story: am I going to kill Rc. completely by burying her under a load of thought and afterthought which she simply can't support? I said somewhere earlier in these notes that I might try to do what Hardy did (or what I thought he did): to elevate a kind of peasant character into something sublime by omitting a great many of the obvious homely details that tend to "regionalize" something. But I'm afraid all that is nonsense. I've just now read Hardy's "Wessex Tales," and they seem to me strongest where they are most explicit, most apparently stenographic of the odd turn of speech and habit that label a man *Wessex* but ultimately make him believable as something more—just *Man*. It is fascinating, for example, to see how Hardy's attempts—in some of the stories, not all—to ennoble the characters have peculiar effects on his form: in such stories he almost invariably has to avoid actual scenes and rely on straight related narrative with only a bare minimum of rather pale dialogue and with a falling off in things like physical description and metaphor. Well, I'll still go on and try *Tess*, but I think I know what I'll decide in the end.

Oxford, 11 April 57

I must think a good deal about the problem of Time in this story—the actual problem of how to suggest the passage of considerable stretches of time. And to convey anything more than the passage of a few days or weeks *may* be well-nigh impossible in a *short* story. That is one reason I must allow this story to spread itself out in more detail. The trouble now seems to be that I see a story which covers—maybe—six or eight months in terms of three, at the most four, scenes. What to do with the interstices, how to suggest that life keeps on, that imperceptibly people change and grow older—to do that in a scenically-conceived story without giving the impression that everybody simply slept or was unconscious during the gaps between the scenes is the problem. Something as vast as *War and Peace*—and as Forster observes, spread out over such a vast geographical canvas—has that tremendous sense of flow about it, no character is ever quite the same person from one chapter to the next, though the modulations are beautiful and delicate and never wrenching. But I haven't got that much space to work in, nor so many pages. Nor so much time, either. So I must find my own way: my early idea about prefacing each section with a letter from Rc. to Wesley may be a way of doing it (it might also be a way of handling the poems—just let her express the matter of the "poems" in these rather intense letters). The really important thing is that Rc. and Wesley emerge in the end as changed people—Rc., at least, if not Wesley. Maybe nothing will change him. And the way she changes is what the story "means." She has learned a tragic fact—about love and responsibility and honesty: now what can she do with the fact which she has so sadly learned?

And another thing: is Wesley going to be much of a character? That is, full and round with sides and a top and bottom? He never appeared, in the flesh, in "A Chain" so I'm not bound to any commitments about him there— except the things Rc. remembered and said about him. Yes, I think he must have a very real life of his own, he must manage to convince me that Rc. might have loved him to distraction—for some reason beyond the physical, which was certainly a big reason too. It's all very well to say, in life, "Why does anybody love anybody else?" And that's almost a satisfactory answer in itself: a complicated interaction of nerves and glands and sounds and smells, and on and on, deeper and deeper into irrationality. But a story must be more responsible than that. It must show you—without being know-it-all in the process—the things that life cannot, or will not, show you as you go through any normal day. So Wesley must come startlingly—if a little appallingly—to life. He must be very much a Presence, not so much sinister as blind. A kind of Ananké looming over and finally crushing Rc.

Oxford, 13 April 57

This really mustn't be a story in which there is a lot of *talk* about emotion. The effect of the emotions must simply be set forth in actions and gestures. Perhaps I can allow myself a poem or two, maybe three or four letters; and of course Rc. will have to do *some* thinking. But it would be wrong, I'm almost sure, to invest her with long meditations on things out of her grasp. Lord David says in his essay on Jane Austen that she realized quite fully that the description of emotion was impossible for her, though she excelled at showing the *effects* of emotion on a character in action. That is what I must try for. Perhaps there is not a large enough range of action for a girl like Rc.—but that's not true: she can run away from home, she could kill herself if she wanted to. That is scope enough for any girl.

Love (and Marriage) in *A Long and Happy Life*

ALLEN SHEPHERD

Reynolds Price has in some quarters been hailed, as Frederick Hoffman observed, "as a special product of Southern writing."[1] Without belaboring the issues of Southern-ness or influences, I should like to consider Price's development of character and theme in his first novel, *A Long and Happy Life* (1962), the characters comprising members of the Mustian family, their friends and acquaintances, and the theme centering upon the rights and responsibilities, principally the latter, of love. The characters are familiar to readers of Price's other works, the short stories collected in *The Names and Faces of Heroes* (1963), and his second novel, *A Generous Man* (1966). Love, in its various manifestations, pervades stories and novels, which makes *A Long and Happy Life* both representative in a sense and indicative of Price's ability to make it new.

The Dantesque epigraph which prefaces the novel may be construed so as to raise several questions concerning how one should read *A Long and Happy Life,* particularly its conclusion. It runs, in translation, ". . . for I have seen first, all the winter through, the / thorn display itself hard and forbidding, and / then upon its summit bear the rose; . . ."[2] This would seem, perhaps, to intimate a good life for Rosacoke Mustian, Price's heroine. But the thesis which Dante illustrates in the passage is essentially that one should not be deceived by false appearances or come to hasty conclusions. In the lines immediately following those which Price quotes, a ship—after a long voyage—finally reaches the mouth of the harbor, where it promptly sinks. Now it may be that the reader's returning to context is not at all what Price had in mind, that it is too literal minded, that he is not "using" Dante in any such way. With or without the epigraph, however, and in or out of context, most readers will surely conclude that Rosacoke hasn't much to look forward to, that she has committed herself to a hard and wintry future. The question, or the answerable question, however, relates not to her future, but to how she blooms in the course of the novel. What the story means is the way she changes, what she discovers, and what she can do with what she has learned.

Reprinted, with permission, from *Twentieth Century Literature* 17.1 (1971): 29–35.

In speaking of Rosacoke as she appears in another Mustian story, "A Chain of Love," Price coined a nice phrase, one which provides a valuable perspective on the novel. He spoke of "the ethic of the freely given gesture,"[3] by which is meant the moral duty of making other people happy, an act being right because it does this or is undertaken to this end. One of the things Rosacoke learns in the course of *A Long and Happy Life* is that it is very difficult to do this because of one's own innocence or ignorance, because one's own motives are usually mixed, because others don't understand or can't respond.

Consider a few examples. Rosacoke planned to give her friend Mildred Sutton a pair of stockings for her twenty-first birthday and to wish her "a long and happy life,"[4] but Mildred dies in childbirth while still twenty. Rosacoke carries a bag of horehound drops to Mr. Isaac, eighty-three and paralyzed, but he doesn't even know who she is. One day Rosacoke finds Mildred's baby, Sledge, who survives his mother, uncovered, and thinking he is cold, covers him up. He wakes, cries, she picks him up, he throws up on her. Rosacoke's brother Milo undergoes his own crisis when his son is born dead. He needs her, asks that she stay with him, but Rosacoke becomes distraught on receiving a letter from Wesley Beavers, cannot bring herself to stay with her brother, and sends him back to his wife. To send him back is probably to do the right thing, but for the wrong reason. Or again, Rosacoke gives herself, in an ultimate gesture, to Wesley. He says, on finishing the job, "I thank you, Mae" (95). He does not even give her in return her name, which would be little enough under the circumstances. In each instance Rosacoke gives, or tries to give, or intends to give, of herself to others. What is significant is not the number of such instances, of which the preceding enumeration is far from exhaustive, but the ethic, the cast of mind, which they collectively dramatize.

Her greatest gift and gamble involves Wesley. He does do what he considers his duty, offering her a trip to Dillon, South Carolina, marriage, a name for her child. This is certainly an appropriate ending, rather than leaving her future wholly up in the air or having her decide on an abortion, an alternative Price considered.[5] But pondering Rosacoke's prospects only brings up another question which has understandably bothered a number of readers. Why does she love him? Is it credible that she should? One might argue that the question is no more puzzling in Price's fiction than it often is in life and that Rosacoke's devotion to Wesley ought simply to be taken as a *donnée* of the novel. But Price does in fact address himself to the question on a number of occasions, and there is one sequence which indicates perhaps more clearly than any other the source and strength of Wesley's appeal, that scene in which Rosacoke—at dusk—approaches the Beavers' house, as Wesley and his brother stand near the front porch, Wesley playing his harmonica. Before she speaks and breaks the spell, Rosacoke thinks:

"There ought to be some way you could hold him there. Anybody who looks like that—you ought to give them anything you have. Anything you have and

they want *bad* enough." So she went on towards him and thought of nothing
but that. (86)

Rosacoke does give everything, but it is not enough to hold Wesley, not at
least as she wishes to. It is Mrs. Mustian who states the thesis everywhere
illustrated in the novel. When speaking of her late husband, who is consistently associated with Wesley, she says, "But Rosa, he changed. Folks all have
to change . . ." (77).

In *The Art of Southern Fiction* Frederick Hoffman notes in this connection
that the novel is "a marvel of vital and other kinds of statistics."[6] And so it is,
with funerals, births, deaths, marriages, pregnancies, all indicative of the continuity of inescapable change. In the narrative we are taken back several generations to Papa, Rosacoke's grandfather, or to Mr. Isaac's mother and father,
forward to Rosacoke's own generation, to Mildred, ahead one generation to
Horatio III, Milo's baby, all of them gathered into the graveyard. The cycle of
change is of course not limited to death; birth is its other name. There is new
life in Sledge, Mildred's child, "that had lived God only knew how, dark and
hard in the orange crate they lined with white and laid him in, his back
curved inwards and his spidery arms and legs twisting inwards to his navel
. . ." (26). And there is Mr. Isaac, a baby for the second time at eighty-three.
Wanting to live to be as old as his father, who died at ninety saying "I don't
understand," Mr. Isaac says to Rosacoke: "I can't die. If you was to shoot me,
I wouldn't die. So I don't pray. I—I—I don't pray no more than that dog
does yonder" (145). But as the narrator then observes, the dog has been dead
for fifteen years. There is one character who seems not to change, almost to
be immune to change. Rato, Rosacoke's brother, home on leave from the
Army, where he is beginning his thirty years as a messenger, hasn't changed,
but he is mentally deficient, which gives him an edge on mutability.

One of the forces that holds things together, gives continuity to change,
orders life, is a sense of family, of kinship. Blood bonds are not always close or
sustaining, or even acknowledged, but they are important, as is extensively
illustrated in the novel. Rosacoke remembers attending a church meeting
with Mildred at which "Aunt Mannie Mayfield stood at age 80 and named
the fathers of her children, far as she could recall" (14). Then there is the
question of the paternity of Mildred's own baby, much on Rosacoke's mind.
Or there is Landon Allgood at Mildred's funeral, asking her, "I'm some kin to
Mildred, ain't I?" (16). There is Mr. Isaac's refrain, "Whose girl are you?",
addressed to Rosacoke. And there is her own family, living or dead or to be
born, in the house or the graveyard or the womb.

At one point rather late in the novel, after she has told Wesley of her
pregnancy and he has proposed his solution, Rosacoke feels, for the first time
in eight years, free, "as if her life were hers" (155). This feeling, however,
doesn't persist for very long, for the ethic of the freely given gesture implies a
debt assumed on the part of the donor, a choice made between love and sepa-

rateness. Rosacoke might set Wesley free by rejecting his offer, but not herself. Throughout the course of the novel what I can only call the life force asserts itself in a whole series of images of sucking and pulling. Since a leech, an old man, and a number of babies are included, one cannot forthrightly say that the image is one of love, but it is possible and to the point to establish some distinctions among the candidates.

Mildred's baby, Sledge, even before his birth, is said to be "sucking blind at her life" (34). Shortly afterward, at the picnic, Frederick Gupton, the baby who will be the Christchild at the pageant, is said to be "pulling hard at her [his mother's] life" (40). Then, as if to illustrate the force on a sub-human level, a leech attaches itself to Wesley's leg, and is said again, with exact repetition of the phrase, to be "pulling hard at Wesley's life" (43). It is Rosacoke who removes the leech and who shortly protests to him that he is answering her questions "like I was a doll baby that didn't need nothing but a nipple in her mouth" (56). Three more representative examples will complete my catalogue. Wesley, after he has escaped again, sends Rosacoke "a giant post card of a baby with a sailor hat on in a baby carriage, hugging a strip-naked celluloid doll and sucking on a rubber pacifier. The caption said, *I Am A Sucker For Entertainment*" (60). Toward the end of the novel, as the pageant is in progress, Rosacoke thinks of standing up and testifying, rather like Aunt Mannie Mayfield, "I am Rosacoke Mustian and the reason I look so changed tonight is because I am working on a baby that I made by mistake and am feeding right now with my blood . . ." (165). And finally there is Frederick Gupton chewing away, despite the paregoric, and at the last after Rosacoke has whispered "yes" to him, smiling in his sleep, "as if," Price writes, "he knew of love" (174).

One need not wax philosophical or physiological to conclude that this train of images defines dependence, or interdependence, of the most basic sort. It is right, then, that both Mildred and Rosacoke should be determined to have their children, with or without acknowledged fathers, and it is right, again in terms of theme, that Wesley should send the grotesque post card, that the leech should be removed from him, that Frederick Gupton should elicit or should be the only one to hear Rosacoke's "yes," that Rosacoke should play the Virgin Mary.

During an early stage of the composition of the novel, Price was concerned that the pageant conclusion would seem too symbolic or ironic.[7] In one sense, the irony *is* very much on the surface and the symbolism may initially seem rather pat, but I think that if one can hold in mind the course of Rosacoke's development from the outset, one will see that those lessons in love and responsibility and honesty which she has been growing into are successfully concretized here, that the chances the novelist took pay off. What was wanted was an ending which would not be a cheat, one which would offer a resolution consistent with preceding action, and which would present a last few words on the donor's ethic. The "yes" Rosacoke whispers to Frederick

Gupton does not signify simply "yes, I yield," or "yes, I accept what seems to be my inescapable fate," or even "yes," founded on duty, desire and love, but "yes" as well to the three gifts laid down by the three wise men: Rato (a brass bowl), Milo (a cheap jewel box won on a gas station punch board) and Wesley (a covered butter dish). The final imperative of the donor's ethic, then, is to receive gladly what is given, to take, if necessary, the deed for the word.

A Long and Happy Life is very much Rosacoke's book. The only other characters of real consequence and of more than one dimension are Wesley and Milo, and possibly Mrs. Mustian. Wesley does not seem to change, or has no wish to. He is a motorcycle man whom Rosacoke loves to distraction. In the motorcycle, she thinks, he has "found the vehicle he was meant for" (11). The defining image of Wesley that recurs to Rosacoke is her first sight of him, high in a pecan tree. He is repeatedly likened to a large, strong bird of prey, an eagle in the tree or a hawk sailing overhead. Thus as Wesley approaches her at the pageant, "her head rolled back and her lips fell open as if she would greet some killing bird" (167). Much as Rosacoke thinks of him, and despite their eight-year acquaintance, he remains something of a mystery.

All of these elements in the relation are suggested in a scene previously mentioned as Rosacoke walks one night through the woods to the Beavers' house to ask—as she tells herself—Wesley's mother what she has done wrong. Riding above her is the hawk, accompanied by strange music, and she wonders, anticipating the conclusion, "if they wouldn't touch her—his wings—and her lips fell open to greet him, but he was leaving, taking the music with him and the wind" (83). As she draws near the house, she hears the strange, sad music of Wesley's harmonica. Then, very briefly, another association is suggested. Wesley's brother is speaking, but Rosacoke can't hear what he is saying. "Like that boy in the picture with her father (him [the other boy] on the left, holding up like a lily the American flag, speaking silence to the wind) . . ." (85–86). Just as Wesley alone hears his brother, so in that picture taken in 1915 did Rosacoke's father alone hear the other smaller boy. From that earlier conversation, Rosacoke is excluded forever; from the present conversation, it would seem, only by chance and distance. The common denominator, however, is a masculine mystery.

If Wesley is an unchanging principle, at least in Rosacoke's life, Milo experiences a crisis and undergoes development, both of which complement Rosacoke's own. Early in the novel, in connection with Mildred Sutton's death in childbirth, Milo observes that "Nothing happens to people that they don't ask for" (49). Later on, as his son, Horatio III, is deposited in the graveyard, Milo is given cause to reflect on this judgment. In taking his own child's baby clothes to Mildred's son, Sledge, Milo is assuredly acting out of mixed motives, the desire to be away from home, wife and mother, the need to be rid of reminders, the wish, perhaps, to assert his own masculine authority, but also out of a need to make a gesture, to give, rather as Rosacoke has done. As it happens, the gesture is well received, but it solves no problems, except minor and immediate ones. Indeed, Milo goes on to be betrayed, as he thinks, by his sister, before being returned to his wife. And again, at the pageant, as Milo, now one of the wise men, offers his gift, he stares at young Frederick Gupton, who obliges by taking Milo's finger and putting it in his mouth. Rosacoke sees on her brother's face "not a frown but the way he had looked that night in Mary's kitchen . . ." (166). Milo has not Rosacoke's desire or ability always to make the kind gesture, the touch, to do the thing which seems right because it will make someone else happy, but such attempts as he does undertake serve to elevate him in Price's scheme of values as "a generous man."

Mrs. Mustian seems intended, more than anything else, to provide continuity and precedent within the family. While the reader senses the possibility of Rosacoke's pursuing Mildred's fate, the more likely model is Mrs. Mustian. Speaking of her late husband, she says to Rosacoke, "He didn't have nothing but the way he looked, and I never asked for nothing else, not in 1930 nohow" (77). The sum of his tangible bequests amounts to a 1937 New Jersey license plate and three children. And so on several occasions Rosacoke desperately wonders what *she* will have if Wesley should leave, "what there would be that she could take out and hold or pass around . . ." (23). Perhaps like mother, like daughter: infatuation, the remembered image of a boy young and serious, decline, departure, the fatal vehicle, in Wesley's life the motorcycle, in Horatio Mustian's death the pickup truck he had walked into one evening.

Such repetitions, parallels and associations as I have laid out are at the heart of *A Long and Happy Life*. I find, however, that in the presence of the heart I am made somewhat uneasy. One can see readily enough that the lives of the characters are intimately and complexly interrelated, which is as it should be. But it is difficult to know just what to make of certain parallels and associations. Thus the implicit parallel between Rosacoke and her mother, extended in that between Wesley and Rosacoke's father, further involved by the possible association of Rosacoke and Mildred. Now to cite another example. Rosacoke is sitting through Mildred's funeral, her mind on Wesley outside. She returns from viewing the body, "feeling stronger with her part done and Mildred turned to the wall where nobody would see." Mildred, I might say, is quite literally turned to the wall, the body having shifted in transportation to the church. Immediately afterward one reads: "And so was Wesley turned away" (20). Now Price uses this device quite frequently, the same phrase applied to two or more characters. The question here is: what association is established between Mildred and Wesley as they relate to Rosacoke? That neither is of any help? That both are beyond reach, inscrutable?

I don't wish to leave the impression that such parallels and associations regularly constitute puzzles; most often they work exactly and well. To cite another minor example, at the time of Rosacoke's father's death, Mr. Isaac had come to the house, given fifty dollars to the widow and said, "He is far better off," a judgment which Price certifies parenthetically, "(which was true)" (70). As Mr. Isaac sits in his wheelchair in the church, waiting to be ninety, Rosacoke, thinking of his "after all this time not knowing half *she* knew," concludes, "I reckon he is far better off" (161). One sees, first, that Rosacoke is still paying off on the gift; second, that the old bachelor has not in fact had Rosacoke's experience nor gained her knowledge; and third, that Rosacoke's hard earned young wisdom is treated with a kind of benign irony which illuminates both her charity and her incompleteness.

Rosacoke's evolution may be traced, finally, through three recurrences of the novel's title. The phrase first appears when Rosacoke, representing white friends, speaks at Mildred's funeral. "There I was just wanting to give her a pair of stockings and wish her a long and happy life and she was already gone" (27). Both the gift and the phrase are freely offered, but the intended recipient is beyond either. The phrase occurs for the second time, somewhat broken up, during the pageant and after Wesley has made his offer, which Rosacoke cannot bring herself to accept. "I looked on it as giving. . . . But I don't want him now. All this time I have lived on the hope he would change some day before it was too late and come home and calm down and learn how to talk to me and maybe even listen, and we would have a long life together—him and me—and be happy sometimes and get us children . . ." (159–160). Price offers no prediction on the likelihood of Rosacoke's hope being fulfilled, but the climactic scene of the novel does fulfill one of the preconditions. "She bent again and touched his [Frederick Gupton's] ear with her lips and said it to him, barely whispered it— 'yes'—and wished him, silent, a long happy life" (173–174). The "yes" rescinds Rosacoke's previous rejection of Wesley's offer, establishes once again her ethic, her continuing vulnerability and her aloneness, since this baby—not even her own—is the one person to whom she can speak. Frederick is, or will be, a Gupton like other Guptons, his mother is even now within a month of producing another, but what is important is that "even in his sleep, he knew of love" (174).

The intricacies and obliquities of *A Long and Happy Life* should incline one to a close and intent reading of the novel, to musing on a single sentence or phrase, and this accurately reflects Price's management of character and theme. While the novel has its share of what Honor Tracy called "warmth and innocence and sweetness,"[8] it is also very carefully constructed, with Price very much in control. Sometimes, as it seems, carefulness becomes self-consciousness, and control manipulation. One is more aware of authorial glosses on the fable than one should be, and of the fact that alternatives are sometimes posed largely as alternatives, and then dismissed. Stylistic resources occasionally show themselves in a technical virtuosity which outweighs the uses to which it is put. These are minor objections, though, not cavils. Finally, however, while he may overcalculate them, Price is a writer willing to take chances, and this problematic novel reflects a number of interesting problems well solved. In the conclusion of *A Long and Happy Life* the meaning of the action finds final focus not in mechanical resolution nor allegorized ethereality but in vital human effort, doomed perhaps to failure, but validating the ethic of the freely given gesture.

University of Vermont

Notes

1. *The Art of Southern Fiction* (Carbondale, Illinois: Southern Illinois University Press, 1967), p. 137.

2. *The Paradiso of Dante Alighieri* (London: J. M. Dent, 1954), p. 165.

3. "A Chain of Love" is included in *The Names and Faces of Heroes* (New York: Avon Books, 1966). "*A Long and Happy Life:* Fragments of Groundwork," *Virginia Quarterly Review,* XLI (1965), 238.

4. *A Long and Happy Life* (New York: Avon Books, 1965), p. 27. Subsequent quotations from this edition will be identified in the text.

5. "*A Long and Happy Life:* Fragments of Groundwork," 237.

6. Ibid., 138.

7. Ibid., 239.

8. "Happily Ever After," *The New Leader,* XLV (1962), 21.

The "Circle in the Forest": Fictional Space in Reynolds Price's *A Long and Happy Life*

SIMONE VAUTHIER

I know that there's something more important, more enduring than fashion and the fads of journalists; and that is the attempt to seize territory from chaos, to clear and tend and fortify a circle in the forest, then to stage games there.

—Reynolds Price

Among many insights into the genesis of *A Long and Happy Life*, the note-book which Reynolds Price kept while planning his first novel offers tantalizing hints at one of the problems he must have then faced: defining once his heroine as "a large, a spacious person," he yet admitted later that he had not "much space to work in."[1] That he solved the problem successfully is obvious: the smallness of Rosacoke's home base does not actually cramp her style, though it undoubtedly defines it. Nor does it hamper the novelist—some critics notwithstanding—[2] in his exploration of the world. The very disparity between the locus of the story and the area of human experience it reveals is an invitation to map out the ways in which Place is made to function in *A Long and Happy Life*.

On entering the Price country the traveller feels no sense of disorientation. From the second page of *A Long and Happy Life* he can take his bearings: he is in Afton, close to Warrenton;[3] Norfolk, Virginia, is a hundred and thirty miles away (p. 7).[4] The action takes place entirely in Warren County, which can be located on any Esso map of North Carolina. What with the images of cardinals and blackberrying Negro children, and the numerous vignettes of dirt roads, sandy patches, clumps of "dogwood, hickory and thin pine," of crossroads store-cum-post-offices, isolated churches and unpainted Negro cabins, the location is well established. "In scene after scene," one critic writes, "the Carolina country comes splendidly alive."[5] Obviously Reynolds

Reprinted, with permission, from *Mississippi Quarterly* 28.2 (Spring 1975): 123–46. Copyright 1975, Mississippi State University, Mississippi.

Price has succeeded in what is, according to Eudora Welty, "the clear intention" of any novelist, making the reader see his picture of the world "under the pleasing illusion that it is the world's."[6] However, the descriptive aspect of the novel and its fidelity to a real landscape need not detain us. As Honor Tracy puts it, "of the ambience, the little town in North Carolina where these simple folk pursue their anything but simple lives, an outsider of course cannot judge; but I can say that it rings true in the way that William Faulkner's Jefferson rings true."[7]

Of greater concern to us is the restricted extensiveness[8] of the fictive territory, mentioned by Price himself. In fact, not only does the whole action occur in a single locale,[9] but the various settings are themselves limited in number, consisting of Mount Moriah Church, Delight Church, the Mustians' house, the Suttons', Mr. Isaac's, the Beavers' porch, Mason's Lake and Mr. Isaac's woods. Nor is any of those places suggestive of vastness. Even exterior locations have something intimate: Mason's Lake is a small sheet of water. Mr. Isaac's woods, although tracts of them remain unknown and mysterious, are not shown panoramically but are apprehended as a series of loci: there is the spring, which the Mustian children once discovered on a hot day, where Rosacoke Mustian, the heroine, cools her feet after she has walked out on her friend Mildred's funeral in quest of Wesley, the boy she loves, the spring which one day she seeks with Wesley in search of something else. There is the broomstraw field where Rosacoke and Mildred unexpectedly came across a deer and the other broomstraw field where she gives herself to Wesley. Less extensive still is the pecan tree in which Wesley was perched on that fateful day when she first met him. The woods, a spring, a tree and a broomstraw field—between these the narration weaves back and forth, never leaving any place for long.

Even the outside world whose presence is dimly felt throughout the story is also restricted in scope. Apart from very brief allusions to Raleigh, Washington, Ocean View—or faraway Oklahoma where Rato is stationed—the outside is chiefly represented by Norfolk, the Virginia town where Wesley works and which, in Rosa's eyes, stands for an alien way of life.

> He said he would . . . take me to Norfolk after Christmas to spend my life shut up in a rented room while he sells motorcycles to fools . . . and staring out a window in my spare time at concrete roads and folks that look like they hate each other. (pp. 179–180)

Norfolk, an industrial center to be sure, but incommensurate with the great American conurbations, yet becomes emblematic of urban America. This is highly suggestive of the figurative treatment of space in *A Long and Happy Life*. Norfolk functions as a synecdoche—representing all the outside world—and as a metonymy connoting the way of life in cities. Further, whereas for Rosacoke the value of Warren County and its closely knit community is defined by the dehumanized environment of the city, for the reader, the existence of Norfolk places the country mores of Afton in perspective, so that the total meaning of the fictional space created by the novel depends on the correlation of the character's perception of a given place and the reader's.

In addition to the topographical limitations, the progress of the narration seems also to have a narrowing effect. It starts with the protagonists on a motorcycle, rushing off in a cloud of dust to a country church, and ends in another country church with a slow-moving Christmas pageant, of which Rosa, as the Virgin Mary, is the still, silent center. The action, in the author's summary, shows that

> the outer world with which [Rosacoke] can communicate—always small enough—grows smaller and narrower from the moment her trouble begins. The point and poignancy of the whole last scene is that this baby [Frederick Gupton as the Holy Infant]—not even her own, someone else's—is the only person on earth to whom she can talk, and speak of her tragic joy.[10]

And yet the "greatness" of Rosacoke is to be able to re-establish communication, through this baby, with loving, suffering humanity, in circumstances that we will investigate later on. What matters here is that when she sees Frederick as one more link in the chain of love, she indirectly indicates that there is no final stop to the road she whizzed on with Wesley at the beginning of the story. Moreover, as the narration focuses on Rosa and her meditations, space seems to dwindle. At one point, exterior space becomes displaced by an interior space.

> [She] fixed her mind on Frederick's weight (that grew every second) and his heat that crept through blanket and costume into her cold side, and soon she was far from him and then farther—from herself and Delight Baptist Church and everybody in it, her mind roaming empty and freer than it had been since the first time she saw the deer in broad daylight at the edge of the broomstraw ring, half hid in trees but watching, waiting (till Mildred said "Great God Amighty"), then going, loud in the leaves.
>
> It didn't last much longer than the deer—her blank roaming. The Angels paused at the end of their first verse, and as they took breath the new sound Frederick made brought her back. (p. 191)

But this self-created space is almost a non-space; unlike the inner spaces which Rosa projects on her environment, it has no landmarks, it is pure roaming. And the allusion to the deer in the broomstraw *ring,* linking the moment with the one epiphany in Mildred's life, recalling even her exclamation, implies that Rosa's "blank roaming" may well be a mystic experience, and as such undescribable. (It must be noted that all the references to time—the deer episode which is introduced as a turning-point, the mention of the length of Rosacoke's trance and its ending—are to be ascribed to the narrator and not to the character.) It is almost as though space and time were for an instant abolished. At any rate the dwindling of space inverts itself to signify dimensionless extensionality. And the conclusion of the novel makes it clear that, despite its geographical and environmental circumscription, space in *A Long and Happy Life* is not conceived of as closed. The extensiveness of the place is revealed as entirely distinct from its extensionality.

But the difference thus illuminated at the end runs like a thread in the texture of the novel. It can notably be traced in the handling of space-time. Although the action covers only a short period—from summer to Christmas—the narration cuts back and forth between this present and the past, to embrace all the significant moments in Rosa's short life and include past loves and losses in the lives of her parents, grandparents and neighbours. If much of the story is told through reminiscences, in fact, these are not necessarily Rosacoke's or Wesley's or any character's, but often the anonymous narrator's. After telling us about Mildred and Rosa's encounter with a deer, the narrator bridges different moments in time, even suggesting possible *durée* in nature, in the following comment:

> If Rosacoke had looked up from Wesley's back at the woods, she might have remembered that day and how it was only nine years ago and here she was headed to bury that same Mildred, and was that black-eyed deer still waiting. . . . But she didn't look up and she didn't remember. (p. 7)

It is sometimes difficult to distinguish between the character's and the narrator's memories because Price has chosen to give the latter a tone of voice resembling the protagonist's, thus bringing the *énoncé cité* as close as possible to the *énoncé citant*.[11] This enables the narration to play with space in several ways, building up a complex system of juxtapositions and superimpositions.

On one hand, it superimposes on the outer space it creates an inner space which is the reflection in the character's mind of some outer locale. In this way, the same place may be, so to speak, duplicated in the narration—a mirroring effect well illustrated when Rosacoke, at the spring, apprehends simultaneously two points in time:

> Looking in it, trying to see her face, she thought of the evening they found this spring—her and her brothers and maybe five Negroes. . . . They halted in a ragged line behind [Milo], and before they could speak, they saw what he had seen—Mr. Isaac there through the darkening leaves, his trousers rolled high . . . little bird ankles. . . . (pp. 30–31)

But the two places thus brought together in the narration may be different, even dramatically contrasting. During the burial service, Rosacoke thinks of the first day "so clear and cool" when she first saw Wesley up in the pecan tree:

... in one tall tree that the path bent around was a boy, spreading his arms between the branches and bracing his feet like he was the eagle on money. It was a pecan tree and she walked straight up under it and said, "Boy, shake me down some nuts." Not saying a word he gripped the branches tighter and rocked the fork he stood in, and nuts fell on her like hail. . . . he stayed up there and when she looked at him once or twice, he wasn't even watching her—just braced on his long legs that rose in blue overalls to his low waist and his narrow chest and bare white neck and his hair that was brown and still cut for the summer . . . and his eyes that stared straight out at sights nobody else in Warren County was seeing unless they were up a pecan tree. (p. 19)

For the shut-in church, warm and dusty, the outdoors is substituted—spreading vast and cool to unseen sights. A memory of life is made to impinge on a death-consecrated moment. The device appears all the more natural as Rosa not only metamorphoses time into space but spatializes her feelings and intuitions. When Sammy tells her she must have a good "hold" on Wesley, the phrase reverberates and what it will "show her, in time," is

a Sunday evening in early November and her having been led on past a hawk by the curious sound to stop in trees at the edge of a clearing and look across a gap through falling night to Wesley Beavers, locked alone with his own wishes in the music he made on a harp with his mouth and moving hands that caused her to say to herself, "There ought to be some way you could hold him there" and then go forward to try a way. (p. 147)

This is less a vision of Wesley (who only appears at the end of the sentence as part of a spatial ensemble where Rosa would like to freeze him) than a visual and kinetic reenactment of an emotion. As a matter of fact, Rosacoke did not walk *past* the hawk, soaring in the sky; *after* seeing the hawk, she heard a strange sound which she at first took to be the hawk's and which drew her on until she realized it was the music from Wesley's mouth-organ (pp. 91–92). Upon the spot in Mr. Isaac's grounds where the narration has her momentarily standing is superimposed another place, a remembered place in which spatial relationships express the relationship between the characters and work as a metaphor for Rosa's desire. Consequently, her shift in position becomes a metaphor for her action, the "way" she finds. By seeing herself in relation to objects in space, she achieves some distance from her self and discovers an issue. The recurring use of the device, while conveying something of the character's inner life and of her stance in front of her limited world, restores to her a measure of freedom. If, according to Gabriel Marcel, "un individu n'est pas distinct de sa place, il est cette place même,"[12] Rosa's situation must be considered as a system of places, "real" and mental, which have a mutual reference to each other, and generate an area of spaciousness for the self.

On the other hand, when the interplay of loci results from the narrator's activity, as in the opening scene when we are told about the broomstraw field, even though it is not visible from the road, nor present to Rosa's mind, the effect, blurring the distinction between space as an immediate fictive reality and space as a mental construct, becomes rather one of depth. Instead of unrolling horizontally before the reader's "eye" a pictorial landscape, the novel adds vertically a number of short but vivid evocations of the same few locations and shapes its own *espace de langage* or territory of words. *A Long and Happy Life*, in that respect, is structured more like a poem or a musical piece than a "traditional" narrative.[13] The recurrence of the same places builds up a slow incantatory rhythm. And, weaving non-spatial motifs, like the deer and the hawk, to the images of the woods, the spring and the broomstraw field, the complex world of words which revolves in the reader's mind acquires great lyrical power.

A Long and Happy Life creates a fictional space that is far from static. The narration constantly oscillates between an inside and an outside. To Rosacoke's mind the inside of Mount Moriah is invaded by the outside where Wesley has chosen to stay. "It was that hot inside and her mind worked slowly back through spring water and shade till she was almost in the night with Wesley . . ." (p. 17). The narration focuses on what is taking place in the church with everyone lining to view the body and "Mildred turned to the wall where nobody could see," and then in a cinematic transition, with the excuse of a similar signifier, shifts back to Wesley. "And so was Wesley turned away. He was squatting on the ground" polishing the wheels of his motor cycle (p. 18). Balancing back and forth between an outside that extends to faraway Baltimore and an inside that contracts to the middle aisle where Rosa walks with her eyes to the ground, the sequence ends with the departure of Wesley and the roar of his motor intruding into the solemnity of the ceremony:

> . . . he bore . . . down on the church like an arrow for their hearts till every face turned to Rosacoke, wondering couldn't *she* stop his fuss, but she looked straight ahead. . . . He was headed for the concrete road, she guessed, and the twenty miles to Mason's Lake and the picnic and everybody there. (pp. 21–22)

Further on, Rosa's letters, full of details about her home life, alternate with the postcards of Wesley, evoking a holiday world of beaches. Or the first paragraph of Chapter II brings together Rosacoke in her room and the road to Mount Moriah:

> But Sunday was bright again and the frost was dew when she woke up, and the road was full of black children creeping towards Mount Moriah, trying their white breaths on the morning air, and carloads of white folks she knew but couldn't see, bound for Delight. Her clock said half-past ten and the house was quiet. (p. 71)

The effect is of course emphasized by the movements of the characters, as in the sequence after the seduction scene, when Rosa, distraught, keeps sallying forth from her house, both a refuge and a prison, in search outside of she does not really know what.

To the polarity of inside and outside is added that of stasis and motion. The narration will sometimes arrest time in a definite space with a picture or a vignette—one hesitates to use the word *tableau* in this context since no canvas is broad enough or crowded enough. So Wesley keeps reappearing up his tree or leaning on his porch. These instances undoubtedly function as clues (Barthes' *indices*) referring to a disposition of Rosacoke's, since in the words Proust applied to a character of his, "le temps ressemble pour [elle] à l'espace."[14] But other instances evince the propensity of the *narration* to freeze time in space: the description, for example, of Rosa sitting and waiting on her porch for Wesley to come while a spider tries "to fill the air with unbroken thread" (p. 69); or the recurring motif of her father's faded photograph (pp. 82–83, 93, 194–195). However, not only do these pictures contrast with the dramatic sequences, thus generating rhythm; in each of them also, the quiet surface is seen, on closer analysis, to be rippled by some faint undercurrent. (Only the boy in the tan photograph is absolutely motionless; but even he is shown in the context of Mrs. Mustian's comment, "But Rosa, he changed," and beside him on the "stiff" paper, there stands a smaller boy laughing "till his face was blurred and the one sure thing about him was an American flag in his right hand and *even that was flapping*") (p. 83—italics added). Quite characteristic is the image of Wesley as Rosa observes him from her retreat in the trees:

> In all she could see—the yard, the house, his brother, him, the trees beyond—his hands were the only moving things. The wind had died completely, his brother watched him as still as she did, and Wesley himself was still as a blind man when his guide suddenly leaves him, embedded upright in the gray air like a fish in winter, frozen in the graceful act, locked in the ice and staring up with flat bitter eyes—far out as anything can be and come back. But his hands *did* move—them and the music—to show he could leave any minute if leaving was what he wanted. (p. 93)

Framed between two references to movement, the idea of stasis is suggested in the ambience, stated directly by the word *still* (used twice, once as an adverb and once as an adjective, which underlines the repetition); it is strengthened by the first comparison, with the immobilized blind man, then by the second simile—an analogy within an analogy within an icon, therefore "embedded" like the fish which is its point of reference—it is further enhanced by the iconic metaphor "frozen in the graceful act" and the insistent precision "locked in the ice." But the core phrase "frozen in the graceful act," fusing immobility and gesture, id-est motion,[15] suggests not so much arrested as suspended motion; encapsulating the meaning of the whole paragraph, it prepares for the restoration of movement—also strongly connoted by the idiomatic phrase "far out as anything can be and *come back.*" The reader, too, comes back to Wesley's moving hands, when immobility is shown up as imperfect, shown up indeed as a sort of illusion which Wesley is willing to accredit but only insofar as it remains understood that he is free to dispel it any time by resuming flight. With its expansions and contractions, its pauses as if between inhaling and exhaling, the fictional space of *A Long and Happy Life* is dynamic.

Furthermore, that the world of *A Long and Happy Life* does not appear to the reader as confined and confining is also partly ascribable to the particular choice of locations and the meanings attached to them. Houses figure prominently in the narrative—more prominently, perhaps, as goals, destinations to be reached than as dwellings. One has a more precise idea of how to get there than of their room-arrangement. But this does not work toward an impoverishment of the house motif. Rather it manifests that, discontinuous as they are, places are not lost in indeterminate space. Unlike the Norfolk flat, houses are inserted in a natural environment in which they blend, like Mary's house, surrounded by trees:

> . . . three *wood* rooms and a roof, *washed by the rain to no color at all,* narrow and pointed sharp up from the packed white ground *like a bone the sun sucked out* when nothing else would *grow.* The only things that moved were *brown smoke* crawling from the chimney and a *turkey.* (p. 86—italics added)

(The shabby cabin participates of the vegetal, the animal—and perhaps the human—kingdoms; it becomes a cosmic house raised by the sun from the earth.) Moreover we are thus reminded of the relative position of the different locations: we learn that there are two ways of reaching the Beavers' house from Mary Sutton's. What Bachelard calls "les valeurs de l'espace habité"[16] are therefore maintained in the reader's mind. Similarly, the sparse furnishings—which remind one of the novel *démeublé* advocated by Willa Cather—[17] may be indicative too of a certain bareness of life. But this bleakness can be of a very different order. Whereas at Mary's the low room with its smell of kerosene and its walls papered with "magazine pages . . . to keep out wind" still shelters baby Sledge, snugly ensconced between four pillows "boxed . . . together like a nest" (p. 87), and therefore testifies to loving care and budding life, at Mr. Isaac's, the rich man's house, the "tired, preserving air" of the dark hall, the picture of F. D. Roosevelt "torn off *Life* magazine, tacked up, crisp and curled and happy" and the yellowed family portraits (pp. 159, 160, 164) speak of life gone by, grown stale and stifling. Indeed the Alston house stands apart in that it is not a "maternal house," to borrow Bachelard's phrase. It is dominated by old Mr. Isaac, kindly but cold and untouched by life; Miss Marina, his sister, is only a lurking presence, "in hiding" in her own home (pp. 159, 166). The Mustian house and the Sutton house, on the contrary, have the intimacy of nests—even if the fledgling Rosa aspires to leave hers.

Albeit rooms may provide the comfort of solitude to exercised souls, to Sissie grieving for the death of her child, to Rosa anxious to escape from the questioning eyes of her family, houses also often are the area of minor confrontations. At home, Rosa must face the teasing of Milo; at the Suttons', she has to overcome the slight feeling of revulsion the baby gives her, a feeling born out of her unconscious fear of maternity. More clearly than any other place, the houses are the settings where the burden of tradition must be assumed, not to mention the lighter chores of a woman's life. Even Mama, generous, warmhearted Mama, can only offer Rosacoke unwelcome advice, the sorry emblem of her dead husband's photograph, and an unconscious lesson in responsibility. Whatever warmth and reassurance houses may occasionally bring, they are also places where the characters macerate in the close air of well-defined, well-set relationships, vegetate in the routine of every-day duties.

In stark opposition to the houses, the outside world is always fresh, however familiar and unseen, always liable to be suddenly revealed or perceived, after long periods of oblivion.

> She looked gradually, at nothing strange, at things she had passed every November of her life and not seen, things that had waited—the rusty bank thrown up by the road and gullied by rain and, beyond in the sun, a prostrate field where nothing stood straight, only corn with unused ears black from frost and stalks exhausted the color of broomstraw, beat to the ground as if boys had swarmed through with sickles, hacking, and farther back, one mule still where he stood except for his breath wreathing white on the bark of a tree that rose up over him straight and forked into limbs with nuts by the hundred and twitched on the sky like nerves because a boy stood in the fork in blue overalls and rocked. (p. 138)

The meaningful events of Rosacoke's life occur in the open air, in a natural setting of woods or fields: the meeting with Wesley up in his pecan tree, her coming across a pregnant Mildred who has been initiated into all the mysteries (but death), Wesley's vain attempt at making love to her, her successful seduction of him, and finally his proposal at which she realizes that she is at long last free of him. But before, and apart from, such happenings, the "bottomless woods" are consistently shown as the area of the unexpected. They are the realm of grace where two little country girls are granted the truly wonderful sight of a deer:

> So they stood up to go, and Mildred's mouth fell open and said "Great God A-mighty" because there was one deer behind them in the trees for quicker than it took to say if it had horns. But its eyes were black and it had looked at them. . . . They were not afraid of any deer, but if those woods offered things like that, that would take the time to look at you, when you had only walked an hour, where *would* they end, and what would be growing in any field they found on the other side. . . . (pp. 6–7)

An embodiment of potency and grace, the deer is "the one wonderful thing she [Mildred] ever saw, the one surprise" of her short life (p. 32); but the woods, dark and sultry as they are, can also offer the mysterious gift of a spring "the size of the evening sun and cold as winter ever got" (p. 30). Beneath the familiar surface, a magical world lies, which can be glimpsed now and then. In a scene with a legendary lilt reminiscent of Eudora Welty's "The Wide Net" and anticipating the author's more mythical narrative, *A Generous Man,* Rosacoke almost forgets Wesley for an instant while she talks to animals, a "biggity" cardinal and "an old blacksnake" (pp. 29–30). Or "the wind . . . [brings] out two things to meet" Rosa (p. 91). Later the sight of a deer and his does will be almost miraculously vouchsafed to Rosa and Wesley, helping bridge temporarily the estrangement between them (p. 101). Nor is the beauty of nature only in the eyes of the beholder. Sometimes her gifts go unnoticed by the characters, though not unmentioned by the narrator:

> So both of them failed to notice the one thing that might have helped—rare as lightning in late December, a high white heron in the pond shallows, down for the night on its late way south, neck for a moment curved lovely as an axe handle to follow their passing, then thrust in water for the food it had lacked since morning. (p. 169)[18]

Kingdom of the unknown, the woods are not without their fearful denizens. Snakes lurk, though rarely seen (pp. 29, 35, 102). "Somewhere in here was a place named Snake's Mouth where all the snakes for miles got born" (p. 157), as Milo once told his little sister to keep her from wandering too far into the forest. Clearly some of the creatures that inhabit the woods are images of sexuality—the elusive snake, the mighty deer and the soaring hawk. The latter two are closely associated with Wesley, who is early compared to a deer (p. 21), and who indeed calls his lovemaking with Rosa "deer-hunting" (p. 137). Association with the hawk seems at first to be a matter of contiguity: Rosa sees a hawk as she hears Wesley's harmonica. But her reaction to the bird, "a killing bird," before she even perceives the connection with Wesley, sounds a muted, mythological note the overtones of which linger in the reader's mind:

> . . . but the hawk saw that and his fine-boned wings met under him in a thrust so long and slow that Rosacoke wondered if they wouldn't touch *her*—his wings—and her lips fell open to greet him, but he was leaving, taking the music with him and the wind. (p. 91)

Only at the end, however, do the sexual connotations of the hawk come out distinctly when the narration picks up this echo of the former scene: Rosa at the pageant suddenly sees Wesley's face "borne forward on a candle," and Leda-like

[h]er head rolled back and her lips fell open as if she would greet some killing
bird, but anybody watching . . . saw her suck one breath in pain. (p. 188)

This is not the place to analyse the symbolism of the wildness and the wild
creatures but whatever its symbolic function, nature is also and above all the
gathering spot of happenings, experiences, feelings which are linked directly
to Rosacoke's and the narrator's sense of life as something beautiful and yet
awe-inspiring, whose very beauty is terrifying. (So it is fitting that Rosacoke's
initiation, of which she makes so much more than a mere sexual encounter,
should take place in the enchanted broomstraw *ring*.) Nature opens up magic
vistas as instant as a deer's flight. Fixed in static images, the spring, the field,
the woods, the fictional space of the novel is yet always slightly shifting, sus-
ceptible of strange and wonderful dislocations, always suggestive, for all its
concreteness, of a somewhere else that would not be so much farther away,
"on the other side," as right here, behind the veil of appearances. *A Long and
Happy Life* does not explore the outside world in which its action is supposedly located: it discovers another world which can only be wondered at.

By contrast with what one may call the realm of the numinous, drabness
seems to stamp the churches: Delight, "wooden and bleached and square as a
gun shell box" (p. 5), Mount Moriah with its "gray paper hornets' nest" in
one window and its close "hot air" (pp. 11, 12) lack spaciousness and antiquity and mystic atmosphere. Yet modest and even unwelcoming as they may
look, they fulfill an important function. Neither private spaces, like the
houses, nor open ones, like the natural world, they are *meeting* houses where is
created a community of the faithful. Therein the individual can feel his true
place in relation to the others and to God. At the beginning of the novel a
detail, foreshadowing the conclusion and the ritual presentation of Frederick
Gupton by which Rosacoke will find renewal, shows how Aunt Mannie Mayfield stood "at age eighty and named the fathers of all her children, far as she
could recall" (p. 11), thus proudly testifying to her place in the chain of
humanity. There the great acts of human life—birth and death—are ritually
recorded and the major events of the Christian drama celebrated. In the
sacred loci human life is made significant, nay given a new dimension. Thus,
if the woods are for Rosacoke the area of meaningful encounters, the church is
the place where the full significance of such encounters is made clear and
becomes a guide for future action. In the outside world, Rosa could run from
her fears, her obligations, her self; inside Delight, "she couldn't,—couldn't
run." " 'I guess I can't run this time,' " she admits to herself (pp. 212, 211).
And yet this is the place where she will experience a sort of trance, in which
she becomes free from the limitations of space-time.

However confined, the church is not closed. On the level of the narration this is rendered through the superimposition of places mentioned above.
In Delight, practically *all* the locations of the story are made to reappear—

the woods, the spring, the broomstraw field, the Beavers' porch, Mr. Isaac's stale bedroom, Mary's kitchen, the near churchyard. Moreover, contrapuntally to this evocation of other locales, the preacher's words and the hymns keep referring to another country, another quest. " 'Now when Jesus was born in Bethlehem of Judaea in the days of Herod the King, behold, there came Wise Men from the East to Jerusalem, saying . . .' " (p. 183). While Rosacoke feels shut-in, is "seeing the far dark wall" (p. 182) of the room, the singers sing of a successful journey to welcome God and the outside world:

> *We three Kings of Orient are,*
> *Bearing gifts we traverse afar . . .*

> (p. 183)

The carols not only evoke the historically and geographically remote world of the Christian drama; they bring into contact two worlds, the earth where "the cattle are lowing" and an ineffable heaven where the singers long "to dwell with Thee there." They oppose life in the here-and-now with its "gathering gloom," life confining as the grave to which it leads

> *Sorrowing, sighing, bleeding, dying,*
> *Sealed in the stone-cold tomb*

> (p. 211)

and a radiant Hereafter, where objects seem to dissolve in infinity, where "*Darkness flies, all is light*" (p. 192). Moreover, the carols briefly suggest the relationship between the outside world and the inner room which must be made ready to welcome Christ:

> *Let every heart*
> *Prepare him room.*

> (p. 177)

They say that "visible and invisible two worlds meet in Man."[19]

Thus the concrete locus of the church, founded on the belief that there is *another* world, becomes the place where in every heart there can expand a dimensionless space, where every one is offered the boundless promise that negates the limitations of space-time. In the meeting-house, the embodiment in the *hic et nunc* of the timeless communion of the saints, two spaces, one physical and three-dimensional, the other spiritual and infinite, coexist in a dynamic relationship. Belief in the second creates and sanctifies the first, which in turn becomes the emblem of the second and makes the sacramental life possible. Mount Moriah calls forth Aunt Mannie Mayfield's testimony but her testifying and that of countless other witnesses, the presence of the living and of the dead in their sunken graves, endow the place with a meaning of its own. In the total economy of the novel, the dialectic of the two worlds is dramatized through the pattern of the action which opens in one sacred locus and ends in another. The physical action in the world between the two loci makes possible the revelation, in Delight, of a transcendent space which was only dimly apprehended in Mount Moriah, when the congregation sang "Precious Name, Show Me Thy Face" (p. 15). Similarly, the visions of the deer and the hawk in a natural setting must be completed by an epiphanic remembering or re-experiencing of them in a consecrated environment before the heroine knows her *place* in life.

Both the dynamic relationship of space and character and the "felt" quality of space are impressed on the reader's mind even as he lets himself across the spatial threshold of the novel.

> Just with his body and from inside like a snake, leaning that black motorcycle side to side, cutting in and out of the slow line of cars to get there first, staring due-north through goggles towards Mount Moriah and switching coon tails in everybody's face was Wesley Beavers, and laid against his back like sleep, spraddle-legged on the sheepskin seat behind him was Rosacoke Mustian who was maybe his girl and who had given up looking into the wind and trying to nod at every sad car in the line, and when he even speeded up and passed the truck (lent for the afternoon by Mr. Isaac Alston and driven by Sammy his man, hauling one pine box and one black boy dressed in all he could borrow, set up in a ladder-back chair with flowers banked round him and a foot on the box to steady it)—when he even passed that, Rosacoke said once into his back "Don't" and rested in humiliation, not thinking but with her hands on his hips for dear life and her white blouse blown out behind her like a banner in defeat. (p. 3)

Space is lived by the heroine as pure (or rather blasphemous) movement and it is presented kinetically ("*from inside like a snake, leaning that black motorcycle side to side, cutting in and out,*" "*speeded up,*" "*passed*"). "Riding like that [Rosacoke] didn't see the land" they went through. But the reader, for his part, is given a stereoscopic view. Perspective is provided by the narrator, who tells us about what Rosa does not see, which, nevertheless, is "there, waiting."

> The road passed a little way from the Mustians' porch, and if *you* came up their driveway and turned left, *you* would be at the Afton store and the paving soon, and that took *you* on to Warrenton where she worked. But they turned right today and the road narrowed as it went. . . . (p. 4—italics added)

The landscape is not sketched in as a mere piece of décor. What we discover is a working topography, seen in relation to a particular trip but also to the everyday activities of the characters, as we follow the protagonists on the road taken and on the road not taken, hanging for dear life, like Rosa, to a prose that is as dizzying, as powerful, as involved and suspenseful as Wesley's driving. In the introduction, we move in towards the center of the novel, with the same snaky and weaving agility as Wesley bearing down on Mount Moriah, regardless of traffic and of burial conventions. After such an opening, we expect—nor are we disappointed—that important as the places evoked are, their relationships and the progress that takes one from this to that are as significant. The characters are seen "on the road" and their journeys—Rosacoke's in particular, but Wesley's and Milo's as well—are important elements in the narration.

On many occasions, indeed, space is the distance between two points, or rather two people, Rosa and Wesley. This distance is expressive of Wesley's aloofness and Rosa's desire. "Désirer, c'est rendre apparent un intervalle," in the words of Georges Poulet.[20] Even when they are together, the protagonists do not seem to occupy quite the same location. At their first meeting he is spread-eagled up in the pecan tree while she picks up nuts, "thinking the whole time he would climb down and help her, but he stayed up there . . ." (p. 19). When she is attending Mildred's funeral service, he is outside, tinkering with his motorcycle before "vanishing in a roar and dust" (p. 23). During the picnic at Mason's Lake she remains on the shore as he shows off in the water; left alone, they face each other for the first time that day, across the small sheet of water (p. 55). On the day she goes to the Beavers' house and takes the decision to do what she can to "hold him there," she watches him from the dark shelter of the trees as he leans up on the porch (pp. 92–94). Yet towards the end of the novel their relative positions shift. When she tells him she is pregnant, he is "downhill from her and lower" (p. 168); after this, she feels free "as if her life was hers" and can afford to look back down at him from the steps of Delight (pp. 174–175); still later, during the pageant, Wesley will kneel to her with his make-believe gift of a butter dish (p. 188). The change of positions (and in particular the functioning of the polarity high/low) has therefore a psychological and thematic significance. From aspiration, "a longing for what is elevated or above one," Rosacoke has moved to acceptance of a boy she now knows to be ordinary, and of *solitude à deux*. However the pattern is not as solid nor the development of the theme as straight-lined as this brief summary might imply. For one thing, the shifts have been described here in their chronological order, whereas the reader is made acquainted with them through a narrative sequence that breaks up temporal succession. To be sure, our very first glimpse of Rosa is of her riding pillion *behind* Wesley but her first *stand* is when she decides to go into Mount Moriah, leaving behind a reluctant Wesley, and climbs up the steps to do her duty to Mildred. "She stopped at the top and looked back towards the road" (p. 9). The gesture illustrates both her independence from Wesley, when it is a question of what she feels "right," and her dependence on him. It initiates a first narrative sequence in which she fears Wesley has abandoned her and feels—wrongly as it turns out—that she is "free" from him (p. 34). This foreshadows the final sequence in which she rejects Wesley and the moment when she enters Delight to do her part in the pageant.

> She got to the steps and climbed and at the top, in the door, turned and not knowing why, not thinking, looked back the way she had come—to the car and the graves and her sorry father, then a little careful, still testing, to Wesley Beavers for the first time since Mr. Isaac's, looking down on him and thinking, the moment she met his eyes, "I am free." . . . (p. 174)

By then she is on the way to achieving a deeper liberation, and the linkage between the two situations, stressed by verbal echoes, underlines the distance she has come since the scene at Mount Moriah. At the same time, it suggests—together with her position "in the door," i.e. in an intermediate locus—that she has not yet made a definite stand, as in the first case, and that the situation may reverse.

In the second place, the reader's and the character's valuation of space may differ, thus modulating the use of locations. For instance, whereas at the end the reader has been made to feel that Rosa and Wesley have never been further apart, Rosa expresses to herself the change in their relations in terms of reduced space: "Now every thing was different. The distance between them—the space—was half what it was that evening. Now Wesley was flat on his feet with his arms pinned to his sides. His wrists had faded white and showed from the sleeves of his sailor jacket (he had grown some in the Navy), and his face was offered up towards her like a plate—with nothing on it she wanted, not any more" (p. 175). While the physical distance between them may actually be less, the indication also translates a subjective feeling of Rosa's. Having ceased to desire Wesley, she no longer is aware of the gap between them. The idol has turned back into a common boy who has outgrown his clothes. This illustrates Ralph Freedman's statement that "the novel always indicates distances between consciousness and objects which create space."[21] But a change in consciousness altering the perspective of the character obliges the reader to modify his, though not necessarily to adopt the character's. In this particular case, Wesley, off Rosa's pedestal (and off his motorcycle), appears as a gangling country youth, more vulnerable, therefore more appealing. The new view sends us back to the previous sequences to test our knowledge of Wesley. The need to collate loci and moments engages us in a spatial restructuring of the novel which is to some extent our own.

As for the movements of the characters, they can, of course, be described in terms of pursuit and flight. Rosacoke "trails" Wesley for the first half of the narration (and a great part of her young life) and flees from him for the third part—until she confronts him and the not-so-rosy future he promises in the final scene. But pursuit and flight take place in definite spaces which, in turn, may stamp action in a particular way. And in the kinetics of the novel, the different characters move on maps with a different scale, as it were.

Wesley, who is a "motorcycle man" (p. 3), travels far more widely over the territory of the novel than any other character. Whenever things get tense, he has the possibility of taking off, and, after the two seduction scenes, he very conveniently goes back to Norfolk.[22] (It must be said however that he sends "funny" postcards that may not answer Rosacoke's need [p. 22] but still evince a desire to keep in touch.) His ability to remove himself to faraway foreign scenes contributes to Rosacoke's wish to "hold him there." On the contrary, the heroine moves on a much smaller area but her movements are more closely scrutinized and therefore seem to acquire greater significance. Throughout *A Long and Happy Life* the girl appears driven to seek in motion an alleviation to her anxiety and fear of loss. Not that her rumblings are necessarily purposeless. Being what she is, Rosa often assigns small duties to herself: a trip to Mary to take a picture of Sledge (p. 85), a call on Wesley's mother (p. 90), a visit to the dying Mr. Isaac (p. 157). But however unselfish her intentions, many of her errands of kindness proceed from, or else turn into, the desire to run away from something. She goes to Mary's in order to forget about Wesley's flying back to Norfolk with Willie Duke, yet once there she soon is "running from Mildred's baby" (p. 90); she flees from Milo's grief on realizing her own burden (pp. 138–139); and when she sees Wesley again after she has given herself to him, she bolts (p. 166). Motion, however, can provide no comfort, because it can only lead from one location to another where Rosacoke will have to confront some face or other of her fear.

But the places which Rosacoke seeks play a part in her development. Even when she fails to come to terms with a reality fraught with so many terrifying mysteries, the mystery of masculinity, of sex, of the link between birth and death, she is compelled, by someone or something, to face it at least for a moment. For instance, Mary asks her:

> "What you so scared of crying for? He [Sledge] come here crying and he be crying when I ain't here to hush him. He got his right to cry, Miss Rosa, and why ain't you used to babies by now?" (p. 89)

Roughly but not unkindly, the woman states one of the facts of life and points out Rosacoke's basic fear of babies, which the heroine will only overcome when she says "yes" to Frederick Gupton in the Christmas pageant (p. 195). Or, when, on one of her night rambles, she meets Sammy and he remarks, " 'I thought you had a *good* hold' " of Wesley, the word *hold* ripples through Rosa's mind (p. 146). This is not truly a moment of insight, since Rosa will only understand later what is involved; yet she experiences then the shock of recognition (the word strikes her mind "dumb") that will make possible the self-perspective she achieves during the Christmas pageant, when many of her fragmentary insights will coalesce.

All the restless motion of the heroine culminates in the stasis of this pageant. While, in the cramped quarters of a country church, "start[ing] back in the Sunday school rooms" (p. 176), a little group of her relatives and neighbors reenact the history-making journey of the Magi bent on celebrating the advent of a new era, Rosacoke's own wanderings come to an end. In her enforced immobility, having renounced most of her former dreams, she finds the strength to "complete" her initial ethical gesture, to start on a new lap of her life-journey. In the religious space created by the Nativity ritual, Rosacoke first realizes that what she had looked on as giving "was like no kind of giving" (p. 179). Then naming, baptizing as it were, Frederick Gupton, she replaces him in the temporal chain of humanity, from the moment he was conceived in his parents' iron bed to his future, to "the ruins he would make and the lives," and she sees Frederick occupying the locus till then reserved to Wesley:

> "Wonder could he dream about that?" she thought, "—about growing up and someday (standing in a field or *up a pecan tree*) seeing a girl that he felt for and testing till he knew it was love and speaking his offer and taking her home and then one evening, making on her some child that would have his name and signs of him and the girl all in its face. . . . (p. 193—italics added)

The correlation between Frederick and Wesley is further enhanced by the use of the thematic configuration of face and name which, as I have shown elsewhere,[23] is frequently associated with Wesley and her love for him. More significantly, however, space here contracts to a locus—field or tree—only to expand indefinitely through time as this locus becomes emblematic of boy's encounter with girl, of human history in a nutshell. Acceptance of Wesley is tied to this new experience of space which has ceased to be motion as in the opening sentence to become time—and what eternity may reside in the mysterious continuity of the chain of love. The "yes" that goes beyond Frederick to Wesley, and in fact to Wesley through Frederick, this silent reverberating circular "yes" is Rosacoke's way of transcending her situation, together with the irreversibility of human time. Through the use of *place* is evinced the "aspiration au sacré" which Georges Mathoré supposes to lie at the root of much of the contemporary emphasis on space.[24] With this, not only a phase of Rosacoke's life, but the narration itself must have a stop. Extensiveness has been reduced to the fork of a pecan tree, extensionality opens out to include time and eternity—the exploration of space could proceed no further in those terms.

The "circle in the forest"[25] which Reynolds Price has cleared in *A Long and Happy Life* may still seem restricted to those readers who are more impressed by the miniature effect of the Price world than by its inner dynamics. It is in any case "territory seized from chaos," reclaimed into the order of form. Against the background of permanence that the countryside provides, the fragility of human hopes, the impermanence at the root of life can take on a new significance. Furthermore the "games" which the novelist has "staged" in his small fictional area are not private games: they turn the spectator into a participant. For the space created by language is to be investigated anew by each reader, metamorphosing into time and altering spacial relationships with each reading. And Reynolds Price, as he tells us, has "always written in the hope of altering, *literally causing movement in,* one or two of three possible things—myself, that person for whom I was writing, or the world at large (though I don't recall ever thinking of the world till a piece was done)."[26] Art may freeze time and motion but only in order to create a new space-time and release new motion in the aesthetic transcending of both permanence and impermanence.

Notes

1. "*A Long and Happy Life:* Fragments of Groundwork," *Virginia Quarterly Review,* 41 (1965), 242, 246.

2. When John Wain, for instance, writes that the novel "is 'Southern' in the sense in which we, the rest of the world, have long since come to understand the term," describing "a rural setting and rather consciously old-fashioned ways" with "a *faux-naïf* quality," he implicitly negates the larger scope of the book (*The New Republic,* May 14, 1966, p. 32). Conversely when Honor Tracy praises the novel for "its extraordinary timelessness," she suggests that it transcends its so-called "Southernness." "There is not a character here," she writes, "in whom we cannot believe, whom we do not seem in fact to have known somewhere" ("Happily Ever After," *New Leader,* August 6, 1962, pp. 21–22). For a scholarly study of the book, see Allen Shepherd, "Love (and Marriage) in *A Long and Happy Life,*" *Twentieth Century Literature,* 20 (1971), 242–248.

3. Reynolds Price himself was born in Warren County, North Carolina.

4. Quotations, identified in the text, refer to the Atheneum edition (New York, 1965).

5. *Times* (London) *Literary Supplement,* March 23, 1962, p. 197.

6. Eudora Welty, *Place in Fiction,* Northampton, Mass., n.d., p. 8.

7. Tracy, p. 21.

8. The concepts of extensiveness and extensionality have been defined by Eugene F. Timpe in his fine essay "The Spatial Dimension: a Stylistic Typology" (Joseph Strelka, ed., *Patterns of Literary Style,* Pennsylvania State University, 1971, pp. 179–197). They refer to actual and potential volume. "The first defines the actual sphere of action or existence. In a sense it means how big." The second "denotes not how big a space is but how big it can become" (p. 184).

9. "Space," "locale," "location," "locus" have here been used to denote in this order decreasing physical extension and increasing definiteness. "Location" has sometimes been preferred to connote the importance of the relative position of a place.

10. "Fragments of Groundwork," p. 244.

11. The distinction has been established by Volochinov, who has shown that "quoting speech" (*énoncé citant*), e.g. the narrator's discourse, and "quoted speech" (*énoncé cité*), e.g. a character's utterance or thought, can either be continuous or discontinuous, either interact or not. (See O. Ducrot and T. Todorov. *Dictionnaire Encyclopédique des Sciences du Langage,* Paris, 1973, p. 409.)

12. As quoted by Georges Mathoré in *L'Espace Humain,* Paris, 1962, p. 16.

13. In this sense, *A Long and Happy Life* belongs to the architectonic novel as defined by Sharon Spencer (*Space, Time and Structure in the Modern Novel* [New York, 1971]).

14. Quoted by Georges Poulet in *L'Espace Proustien,* Paris, 1963, p. 135.

15. One is of course reminded of the "frozen moment" in Faulkner's novels but the comparison cannot be pursued here. The inner tension of the passage—its core metaphor (*frozen in the graceful act*) suggesting grace, the supporting images evoking awkwardness of gesture, or stance (*blindman*) and defective sight (blind, *flat bitter* eyes)—make it a good example of the sour-sweet effects which this deceptively simple novel can achieve.

16. Gaston Bachelard, *La Poétique de l'Espace,* Paris, 1957.

17. "Leave the scene bare for the play of emotions," advocated Willa Cather ("The Novel Démeublé" in *Not Under Forty* [New York, 1936, p. 51]). Without going into a discussion of the use of material objects and settings in modern fiction, it should be noted that in its Japanese-like bareness, place in *A Long and Happy Life* is very unlike Faulkner's space, "un espace encombré, surchargé, proliférant" (André Bleikasten, "L'espace dans *Lumière d'Août,*" *Bulletin de la Faculté des Lettres de Strasbourg,* Décembre 1967, p. 406).

18. Allen Shepherd, in a stimulating essay which appeared after this article was completed, has shown that in *A Long and Happy Life,* although "natural phenomena display no care, comprehension, much less compassion," the heron might have helped "by offering, being, an image of sustaining natural beauty, a sign, by being received as a messenger" ("Notes on Nature in the Fiction of Reynolds Price," *Critique,* 15, No. 2 [1973], 85 and 86).

19. T. S. Eliot, Choruses from "The Rock," *Selected Poems,* London, 1962, p. 123.

20. Poulet, p. 61.

21. Ralph Freedman, "The Possibility of a Theory of the Novel," in Peter Demetz, ed., *The Disciplines of Criticism,* Yale, 1968, p. 73.

22. This may be, on a reduced scale, Price's version of the "turn[ing] on the poles of city and country" which he sees as typical of the great novels of the 19th and 20th centuries, whereas "the possibility of an entirely urban novel" is "a central dilemma" of contemporary fiction (Wallace Kaufman, "A Conversation with Reynolds Price," *Shenandoah,* 17 [Spring 1966], 18–19). To Price, "city life is, by definition in an age of potential nuclear destruction, impermanent" while the countryside "has at least the advantage for the artist of permanence. It can provide for him the objects of meditation, in the presence of which the literally human qualities of his life can be understood, calmed, controlled and shaped" (ibid., p. 19).

23. "Nom et Visage dans *A Long and Happy Life,*" *Recherches Anglaises et Américaines,* V, 1971.

24. Mathoré, p. 287.

25. For the context of the phrases quoted in the next sentences see the epigraph to this article, which is a citation from "A Conversation with Reynolds Price" (p. 18).

26. "Dodging Apples," *South Atlantic Quarterly,* 1971, pp. 1, 8.

Reynolds Price's *A Long and Happy Life*:
Style and the Dynamics of Power

GLORIA G. JONES

Although critics have identified several modern male writers as "feminine," most have been reluctant to define the term or explore its implications. In *Femininity and the Creative Imagination: A Study of Henry James, Robert Musil and Marcel Proust,* Lisa Appignanesi gives her distinction between masculine and feminine writers:

> The predominantly masculine writer has a tendency to see the importance of events in terms of the collective: he will externalise activity and judge it by collective, transpersonal standards. The predominantly feminine writer has a tendency to internalize activity. (23)

This internalizing could refer to "stream-of-consciousness" exploration rather than physical action to resolve conflict between characters, or the term could also mean that we should attend closely to the less obvious elements of style in interpreting "the importance of events." Consequently, we must rely on more than content or theme as the primary medium for revealing the social and cultural views about women, their placement in the hierarchy and the shifts of power in male/female relationships. Indisputably, content does illuminate these. But as Domna Stanton points out,

> women's oppression, or more precisely, our *repression,* does not merely exist in the concrete organization of economic, political, or social structures. It is embedded in the very foundations of the Logos, in the subtle *linguistic* and logical processes through which meaning is produced. (74; emphasis added)

To discover what "the subtle linguistic and logical processes" disclose, we need to narrow our focus and look specifically at all the elements of what we call style—imagery, alliteration, metaphor, diction, rhythm, and syntax—to determine how "feminine" writers "internalize activity," both in the consciousness of their heroines and in their own conscious and unconscious stylistic choices. To demonstrate how these elements support and mirror content

Reprinted, with permission, from *CEA Critic* 56.1 (Fall 1993): 77–85.

and how skillfully one male writer illuminates his female character's point of view, I will examine three passages from Reynolds Price's novel *A Long and Happy Life,* which centers around the changing relationship between a male and a female—a relationship that begins with a dominant male and a tentative, unsure female but culminates in equality.

The first passage is the opening paragraph of the novel:

> Just with his body and from inside like a snake, leaning that black motorcycle side to side, cutting in and out of the slow line of cars to get there first, staring due-north through goggles towards Mount Moriah and switching coon tails in everybody's face was Wesley Beavers, and laid against his back like sleep, spraddle-legged on the sheepskin seat behind him was Rosacoke Mustian who was maybe his girl and who had given up looking into the wind and trying to nod at every sad car in the line, and when he even speeded up and passed the truck (lent for the afternoon by Mr. Isaac Alston and driven by Sammy his man, hauling one pine box and one black boy dressed in all he could borrow, set up in a ladder-back chair with flowers banked round him and a foot on the box to steady it)—when he even passed that, Rosacoke said once into his back "Don't" and rested in humiliation, not thinking, but with her hands on his hips for dear life and her white blouse blown out behind her like a banner in defeat. (3)

Syntactically, the most obvious feature is that one sentence constitutes the whole paragraph. The phrases, varying in length, are strung together with commas, a single set of parentheses, and one dash. Most of the phrases that describe Wesley begin with present participles—"leaning," "cutting," "staring," "switching"—and are concrete, visual and physical. The only present participles used to describe Rosacoke are semantically negated—"thinking" by "not," and "looking" and "trying" by the idiomatic phrasal verb "given up," which implies a resigned abdication of the actions of "looking" and "trying." Using subordinate clauses to modify Rosacoke—"who was maybe his girl," "who had given up"—further portrays her as submissive, not in control on this ride. The only word she speaks, "Don't," is a plea, requesting cessation of Wesley's action but "said once into his back," not loud, not forcefully, and with no successful result. Even the verb for which Rosacoke is the subject—"was laid"—is passive in voice and meaning. And her vulnerability is underscored by the past participle "spraddle-legged," a phrase that, by itself, has sexual implications, implications intensified by the earlier use of "laid" and "sleep."

These two words are part of the first metaphor that characterizes Rosacoke—"laid against his back like sleep." There is physical closeness between these two characters, but emotional closeness is called into question, first by the "maybe" in "who was maybe his girl" and then by the phrase "rested in humiliation," containing one more verb emphasizing passivity. The words "sleep" and "against" set up a kind of dichotomy. In sleep, we are unconscious, not in complete control, and we lie *on* something, not against it.

So what we sense is an almost unwilled and unwilling pressing against Wesley's back, not by choice but by circumstance. Moreover, the circumstance is not joyful, as the final metaphor characterizing Rosacoke tells us—"her white blouse blown out behind her like a banner in defeat." This metaphor is straight out of a 1928 poem by Robinson Jeffers entitled "Hurt Hawks," which narrates the events leading to the death of an injured hawk. In it, the hawk's broken wing "trails like a banner in defeat." Whether Price's echo of this line is conscious and intentional, unconscious, or simply coincidental does not matter. Anyone who has read the poem would see the parallels between the injured hawk and Rosacoke. Neither is in control of events; both are at the mercy of someone else. And both depend on an outside agent for resolution. The hawk awaits intervention to end his life, and Rosacoke, "not thinking," places "her hands on his hips *for dear life*" (emphasis added).

Wesley is the one in control here, and this control is signaled in the initial phrases. The limiting word that begins the paragraph is not tentative in meaning like the "maybe" in "who was maybe his girl." "Just" defines and emphasizes the physicality of Wesley's movement—"Just with his body,"— and the metaphor that follows—"from inside like a snake"—is functionally bifurcated. It describes both the movement of Wesley's body and the movement of the motorcycle "cutting in and out of the slow line of cars." And the animal imagery introduced with "snake" continues with "switching coon tails" and even Wesley's last name, "Beavers."

The initial phrases also establish the rhythm of the paragraph, a rhythm sustained by the generative nature of the sentence. Phrases and clauses of varying lengths build upon each other, moving us forward. The alliteration in "sheepskin seat," "side to side," and "laid . . . like" accelerates the rhythm while that in "blouse," "blown," "behind," and "banner" slows it down. Both the syntax and the diction sustain the movement. We see the body leaning with the motorcycle, controlling and aiming it, but the vision is of the man and the machine as one—snake-like, smoothly going forward. And we go forward, searching for the name of this man described, but anonymous, for six lines. We anticipate a subject and verb, but we must hang on, along for the ride, until we get them. It is as if we are propelled toward our syntactic destination just as the motorcycle cuts "in and out of the slow line of cars to get there first." Even the visual interruption of the parenthetical information on the truck and its contents does not break the rhythm. It is sustained by the continued use of participles, both present and past—"lent," "driven," "hauling," "dressed," and "banked"—and is tied to the main passage by the repetition of "passed" in the phrases immediately preceding and following the parentheses—"when he speeded up and passed the truck" and "when he even passed that."

There is an intensity in this first paragraph that forces us to question what is going on between these two people. Wesley emerges as a dominant, physical, almost animal-like, controlling force; Rosacoke is submissive and tentative. And even though the point of view is technically third person, the perspective is Rosacoke's: She questions whether she is Wesley's girl; she is the humiliated one—the one who gives up. Rather than simply mirroring or supporting content, the syntax and attendant elements of style create and broaden our sense of Wesley's supremacy.

However, Wesley does not remain dominant throughout the novel. A second passage, from the middle of the novel, illustrates how Price conveys stylistically and linguistically the shifts in balance that begin to occur in the relationship:

> But Wesley didn't need any light. He started above her and even if the sun had poured all over him, she couldn't have seen the one thing she needed to see, which was down to where he was locked already at the center of what she had started, where he was maybe alone or, worse than that, keeping company in the dark with whatever pictures his mind threw up—of some other place he would rather be or some girl he knew that was better. But he didn't speak to tell her *where* he was. He only moved and even that was a way he never had moved in all the evenings she had known him—from inside the way he did everything but planned this time fine as any geared wheel, slow at first and smooth as your eyeball under the lid, no harder than rocking a chair and touching her only in that new place, but soon taking heart and oaring her as if he was nothing but the loveliest boat on earth and she was the sea that took him where he had to go, and then multiplying into what seemed a dozen boys swarming on her with that many hands and mouths and that many high little whines coming up to their lips that were nothing like words till the end when they came so close they broke out in one long "Yes," and what he had made, so careful, fell in like ruins on them both, and all she had left was her hands full of broomstraw and one boy again, dead-weight on her body, who whispered to her softer than ever, "I thank you, Mae" (which wasn't any part of her name) and not knowing what he had said, rolled off her and straightaway threw his flashlight on the sky. (104)

In doing close readings, we look for repetition of key words or phrases, perhaps used with variation, to signal that a change or shift is happening or will do so. In this passage, there is again reference to the way Wesley moves, once more "from inside the way he did everything." But there is a difference here. No longer is his movement instinctive and animalistic, "like a snake"; it is now planned and mechanistic, "fine as any geared wheel." And while the imagery in the first passage characterizes Wesley's motion with visual, physical verbs—"cutting" and "switching"—the imagery in this second passage is tactile, with the motion being metaphorically described as "smooth as your eyeball under the lid" and "no harder than rocking a chair." The "Just" in the first passage is replaced by another limiting word, "only," again setting boundaries on how.

The first sentence takes us back to an image in the first passage. Rosacoke, because of the speed and movement of the motorcycle, "had given up looking into the wind." Consequently, she cannot see. In this passage, Wesley's dominance is again revealed: "But Wesley didn't need any light." Rosacoke, however, "even if the sun had poured all over him, . . . couldn't have seen the one thing she needed to see." She is still without sight, and as a result, she is again dependent on Wesley.

Because the event being detailed is lovemaking, we expect the language of touch. And although the "geared wheel" metaphor is somewhat unusual, the participle "oaring" completely surprises us. Not only is this word seldom used as a verb, it is also outside the lexical field of sexual intercourse. Here, it is a transitive participle with "her" as its object. Once again, Rosacoke is not in control; Wesley is manning the oars. This nautical imagery continues but doesn't play out to a logical conclusion. Wesley becomes the "loveliest boat on earth and she . . . the sea that took him where he had to go." But again Wesley is the moving object, and Rosacoke is the substance on which he operates.

Also outside the lexical field of lovemaking are the next two participles used to describe Wesley's movement—"multiplying" and "swarming." The mathematical "multiplying" does not modify a stated noun or pronoun; it conveys the verbal image of a concept—the way Wesley moves—the sense that he (or his hands) becomes more than one: He "seemed a dozen boys." Wesley becomes plural; he is "swarming on her." But we note that even though the noun "boys" is masculine, it is not *adult* masculine, perhaps a hint of a change in dominance. The metaphorical use of "swarming" calls up visions of numerous bees, certainly more than a dozen, buzzing around Rosacoke, lighting and retreating and lighting again, making "that many high little whines," sounds that "were nothing like words." And throughout this, Rosacoke remains the recipient, not an active participant.

The use of these present participles contributes to our perception of Wesley as the dominant force in this passage. He is "touching," "taking," "oaring," "multiplying," "swarming." But the final participle describing Wesley is negated; "not knowing" is reminiscent of Rosacoke's "not thinking" in the first passage. For the first time in either passage, a negative modifier refers to Wesley, a signal that the tenuous balance in the relationship is about to shift. No longer is Wesley in control; Rosacoke has knowledge that he does not, and this knowledge precipitates the shift.

Until now, the negations have semantically reinforced Wesley's dominance. He "didn't need any light"; one in charge can function without it. He "didn't speak to tell her *where* he was"; "he only moved," subjugating her without words. "Knowing" is the first participle referring to Wesley that is nonphysical, signaling that he is not in control in the internal world. Using parentheses to set off what Rosacoke knows further isolates Wesley. It physically removes these words from Wesley and is to the reader like an aside to the audience of a play. We now know what Rosacoke knows and what Wesley either does not know or does not realize he has said. Unlike the first passage, in which the parenthetical information is an embellishment, purely description, these seven words—"(which wasn't any part of her name)"—are as important as any in the paragraph. And because he is not knowledgeable, Wesley can only continue to be physical, so he "*rolled* off her and straightaway *threw* his flashlight on the sky" (emphasis added).

His calling Rosacoke "Mae" sends us back in the paragraph to the phrase "where he was maybe alone," indicating the possibility that Rosacoke was not connected to the activity in *his* mind, that there was some girl "he knew that was better." But the "maybe" here recalls the use of the word in the first passage to question Rosacoke's relationship to Wesley—"who was maybe his girl." Its use here and the answers to the implied questions in both instances—Was she his girl? Was he alone?—force us to reassess what has preceded it in the text and to view what follows it in a different light. In a sense, we read both sequentially and recursively.

Unlike the first passage, which was only one sentence, this paragraph consists of four. But like the first paragraph, its syntax parallels in rhythm the event being narrated. The initial one-sentence paragraph is much like the motorcycle ride: It moves and weaves, imitating the action. This passage begins with a short sentence of only six words. The second sentence picks up speed, layering subordinate clauses within subordinate clauses and mimicking the complexity of Rosacoke's thoughts and emotions. The third sentence is shorter, only ten words. And then a single sentence, more than twice as long as the three preceding sentences combined, makes up the rest of the passage. This sentence builds rhythmically, relying on present participial phrases to sustain the movement—"rocking a chair," "touching her," "taking heart," "oaring her," "multiplying," and "swarming." It surges forward, intensifies with Wesley's "one long 'Yes,'" and then slows down, with no more present participles except the negated "knowing." All the other verb forms in the last part are either past tense or past participles—"had made," "fell in," "had left," "whispered," "wasn't," "had said," "rolled," and "threw." The movement of the sentence parallels the activity of sexual intercourse; it builds, reaches a pitch, and then slows down. Even the diction signals a change—"fell like ruins on them both." And for the first time Wesley is not moving and active; he is "dead-weight on her body." What begins as a passage with Wesley still physical and in control ends with him inert. And there is a significant shift in point of view. The first passage partially reveals Rosacoke's consciousness. This midnovel excerpt is completely from Rosacoke's perspective. Wesley surely would not describe himself as "multiplying" and "swarming," but Rosacoke's state of mind permits no tender descriptions of the lovemaking. The shift in dominance is subtle, stylistically hinted rather than blatantly stated.

The final passage I will examine is the next-to-last paragraph in the novel:

> She looked to Wesley. There was nowhere else to look. He was kneeling tall back of John Arthur Bobbitt with his face and his eyes on her, having offered his duty and with nothing to do but wait for her answer so he could plan his life, still not frowning but not glad, smiling no more than her father when he was a boy before he changed, in a tan photograph on a pier by the ocean with another boy blurred beside him. She stayed facing him. He held her like a chain. Then she drew one breath, hard, and said what she suddenly knew—to herself—what he had showed her, "Wesley knows me. After all Wesley knows me." And she knew that was her answer, for all it meant, the answer she would have to give when the pageant was over and Wesley drove her home and stopped in the yard and made his offer again—"Are we riding to Dillon tonight?"—because it was her duty, for all it would mean. (195)

Immediately, we notice that Wesley is no longer the dominant figure. The paragraph affirms the shift that began in the second passage. Both of the other paragraphs start with Wesley—the first with the power in his movement, the second with his visual acuity. But "She" (Rosacoke) is the first word here. And for the first time, she is able to see: "She looked to Wesley." Her looking is not negated syntactically or semantically, although it is qualified by the next sentence: "There was nowhere else to look." However, figuratively, the qualification expands rather than limits. While it could simply mean that Rosacoke's vision was blocked by other things, it could also reveal her coming to terms with their relationship. I favor the latter and believe the word choice in the first sentence encourages such an interpretation. After all, Rosacoke does not look "at Wesley"; she looks "to Wesley." Looking "at" is simply a viewing; looking "to" implies anticipation and hopeful expectancy. And "nowhere else to look" foreshadows her acceptance of Wesley as her future.

However, the most important revelation in this paragraph is Rosacoke's decisiveness, a decisiveness evidenced by the verbs used—"She looked," "She stayed," "She drew," "She knew." There are no more subordinate clauses describing her; there are awareness and determination. And the diction indicates a balance in the awareness: "She suddenly *knew* . . . Wesley *knows* me' " (emphasis added). Although the metaphor "He held her like a chain" sounds negative, it does not mean submissive bondage. The chain here goes in both directions, as Price's word selection illustrates, the syntax simulating a chain's circular interlacing of elements that can be connected at each end. In the third sentence, we find the phrase "having offered his duty." In the last lines, "offer" and "duty" are repeated again: "made his offer again" and "because it was her duty." Using "answer" twice in the seventh sentence echoes its use from the third. The words "for all it meant," referring to Rosacoke's "answer," are repeated as the final words in the paragraph, once more with reference to Rosacoke's "answer" but in the present tense with the modal "would"—a look to the future and bringing us right back to the first sentence—"She looked to Wesley."

The repetition of these words not only works syntactically to augment meaning but also contributes to establishing rhythm. The sentence length is more varied in this passage than in the other two. It begins with a sentence of only four words. The second sentence is only somewhat longer, with six words. The third is much longer, relying on participial phrases—"having offered," "still not frowning," "smiling no more"—to sustain the movement. Following this sentence are two like the first two—four words and six words each. A longer and then a shorter sentence come next, preparing us semantically for the revelation and resolution that unfold in the final and longest sentence in the passage, a sentence that ties together all the verbal threads that loop throughout the paragraph.

The repetition of key words and sentence patterns sets up a balance that parallels the equilibrium finally achieved in Rosacoke and Wesley's relationship. Rosacoke is no longer subordinate—syntactically, semantically, or actually. Price gives us hope that Wesley's dominance, revealed verbally in the first passage and continued and eventually undermined in the second, no longer exists.

When I chose these excerpts, I had no idea how interconnected and tightly woven they would turn out to be. I knew that I agreed with Constance Rooke's assessment that there is an "extraordinary density of images in this novel," and I concurred that certain "subtleties of theme . . . emerge from those image patterns" (36). I did not, however, imagine the elaborate tapestry that would materialize from weaving this imagery into syntactically protracted sentences that mirror, foretell, and underscore the events described in the text. Making the effort to penetrate Price's remarkable design, however, is rewarding. What is revealed is not just that meaning, character, and plot are illuminated by such an examination but also that the stylistic elements are an integral part of the text and serve as much more than embellishment. They are indeed the primary medium through which the delicate shifts in power between Wesley and Rosacoke are revealed. And Price subtly illuminates his female character's mind as Rosacoke moves from being subordinate and object to being independent and subject, both semantically and syntactically.

Works Cited

Appignanesi, Lisa. *Femininity and the Creative Imagination: A Study of Henry James, Robert Musil and Marcel Proust.* New York: Harper, 1973.

Jeffers, Robinson. "Hurt Hawks." *An Introduction to Literature.* Ed. William M. Chace and Peter Collier. New York: Harcourt, 1985. 402.

Price, Reynolds, *A Long and Happy Life.* New York: Antheneum, 1962.

Rooke, Constance. *Reynolds Price.* Boston: Twayne, 1983.

Stanton, Domna. "Language and Revolution: The Franco-American Dis-Connection." *The Future of Difference,* Ed. Hester Eisenstein and Alice Dardine. New Brunswick: Rutgers UP, 1988. 73–87.

Price's *Love and Work*:
Discovering the "Perfect Story"

GARY M. CIUBA

The good hearts of Reynolds Price's novels live by stories. By day his narrators offer stories to listeners as nourishment, admonition, and entertainment, while at night they continue to create fictions in their own dreams. They read tales in letters and diaries and, like the resilient Kate Vaiden, may even record family history to trace the design of a life's masterplot. Although Price has celebrated this vital passion for narrative as typically Southern (*Common Room* 168), he also hears in his regional tradition the telling sign of a universal hunger. In "A Single Meaning," his preface to translations from Jewish and Christian Scripture, he explains that the "root of story sprang from need— need for companionship and consolation by a creature as vulnerable, four million years ago and now, as any protozoan in a warm brown swamp" (*Common Room* 249). As Price listens to the story of all stories in Genesis, Adam first speaks not to assert his authority over beasts and birds but to search for an end to his aloneness, to find the fit helpmate that he lacks.

The descendants of Adam and Eve continue to yearn for such solace. Price speculates that primitive men and women told stories as a way of opposing the chaos around them. By revealing patterns in nature—phases of the moon, cycles of growth, alternations of seasons—such protonarratives eased the daily struggle to survive through acknowledging predictable sequences around which a stable, understandable life could be built. Once apparently random happenings now became part of a grander plot unfolding in time. As questions about what-happened-when inspired conjectures about why it happened at all, chronology led backwards to etiology and theology, to the venerable tales of myths. Since Adam, the first narrator, Price's storytelling humanity seeks "credible news that our lives proceed in order toward a pattern which, if tragic here and now, is ultimately pleasing in the mind of a good who sees a totality and *at last* enacts His will. We crave nothing less than perfect story" (*Common Room* 249).

Having found his greatest satisfaction in the narratives of the Old and New Testaments, Price has sought to intimate the story *par excellence* in his

Reprinted, with permission, form *Renascence* 44.1 (Fall 1991): 45–60.

own fiction. (See Sadler's essays which survey how ordinary events and commonplace objects become almost supernatural emblems in Price's life and writing.) In *A Long and Happy Life* (1962), Rosacoke Mustian honors the numinous radiance of creation and at the end witnesses that holiness become incarnate love as she plays the Madonna in the Christmas pageant staged at Delight Baptist Church.[1] While her brother Milo pursues a mythical quest for the python Death in *A Generous Man* (1966), the adolescent Adam falls and rises as he learns about what selfless gifts will outlast an already menacing mortality. Price's early pastoral romances not only look for the glimpses of cosmic design that he has long admired in the comedy of Eudora Welty, but also listen for echoes of the divine narrative in which his Warren County farmfolk are the consummate characters. *Love and Work* (1968), Price's partly autobiographical third novel, is his most searching examination of the role that he has continued to pursue in his latest work of fiction, *Tongues of Angels* (1990), and in his recent memoirs, *Clear Pictures* (1989): the artist as a witness to sacred story.[2] While never quite cultivating the self-reflective gamesmanship that its author dislikes in much metafiction, *Love and Work* recounts the exhaustion caused when both life and literature are severed from what Price respects as the ultimate narrative. Thomas Eborn, novelist *manqué* as well as failed husband and frustrated son, is a storyteller who does not know the entire story. As Ida Nolan, his mother's Irish Catholic friend, criticizes his incomplete fiction in the prologue to her own seemingly incredible tale, "There's another story—or there's more to yours" (143). *Love and Work* tells how Eborn learns but cannot yet live out Price's "perfect story."

The story that Eborn knows throughout most of *Love and Work* recites an almost fatalistic tale of the end: the decay of the flesh, the demise of love, the supremacy of death. Eborn's grim elegy repeats an outcry that Price hears as well in Scripture. While classifying the various types of stories in the Old and New Testaments, Price notices that in opposition to their consoling message is another claim voiced in sermon and poetry: "*I am here alone, there is no one beyond me, I will soon dissolve.*" The preacher in Ecclesiastes sees the death of the righteous; the psalmist imagines dead who "have gone down to silence" and do not praise God (*Common Room* 256). Eborn reads this lament most starkly in the diary from 1955 that he discovers at his mother's house on the day of her death. Lou Eborn's red-leather journal relates the baffled defeat of her husband's last month alive. Although Tom's near-blind mother usually read herself to sleep with popular periodicals and devotional tracts, Eborn admires her surprising literary skill in chronicling how her cancerous husband literally went "down to silence": initial inconclusive tests, bronchoscopy, surgery, tracheotomy. As a novelist he commends the skeletal efficiency of her prose and the deft shift from past to present tense as she sensed fate daily overtaking her. But his mother's artistry only makes more evident both the morbid truth and the apparent lies which Tom discovers in her narrative. Since Lou kept the diary from that first Sunday in January when her exhausted husband became unwell after shovelling snow, she seems to have foreseen "in the first small sign, the sprawled hideous rapid death" (23). Already schooled in loss as an orphan, Tom's prescient mother sensed the same encroaching dissolution that now haunts her son. The terse eloquence of her calendar entries preserves for Eborn the only story: death may begin in any instant; every moment is mortal.

Although Lou's diary in form and content makes a literary record out of ravaging temporality, her novelist-son faults the fraudulent love behind such a primitive work of art. He objects most fiercely to the selfish sentimentality in his mother's final line on February 20: "*No one will ever know what it did for me when I saw him breathe his last at 8:21 pm*" (25). Since Eborn ordered his mother out of the hospital room at his father's death, he protests, "Did for *her?* It had not *been* for her. He had not been hers. She had not *seen* the last breath" (25). Lou's understated grief for the husband who was her one goal and gift rejects precisely the claim that "*I am here alone, there is no one beyond me.*" But embracing such isolation, her son vows that henceforth everyone whom he knows must die alone. The solitary Eborn understands love not as spiritual identification but only as the proprietary passion declared again in a 1928 letter from his father, which he finds beside his mother's equally avaricious diary: "*Can't we ever understand that you are mine, I am yours?*" Tom rages against that ownership as "The fatal error of their lives (his parents), fatal error of Western Man! . . . No one was anyone else's, ever" (27). Yet in denying this essential connection Eborn denies the sole defense against the death recounted in his mother's journal. As he discovers at the end of the novel, not only did his parents live out the hated genitive of possession, but they also belong solely and supremely to each other, forever.

Tom hears his parents' story of inevitable disaster resonating throughout the entire novel. When the telephone rings, on the first page, he suspects that it announces bad news. Earlier that morning Eborn was disturbed by an ominous dream about being separated from his injured friends after a car crash. And later that afternoon he dreams of a domestic day of the locust as a horde of maggoty invaders swarms over his yard and front steps. Tom frequently speculates as he leaves his house whether stored combustibles or an electrical malfunction might not blaze out in his absence. Or he wonders whether his wife will be killed when she goes shopping. When his first dream seems to have come partly true, Eborn stops to help the dying victim of a car accident and dreads that he may have caused the calamity by somehow willing it. After returning to his darkened house, he fears that Jane has committed suicide or been murdered. If his father's death could begin merely with tiredness after shovelling snow, then no moment ever rests in sure safety but may conceal an ambush, open out onto loss.

Eborn turns from such apocalyptic presentiments to his writing as his single refuge from the threatening waste and wreckage. As he drafts an essay on work itself for his college magazine, the professor and author recognizes the story that should inform the creation of all of his stories. Alluding to the second chapter of Genesis, he suggests that the *"only abstract reason for working may in fact be that a God exists who created man and set man to work to glorify His creation. . . . If a man does not acknowledge such a God—and his own duties to God—then perhaps he is a fool to work"* (7–8). Adam's stewardship in Eden should teach the novelist, who has not yet planted the fence of climbing roses that he had intended, that all of his toil is only the praise owed God through caring for his particular plot of the world. Ardor alone compels humanity to undertake that which is arduous as a joyous debt to creation and its Creator. As Price's own title indicates, what Tom regards as the polarities of his life are not really disjunctive. Rather, work must be performed out of love, and love must be nurtured by daily work. Yet if Eborn seems to honor the God who worked six days in making the world by his words, the author foolishly takes Hitler's motto for the concentration camps rather than the sacred story from Genesis as the rationale for his own literary creation: "Work Makes Free." Work frees him not just from bodily needs but also from loving those whom he will lose in death. Ultimately, it delivers Eborn from his own flaws because the devotion to his craft exacts the highest degree of physical and artistic performance. In this aesthetic version of salvation by his own good work, Tom's writing frees him *"for the attempt to understand, if not control, disorder in the world and in those I love"* (40). His fiction may even enable him to create some alternative and orderly cosmos that at least will last as long as he does. But while glorifying his work as a sanctuary from certain devastation, Eborn excludes from his own stories the very passion that inspired his mother's diary. Jane detects this central lack of love when she reads her husband's artistic apologia. His writing is too self-enclosed; its end is only the narcissistic Thomas Eborn. Whereas his essay exalts the artificer who labors by and in behalf of himself, Jane affirms the travail done with and for another: "Tom, we are my work" (52). Citing her domestic duties as janitor, cook, and housekeeper, Tom's wife undertakes works of love that go beyond all of his vaunted love of self-serving work.

Even the workaholic Eborn senses his own radical imperfection. Feeling an enormous vacuum around his own chilled heart, he returns to his mother's house to search through her checkbook, bills, and policies for some clue to the message which Lou had wished to tell him on the day that she had died. When he had refused to answer her call because he was working, his mother simply instructed Jane, "Tell Tom to phone me when he's free. I'll tell him something" (12). Eborn later asked both Ida and Lou's sister about this cryptic revelation, but neither claimed to know his mother's secret. Price thus builds Eborn's own incompleteness into the mystery of his plot. As in *A Generous Man,* his seekers live in ignorance of what only some final, wonder-filled story will reveal as a transcendent resolution.[3] However, Tom finds no answer in his mother's accounts, merely "all her meaningless incompletions, the only unfinished business of a life which had surely finished twelve years before" (57), the terminal insignificance of a wife who had really died along with her husband. Eborn tries to purge his family of such dissolution by ceremonially burning all of Lou's long-treasured papers. He leaves his mother's house purified, "aimed for his work," and on the drive home he seems to glimpse the perfect story (60).

Although Eborn usually creates in agony and celebration, he achieves the supernal calm and clarity that he had often admired in Greek metaphysicians for whom "the slim probe of reason could consciously pierce its way to order, completion" (61). He beholds with such rare certitude the entire center of the novel which he had already started that the fluid progression of scenes seems to "guarantee final light, comprehension, truth" (61). Inspired by Jane's cousin who had committed suicide, he imagines a novel truer even than life. At her funeral Tom objected, "This is not the ending. What if she had lived? Make her live. Live with her" (62). He now plans to tell the story of a woman saved from suicide by a husband who gives her this new will to live. Eborn is at last beginning to see beyond the end that had dominated his imagination, and so he discovers new possibilities for his previously foiled creativity. If the husband in a moribund marriage can become the Orphic artist, he may work against death by using fiction to preserve life. Yet Tom's inspiration is an arrogant delusion for such an ungenerous man. Eborn never actually writes this novel about marital resurrection because his rancor as Jane's spouse denies him the felt life of an animating heart.

Price exposes Eborn's fantasy as a savior in fiction by the car accident that the novelist witnesses while envisioning his perfect story. Although he tries to help the police officer extricate the vaguely familiar youth from the wreck, Eborn fears that his delay in responding may have caused the young man's death. He can save neither in art nor in actuality if he does not work out of immediate love. But his futile effort at least dispels his fictional pretensions to a romance which is far easier to live out in his imagination than in his own marriage. And his failure returns the writer to the more onerous world of attachments and responsibilities, which he thought he had burned so decisively earlier that afternoon. As he drives home under a vulture-filled sky, he can no longer dream of his ideal narrative remote from time and death, for the egotist is obsessed with the omnipresent threat of his own destruction. Everything that he sees may be a "possible site of his imminent death, his hundred-and-sixty pound contribution to the daily meat-take of summer roads" (70). Unlike the tubercular Keats whom he admired for his ability "to do one's work above the pink froth of dissolving lungs," Eborn must write out of his very affinity with, but not absorption in, dying life (47).

Eborn discovers a way to understand the role of story in his own waste-filled life through Homer's story about Odysseus' meeting with his mother in the underworld. Haunted by the car accident, Tom comes to see the youth's self-destruction as an emblem for how Eborn himself deliberately devastated his whole family by burning his mother's papers. "Perhaps I've destroyed what cannot regrow; hacked all of us—Father, Mother, me and therefore Jane—loose from our only tether, the past; our proofs as a constant need and use for love, however less strong, less lasting than our skins the love must be" (76). The adrift artist needs to reconnect himself to the severed bonds of family history. If he still does not recognize how love may outlast time, he does understand how the remembered ties of the past validate love. The instructions of Circe and Tiresias teach the novelist how to rediscover these fundamental ligatures. Lou Eborn's son recalls that when Odysseus offered his mother's ghost the blood of a sheep, she revealed news about his grieving family in Ithaca. Tom senses that the hovering shades of his past require his own heart's libation and hopes that in return for such tribute they will offer "their knowledge, plan for our future, hold on our present, which they easily steer" (77). Eborn rejects his earlier nihilistic view of the past as a record of ineluctable ruin. Instead, he comes to see family spirits not just as the pitiful and vanquished dead but as possible guides to his own destiny. The novelist realizes how he can learn this news, perhaps the secret which his mother took to her grave, after reading a friend's gracious poetic tribute to Lou Eborn. The elegy recalls such hardy examples of her love that it exposes the earlier romanticized novel which Tom planned purely in his mind, making him feel "condemned in his own baroque retreat, his filigree shields that had shattered at a touch" (81). Yet Eborn objects that the poem has not remembered the whole truth of his mother's life. And so he resolves to tell the complete story. He will recover the lives which he destroyed that afternoon in the fire and will return to the very origins of his own life by imaginatively recreating his parents' past. Offering the dead his services as a storyteller, Eborn hopes that in exchange for his vitalizing blood as an artist, the ghosts may speak through him the news that he needs.

Eborn's novel raises the dead. In three days Tom writes an account of how Louise Attwater and Todd Eborn first met at an iceskating party in February 1923. Although inspired by only a few facts and a picture of his parents from 1928, Eborn works "as if transcribing, not inventing at all" (83). The novel is the quickening medium for the return of their spirit-filled flesh. Lou and Todd appear not as shadowy revenants from a classical nether world but as the vibrant hearts and bodies of forty years ago. They seem especially lively because Tom's narrative uses the historical present to make their meeting now happen once again. But the tense of his verbs also locates in time a truth that Eborn will later discover as more profound and poignant than the vividness of any writer's technique: the dead indeed do live in their love.

Although Tom's fictional recollection celebrates the vivacity of the love that drew his parents together, it also foresees the tide of loss that would later overwhelm them. Since both Lou and Todd have borne the pain that Eborn finds so unbearable, they play the whole scene on the edge of heartbreak.

After her father's death the orphaned Lou resolved that *"no man will hurt her again, pierce deep enough again"* (88). Rather than be so vulnerable, the disheartened daughter feels a *"need and readiness for ruin"* that will make her glad when she is dust (103). And when she finally steels herself to risk loving the playful young man who has just returned from buying illegal liquor, Todd pretends that he has been shot in the snow by the bootlegger's daughter. Lou sees the story of her lifelong abandonment, *"Lost . . . They all fly from me"* (104). Already becoming the alcoholic who would cause such hardship to Tom's mother, young Todd drinks to flee his own inescapable pain. His ache is the same compulsion later felt by his son—duty to the people that he must love, especially to his mother. Eborn ends this first scene with a moment that embraces the frustration of his parents' next thirty years together. When Todd pursues Lou toward the woods, she withdraws her hand but holds her eyes on his face and acknowledges, *"Everybody's caught"* (104). The restless bondsman is once more captured at heart, and the perpetual orphan again dares to love a man who will hurt and leave her.

Eborn has imagined the sorrowful ends of his parents' inextricable lives as implicit in their very beginnings. Yet in re-creating the single moment that contains their whole future, he also rediscovers the primal love with which he had lost all connection. Like Rosacoke and Wesley in *A Long and Happy Life,* Lou and Todd move toward each other by some kind of magnetic inclination. Eborn shows the motions of their ebullient love by choreographing their entire first meeting as a duet of turnings and followings, leanings toward and hearkenings after. They seem drawn together by forces of nature, fundamental laws of physics, that culminate when Todd catches Lou and then trails after her. Eborn's art has caught his parents for all time in their permanent and exclusive mutuality as they fix themselves upon each other.

In writing the first scenes of his parents' life together, Eborn reclaims a larger part of the story than he had ever previously intuited. This new comprehension makes his initial chapter already seem part of a greater artistic unity. When Tom begins their story, he feels no dread at "a finish delayed years from now" (83); and after he ends, he foresees other scenes—the Depression, his father's alcoholism, his conception and birth—extending before him. The dutiful son has given of himself to the past and so been gifted in return with an appreciation of how his parents loved in the face of ultimate loss. He now sees beyond his essay's earlier justification of work as the sole defense against death. Eborn admits that Jane's critique of his essay made him realize that he had wrongly diminished his mother's and his wife's lives as well as his own marriage: "There were pure kinds of work that involved no products so were hardest of all, being fueled by nothing more visible than love. These scenes will be a chart of one kind, a work of love which will find exactly that—that love can be work" (110). Yet if Tom's novel begins with the kind of passionate quandaries that have repeatedly fascinated Price in his own novels, Eborn's subtle text finally fails in the context of his creator's more comprehensive fiction. Although his work-in-progress is a love story, Eborn is still not willing to perform that invisible labor which his tribute to his parents recalls. After crafting the opening chapter in virtual seclusion for three days, he immediately calls his friend Ted to be the first to hear his work rather than waiting a few minutes for Jane's return from work and grocery shopping. When his wearied and resentful wife finally does read his manuscript, she dismisses it as "easy lies" (111). Jane judges its moral rather than literary value. Her husband's story is facile and false because it was written by a hypocrite. So great is the division between his love and his art that even while loathing his wife, he plans to write the second scene tomorrow, *They Love*. Since Eborn has refused to bear the very responsibilities that his parents accepted, he cannot deny the truth of his wife's criticism. Suddenly, his work to raise the dead seems dead itself.

Eborn has long fancied that his writing was an essentially religious discipline. For twelve years it has seemed to offer "an unhurried steady attention to mystery (whether threatening or buoying)" (120). Eborn imagines his work much as Price describes Faulkner's awestruck art in an essay on *Pylon*, "the icon which both portrays and worships the unseen god" (*Common Room* 30). If Tom had not achieved "*comprehension*," the novelist consoles himself that he had performed a "*celebration* at least, a seemly dance round the shrouded god or as firm a wall as man could build to hold off madness, idleness, loss" (120). But when Eborn receives a phone call from Ida Nolan telling him that she has seen a mysterious light and an open door in his mother's house, the news challenges the soundness of his reverently constructed house of fiction. As the novelist explores the family home that has been violated, he recognizes that his work has neither paid hierophantic tribute to the hidden realities at the heart of life nor erected a barbican to oppose the chaos outside his art. Rather, the trespassers confirm his belief that the core of life is rampaging loss and prove that the artist can create no bulwark against the inexorable destruction. Eborn, therefore, dismisses his work with Jane's verdict of "easy lies," but for the wrong reason. He does not recognize his failure to love but only the failure of love itself. Tom feels that his fiction has repeated the delusion taught him by his parents "that love is possible, however scarce; that the aim of life, the end of human effort, is the comprehension, loyalty, generosity which come at last (the light in the circle) to the few who can try" (120). Whereas Lou and Todd at least worked at preserving what they never recognized as a lie, Eborn rejects both his life and art as deceptive artifice. The novelist sees through the romance that he has been recounting for the last three days to the pure end of nothingness. And so the disillusioned worker longs for the eternal repose that Michael Kreyling has shown as an Augustinian ideal, attractive but finally inadequate, in much of Price's own unquiet fiction ("Motion and Rest" 856–857). Eborn simply wants to stop, "never to move; to finish here, now" rather than face the steady depletion that has taken his parents and now claims their home (121).

Eborn seems to discover justification for such closure in the one token left by the housebreakers. Although the intruders have not stolen any family possessions, a police officer discovers a single "sign" of their desecration in a dry turd neatly left in a dark corner of the breakfast room (131). Tom immediately understands its significance for him alone. "Personal," he thinks, recalling the same word that Jane used when she announced long-distance phone calls from his mother and Ida (12, 112). This ominous summons always seemed to herald some message, and only minutes before, Eborn had been scrutinizing his mother's picture for some sign of this revelation, the news that she promised to tell him on the day of her death. When Eborn sees the excrement, he understands its climactic import in a life that rushes to its close in an affronting void. "Of course it's the last of the last straws," he concludes, "a high-school notion of the symbol for *finished*—signed and sealed" (132). The novelist reads an eschatological truth in the scatological sign. The excrement makes offensively palpable the sad waste to which all human existence eventually comes, an inevitable and undignified terminus more powerful than either love or work. Like Eliot's visionary speaker in "East Coker," Eborn despairs that the end of life is "dung and death" (183).

As a listener to and teller of stories, Price cannot accept such a dispiriting finale. In discussing how Scripture confirms and comforts its hearers, Price decides that "Only the story which declares our total incurable abandonment is repugnant and will not be heard for long" (*Common Room* 256). *Love and Work* seriously considers such dereliction but rejects it as absolute and irremediable. If the excrement seems to validate Eborn's vision of futility, both Jane and Ida point beyond this repugnant end toward a surprising continuation and a more complete story. When Eborn looks away from the "sign" which the officers discovered, he searches Jane for "a sign from her at least—regret, tears even, or the taut flush of triumph." As she cries, he sees a possible answer to the empty finality, "Their single chance, single guarantee, of continuation" (132). Earlier Jane had been unsure whether she could remain married to a husband who yearned for only utter cessation. But her tears come like a revelation—"There they were" (132)—proof of her willingness to continue in spite of what appears so radically conclusive. Beginning to clean up the excrement, she works in and at love, but unlike Tom, never for self-gratification or the saving sake of the work itself. When her husband recognizes his own responsibility and asks her to stop, Jane hesitates and then foregoes what could easily lead to the spiteful pleasure of wifely martyrdom. She decides not to turn on him or leave but to sort dishes as he has asked. Like the pregnant woman who witnesses the car accident, Jane bears her burden and helps to her limit. Her constancy finds its strength in a love that may even outlast what seems like the end.

Ida Nolan tells an even more joyous version of the same denouement. "This is not a short story. You could tell it better, Tom—really beautifully," his mother's old friend apologizes for her homespun eloquence (139). As an unskilled artist she cannot construct the "filigree shields" that Eborn has designed as his own life's work (81). Rather, Ida speaks as a fellow author only because she instructs with a transcendent authority, "but it's God's plain truth. I'm the one alive that knows it, so it looks like it's me that's been picked out to tell you. You may not believe me—I tried to escape it" (139). This Irish Catholic woman, whom Tom has always found slightly silly, tells her story for some of the same reasons that Tom himself uses to justify his art. Just as Tom writes because it is *"my gift (forced on me by birth and growth)"* (40), so Ida bears her good news only after she first tried not to come to the house that had been so strangely entered. And like Tom's own supposedly iconographic art, her startling report testifies to a mystery that belies his pessimistic materialism: Ida announces that Tom's parents have visited their home tonight. Tom finds her claim so absurd that he can only fancy Todd and Lou haunting the shabby house as paunchy and wobbly versions of the ghosts from *Wuthering Heights,* "Heathcliff and Cathy wheezing and varicose, hemorrhoidal, dry; dead too late!" (143). Since spirits live in the mansions of perfervid imaginations, not in squat, red-brick two-stories, the novelist opposes this grotesquely comic reverie with his blunter rendition of the truth, the emptied story of ultimate endings by which he lives. He informs Ida that "nothing was stolen; but something was left—in plain shanty-Irish, a coil of shit on this breakfast room floor. As human as that. End of story. Sorry" (143).

Shaking her head and smiling, Ida narrates a romance that challenges Eborn's biological reductionism. She uses the genre of fabulation which most explicitly contradicts his naturalism, which is defiantly fabulous: she tells a ghost story. "Not ended, Tom. Your Mom and Dad *win.* There's another story—or there's more to yours" (143). Ida reveals the secret that Lou confided to her friend and meant to share with her son on the day of her death. After Tom's mother woke the night before from her customary late evening nap in front of the television, she saw Todd Eborn once again sitting in his usual chair. Lou's account of this visitation is so credible because of its absolute naturalness. Totally unafraid, she saw no Gothic ghost but her very ordinary husband. She even left him to walk calmly to the bathroom, where she thought that he needed a haircut.[4] Price's very prosaic apparition lacks the supernatural aura of Brontë's hauntings or the pathetic farce of Eborn's own fantasy because Todd's return after death so perfectly accords with these two lives that have been so long joined at heart. Lou's tale answers the threnody that Price sometimes hears in the Bible, *"I am here alone, there is no one beyond me, I will soon dissolve,"* by affirming a continuity between the seen and unseen world, a community of the living and the dead in perduring love. Sensing the sacredness of Lou's story, Ida felt like blessing herself or genuflecting. However, she contented herself with telling her friend what Lou already acknowledged: the vision was a message from God. Although Tom completely believes his mother's report, he does not at first understand it. At best the tale seems a "corporal summons from a standard night to the sill of death," a proleptic image of Lou's own mortality (146). But Ida points out what Eborn himself sees in the novel's amazing climax. Tom's parents still possess the house in their love.

Price uses the end of his novel as a criticism of Eborn's vision of endings. "We cannot, of course, be denied an end," Frank Kermode concedes in *The Sense of an Ending;* "it is one of the great charms of books that they have to end." However, ". . . we do not ask that they progress towards that end precisely as we have been given to believe. In fact we should expect only the most trivial work to conform to pre-existent types" (23–24). Eborn's "sense of an ending" is as banal and predictable as the excrement which for him typifies the end of human life. But Price stages a much more revealing peripeteia that works precisely in the way that Kermode describes such reversals. By "upsetting the ordinary balance of our naive expectations," it succeeds in "finding something out for us, something *real*" (18). Eborn's surprising vision of his parents' ghosts confirms that he has been wrong about the end of the story. Their presence both inspires and accuses, validates his work but exposes his failures in love. Lou and Todd first appear like Greek shades—murky, somewhat shameful figures who seem to verify the artistry of their son's recent attempt at fiction. The novelist's words have come back to haunt him. He senses that their secret message corroborates "What he'd already known— the hungry dead—and worked to help. So his work, his *knowledge,* was true, not lies. That at least could continue" (147). Whereas his writing had once seemed at an end, the specters sanction his fictional raising of the dead as a son's offering to placate his parents.

Eborn's vision finally takes him beyond such self-congratulatory vindications of his craft. As the room is filled with the same strokes that pressed down on Eborn when he tried to rest on the day of his mother's death, the sanguine novelist beholds the luminous center of Price's cordate world. "Filling with what?" the visionary wonders. "Light. Theirs. There, pumping from them like arterial blood till they showed quite clearly, in their perfect youth, years before his birth" (147). When Ida first told him about Todd's return, Tom wondered whether his father appeared as the winning youth whom his mother first met or the wracked victim at the end of her diary. As he gazes into the sustaining rhythm of their lives, the systole and diastole of the heart, Eborn beholds them virtually reborn as the vital figures summoned in his story. Unlike the sexual pumping which Eborn had worked at when he feigned orgasm while making love to Jane, this pulsing light throbs with the unstinting, engendering love of a lifetime. The childless Tom feels in his flesh the creative passion which generated his own being and his parents' unending partnership. Eborn notices that "they did not smile. Nor look at him. They do not move! He sees that, always from the first, they have faced one another only, static in ecstasy, sealed in their needlessness, one another's goal—won at last and for good. Oh won at the start—gift not reward" (147). Like Lou's diary which shifted from past to present tense, Price's narrative here deftly embraces all the time in the lives of Tom's parents to dramatize the immortality of mutually generous hearts. What Eborn imagined in the first scene of his novel is the eternal truth of his parents' love. Turned away from their son and toward each other, they lived in exclusive attention and attachment. And the complete story is that they still do, dwelling in utter reciprocity beyond death. In this everlasting exchange, he is hers, and she is his. The possessive pronoun so hateful to Eborn does not indicate ownership but the inseparable union of his parents who, linked by a copulative verb, found their fondest ends in each other. Lou and Todd have not been so much caught in their love as their son's novel suggested; rather, as perpetual gifts, they pour forth forever their common self-donation. They continue after death as they did from their first meeting that Eborn has envisioned, vibrantly in tandem. Their son smiles "to be their one product, their hope, the agent now of their rehabilitation" (147). Yet if the author whom they produced now prides himself on reproducing his parents through his art, the novelist is deluded. Eborn did not save them in fact but has preserved them only in fiction. Lou and Todd's love, not their son's work, raises them to everlasting life.

Although Eborn's vision of his parents at first seems an artistic epiphany, it turns into an approximation of the last judgment. Tom stares at the imperishable wellsprings of Price's fictional world only to discover his own isolation from their brilliant confluence. Love abounding terrifies the closed heart because it manifests by contrast the sinner's lovelessness. Eborn seems to shut his eyes and lips, even ears, to the "roar of light" radiating from these binary stars (148). Although the unlaved and unloving son considered himself "their one product," he shields himself from their illumination, "their effortless product, only product" (147), divorcing himself from his very origins in their astounding generosity. He can disown such magnificence but not annul it. "He knows that he must stand in it all his life—and worse, beyond—in full sight of them, their atrocious joy; but separate, lidless, scalding in their trail" (148). The lavish immensity of his parents' love, filling the room to bursting with light, reveals and condemns his own constricted affections. The searing pain of his life and after his death is to exist before such blazing plenitude in his own infernal deprivation.

Until this end, Eborn has known only the dejection which both Price and Scripture regard as providing questionable inspiration for genuine narrative. In "A Single Meaning" Price claims that the laments sometimes heard in the Old and New Testaments "do not, from the point of view of Biblical narrators, constitute a story at all." They lack action, characters worthy of attention, and, most importantly, some final consolation (*Common Room* 256). *Love and Work* makes its story out of Eborn's inability to discern the more complete story of his own and his parents' life. On the last page, Tom seems to glimpse a less disconsolate reading of human endings when he tries to say "The dead have their own lives" (148). His parents do not depend on the haunt of memory or the propitiatory rites of his fiction for some shadowy Elysium. Rather, they live on their own, and they abide in their love. In their final apotheosis these good hearts have become household gods in the domestic world of Price's fiction.[5] However, their son falls silent when he attempts to utter his terrifying and transcendent conclusion. "The room, though, is still. No one has breathed" (148). Seeing without speaking, Eborn is a failed version of Price's *homo narrator*. He can only give voice to his vision in a novel and in a new life if he accepts his part in the consummate narrative where labor finds its completion in a love that lives even beyond the apparent end of the story.

Notes

1. Rosacoke's reverence before creation resembles Price's own early nature mysticism as described in *Clear Pictures* 234–239.

2. Price told Constance Rooke that whereas his earlier novels focused on familial and erotic love, his fiction beginning with *Love and Work* shows in addition "a more conscious sense of a supernatural element in the lives of the characters, though it's present in *A Generous Man* too. That element is largely detectable by its absence from their lives, rather than in any conscious obeisance they make to such a reality" (706).

3. Daniel (51–52). Rooke (*Reynolds Price* 80, 83, 86) and Shepherd (54–55) have noticed how several minor characters as well as the novel's many references to myth, dreams, superstitions and numerology continually expose Eborn's blindness to the transcendent story in which he participates.

4. In discussing the ghost of Tommy Ryden in *A Generous Man*, Price also describes the appearance to Todd Eborn: "What has interested me always about ghost stories—respectable, well-authenticated ghost stories—is that ghosts almost always appear in unexceptional corporeal form. That is, they do not appear as filmy, vaporous emanations of light but have simply— and terribly—the opaque reality of a live person walking through a room or sitting in a chair" (Kaufman 82).

5. The return of the Eborns follows an ancient tradition for hallowing a home. In "Homeless, Home," Price observes that both Jews and Romans only regarded dwelling places as homes when they were sanctified "by the presence, over sizable reaches of time, of spirits: transcendent gods or the souls of dead parents, who were either loved in life and memory or feared in death." He wonders whether real homes "are possible only for a people convinced of man's immortality" (*Common Room* 233–234).

Works Cited

Daniel, Dan. "Amazing Crossroads in *Love and Work*." *Reynolds Price: From* A Long and Happy Life *to* Good Hearts, *with a Bibliography*. Sue Laslie Kimball and Lynn Veach Sadler, Co-Editors. Fayetteville, NC: Methodist College Press, 1989, 46–53.

Eliot, T.S. *Collected Poems: 1909–1962*. New York: Harcourt, Brace & World, Inc., 1963.

Kaufman, Wallace. "Notice, I'm Still Smiling: REYNOLDS PRICE." *Kite-Flying and Other Irrational Acts: Conversations with Twelve Southern Writers*. Ed. John Carr. Baton Rouge: Louisiana State UP, 1972. 70–95.

Kermode, Frank. *The Sense of an Ending: Studies in the Theory of Fiction*. New York: Oxford UP, 1967.

Kreyling, Michael. "Motion and Rest in the Novels of Reynolds Price." *Southern Review* 16 (1980): 853–68.

Price, Reynolds. *Clear Pictures: First Loves, First Guides*. New York: Atheneum, 1989.

———. *A Common Room: Essays 1954–1987*. New York: Atheneum, 1987.

———. *Love and Work*. 1968. rpt. New York: Ballantine, 1988.

Rooke, Constance. "On Women and His Own Work: An Interview with Reynolds Price. *Southern Review* 14 (1978): 706–725.

———. *Reynolds Price*. Boston: Twayne, 1983.

Sadler, Lynn Veach. "The 'Mystical Grotesque' in the Life and Works of Reynolds Price." *Southern Literary Journal* 21.2 (1989): 27–40.

———. "Reynolds Price and Religion: The 'Almost Blindingly Lucid' Palpable World." *Southern Quarterly* 26.2 (1988): 1–11.

Shepherd, Allen. "*Love and Work* and the Unseen World." *Topic* 23 (1972): 52–57.

A Time to Bolt:
Suicide, Androgyny, and the Dislocation
of the Self in Reynolds Price's *Kate Vaiden*

JOSEPH DEWEY

Kate Vaiden's life is shaped largely by the dark logic of suicide. Before she is eighteen, her world of rural North Carolina is shaken three times by the irrational stroke of self-destruction: when Kate is eleven, her father shoots first her mother and then himself; her first boyfriend, a Marine recruit, days from completing basic training and returning presumably to elope with Kate, stands up during a drill in which recruits crawl under live machine-gun fire, taking four shots in the back; later, when Kate nears eighteen, the father of her child shoots away most of his heart in a bathtub. In a novel concerned with the education of its heroine, the act of suicide is critical here for what it fails to teach Kate. By eighteen, the threshold age of maturation, Kate learns not the terrifying waste of such an irrevocable stroke or the absolute price of withdrawing from experience within such a self-involved gesture. Rather she comes to learn its persuasive argument—the necessity of sacrificing the self to preserve it. Taught by such self-consuming rationale, Kate emerges from her adolescence paying inordinate attention to the self: she learns that to touch another, to allow another to touch her, is an unwarranted invasion. In recounting her emotional experience, Kate is drawn to the bloody language of warfare, violation, surrender, wounding, and attrition; indeed, her adolescence is framed against World War Two. The implosion that destroys her parents, the awkward sexual initiation with the doomed Gaston Stegall, the contradictory affair with Doug Lee that nevertheless produces the child she will abandon within its first year—each experience teaches her that to be touched is somehow to be diminished. The self, she learns, is something to be protected. She can understand neither betraying it voluntarily to the illogic of family nor the willingness to endure love (people gazing at each other like "hypnotized frogs").[1] Kate argues herself out of the passive condition, the experience of overwhelming emotions that can never be predicted, controlled, or explained.

Reprinted, with permission, from *Mississippi Quarterly* 45.1 (Winter 1991–92): 9–28. Copyright 1992, Mississippi State University, Mississippi.

For example, first love, often the liminal experience of adolescence, teaches Kate not the stunning surprise of fusion but rather the dreary inevitability of fission. Her initial experience comes on the fox hunt with Gaston Stegall, two years her senior in school. Against a backdrop that suggests the animal instinct to hunt and trap, Kate is initiated into sexuality as wonderless biology. Kate follows Gaston into the woods (much as the bitch takes the lead chasing the fox into the woods) and spies him masturbating: "he held his penis like a wingshot quail"; it seemed a "blind and feverish animal that might not survive." More curious than aroused (she asks, "Is it sick?"), Kate intervenes not to experiment with contact but rather to finish the job: she "milk[s]" him "dry" (pp. 40–42). This initiation (Kate is twelve) encodes the sexual act in a repellant vocabulary of pain (Kate eases Gaston's "hurt"; erect, Gaston groans that he feels near death, that something is the matter "with this") and isolation: as Kate completes the job, despite Gaston's enormous relief, both stay necessarily unviolated. There is no confluence, only the sparkless friction of glandular relief. As the relationship persists over two years, Kate, although baffled by such need, is fascinated by the novelty of ministering to Gaston's struggling penis (Kate less a lover, more an unlicensed paramedic). Their relationship is starkly phallocentric: Gaston's demanding organ is a "live handy pet with elaborate features," which she must keep calm. Sexuality, denied its tonic wonder, is a paltry matter of unilateral relief, unburdening the pain of Gaston's unspent seed. Despite his cautious invitation ("Ain't you hurting yet, nowhere at all?"), Kate cannot coax sufficient response to participate ("I was not. I was happy").

When Kate disposes of her virginity with Gaston in a mossy creek bed near where her parents died (the ascendant impulse to love plotted against the curving line of death, their green bower is, in fact, part of a cemetery and nearby is "damp gray" quicksand where years earlier a pony, an animal Kate associates with potent sexuality, struggled to its death), the act falls far short of Kate's expectations. With curiosity, she had read a smutty poem at school, "Rhonda's Road to Womanhood," its "ruled dingy pages" of rhymed couplets describing the lusty satisfactions of a secretary (ironically Kate's eventual profession) once she finally yields her virginity. To Kate, the poem is like "grabbing a live wire and not letting go" (p. 37). The act itself does not engage her: during Gaston's heaving struggles she pictures her own face in the beech leaves overhead, potential union reduced to crude narcissism. Two innocents making love in a green bower—finally a disturbing parody of Eden that occasions no cataclysmic epiphany on the possibility of bursting through the self, rather only Kate's banal invitation to repeat the act ("You just got to name your day"). Kate must counsel herself to enjoy the act; it is a gift, she decides within the fascism of her ego, that she is giving not to Gaston but rather to herself. And later she admits only that Gaston's dependence satisfied her, his gratitude for her "slim supply of human traits" (p. 83). When Kate studies Gaston's easy features "hoping to guess what people saw in love," nothing strikes her (p. 73). She will repeat the gesture two years later on a train with Doug Lee, with similar conclusions ("I didn't see one cell I wanted for life" [p. 181]), shortly before a stop where she bolts.[2]

What, then, is the reader to make of Kate's closing decision to return to North Carolina to track down her abandoned son? It would seem a most miraculous change of heart. Diagnosed at fifty-seven with cervical cancer and given only five years to live, Kate, on a package tour of Rome and the Vatican, pauses in the Catacombs to contemplate the brown bones of St. Peter, the "biggest quitter in human history" (p. 288), whose storied repentance suggests to her the possibility of her own forgiveness. Flying home, Kate resolves to find her son, now forty, and back in North Carolina, she secures his phone number in Norfolk. When she calls, she receives only a recorded message and leaves one of her own ("I'm the burglar and I'll be right over" [p. 306]). The book does not close with reunion. Kate must steady herself for that reunion, she says, by first writing out in full for her son the facts of her life. Far from admitting another into her hermetic private sphere, Kate's last action is to bolt her door and switch off the lamp, neither gesture promising the illumination of reconnection. The nearest she will permit her son is an anonymous message on an answering machine—the message an unambiguous warning that associates reunion with robbery, with leaving something diminished.

This (melo)dramatic impulse toward motherhood is, finally, suspect, superficial. In the Catacombs, Kate is allowed ten seconds to view the "few scraps" of St. Peter's bones (later she reads in a single sitting the gospel of Luke, with its complex theme of forgiving the outcasts). Kate has never been strong on religion ("Church . . . is an optional thing I can take or leave" [p. 203]).[3] A startling vision she has during Christmas, far from asserting the spiritual, is a gruesome image of a baby pushing its oily head slowly out of its mother; during a Good Friday service, she wonders how iron nails might feel deep in her palms and the soles of her feet. There is little of the spiritual about Kate's sudden reformation. She is impressed not by the faith of Peter nor by his rigorous road toward the dislocation of the self through the earnest petition for forgiveness, but rather by the aptness of her own easy appropriation of the Peter role. A betrayer, she will seek her son and receive forgiveness, acting out a sort of *Reader's Digest* (among her favorite reading) parable of the Prodigal Mother (Luke alone records the Prodigal Son). Appropriately, her decision to move toward commitment occurs as she flies over Greenland— despite its name, an uninviting sheath of ice. Kate, pressured by mortality, hungers for company. It is the same sort of reductive affection she defined forty years earlier on the fox hunt with Gaston—the elemental rule of need. Kate postpones her reunion from spring until fall, away from the promise of growth to a time that bodes only the natural concession to dying (forty years earlier, Gaston had promised summer as a time to "come back to life" [p. 68]). Though she begins to negotiate the reunion with her son, Kate cannot complete the act itself. Internal growth for her is best suggested by the malignant spread of the cancer itself. Unlike the heroines of Defoe's *Moll Flanders* and Willa Cather's *Sapphira and the Slave Girl* (which Kate reads), books that move toward powerful reunions of mother and child, Kate staves off immediacy. Distance closes the novel. The reunion between mother and child is only a near-collision of voices.

The response to Kate, then, must be archeological—turning over the fossilized bits of her heart, to coax from them an explanation of why. As a daughter, she divides unevenly between her dead parents what thin affection she can generate; she is an ungrateful ward, a mercurial lover, an indifferent friend who demands nevertheless enormous attention, a radical failure as a mother. Relational identity completely fails her. She tries family after family, some blood-kin (her Aunt Caroline, then her cousin Walter Porter in Norfolk, and finally her infant son); she tries relationships with strangers (Daphne and Cliff Baxter, whom she meets on a train to Norfolk; later the blind piano tuner Whitfield Eller, who had taken in Doug Lee). No arrangement will work. Kate hungers most purely for solitude. But Price resists recycling the Dickensian orphan who struggles because of abandonment with feelings of being unworthy of the investment of love. Kate is simply never open to others. Her earliest memory is of being left alone at five months in the backyard and feeling not panic over desertion by her parents but rather a calm self-sufficiency. She recalls Sunday breakfasts when, at the age of three, she would realize in regular epiphanic jolts that her parents had a deep partnership that could not ever completely include her. "I'm not in this, this is all for them" (p. 5). Even before puberty, she discovers the satisfaction of masturbating—easy relief without the interfering complications of a partner. She daydreams (long before Hiroshima, as she confesses) about living alone in a ruined, dead world. She confesses to Gaston her sense of kinlessness—indeed, she calls her parents Dan and Frances.

In this, Kate tests a dilemma central to Price's fiction—the male urge to be (autonomy) against the female imperative to be part (nurturing). Kate sorely taxes gender definition. On a long train ride, she recalls her father's joke that kissing her elbow could change her into a boy (a contortion she finds frustratingly impossible). As the train pulls along, she wills herself into a boy, Marcus, who has no friends and a habit of taking "long, thirsty hikes" in the hills (p. 13)—the embodiment of the male stereotype of frank autonomy. In her maturation, she expresses only ironically the traditional feminine sensibilities—tenderness, cooperation, domesticity, passivity, and urgency toward communion. She bonds once—with a gray mare given to her as a gift. She dreams of learning the horse's language (she reads *Doctor Doolittle,* about another droll misanthrope soured enough on human relations to turn to animals); but even that impulse fails her: she neglects the mare until it must be given to a family to raise. She is, by her own confession, not a very good she—if a woman is to find identity bound up in her biological ability to bear children and by the demand to provide the appropriate nest. Such biological totalitarianism, however, drives a woman to reject as peripheral critical questions of who she is, to allow her single, potentially powerful voice to disappear within the cacophony of the house.[4]

But Kate most dramatically speaks. In her reaction against any potential involvement as toxic, she argues a radical masculine sensibility, what Price has epitomized elsewhere as the "wanderer, the buccaneer, the rogue" (*Conversations*, p. 149). As Kate defines her self, she asserts, unconsciously, the fullest range of masculine stereotypes—a peculiar hardness of heart; a fear of emotions; a compelling concern for strength or at least the appearance of being strong; a willingness to jerry-build a life from impulsive gestures, a determination to assert autonomy at inestimable emotional cost to others; a perception of relations as a stifling trap; a conviction that vulnerability leads only to diminishment. She is restless, her "butt smoking" (p. 284); she is hungry (assigned to write on any of the deadly sins, Kate selects gluttony and tells of a boy who ate everything but "never got fat" and "never got full" [p. 147]; in any emotional crisis Kate eats enormous meals, yet stays "thin as a file" [p. 35]). This rebellious discontent with the narrowest interpretation of female possibilities separates Kate, finally, from the other women she watches settle into the dust in Macon, housewives casually defined and lightly valued, finally gender bound and fiercely unhappy.

That Kate resists should be the stuff of feminist heroics. After all, in the very process of autobiography, Kate participates in a subversive act of authority. Pen in hand, Kate rebels against traditional limits of female narration, so ably defined by Joanne Frye.[5] To recount an individual life is to scribble a unique identity against its internment within the hurried push of time. Yet, in the novel genre, women have been defined within the claustrophobic expectations of the love story. Against the obligations of gender, female narrators cannot lay claim to a voice without appearing to sacrifice what defines them as women, the self-denying process of reproduction. For a woman character, to say "I" is ultimately to rebel. When, at the age of eighteen, Kate determines to fly solo (she admires Amelia Earhart), she would seem, to borrow from Price, to say "nonsense" to the "harem-wife-mother stereotype" (*Conversations*, p. 210). Indeed, after Gaston's suicide, Kate glimpses what a future might have offered as his wife. Gaston's father stops by to see Kate and over his shoulder Kate sees the mother, waiting patiently in the car, her teeth missing—voiceless and toothless, domestic and domesticated. What Kate finally claims is the radical act of author-ity, the traditional male privilege of self-definition. Indeed, Price's fiction values introspection, the arduous struggle of sorting through errors of the heart to earn "that small clearing in the jungle which may be empty of all but a polished mirror."[6]

Why, then, is Kate so fiercely unsatisfied? With her own time dwindling, she is preoccupied with guilt; repeated references to Judgment Day unconsciously surface in her discourse as she prepares to assume the maternity she could not coax forty years earlier. Happiness has eluded her in her forty years alone; she finds affirmation only in the joyless act of surviving great stretches of time ("You pray to die when you pass a calendar—all those separate days stacked before you, each one the same length and built from steel. But then you butt on through them somehow" [p. 201]). Price resists the resolutions of so many of Kate's romances—a woman requiring the dreary intervention of a male to complete her identity. But, if creating an I (rather than sinking it within the gender expectations of a she) defines Kate's rebellion, it defines as well her own elaborate act of strategic suicide, a strategic martyrdom (she admires Joan of Arc): to protect the self, she destroys it. Kate is, finally, more dead than alive (her tendency to fall into profound sleeps, "dead as a chloroformed dog" [p. 129], underscores her lifelong emotional inertia). She elects at eighteen to pass on what she cannot control; she numbs her heart and, in so doing, finds that time, which presses so heavily on her as a teenager, spins furiously by, which accounts for Price's decision to spend an enormous part of the book reviewing Kate's adolescence and then running rapidly through nearly forty years in the closing twenty pages. When, at eighteen, Kate bolts from the blind piano tuner's unexpected invitation to marry (extended to her not surprisingly as they pass a cemetery), she closes out her emotional life; without the burden of a beating heart, Price argues, time is all too navigable. Kate at fifty-seven stands against time—she has survived. It is the desperate strategy of suicide, the joyless withdrawal from experience. Kate's description of her own bedroom, which she visits while looking for her son, defines her own condition: "It might just as well have been a Williamsburg dummy, a rebuilt historic landmark, soul omitted" (p. 280).

During the same visit, Kate notices a houseplant, a Wandering Jew, that has been overtended, overwatered and now hangs in limp and dying tangles. Kate performs a similar act of compassionate destruction on her own wandering heart. Unlike Gaston, destroyed by the meanness he found in basic training; unlike Dan, destroyed by the revelation of the heart's impossible fickleness; unlike Doug Lee, destroyed by a heart unable to trust its expression, Kate will not be broken by the abundant meanness she witnesses. Yet, ironically, in disconnecting herself at the spare age of eighteen, in her final act of bolting, Kate commits emotional suicide, like Gaston in boot camp, long before she ever engages the war itself. She survives by refusing her heart, like the Roanoke River, whose unmatched beauty Kate fondly recalls, but which is now dammed, its energy restrained at enormous sacrifice. Her pride in her ability to survive her own adolescence recalls an obscure poem by Alfred Noyes that Kate recites as a child, "A Victory Dance," a macabre account of the grotesque remains of dead soldiers watching with ironic pleasure the victory balls that signaled the end of a war. In her determination to survive, she passes on the rawness of the heart itself as she cites the power of the passage in Mark in which Jesus at Gethsemane begs to avoid the suffering. She retreats from experience, recalling the story Gaston tells of Robert E. Lee's young daughter Annie, who retreats deeper into Virginia from the approaching guns of the Union army—retreating, only to die from cholera.

Despite such self-destruction, however, Kate's voice is disarmingly seductive—her apparently uncompromising honesty in recounting with deadpan earnestness each vicious act of emotional treason against her family seems to salvage the damning comparisons Price draws to her—a dead river, a dying houseplant, an empty historical landmark eerily alive simultaneously in two tenses. Defining the problem of Kate, however, begins with just this problematic gift for talk. Recall her school teacher's criticism of Kate's "tendency to talk" (p. 33). Kate is a creature of language; indeed, she engages the reader as a pure creation of words. Price offers no physical detailing of Kate; she is her voice, self-generating, self-sustaining, indefatigable. Kate does not act in the narrative present; rather she talks. Again and again she is associated with the power of her voice. When she presses a distraught Doug Lee about why he continues to pursue her, he acknowledges the attractive power of her voice: "You could talk your way through granite rock" (p. 216). Kate is all too determined to speak. Indeed, she is addicted to confession. Like some manic Ancient Mariner, she recounts her life in full on six separate occasions, reduces the act of autobiography to banal habit. Despite her apparent privileging of her abandoned son, he is simply the latest person she tells, save that now Kate talks against the prognosis of cancer, recalling Scheherazade from the *Arabian Nights* (a favorite reading of Kate's)—language itself now a vehicle for preserving the I against its "death," the commitment to an uncertain We.

This absolute dependence on language signals Kate's handicap. Here, language is debased and counterfeit; it is never a vehicle for honest confession or humane engagement. Kate's family is riven by buried secrets and by infidelities hastily exorcised by piles of poor lies. The power of the secret is the last lesson Kate's mother teaches her. The night she will die from the brutal exposure of her own secrets, Kate's mother makes Kate a "secret garden" by pressing a small piece of broken glass against wildflowers buried in a bowl-shaped depression in the ground. Kate visits the spot repeatedly and, indeed, the flowers stay remarkably fresh, suggesting the persistence of secrets that stay fresh despite being buried. Secrets corrode virtually every relationship in Kate's experience, each one a charade of commitment that, in turn, must be perpetuated by lying. Characters consistently opt for lies, effortlessly lying to spouses, to children, to friends, to police officers. The central event of Kate's boneyard adolescence, her parents' murder-suicide, is never explained, certainly not in the obvious lies Swift belabors in the kitchen the night of the shooting. His skin splotched like a leper's, his eyes bolted to the floor, Swift is the very caricature of the unreliable narrator as he stumbles through a poor account of what happened in the cemetery when Dan caught Swift and Frances together; even Caroline, Swift's long-suffering mother, doubts the veracity of the story. The reader, indeed Kate herself, will never wholly understand the act—not from Swift's revisioning and not even from a letter written by Dan himself the night before he completes the agony of his own heart in the act of suicide. In the narrative present, Kate is given the letter by Swift, now in a nursing home. The letter promises resolution (in fact, Price encourages such expectation by having Kate refer to the letter early on but withholding its contents until nearly the close). The letter, finally revealed, is yet another aborted attempt to put into language the fierce confusions of a crippled heart. It reads like a telegram from a war zone, full of contradictory terrors of living within a world that might detonate in a fragile moment. Completing it, Kate (as well as the reader) confesses, "I was still blind" (p. 305).

The debasement of language is further underscored by the dependence on telegrams and letters. Whenever Kate bolts, she turns to the convenience of Western Union. Such elliptical fragments of language do not threaten even the possibility of disclosure; indeed they are nonengaging subversions of whatever potential language offers for fusion. For Kate, telegrams are far easier than the awful immediacy of the telephone, of language unmediated, much as elaborate confession, pages of introspection, is far easier than the briefest face-to-face encounter with her grown son. Gothic secrets, baroque lies, hasty telegrams—language within Kate's experience is a convenience, a way to evade truths and the raw spontaneity of simple engagement. Language, here, measures distance. Recall that Kate responds more powerfully to an erotic poem than to the act of love itself. A voracious reader, she finds delicious escape in the romances she trolls from the local bookmobile. Years later, as she works her way up through a law firm, Kate engages finally not people at all but simply clients—the perfect frictionless community created solely by language in a profession that goes about its charade of encoding the raw mess of experience ("divorce, child custody, murders" [p. 281]) into neat affidavits.

Even love letters frustrate despite their apparent privileged claim to privacy and their promise of exercising the vital consolation of language to pull together hearts apart. The letters of Kate's parents, written during an eight-week separation shortly after Kate's birth, reveal little of the potent emotions that connect these two people. The letters are rather tepid. To read the exchange Kate offers as proof of her parents' happiness is to hear how much cannot be said—Frances's problems with the lingering infatuation of Swift, her dissatisfactions with the poverty of marriage; Dan's desperate uneasiness over the thinning of his wife's affections, his unholy dependence on her. The letters ironically insist only on reassurances. Gaston's single letter from boot camp is equally perfunctory, saying more in what must be withheld from the cheapening approximations of language. Indeed, Gaston's letter indicates nothing that would anticipate (much less explain) his decision to stand up during the drill. Ironically, after Gaston's death, his father brings Kate a letter Gaston had written to her the night before his suicide. But Kate coldly refuses it, fearing, the reader suspects, it might hazard too close to revelation.

When Kate uses language, when she indulges her fondness for disclosure, it never secures a closure of hearts: people do not believe her; they abandon her in understandable horror; they indulge cold pity; they even fall asleep. She fares no better with the reader. The more she explains, the less we understand. We hear the voice, emerging from the warfare of her adolescence, as the children in Macon during World War Two gather about the radios and listen to the "big, strong" (p. 155) voices of Princess Elizabeth and Queen Wilhelmina addressing their populations during the German air war, voices that despite their apparent clarity are separated from Macon not merely geographically but more dramatically by situation as well. The voices offer only the illusion of nearness. Indeed, Kate's signature speaking device, her effortless way with similes, represents another dodge away from reality, an oblique and indirect approach to the world "as if," a part of her larger resistance to experience.[7]

Despite her declaration that as a legal secretary she can perceive the moment when clients start to lie (one thinks inevitably of Nick Caraway, who so protests his honesty), Kate labors under a destructive illusion—the possibility of explanation. Pressured by mortality, she is determined to bend her experience to the rigid logic of plot. Yet Kate matures in a mid-twentieth-century world that defies the presumption of explanation: what occasions her orphaning, for example, is the funeral of her youngest cousin after a pointless motorcycle accident, itself happening shortly after the Vaidens' dining-room ceiling suddenly caves in. Kate's enormous faith in the suasive power of the tongue directs her to presume explanation for experience that is profoundly emotional. The more she talks, the more the events themselves undermine the very premise of accountability. Price carefully manipulates uncertainty. Here, the central event of suicide is critical. Self-destruction, given its cold absoluteness, must necessarily beggar explanation and raises questions of motivation that must defy whatever note is left behind. Kate cannot abide such mystery (she reads shelves of Nancy Drew). She assigns a reason for each act—that those who come near her are doomed. It is an unconvincing, even disturbing assertion of ideological egotism, a casual positioning of herself in the center of what is a complicated, ambiguous emotional chaos only marginally influenced by her presence. These suicides, in turn, have each taught Kate only irresolvable contradictions; hurt badly by abandonment she will hurt others with the same gesture. Loved, she will withhold her heart; approached, she will bolt. Tallying up her experience against her explanation cannot "solve" Kate. For all her homely pretense to full disclosure, the mystery of her actions remains (as with any act of suicide; indeed Kate's lengthy narrative, finally, is a sort of tediously long suicide note).

As a child, Kate is fascinated by her school teacher's paperweight—a seahorse, so apparently alive, suspended in a block of glass. Much later, Miss Limer, when she gives the paperweight to Kate, confesses that it is a *memento mori* of her own emotional catastrophe, a souvenir sent from her lover shortly before he married another woman, a wounding that has left her (like Kate) within the dry logic of isolationism (her name suggests her souring). At the close of her life, Kate, another relic of abandonment, is much like the perfectly preserved seahorse. She hangs suspended in her text, immured in language; for all the apparent revelation, Kate stays, like the seahorse in glass, untouched and untouchable, dead despite the appearance of life, distant despite the illusion of nearness, mysterious despite the suggestion of clarity. The reader recalls Kate's difficulties in high school with the Pythagorean Theorem, the reassuring theorem that argues that knowing two sides of a triangle will solve the mystery of the third side. Such reliability is denied by Kate; if the reader and the text form two sides, Kate is the defiant third, unknowable as she deadpans her way through each impulsive urge to bolt. Kate confesses ironically just such a predicament when, talking about the criminals she has met in the law firm, she acknowledges, "the worse the crime, the less you know" (p. 55). Investing in the possibility of explanation and finding problematic comfort in language, Kate thins into a voice, like Amelia Earhart disappearing into the dark Pacific void.

Against Kate's internment within language, Price sets the difficult struggle to touch, to seek violation of the private space Kate protects. Gaston, Dan, Frances, Doug Lee struggle with the very emotions Kate rejects— "[s]urprise and pain and being captured" (p. 20)—struggle with the wildest impulses of the heart that compel us to hazard the trick of unmediated connection. These characters are not creatures of language (Gaston's graduation pin is for penmanship, involved more with the medium than its message). Unlike Kate (who ironically describes her absorption into language when she concedes, "touch me; I answer" [p. 3]), these are touching creatures, some gentle, others wielding ice picks in wild attempts to dislocate the self. Kate cannot touch: she even has "corpse-arms," as Gaston tells her while she cleans the chalk erasers after school, her arms coated in dust—"You're dying from the fingers up" (p. 68). Significantly, the single most destructive decision in Kate's experience is determined by unreciprocated touch: when she offers her newborn child her finger to hold and the baby simply turns away, she feels justified in abandoning the infant.

Yet, given the casualties of touch strewn about the North Carolina hills, for Kate fashioning the I might seem the only way to survive, and her advice, that time can only be endured, might hang unironically as the last best word. Yet Kate learns only part of what her experience could teach (after all, she is shuffled in and out of a number of schools, leaving her education haphazard). What Kate never acknowledges, her fingers dead, her heart hibernating, her cervix tumorous, is the miracle of the passive condition. There is, after all, no shortage of teachers. For all her professed independence, Kate depends to a remarkable degree on Good Samaritans (another Luke parable) who, despite her characteristic ingratitude, provide a support system that alone ensures her charade of independence. For example, Fob, the wealthy tobacco farmer, supports his inexplicable faith in Kate with a gift of considerable money. Noony, the black cook in Kate's adopted home, instructs Kate in the heart and, despite an accurate assessment of Kate's vast egotism, offers her refuge in her shack when Kate reappears in town pregnant and alone; Tim Slaughter, a cabdriver in Norfolk, picks up Kate when she arrives there alone, without luggage, and against Kate's suspicions, dedicates himself to her well-being, taking her in when she initially abandons Doug Lee after his proposal; Aunt Caroline takes in Kate's mother and then Kate and then Kate's son when each in turn needs a home; Whitfield Eller, the blind piano tuner, gives Kate a place to stay, employment, and an offer of marriage when she finds her life ragged after the suicide of Doug Lee; Daphne and Cliff Baxter, strangers Kate meets on the train to Norfolk, a couple who face drastic separation (Cliff is a day away from overseas duty), make room for her in their tiny hotel room; and even the nameless tourist in Rome, a stranger in an American rain-coat, gives Kate his unused ticket to the Catacombs, which will trigger Kate's impulse toward reunion. Yet Kate cannot shake suspicions about these Good Samaritans: she is certain, for instance, that Fob will expect some sexual favor; when Tim Slaughter and later Whitfield Eller simply touch her, she bolts within hours. We must learn the potential of touch by listening to one numb, by her own admission, to its possibilities, a narrative strategy that recalls the Emily Dickinson poem that particularly attracts Kate: "Success is counted sweetest / By those who ne'er succeed."

Given such enormous exposure, Kate fails then not as a woman, or a lover, or even a mother; she is ultimately a bad student. She never suspects the possibility of sympathetic closure, the bolting possible between hearts, largely because she exercises her heart within the dark frame of the immediate family and later within the tight algebra of procreation. As Price has argued throughout his work, the miracle of the relational world is seldom expressed in the family (he has described the family as the "most destructive force there is, except for tornadoes" [*Conversations,* p. 211]) or in the sexual politicking that inevitably erodes marriage ("One of the saddest things I'd have to say is that . . . I have never watched more than two marriages that I envied" [*Conversations,* p. 214]). Rather it is felt in the compelling mystery of strangers opening themselves up to others—the fragile miracle of a moment's generosity, of unexpected, unambiguous kindness. To complete the equation of the self, Price argues, requires others to determine its value, to measure its potential for expansion.

Kate, then, closes her narrative locked within the irresolvable dilemma so characteristic of Price's fiction: the distrust of the unviolated self and the terror of commitment, the heart's tendency to err.[8] Yet *Kate Vaiden* itself represents a critical shift for Price. Price here offers resolution, a way for the self to break from unendurable loneliness into intimate communion and yet preserve its autonomy, an achievement that elevates language and its potential for fusion rather than reveals (as Kate's confession) its utter poverty and the necessary distance it places between hearts. Such a dislocation of the self is not achieved by Kate, victim of her own experience. Rather it is realized in the fusion of the author and the first-person narrator—a fusion to which Price himself tirelessly directed attention—that combines the imperatives of touch and tongue because touch can come only through the magnificent accomplishment of language itself. This experiment with objective narration is a critical break for Price. Although long fascinated by female characters, Price never approached the feminine sensibility within the intimacy of the first person. In allowing Kate to speak her own story, he defies artificial boundaries imposed by gender to create what he described as a "reversed gender novel." He has decried the "ghettoization" of the American novel that decrees that men write only about men, women about women—a practice that has denied a generation of writers imaginative access to "half the human race" and, as a result, to an "immensely useful species of fiction"—creative androgyny.[9]

Nevertheless, for a male writer to enter the feminine psyche would seem a most dangerous act of trespass and forced colonization. When male writers have fashioned first-person female voices—Defoe's Moll Flanders, Richardson's Clarissa, James's governess, Joyce's Molly, to name the most obvious—the results have been predictably uneven: androgynous tension is difficult to sustain. In the estimation of Anne Robinson Taylor, the women inevitably seem "transparent, unconvincing masquerades" perpetrated either by unpleasantly "feminized males" or by males exorcising misogynistic angers, Freudian anxieties, or childhood traumas.[10] Worse, the women gravitate toward unconvincing extremes, either the great-breasted maternal force or the bawdy erotic life force. It is, perhaps, the wisdom of the moment to concede what Faulkner himself confessed in avoiding the creation of a voice for Caddy, another mother who abandons a child. He argued that he was finally "incapable of understanding" the female interior.[11]

Price rejects such restrictions. Although he has long been fascinated by the workings of the female imagination (following *The Surface of the Earth,* he confessed a tremendous awareness of "the reality of being a woman" [*Conversations,* p. 150]), Price here engages signal moments in female development— the onset of menstruation; the initial tentative attempts at make-up before an unflattering mirror; the receptive sexual experience; the immediate certainty of conception; the profound discomforts of pregnancy; the warm onrush of labor and delivery; the struggle with the demands of mothering; the cooling of menopause—a careful re-creation that requires complete abandonment of male privilege. In stepping so compellingly within the interior life of a female narrator, Price achieves the unironic We, an authentic violation of the self that nevertheless preserves intact its necessary autonomy. The voice of Kate is no straining falsetto. Language here bolts. Price finds in first-person narration the enlargement of the self against the apparently intractable barrier of gender through the vehicle of language. Although Kate displaces gender by embodying male gender stereotypes, she cannot make the requisite leap beyond immense self-involvement. Therefore, gender considerations are finally irrelevant as Kate is no longer fully human—recall the talk Kate has with Miss Limer about the seahorse paperweight and the indeterminacy of the creature's sex. Biography tempts—after all, Price, like Kate, completed his narrative against the sudden pressure of mortality. Like Kate, Price was diagnosed with cancer, a particularly debilitating sort of spinal cancer. As Kate tidies up her small, private room, Price bursts through toward what he has described as a "vast and common room" ("Men Creating Women," p. 20) to explore the fullest impulses of the human self by exploding gender altogether. Kate's voice emerges from a most radical tension: the reader cannot afford to forget that the I here is the creation of a male.

Yet, such a reading frustrates affirmation. Must the potential for such androgyny be relegated to a self-conscious aesthetic exercise, a highly artificial union of author and narrator that denies genderlessness in any practical arena? Must it stay, finally, a metaphor? Price's interest in androgyny lends unsuspected importance to an apparently secondary character, Kate's homosexual cousin Walter Porter, with whom Kate lives for four critical months following the death of Gaston. Against Kate's considerable centripetal collapse into the protected self, Price sets the ascendant example of Walter Porter, whose heart compels him outward to construct not merely the I but rather to complete it by insisting on a We within the same explosive universe of meanness that drives Kate inward. Unlike Kate, Walter can only define himself relationally (he spends his evenings sending birthday cards to "thousands of friends . . . he never saw" [p. 135]; he refuses to eat dessert without company) and, as such, brings to the narrative a tonic presence, a gift for sympathy, the very essence of the traditional feminine sensibility. Unlike the narrative experiment in androgyny, Walter offers the experience of it.

When Walter is introduced, the other members of his family have defined only a most toxic sort of love—incest, betrayal, murder, suicide (indeed, the family poetry recitations feature Byron's lurid "Bride of Abydos"). His return to Macon for Thanksgiving to re-engage his family, who had years earlier driven him away, follows Kate's fox hunt. Against that reduction of love to predatory satisfaction, Walter brings to the narrative the impulse toward unconditional love, an unabashed impulse to touch honestly without qualification, without agenda. "Where other people would nod and smile, Walter would rise up from where he was reading and cross the room to touch you . . . just warmth like a dog's, that constant but drier" (p. 50). Although Kate denigrates the impulse to touch with such immediacy (later, when Walter strokes her neck, she prepares for something "funny"), she is drawn to him. Unlike the rest of the family, who attend politely to Kate after the murder-suicide, Walter tries not only to comfort her but to listen to her. In contrast to Kate's tendency to shape distance through language, Walter listens, enters empathetically into her private space (all he talks about is her schooling, her friends). And when he talks, he speaks the only kind words

about the father, revealing an openness of heart that defies the colder judgments of the mother's family, who demand Dan's burial miles away.

Comparisons against Kate are critical. Like Kate, experience has taught
Walter the price of a beating heart. As he tells Kate, "You've been through
some Hell . . . but Hell is a place I've served time in" (p. 59). His homosexu-
ality has cost him his family, his roots. More than bearing the suffocating
homophobia within his own family, Walter has involved himself since leaving
Macon with the emotionally damaged orphan Doug Lee, seven years his
junior. Despite the ugly comments that Kate overhears about Doug Lee and
Walter as roommates in Norfolk, their relationship is decidedly asexual.
Indeed, when Walter tells Kate the background of his relationship with
Doug, what impresses the reader is how little the bonding has to do with sexuality. Walter tells Kate that ten years earlier, as Doug Lee's Sunday-school
teacher, he could not bear to see the child placed in a state orphanage following his abandonment by his parents. Rather he negotiated a near-adoption
that, after two years, sufficient community whispers had forced to be
rescinded. Walter, however, will not allow Doug to be returned to the "dim
dormitories" (p. 31) of the orphanage and together (Walter is only eighteen
years old) they bolt to Norfolk. Unlike Kate, who will at the same age decide
against the possibility of such commitments and will bolt in her own fashion,
Walter bolts his heart to another in a gesture that has less to do with the sort
of affection Kate understands—naked need and the pain of unspent seed—
and more to do with the sort of love she cannot understand—naked vulnerability and the irrational gift of the self. Against Kate's deconstructions of family, Walter struggles to shape one about Doug Lee, who is rabidly hostile even
to the idea. Price underscores their differences with the pictures on their bedroom walls—rooted trees (Walter) against harborless ships (Doug). Doug Lee
dismisses Walter's nurturing; debts to Walter, he says coldly to Kate, have
been settled in acts of sexual gratification. Later, when Kate angrily rejects
Walter's simple offer of help while she is pregnant by saying that he doesn't
owe her anything, Walter is genuinely stunned to hear affection negotiated so
casually. It's not that I owe you, he tells her, but that I love you.

Thus Walter can seem a warning against the emotions: he is used,
betrayed, and then abandoned by Doug (who twice tries to kill him) and
Kate (who fathers her child by his lover). Unlike Kate, who keeps leaving
families, families leave him. Yet against characters who, touched once by the
fierce heat of the heart, recoil into protective self-enclosure or those who, lev-
eled by the heart's manic potency, waste lifetimes determined to extricate
explanation from such ruin, Walter argues the resilience of the unexamined
heart. Against Kate's charade of autonomy, he acknowledges contingency, the
fundamental blessing if "we reach out and take what's in front of our eyes" (p.
171); puzzled, Kate appropriately sees only a wall. Against Kate's strategic
hibernation, Walter has the strength to engage the heart's uncertainty for the
"chance to make something last" (p. 171), intervening again and again in cir-

cumstances. And unlike Kate, whose thin heart is dead long before the cervical cancer will complete the job, Walter's great heart beats even after he is dead, for he wills to Kate's child his considerable possessions and property. Wounded during the Easter season in the palm of the hand by an icepick wielded by Doug Lee, Walter parallels, without irony, the Christ (another disturbing androgynous presence). He defines the self to offer it to another.

There, of course, is the problem. Contemporary readers are far more likely to credit the irrational meanness of Kate than to credit equally irrational goodness; what is reflected is a problem as old as *Paradise Lost* (not lost on Price, himself a Miltonist): the wicked are far more attractive than the good. Kate acknowledges as much when she confesses that a lifelong reading habit has convinced her that the "wicked alone bear reading about."[12] Yet, given Price's interest in the imaginative possibility of androgyny, Walter is more than another dreary Tobacco Road Christ figure. Unlike Kate, whose defiance of gender leaves her within the dry closure of problematic self-examination, Walter's defiance of gender pulls him consistently toward rather than away from people. His strength is his heart and its instinctive ability to live within the tension of masculine and feminine. Walter exhibits with unaffected directness the traditional gender definitions of the female: he is emotional, fragile, vulnerable, instinctively protective; but he demonstrates as well the masculine hunger for unconditional autonomy and unapologetic self-definition—his radical declaration of homosexuality in the 1920s rural South (Kate hears of an uncle who, confronting his own homosexuality, opted to hang himself in the barn). Touched again and again by catastrophe, Walter resists the temptation of surrenders—alcohol; convenient marriage; radical self-involvement; suicide, emotional or physical—and persists in his engagement of experience. Indeed, he possesses the only strength Kate does not—the strength to be weak, to relinquish the pretense of control by opening a heart completely, to trust in the heart against the considerable evidence of human meanness. That strength, Price argues, is not what makes us male or female but rather what makes us finally human.

The strength to be weak—here is the lesson of Price's parable. When Walter, who works for a railroad, inspects the Ringling Brothers circus before transporting its animals across the Shenandoahs, he is enthralled by a huge gorilla, "black as a hot night," who, behind bullet-proof glass in a massive case, is advertised as bloodthirsty, posters showing him dismembering a native. The circus manager, however, contemptuously dismisses the gorilla as a "sissie" who refuses to act like a male gorilla. Yet as Walter watches, the gorilla, with arms like the "hindquarters of a horse," lumbers to an inflated tractor tire that swings in his cage and effortlessly turns it inside out—"no six men could have done it" (pp. 50–51). Weeks later, when Walter is cleaning up a train accident in the Shenandoahs, he jokes with Kate that the gorilla has been sprung free at last. That is the larger victory of the novel—setting free the androgynous voice, successfully balancing the I and the We. With the requisite courage and imagination, Price disturbs the easy assumptions of gender to explore the possibility of shared rather than tensive gender, to arrive (as Walter Porter does) at a necessary time to bolt, to dislocate the self and to explore that facet of our human makeup not available to those too consciously bound to gender. The voice of Kate Vaiden may be intriguing because it is Kate's, but it is important, finally, because it is Price's.

Notes

1. Reynolds Price, *Kate Vaiden* (New York: Atheneum, 1986), p. 46.

2. Price himself develops the multiple meanings of the word "bolt," which he uses throughout the text to mean both the active (to run suddenly without explanation) and the passive (to be firmly attached to another). The novel, as well, uses "bolt" in a variety of other meanings, creating from it something of a motif.

3. Price himself has argued rather strongly against the possibility of the institutional church providing "spiritual nourishment," the sort of experience necessary to conduct "successful negotiations with the supernatural" or to confirm "self-transformations" (*Conversations with Reynolds Price,* ed. Jefferson Humphries [Jackson: University Press of Mississippi, 1991], p. 248).

4. The argument here is based on the important work of Carol Gilligan, who has defined in psychological terms the problem of autonomy and compassion central to the development of the female sensibility (see *In a Different Voice: Psychological Theory and Women's Development* [Cambridge: Harvard University Press, 1982]); Adrienne Rich, who has so eloquently examined the struggle to define the self against the imperative of reproduction (see *Of Woman Born: Motherhood as Experience and Institution* [New York: Norton, 1976]); and Lucinda Mac-Kethan, who traces the female struggle for voice within Southern literature, where the urge toward individuality is complicated by a persistent agrarian culture that idealizes women and, hence, denies them individuality or growth (see *Daughters of Time: Creating Woman's Voice in Southern Story* [Athens: University of Georgia Press, 1980]).

5. Joanne S. Frye, *Living Stories, Telling Lives: Women and the Novel in Contemporary Experience* (Ann Arbor, Michigan: University of Michigan Press, 1986).

6. Quoted in Constance Rooke, *Reynolds Price* (Boston: Twayne, 1983), p. 4.

7. Kate's striking way with metaphoric language is most curious and most insistent. Initial critical response found such a deliberate speaking device "highly distinctive" (Robert Tower, "Ways Down South," *New York Review of Books,* September 25, 1986, pp. 55–56); "homely" if a bit unbelievable for its cleverness (Walter Clemons, "The Ballad of a Country Girl on the Run," *Newsweek,* June 23, 1986, p. 78); "exhaustingly rich" (Robert Wilson, "Confessions of a Country Girl," *New Republic,* September 22, 1986, pp. 40–41). The disturbing connection to Kate's larger strategic withdrawal from experience has not been drawn out.

8. This central dilemma in Price's work has been pointed out by Allen Shepherd, "Love (and Marriage) in *A Long and Happy Life,*" *Twentieth-Century Literature,* 17 (1971), 29–35; Clayton L. Eichelberger, "Reynolds Price: 'A Banner in Defeat,' " *Journal of Popular Culture,* 1 (1972), 410–417; and to a much greater extent in Rooke's introduction to her Twayne book on Price.

9. The following discussion of androgyny draws together a remarkable series of works on the subject written, for the most part, during the 1970s, most critically the work of Carolyn Heilbrun (*Toward a Recognition of Androgyny* [New York: Knopf, 1973]), June Singer (*Androgyny: Toward a New Theory of Sexuality* [Garden City: Anchor, 1976]), and Robert Kimbrough (*Shakespeare and the Art of Humankindness: An Essay toward Androgyny* [Atlantic Highlands:

Humanities Press, 1990]). Price's remarks are taken from his essay "Men Creating Women" (*New York Times Book Review*, November 9, 1986, pp. 1, 16, 18, 20), which appeared shortly before the publication of *Kate Vaiden*. It is, of course, a matter of necessary subjectivity whether *Kate Vaiden* is the "great androgynous work" that Heilbrun confidently argued (p. 171) would be produced by the sexual revolutions of mid-century, but Price tackles the possibilities of consciously rejecting the limitations of gender indoctrination.

10. Anne Robinson Taylor, *Male Novelists and Their Female Voices: Literary Masquerades* (Troy, New York: Whitston, 1981), p. 2.

11. Quoted in Louise Westling, *Sacred Groves and Ravaged Gardens: The Fiction of Eudora Welty, Carson McCullers, and Flannery O'Connor* (Athens: University of Georgia Press, 1985), p. 64.

12. Walter has been ignored by initial critical responses to the novel; Rosellen Brown ("Travels with a Dangerous Woman," *New York Time Book Review*, June 29, 1986, pp. 1, 40–41) alone mentions him, only to dismiss him with the withering epithet "saintly," any admiration leavened with disbelief. He is wholly overlooked in the only published essay on the novel (Lynn Veach Sadler, "The 'Mystical Grotesque' in the Life and Works of Reynolds Price," *Southern Literary Journal*, 23 [1988], 27–39), which rushes to embrace the apparent strength and honesty of the title character.

Lunging in the Dark:
Blindness and Vision, Disappointment and Aspiration in Reynolds Price's *New Music*

R. C. FULLER

You can't ask Fate for road maps. . . . You lunge, in the dark.
—Neal Avery from Price's *Night Dance* (108)

In his trilogy *New Music,* Reynolds Price understands life as a metaphor of aspiration, a drama in which our role as observers, our attention to the stage's visions, draws us imaginatively inward to become actors in a fantasy beyond mere shimmering surfaces, even beyond existence itself. Contemporary audiences of his dramas and readers of his fiction, seemingly blind to these mysterious flights, often interpret Price's writings as "basically lyrical, realistic" (Kaufman 81). Price himself avers, however, that while his works negotiate with the real, mundane world that all human beings perceive through their natural senses, he also emphasizes that this same world's capability of "swelling at moments of intensity to a mysterious, transfigured world lies only slightly beneath the surface." During such moments of "swelling," all manner of unrealistic events occur: "the return of dead, outrageous coincidence, great rushes of communication between people" (79). Their prevalence and permeance across the pages and the stages of Price's trilogy certainly portray a world with the potential to transform itself: *Night Dance* features what Price calls the "strange, unexplained moments" of the dead returning twice (Evett 8–I), and both *August Snow* and *Better Days* feature numerous "unashamed" soliloquies showing secrets that transform perspectives on the characters (Price, *New Music* 9). Thus, Price's plays "behave quite unrealistically" yet with what he calls "a hyperrealism, a truth which is beyond question" (Kaufman 81).

Through their "hyperrealism," Price reveals life billowing like a dream, but the dream is unquestionably true. Price's world is self-consciously theatrical, but the theatrical elements are more honest and expansive than this world. In this manner, Price understands theater is the art of seeing, the psychology and the theology of bearing witness to hidden mysteries.[1] His hyper-

Reprinted, with permission, from *Southern Quarterly* 33.2–3 (Winter–Spring 1995): 45–56.

realistic images of the dead and alive lift the shrouds off their secrets and demand attention.

Moreover, in this trilogy, Price stages several of these hyperrealistic scenes for the audience only: no characters are privy to them, and they do not advance the play's plot. By theatrical convention, only the audience, of course, sees and hears the many featured soliloquies. Thus, Price consciously emphasizes the audience's role as witness. These characters acknowledge this audience of strangers and tell them secrets that even their closest family members do not know. Neal, the protagonist of *New Music,* even addresses audiences directly and, in his last long soliloquy, imagines how we would respond if we were in his shoes. This presentational device forces us as audience members to reflect on our position both inside and outside of the play's world. Similarly, *Night Dance* concludes with the hyperrealistic image of two ghosts *alone* on stage dancing together. Again, Price instructs his audiences to behold this scene (without us, no one would see it) and urges us imaginatively to reconsider how we look at our own worlds. Thus, he counsels us about our vital viewing role as we lunge through the dark of life's theater with no road map.

The mindful interaction of seeing and being seen that defines Price's dramas discourages scholars and other die-hard-readers-turned-audience-members from searching for influences from this writer's extensive list of novels on the form of his plays. The theater's reflective perspective distinguishes its art, and, surprisingly enough, the effect sways in the opposite direction. As Price himself explains, "the method of my fiction is tremendously influenced by the theater" (Evett 8–I), and when he talks of the influences on the hyperrealistic happenings and tone of many of his novels, he lists *The Tempest, The Winter's Tale, The Magic Flute* and Japanese Noh plays (Kaufman 81). Thus, while Price has most frequently chosen the novel as the form for his writing, he has also often chosen the double-vision of theater and found ways of suggesting it in various genres.

So, we must keep the image of this mutually reflecting relationship in theater before us as we grope for some understanding of Reynolds Price's *New Music;* otherwise, we are like Jonah blindly sailing away from our Nineveh. However, as with Jonah, this task of bearing witness is not always easy. In our case, this is especially difficult because this aspect of the dramatic event seems as intangible and ephemeral as Bottom's bottomless dream in Shakespeare. Moreover, observing the phenomenon of seemingly endless reflection in Price's art—observing observers observing and at times being observed by the actors—creates a mysterious sort of "vertigo" that is hard to view directly without getting a trifle dizzy (Cope 4).

Luckily, the palpable experiences of the Avery family, three generations of observers, offer guidance and deceptively level ground. As their surname "Avery" suggests, they "aver," they bear witness to their visions with their voices. They have keen eyes, love language and understand the "first principle" of southern storytelling: *"Be as clear and entertaining as truth and brevity allow (and if the truth is boring, don't hesitate to stretch it)"* (266). Roma, the widowed matriarch of the Avery clan, is "a looker," one who studies the world with her "great wide eyes" (177). Moreover, she remembers "every word she'd heard" and feels compelled to comment (often harshly) on everything she sees and hears around her (178). Her late husband Britt called her "a *truth* monger" (39), and she calls her talk "my Famous Fountain of Truth" (65). During the last three years of her life, however, she is blinded by cataracts and "hates most minutes she breathed after that" because she can no longer witness the world about her (177). Without that ability to reflect her vision of things, she grows more bitter.

When Roma strokes her eyes and tells us in soliloquy that her father "shows" in her son Neal's eyes, she implies that this gift for observing runs in the family and has been passed on to a third generation. Later, she explains in detail the power of Neal's gaze in his youth: "he watched it [life] so close. Most people's eyes are like fish in a cave—just not *there*. Neal saw all the world, in his own hot light, and could grin back at it" (140). Price's trilogy focuses on Neal as a "close" witness who ages from twenty-two to fifty-nine over the course of the three plays but sees himself "stuck in the shoals" for much of that time, unsure of his identity, his purpose and his actions (153). In the first play, *August Snow* and in the time prior to it, Neal clearly represents what his first name means: "the champion." Especially from the perspectives of his mother, his wife Taw and his best friend Porter, Neal symbolizes "the golden boy" (115), "the king" (142), even a saint or a god (140). In his review of the original production of Price's trilogy at the Cleveland Play House in 1989, *New York Times* theater critic Mel Gussow takes issue with Neal being "the object of everyone's love and admiration" because there is little "to justify such a supposition": "Neal does not really stand out, except in the eyes of his beholders" (16).[2] That, however, seems precisely Price's point. For example, Neal himself fully realizes that his "beholders' " suppositions are unjustified. From Neal's own perspective, he recognizes his own human limitations, even frailties. In soliloquy, Neal reveals to the audience:

> The trouble, my whole life, has been this—people fall for me, what they think is me. . . . They think life can't go on without me—when I know life can go on in the dark if they blind you, butcher you down to a torso, stake you flat on a rank wet floor and leave you lonesome as the last good soul.
> Neal Avery can't save the *shrubbery* from pain, much less human beings. . . . It may be why I'm soaked to the ears so much of the time—*I know I'm me,* an average white boy with all his teeth, not Woodrow Wilson or Baby Jesus or Dr. Pasteur curing rabies with shots. (36)

From Neal's perspective, his name "Avery" means "average," and if he is "champion" of anything, it is only the average.[3] The weight of these impossible expectations established by Neal's loved ones' visions of him causes him to question his identity quite seriously:

Who on God's round Earth do they think I am? Who would patch their hearts up and ease their pain? If I stand still here for many years more, won't they wear me away . . . with the looks from their famished eyes? (36)

Neal feels required to satiate the starving looks of Roma, Porter and Taw, and they all use similar metaphoric language to describe their relationships to him. Roma compares herself as a devouring mother to a"she-wolf" (142), Porter admits that Neal was his "daily bread" for "long years" (109) and later tells Taw (who seems to agree with him) that "we ate Neal up . . . you, me, and Miss Roma" (115). All three have created images of Neal that they require to feed their own narcissistic needs and transform their own pains. As their language suggests, they swallow their god-image of Neal, like the Eucharist, to nourish their own hungry hearts. His image serves as food for their own psychometabolic processes. By consuming their images of Neal with their eyes, they also introject the qualities that they have projected onto him, incorporating these strengths into themselves and creating needed changes.[4]

But while Roma, Porter and Taw bask in the "hot light" of Neal's eyes and smile, nourishing themselves on their inflated vision of him, Neal weakens and feels that "they wear me away" (36). No one feeds his own "special need worthy of care" (59). From Neal's perspective, he senses the dark psychological pain of constantly feeding others' inner cravings: the harsh cannibalism of the Eucharist. At first, we might think that their grandiose image of Neal would also build him up and nourish him. As Neal himself admits, "for a while, I was one splendid boy" (187). Overall, however, they deplete him and make it difficult for him to change himself, to transform himself from boy to man. Not only do they nourish themselves on his exaggerated image, but in order to do so they must also greatly exaggerate his dependence on them for his self-image. By inflating their image of him, they also inflate his dependence on their eyes for his worth.

As his parent, Roma's effect on her only child Neal has been lifelong (longer than that of Taw or Porter), and it has undoubtedly intensified since her husband's recent death. Not too surprisingly, her parental hunger relates directly to Neal's inability to separate fully from her and enter adulthood. In his paper on "The Dark Self," Peter Mudd helps explain how parents who feed narcissistically on a child's reflection fail to mirror back an appropriate parental image for the child to introject. In their mutual reflection, while Neal feeds his mother's "famished eyes" and aids her psychometabolic process, she does not, ironically, feed her son appropriate food that would nourish his metamorphosis into manhood. What she provides Neal is as "healthy as a sack of rat bait" (Price, New Music 22). Because of Roma's narcissistic needs (which she openly admits throughout the first two plays), she actually inflates her own importance as image-creator to secure Neal's dependence on her. As a result, she does not allow Neal to grow up: "The parent who fails to reinstall the self becomes . . . a glutton who feeds on the idealization process and cannot tolerate its appropriate gradual reduction. . . . [This] undermines the development of personality" (Mudd 14). Consequently, a parent, like Roma, "who feasts on the self-projection" she has placed on her child, engenders conflict for him by obscuring the "true self of the child" beneath the eternal omnipotent power of the adult. In short, for a boy like Neal, his true self is sacrificed to Roma, or rather to his inner "parental deity" (11): a mythological infanticide similar to those of Isaac, Jephthah's daughter and Jesus in the Bible.[5]

As a result, what inflated him as a boy now deflates him as he tries to live up to it as a young adult. He has given up all his authority to the demands of the deities he has incorporated into himself, and the weight of their impossible expectations threaten his inner life and create much of the initial tension for his character in the play. Because he cannot possibly live up to their images of him, he feels constantly disappointed with himself. In his soliloquy, he considers whether he should "flee for life, for my good and theirs," and certainly, as he admits, his tendency to be "soaked to the ears so much of the time" represents his current attempts to escape the pressure of being a martyr devoured for others' nourishment (36). Rather than strengthening his view of himself, however, the alcohol has "blurred" his "vision" further (23), making him "blinder" than Taw "ever dreamed" he could be (8). As a result of his increasing blindness, Taw issues Neal an ultimatum about his alcoholism: he must stop drinking and stay at home providing "loyal attention" or she will pack her bags and leave him after only a single year of marriage (7). She will not allow the "hot light" of his eyes to be cooled by alcohol. Thus, Neal must give up his wife's love or his love of liquor. If he chooses the latter, that means he will also have to find another means of flight and transformation.

Taw initially suggests that they physically flee together, leave Neal's small-town home in eastern North Carolina, "go someplace and breathe." She feels that Neal is "strangling" because of Roma and Porter's suffocating needs. According to Taw, physical distance may loosen the rope around Neal's throat (28). Likewise, however, in subsequent scenes, Roma and Porter tell Taw that she too "smothers" Neal and makes it difficult for him "just to draw his next breath" because of her close proximity and the pressures of marriage (39, 57). Interestingly, each of these three who love Neal can see how the other two choke him, cutting off his breath, his ability to aspire. All of them, moreover, encourage the others (and begrudgingly agree) to "step back" from Neal so he won't feel stifled and can get some "air and room" to grow (56, 58).

Ultimately, Neal does not physically flee. He cannot abandon his responsibility to Taw (bonds to her as her husband), to Roma (bonds to her as her son and to his father's clothing store, hounds and horses), and to Porter (bonds to him as his friend). However, Price's trilogy is less concerned with Neal's action—whether he flees or not, whether he drinks or not—than with his "mind." As Taw explains when they reunite at the end of *August Snow,* what she really wants is for Neal to be *"present"* in his "right mind" with "clear eyes" (81–82). More than a change in Neal's behavior, he needs to transform his mind's perspective of his role in the lives of those he loves. He struggles with no less than transforming his inner deities, gradually reducing the claim they have on his life, and resuscitating his true self.

No doubt Taw, Roma and Porter's "stepping back" will help relieve some of the immediate pressure to save them that Neal feels in his daily life. But more importantly, Taw's suggestion of "fleeing" helps change Neal's inner perspective. When she envisions an action that focuses primarily on his own needs, she helps trigger his imagination with three different visions: a memory, a fantasy and a dream. During his discussion of fleeing with Taw, he recalls his memory of first seeing her months before she ever saw him. In other words, as he contemplates Taw's ultimatum, he remembers that before she ever met him or asked him for anything, he observed her from a tree and decided he would "volunteer" to "take and keep" her (30). This picture reminds him of the power of his own free vision—that he chose the role of Taw's protector before she even knew him. Rather than associating her with the powers of his parental deities, he realizes that he placed claims on her long before she ever placed claims on him. He recognizes the power of his own vision and takes responsibility for it. Similarly, in a later scene, he admits his own free choice again, this time in his relationship with Porter. Here, Neal fantasizes about fleeing together: future adventures to Mexico with Porter. Once more, at this point, Neal's action regarding this flight is less important than the validation he gives his imagining and his admission that he "may want that" (34). He consciously becomes aware that he is not just being acted upon by the needs of others, but he is also acting upon his own needs. He envisions a future for himself and admits that the trip to Mexico may indeed be what he aspires to. In other words, he is breathing again and increasingly understands his life as a metaphor of aspiration.

Finally, in the concluding scene of *August Snow,* Neal dreams of a flight that magically transforms him:

> I run the last step over the ledge and fall through space toward a sharp rock valley. . . . I'm bound to die. Then my arms stretch out on the wind rushing by. And—God!—I rise fifty yards in a sweep before I level off and glide. I'm scared cold-stiff but I flap my arms, and this time I understand I've learned to fly.
>
> The sun breaks out . . . I'm climbing and banking and looping-the-loop while all the cruel children line up on the ledge . . . and beg me to land and teach them how. I just glide on. (80)

The image of the young boy flyer in dreams has often been associated with the *puer aeternus* who finds it difficult to develop or trust his own masculine powers because the male ideal in the person of the father was destroyed, in Neal's case, destroyed by Britt Avery's early death and Roma's portrayal of her late husband as a "son of a bitch . . . frying in Hell" (46). In this respect, Neal's dream of flight most closely resembles the Egyptian myth of Horus who rises hawklike above his dead father to redeem him. As James Hillman explains, "In a young man's life . . . the puer represents the necessity of seeking the fathering spirit, the capacity to father. The Horus image of flying higher and further connotes a spiritual fathering" (167). Thus, the image of the puer in flight, the eternal youth, is transformative: it mentors him, helps spiritually initiate him into manhood by redeeming the father, and envisions his achievement and escape from within the life he has chosen. Even though he physically does not roam, in this dream, Neal gains the power to flee via his imagination. The dream affirms Neal's imaginative power to conceive his own separation from the "cruel children," to achieve his own individuation. Neal's initial fears of becoming "the thing" that Taw wants him "to turn into," of becoming "housebroke" like an old hound, are defied by his dreams' image of his freedom while he lies sleeping at home in his Morris chair (5, 78). Afterward, moreover, Taw suggests that his metamorphosis in the dream (to a flyer) has created a change in him in the outer world as well. She calls him a "whole new man" and observes his "clear eyes" (82). Neal's transformation into manhood has been assisted by his reflection on his creative image of himself in the dream (as certain nourishment for his psychometabolic needs as the food Taw passes him in a bowl at their supper table). At the end of *August Snow*, Neal has begun to realize his need for the food his own visions supply.

Nevertheless, Price astutely recognizes that our individuation involves a complex process of transformations: major conflicts rarely resolve themselves so thoroughly at a single point in life that we feel completely free and they never rear their Medusa-like heads again.[6] Most of our major conflicts remain ours for life, and Price's trilogy allows him to show how Neal's struggles manifest themselves at various times in his life. *August Snow* ends in 1937, a time Price chose "for the imminence of the Second World War, a coming storm of which the characters are oblivious, though the audience is not" ("Genesis" 7). *Night Dance* begins in 1945, at the end of the war, as the characters face the tragedies of the "bodies that stump back here" and the prospects of peace (155).

The war creates new "storms" for Neal, who is now thirty years old, and he again fights blindness regarding his identity and personal path. He initially struggles with having been excluded from serving in the war because of his two flat feet (34). This makes him again feel inadequate as a man and feel alienated from his other male friends like Porter Farwell and Wayne Watkins (another childhood friend), who were drafted and served. While these buddies proved themselves on the world's stage, Neal was stuck at home with no outward opportunity to prove himself as a warrior or a "champion." Instead, because he was rejected by the army, he feels like damaged goods. News of Wayne's death on Okinawa after the Japanese surrender intensifies Neal's feelings of pain, injustice and self-blame. When Taw accuses Neal of drinking again, Neal defends himself: "Give me *some* human credit. I loved a boy for years; he's gone. I never marched as far as the city limits; Wayne went round the world and is dead for his pains" (90).

Taw and Neal have been given the burden of delivering this news to Wayne's wife Genevieve (who lives above them and has also been their long-time friend and landlady). When she excuses herself from their company and shoots herself, their sorrow and survivors' guilt, of course, multiply. They grow increasingly "sad and ragged" (157).

In the hospital, before she dies, however, Genevieve calls Neal to her bedside. While she fails to hold on to life, a few moments after her death, standing in her "blood-soaked" gown, she appears to Neal (118). To Neal's credit as a witness, he completely believes in this hyperrealistic image of the dead returning and never doubts Genevieve's resurrected presence. Like Michael Egerton's friend in Price's earliest story and Bridge Boatner in his much more recent novel, Neal suffers the brutal vision of another's passion and pain, allows his eyes to take it in fully and accepts its message of grace, of life beyond death and the surface of things.[7]

In addition to her appearance, Genevieve's words also offer guidance. She testifies that Neal once again is "going blind fast" when he needs "new eyes" (124). Despite his patient observation of Genevieve's ghost, he has for-gotten that "You must stand in your life; it's all you've got" (123). Instead, Neal continually compares his outward journey with other men's and finds himself lacking. For instance, when Taw advises that they "don't have a lot to show—on paper, in the sky" but they are "walking the path most humans walk," Neal calls her a liar (156). Likewise, he becomes defensive with Genevieve's ghost and tells her that he's as "realistic as a week of migraines" (124). To a ghost, however, realism is of little value. She reminds him of the symbolic, the metaphor of aspiration that is his very life no matter what soil he stands on. She challenges him to see with "new eyes" and recognize that the warrior's battle rages on in Neal's inner life as he continually tries to con-quer his own disappointments and the threats of alcoholism.

Specifically, she also tells Neal to have a child in order to bring a new pair of eyes into his home: a constant reminder of youth's imaginative per-spective. Her words, moreover, "Get you a child" (123), symbolically suggest Neal's need for spiritual rebirth. Throughout the play, Genevieve and Wayne, even in their deaths, are clearly foils for Taw and Neal. After witnessing Genevieve's suicide, for instance, Neal imagines his own: "I may be a ghost. Maybe I died too. Maybe I drove out toward the river, once Gen was gone, and plugged my brain with cold lead shot" (158). His suicidal fantasy reflects his need to die metaphorically in order to be reborn into his own identity, into his own true self. His death impulse serves a "transcendent function," helping him "to climb across" to his new life (Mudd 13).[8] Similarly, in this context, Neal's need for a child symbolizes his current need for personal renewal and transformation. Neal calls himself "an antique" (155), and Porter calls Neal "worse" than dead (141). In the final moment of this second play, the resurrected dead, Wayne and Genevieve, dance together on stage, and Neal and Taw have exited to the bedroom with hopes of conceiving their child. When Wayne describes the other couple as "dead to the world," however, he suggests not only their sleeping, but also their dying to the world's limited perspective and being born into their imagination's unlimited perspective.

In *Better Days,* the third play of the trilogy, Roma's death is the slow burn that further transforms Neal by finally freeing him from the fate of forever feeding his mother's narcissistic needs. The first scene begins after Roma's burial as the family tries to negotiate this transition in their lives. Surprisingly, and much to Taw's chagrin, Neal announces his intention for them to move back into his childhood home where they have both experienced much meanness and pain. Because he has internalized Roma's demanding hunger, Neal, even at fifty-nine years old, even after her physical departure, is unable to separate fully from her and is, at first, ready to crawl back in this symbolic womb. When he and Porter read Roma's will, however, Neal learns that his mother has left the house to his son Cody instead. Again, Neal faces disappointment as he realizes his mother's lack of "trust" in him and her displeasure that he never stood up to her (221). But by carefully observing the world around him and slowly building his confidence about his power as a witness, he begins to doubt his mother's perspective and the negative authority of his inner parental deities that Roma's disapproval triggers for him.

For example, Roma justifies the decisions in her will by noting Cody's perfection which "has not given less than complete satisfaction" (221). No doubt Neal recognizes such a statement as similar to the inflation he received before Roma felt betrayed by his union with Taw. Moreover, his eyes have witnessed the "sad damned sight" that falsifies Roma's claim (233). Thanks to a generous commanding officer, Cody has been given "compassionate leave" from the Vietnam War to attend his grandmother's funeral (180), and Neal witnesses the changes that have taken place in his son. As much as he has admired Cody's strength and goodness (227), Neal cannot deny what his eyes and ears now tell him: Cody admits he is "a trained killer" in a "dumb and vicious" war who loves power, "can't wait to lengthen his gory list," and has "very-nearly-lost-his-mind" (227–28, 231).

Witnessing this not only lessens Roma's authority, but it also reminds Neal that boys' deeds in war do not necessarily make them men and heroes. At one point in *Better Days,* Neal is surrounded by three different veterans of wars, and all three discredit the heroism of service. In addition to Cody, Porter calls stories of his heroism "lies" (189), and Dob Watkins (Wayne's father) avows, "They ought to just shot me on Armistice Day. What they sent back here won't me—nobody *I* respected" (184). Their testimonies once again deflate Neal's idealized image of military service and his craving to participate in order to make himself a man. Their stories remind Neal that the heroic journey cannot always be found outwardly, and, thus, they indirectly lend authority to Neal's victorious inward battles.

While his powers of observation strengthen his sense of individual authority, when he witnesses Fontaine Belfont, his mother's lover in the years after his father's death, Roma's grip on him loosens even further. Fontaine, who misses Roma's funeral because of a flat tire, introduces himself to her family later at the house and speaks frankly of their relationship. From Fontaine's presence and words, Neal fully realizes his mother's "Self-Sufficiency" (255). Despite Roma's constant complaints to Neal and feelings of betrayal and jealousy, the truth that Fontaine demonstrates is that she created a life all her own and of which Neal was no part. Like Thomas Eborn in Price's *Love and Work,* Neal, by witnessing such news about his parent, finds freedom from guilt and duty. Now, Roma can no longer trigger his own demanding deities. Like his mother, he has the right to create a life of his own. This validates his own life as witness and gives him a surprising sense of hope for the future where he had none before: "I am the one with hope. Who'd have ever guessed that? Roma Avery's son, the world's oldest boy. There's time for us all. I can see that far" (262). His time has come, and, with no accusations of blindness from any sources, he envisions spending his future as an observer who will "watch my son . . . making his own path, renewing our line" (227). Well, early in the play, Cody has made it clear that their "safe clean lovable town" is "dead" with nothing to offer him, but by the end of the play, he is making plans to visit at least and to share the house with Fontaine and Porter "if I come home alive" (261). Of course, there's no certainty because the war could interfere, but we also know in the audience that at the time of the play's setting (July 1974) the Vietnam War is in its final months, so we, like Neal himself, are encouraged to envision "Better days" (263).

By relying on the audience's knowledge to mirror Neal's vision of hope, Price again emphasizes our part in the theatrical event: we are needed as witnesses to make the play's final perspective complete. Throughout the three plays, as well, hyperrealistic scenes for our eyes only, soliloquys that directly address us and Neal's palpable experience as an observer remind us of our vital role as spectators: again, without witnesses, theater cannot exist. Moreover, Price reminds us that just as Neal's vision allows someone "as torn as me" to still see "life" and "hope" (228, 262), so too the power of our imaginative visions renews our own lives.

Fully witnessing the theatrical event offers both psychological and theological metaphors of salvation. For example, to participate fully in Price's imaginative world requires us to use our minds to leave the logic of our concrete world. Like Peter Mudd's articulation of transcendent function's needs, the experience of theater suspends our tight hold on literal destinies and controlling strategies. As viewers, we must be willing to "die" in the service of the play becoming "alive." In this manner, the play's suspension of our disbelief in the audience frees our imaginations to play. The metaphorical sacrifice of our doubting selves to the theatrical experience ironically breathes life into and animates the greater potentialities of our hidden selves. When the status of the active ego is relativized during the play, personality itself becomes more pliable, inner deities more transformable, and we too are renewed. Likewise, theologically, Price understands humankind, in "this prodigious theater" of the world, as the "indispensable spectator" who imitates "the *oculus infinitus* which is God" (Cope 27). In this view, seeing is an act of creation by which God's divinity is perceived in the diversity of others' eyes, and, by analogy, human vision is also creative, reflecting divinity and the diverse theater of human identities. Thus, each new human reflection transforms the face of the deity and its demands.

For Price, the theater embodies "our mutual room" where we sit in the dark and watch "other members of our species—all shades of gender and private need" lunging on a stage ("Vast Common Room" 377). Reflection on his trilogy offers loaves and fishes for our own diverse personae and their needs.

Notes

1. To understand theater as a way of viewing, an art of seeing, is to recognize the etymology of the word *theater*, which means a place for seeing and comes from the same root (*thea*—the act of seeing) as theory, connecting it closely to observation and belief.

2. My continued appreciation goes to Charlie Owens and the rest of the staff at the Cleveland Play House who assisted my research by providing information about the original production of *New Music* and by making it possible for a poor graduate student to see the entire trilogy in 1989.

3. The word "average" comes from the French word "avarie" (very close to "Avery") which means "damaged goods."

4. The suggestion of the Eucharist also connects Neal's sacrifice of himself archetypally with Dionysos, the patron of the drama. Like the Christian disciples and others, the earlier participants in the Greek Dionysion mysteries also ritualistically dismembered and ate the god and drank him as well as experienced the drama's passion to incorporate the divine spirit into themselves.

5. Appropriately, Price has translated the Old Testament stories (Genesis 22 and Judges 11) of Abraham's near sacrifice of Isaac and Jephthah's sacrifice of his daughter—archetypal predecessors of God's sacrifice of his son Jesus. For more information, see Price's *Presence and Absence: Versions from the Bible.* (Columbia, SC: Bruccoli, 1974). Certainly this testifies to Price's longtime fascination with children's symbolic sacrifices of themselves to their parents.

6. Actually, according to Price, the drama of Perseus is the central myth of the artist's depth journey with artist in all roles, Perseus and Medusa and Athena's mirror-shield (see "Dodging Apples," *A Common Room* 186). For Price as a writer, the "mirror-shield" represents the self-reflective distance of the narrative act. In addition, the Medusa symbolizes those cavernous aspects of ourselves that we cannot look on directly without turning to stone with fright. For Neal, while his mother sometimes acts like a monster, his real Medusa is his monstrous inner fear of his internalized maternal deity.

7. The narrator of Price's earliest story bears witness to the Christ-like suffering of his friend and fellow camper "Michael Egerton" (62). Similarly, in Price's recent novel, *The Tongues*

of Angels, camp counselor Bridge Boatner bears witness to death of his camper Rafe. Despite the pain involved in such observations, Bridge testifies: "Only the endlessly watchful life is worth living and will be rewarded. . . . You watch your particular set of objects because you love, or at least respect them on faith. . . . Then you go on watching with an even deeper, though maybe more painful, devotion" (30–31). Bridge especially associates the "reward" of witnessing with the grace of forgiveness.

     8. Mudd further explains: "The transcendent function is the [imaginative] capacity to die because it requires the suspension of the exclusivity of structures [like deified parental images]. . . . Without the transcendent function as an operational psychological reality . . . the personality [will be] impoverished" (17–18). In other words, Neal's suicidal fantasy suspends the power of his ravenous inner parental deities and thus nourishes his developing personality.

Works Cited

Cope, Jackson I. *The Theater and the Dream: From Metaphor to Form in Renaissance Drama.* Baltimore: Johns Hopkins UP, 1973.

Evett, Marianne. "*New Music* Comes Together." *The Plain Dealer* [Cleveland, OH] 15 Oct. 1989: 1–1+.

Gussow, Mel. "Love and Loss and the Salve of Time." Rev. of *New Music.* Cleveland Play House. *New York Times* 4 Nov. 1989: 16.

Hillman, James. "The Great Mother, Her Son, Her Hero, and the Puer." *Fathers and Mothers.* Ed. Patricia Berry. 2nd ed. Dallas: Spring, 1991. 166–209.

Kaufman, Wallace. " 'Notice I'm Still Smiling': An Interview with Reynolds Price." *Kite-Flying and Other Irrational Acts: Conversations with Twelve Southern Writers.* Ed. John Carr. Baton Rouge: Louisiana State UP, 1972. 70–95.

Mudd, Peter. "The Dark Self: Death As a Transferential Factor." Eleventh International Congress for Analytical Psychology. Paris, Summer 1989.

Price, Reynolds. "The Genesis of *New Music.*" *Curtain Times* [Newsletter of the Cleveland Play House]: 7.

———. "Michael Egerton." *The Names and Faces of Heroes.* London: Chatto and Windus, 1963. 54–63.

———. *New Music.* New York: Theatre Communications Group, 1990.

———. *The Tongues of Angels.* New York: Atheneum, 1990.

———. "A Vast Common Room." *A Common Room.* New York: Atheneum, 1987. 371–77.

Reynolds Price and Religion: The "Almost Blindingly Lucid" Palpable World

Lynn Veach Sadler

Reynolds Price has woven standard southern strands—loosely religious strands—into a unique and simultaneously typical experience. The same is true of the pattern his life has woven: one unique and yet a powerful archetype of sensitiveness and suffering transformed into creativity. The result is a world of common objects and ordinary people meaning more than they or we know, being "almost blindingly lucid" with a meaning beyond themselves. Price's use of symbols may not be conscious, but he is conscious of the fact that objects in his works become symbols in the wholeness of a narrative, as daily objects and acts become symbols in the wholeness of God's [and gods'] time: "Any sense that certain objects have become symbolic—such as the python in *A Generous Man,* or, say, the deer in *A Long and Happy Life*—comes to me, if at all, only after the story is done and the whole can be seen. Python and deer were, for me, first—and indeed finally—python and deer, *things* grander in their own mysterious life than I or my characters could ever make them by meditation" (Kaufman 79). His pattern for the craftsmanship of his work is the Bible: "it seems to me perfectly clear that the great stories of the Bible reveal that the most complex imaginable human situations and thoughts can be contained in sentences of the utmost syntactical simplicity and lucidity" (Rooke 718).

What are the typical southern strands of the religious underpinnings of his works? He lets us see them in his own summary in the introduction to *A Palpable God* (1978) and immediately makes them larger than southern as he expresses his belief that the human need to tell and hear stories is second after nourishment and comes before love and shelter, an extraordinarily high opinion of the human that may account for the fact that he has "never written about what seems to me a really bad person" (Cockshutt 54). He believes that the Bible is the origin of narrative and, in particular, that Adam invented narrative in Genesis (*A Palpable God* 8).

Like so many of us southerners, Price was nourished early on books: standard children's fare (the Hardy boys) but especially the Bible. His mater-

Reprinted, with permission, from *Southern Quarterly* 26.2 (1988): 1–11.

nal grandmother gave him Josephine Pollard's *Wonderful Stories of the Bible* when he was three. Before he could read, he loved its pictures as well as the rich oral renditions by his family of its own lore and of biblical tales. His parents, "religious but not churchly" (*A Palpable God* 11), a phrase equally applicable to Price, gave him Hurlbut's *Story of the Bible* when he was four. In his "pious adolescence" (12), stories of Jesus resurfaced as a major influence; and his second sizable narrative, written when he was thirteen, was a play about the Magi. A course in the Bible taken as a freshman at Duke became one of the "lights" of his undergraduate experience, and he took classes with Weston La Barre "in a long attempt to disprove to myself the preposterous claim of the earliest stories I had known and loved" (45). Again, like so many of us, he seems to have felt embarrassment that the Bible and religion had such a hold. A Methodist who has not been an active member of a church for over twenty years, he sees such Christian values as are visible in his words as tending "to be what Aldous Huxley called the perennial philosophy, the basic values present in all the great religions—values of charity and selflessness, which seem to me actually at the center of any possible durable ethic for human continuance on the globe" (Rooke 706–7).

Price's earliest experiences, then, draw visual and biblical narrative together, and his first narrative memory is purely visual: his bedridden paternal grandmother slaps his mother, who is in the act of bending to kiss her—an image surely "almost blindingly lucid" to the child hearing about it and seeing it through his imagination. In that narrated picture resides the lucidity of craziness or animosity as well as blindness to motive and reality. Similarly, the Bible pictures that inform Price's childhood reveal and withhold revelation. Unusually, for example, Jesus raising the dead girl becomes for the young Reynolds Price the conduit for the fact that children are serious people and can die. Elsewhere, he describes such pictures as enabling him to imagine significant deeds by children and recalls his near epiphany at his first Christmas pageant, when he was four or five: "I wouldn't have been able to state my personal logic, but the substance was something very much like this—*A child is the center of Christmas. All these adults are gathered to watch him. A child is the center of an entire faith. I am a child. I matter in the world*" ("Child's Christmas" 212). In his first novel, *A Long and Happy Life* (1962), Rosacoke Mustian works out what to do with her life as she plays Mary in the Christmas pageant.

In the grasping after meaning first in the "almost blindingly lucid Bible stories" (*A Palpable God* 11) and then in his own works, Price cuts back to the rich emblematic tradition that died out with Bunyan, who would be very much at ease with the inchoate reach toward the figurative by the untutored Price characters early (e.g., Rosacoke's hawks and deer) and late (Kate Vaiden's voluble wielding of metaphor and simile in the most recent novel, 1986). In deriving from biblical narrative the belief that a story is an account of something seen and made visible in the telling, of something known especially by the narrator but partially by the audience (14), he cuts back to Milton (the "fit audience . . . though few"), whose *Samson Agonistes* was the subject of his thesis at Oxford; Price published a version of it in *Things Themselves* (1972), as well as an article interpreting the poem ("Poem Doctrinal and Exemplary to a Nation"), and teaches a course on Milton at Duke. Indeed, his contribution may be the ability to see and unite both of these strands.

That dual, oxymoronic vision—Bunyanesque and Miltonic, simple and complex, perhaps the secret also of our "southernness"—is of long standing, too, in Price's canon. The humble characters of *A Long and Happy Life* and *A Generous Man* (1966) are presided over and enlarged by epigraphs from Dante's *Paradiso* and *Purgatorio,* respectively, though the author and the audience, rather than the characters, must derive meaning from the juxtaposition. Similarly, though its characters are more sophisticated and complex, *The Surface of Earth* (1975) draws on Augustine's *Confessions* to suggest a resolution of the opposition between the agitation of life (the surface of earth) and the calm beyond it. Normally, Price's characters, whether educated, are too apt to be members of "The Church of Getting Through Time" (*Private Contentment* 130). Writer Charles Tamplin, from whom more is expected because he knows more (and, from the reader's point of view, because he is in a large sense a mirror of Price), is one of the greatest offenders against the "blind lucidity" of the everyday; he would "kill a day as painlessly as possible" while mouthing the connection between the palpable and the "unpalpable" worlds: "Charles Tamplin felt himself suspended, space and time. This might as easily be Galilee as Oxfordshire, before Christ, before green hills burnt to sand" ("The Happiness of Others," *Permanent Errors* 8, 9). Price seems to struggle throughout his career with preventing the overlays of learning and the artist's ways of knowing from interfering with primal knowledge of the unseen world. While neither his largely untutored nor his "tutored" characters are entirely successful in marrying the seen and unseen worlds as a daily practice, he suggests greater success for the former.

Finally, however, Price cannot escape the dominance of these early influences, and their interpenetration in his life seems to have imbued him with a sense of calling to set them right in the view of, perhaps, the sophisticated who have outgrown them. A former Rhodes scholar at Oxford, who has been nurtured by the likes of Eudora Welty, Lord David Cecil, Stephen Spender and W. H. Auden and who now lives by choice in North Carolina in a house filled with art, he has been haunted by the Depression ("my generation's Civil War," Kaufman 89), though he was born as late as 1933, and the financial humiliation it meant to his own family. Although he has visited New York frequently for its culture, he is bold enough to claim that "there is no real literary establishment in America" and to describe New York as inhabited only by "publishers and agents giving drinks and lunch to each other" (Cockshutt 56). While refusing the label of "southern writer" as condescending, he has lived for years by a pond in the beech trees near Durham, North Carolina, a

setting that is both southern and Thoreauvian but also domestically ceremo-
nial and "artistic." One of his proteges, Anne Tyler, applauds his "great good
fortune to know his place, geographically speaking," and to have "a feeling
for the exact spot on earth that will properly contain him" (82–3). It is questionable whether the origin is "good fortune": the sense of oneness between
that place, with its impacted culture, and Price as writer seems to have been
hard-won. Southerners are frequently born sensitive to the skepticism of out-
siders.

Although Price learned from Eudora Welty the validity of "the normal
daily world of the vast country called the American South" ("Form of Thanks"
125), he can still (with the rest of us) smart at others' easy dismissal of that
world while knowing that it can be cloyed with conservative religion and
soured by racism. He has recently described "the two realities which undergird
all that we mean by American Southern culture" as "the presence in society of
a great many, sometimes a majority, of black men and women *and* a universal
adherence to the Christian faith" and deems "the belief in the divine nature of
a single real human figure called Jesus" to be "still the most unifying fact
[about the South]. Fifty years ago it was even more so" ("A Child's Christmas
in North Carolina" 208, 212). Both are present in his works and his life. His
black figures are memorable but tend to remain simply a part of the palpable
world Price is depicting; as examples, they run from Mildred Sutton, pare-
goric-drinking Landon Allgood, and Sammy Ransom in *A Long and Happy
Life;* through Uncle Grant thrusting himself into Price's memory during his
days at Oxford and then into *The Names and Faces of Heroes,* as Wash becomes
Miss Lillian Belle's audience in "The Anniversary" (also in *The Names and Faces
of Heroes*); and on to Noony in *Kate Vaiden.* The Christian mythos is far more
pervasive in the lives of the people in his works than the presence of blacks.
His very first story, "Michael Egerton," is set in a summer church camp whose
athletic teams are named for books of the Bible (Colossians, Ephesians). Miss
Ellie, of "Troubled Sleep," is unique for refusing to call John "the Baptist."
Rosacoke's undimmed image of Wesley (a name, of course, drawing on
Methodism) in the pecan tree in *A Long and Happy Life* is a domesticated version of Zaccheus in the sycamore tree trying to catch a glimpse of Jesus (Luke
19: 1–10). In a very large sense, then, when Price traces "the origin and life of
narrative" (a phrase used in the title of the introductory essay of *A Palpable
God*) to the Bible, he makes "almost blindingly lucid" the worth of his time
and his place (though his motivation in the search described in that essay leads
in other directions). His point is obviously well taken when Anthony Burgess
would require "A Single Meaning: Notes on the Origin and Life of Narrative"
in every creative writing class (cited in Kreyling 522).

Price's view of his own work and of the creative process is at once much
more mundane and much more generally religious than might be supposed.
He insists that his stories arrive as "sudden visual pictures" rather than as
"visions": "I don't mean to imply some mystical, quasi-religious process. It's

not that. It's a simple matter of reverie, a sudden daydream." It is the work of a "day-laborer, a hod carrier, a hoe carrier, a hoe swinger" that he believes is "in any serious novelist" ("The Creative Process" 207, 208). He is equally sure, however, that "the 'scientific' method of literary study has often been more nearly theological-expository." He points out, for example, that "A number of the New Critics . . . were sons of ministers or were reared in strict Protestant-Jewish traditions of scriptural scrutiny—and some of their more extreme techniques resemble nothing so much as the ruthless squeezings given to the book of Revelation [sic] in thousands of fundamentalist churches today" ("Dodging Apples" 2). He says he writes because of his bent to write and because he would "understand what is mysterious—in the behavior of the visible world, the behavior of God, of my friends and enemies, strangers, finally of myself" (5). That first story, "Michael Egerton," derives from a literal image of the title character and was developed as the exploration and explanation of its mystery. Ultimately, for Price, "the novel, east and west, has traditionally been, as distinguished from the poem, an instrument of reason intended for discovery and comprehension and then, of necessity, forgiveness—in fact, the supremely Christian form, the new dispensation which rose to augment, if not supersede, older pagan forms (the psalm, epic, lyric, drama) which were hymns to mystery, human and divine" ("*Pylon*" 60–1).

Despite his utilitarianism in approaching writing, Price may be working out a little uneasiness also, at the intrusion of mystery into his life. He knew by age five, for example, that his alcoholic father reformed after vowing to stop drinking if God allowed his wife, thought to be dying in childbirth, and baby (Price) to live. This episode has exerted itself throughout his career to date, early in the short story "The Names and Faces of Heroes" (*Names and Faces* 162–6) and most recently in "A Tomb for Will Price," one of the poems of *The Laws of Ice.* He had actually thought to write his first long novel on this subject, which he links with Abraham's sacrifice of Isaac. His first approach had in fact been a series of meditations on the narrative implications of Rembrandt's treatment of the story. Price called them "Four Abrahams, Four Isaacs by Rembrandt" and included them in *Things Themselves,* a collection of critical essays. He began studying the Bible and translating the thirty stories of *A Palpable God* to help him find his way in the novel that became *The Surface of Earth,* in which he makes use of both the story of the sacrifice of Isaac and of Jephthah's daughter. His second motivation was the "hard time" he was having in his life and thence the need to turn to "old supports" (13) that, as if by design, taught him about his trade. He learned in particular that a writer cannot tell his/her audience a story it does not wish to hear (23); that narrative must leave at its end an ultimately consoling effect (24), in consonance with Price's view of human existence as a "divine comedy"; and that the first and final aim of narrative is compulsion of belief in an ordered world (34). Price's earliest characters often know such lessons intuitively. Rosacoke is always looking for signs to direct her. Price's own house plays host to a col-

lection of objects (e.g., cow vertebra, a steel egg, death masks, a personal letter from General Eisenhower) that, individually or as a whole, give instant
credence to the "almost blinding lucidity" of life. The same kind of clutter of
objects may collect in a novel (e.g., a turtle, mica, oyster shells, a weasel's
skull in *A Generous Man;* those of Charles Tamplin's room in "Scars" [*Permanent Errors*]), but the only lucidity brought is to a receptive audience.

Critics have noted the deeper world in Price's works. For Theodore
Solotaroff, for example, *Love and Work* is a novel "about the unconscious and
its circuits of love, fear, and punishment—what used to be called God. There
is more than a hint of the spiritual in Price . . . which takes a psychological
rather than a theological form: a powerful sense of dark unseen forces and
influences that are only partly explained by the description of emotions and
that require not just attention but supplication" (29). Thomas Eborn, the
principal character, is more educated and more articulate than the Mustians,
but his dreams and his visions of the dead at first glance seem more appropriate to them. Again, however, the writer (Eborn) and the larger, "unseen"
world must fuse. Eborn's problem is that he lacks the capacity to dwell in
mystery, feels embarrassed by it as by love. Instead of using his learning and
his intellect to open the unseen world, he has used them to wall himself off.
By imposing an artificial order, he has prevented himself from seeing the
world's ultimate order in diversity. A ghost appears also in the much earlier *A
Generous Man,* and the child (Price) in the title story of *The Names and Faces of
Heroes* has a vision of his father's death. Price's response is this: "I do strongly
suspect, even avow the existence and presence of forms of reality quite
beyond those forms which we encounter in our daily routines. And whether
or not those forms do manifest themselves—ever, in observable, sensually
perceptive ways—certainly there can be no question that the dead linger,
most powerfully, in our lives; the meaningful dead, those people who by the
time most men have reached the age of twenty-one stand as one's ancestors
on the black side of death in relation to our present continuing lives. That's
all" (Kaufman 83).

Price's life appears infused with such near-mystical events, or he interprets them as near-mystical. His relationship with his mother, for example, is
equally momentous and unusual. We infer that she has lived a life somewhat
outside normal boundaries, though in what ways he never makes clear. She
was plagued by a sense of being orphaned (though she was reared by her elder
sister) and impressed on Reynolds a fear of abandonment. His curiosity about
her life before his birth prompts the writing of his latest novel, *Kate Vaiden;* and
an earlier poem, "A Heaven for Elizabeth Rodwell, My Mother" (1984;
included in *The Laws of Ice,* 1986), deals with hard events she had to endure.
He had already imagined her life with his father before him in "Late Warnings" ("My Parents, Winter 1926" and "The Knowledge of My Mother's Coming Death," published in the "Elegies" section [II] of *Permanent Errors,* which
has his parents' picture on the cover). The ambiguity that surrounds his rela-

tionship with them is evident even in his inclusion of these sketches and revelations in *Permanent Errors:* are these particular errors theirs or his or those of a world wrong for them in the time they had to live? While the question of lineage and its responsibility for what one is and is not is characteristically southern and recurs throughout Price's works (is even parodied, along with other "Southern paraphernalia," in *A Generous Man*), the nexus of mother, father and son seems to demand an unusually large place in Price's fiction, particularly in light of his having had a younger brother but seeming to suggest often that he evolved essentially as an only child. Much of the family material recounted in *Permanent Errors* is used in *Love and Work,* in which Eborn's mother also dies of an aneurysm. The need to write at least partially about his mother in *Kate Vaiden* forced him to abandon his vague plans to produce next a picaresque story about a man looking back with pleasure on his youth. One has to infer finally that Price feels a more than ordinary relationship to his parents and feels that, in this relationship, palpable and unpalpable meet.

Price must also wonder at the collection of coincidence in his life and the question of whether he could have "imagined" his fate in his writing. Today, of course, he has spinal cancer, detected in May 1984, when he had just read the first part of *Kate Vaiden* to Eudora Welty, and is confined to a wheelchair. One result has been a stoical overturning of depression and bouts of memory loss: "I certainly would not have chosen it. But I *have* chosen to deal with the thing and not let it deal with me. It's already done its worst with me; now I have to do my worst with it" (Shapiro 70). Another reaction has been an incredible increase in creativity: "The X rays or God have speeded up my creative metabolism" (Shapiro 70). He was back at work three months after the diagnosis. He agreed to write the play (*August Snow*) Hendrix College, in Arkansas, had requested for its drama students to perform in the fall of 1985. Then he went on to finish *Kate Vaiden* and write most of the poems in *The Laws of Ice* as well as two more plays. He is working on a collection of essays and has another novel in mind. Price's decision to make Kate Vaiden the victim of cervical cancer, then, is hardly surprising. However, earlier examples seem almost ironic auguries. In "A Chain of Love," his first published short story (1958), Rosacoke, staying in the hospital with her grandfather, is attracted to the room of the dying cancer patient across the hall. In *Love and Work* (1968), urbanism becomes "literal cancers (proliferation of unneeded cells)" (19). The dog, old Peter, in "A Dog's Death" (*Permanent Errors,* 1970) breaks out in "tumors" and has to be put to sleep; he gets linked with Charles Tamplin's willful loss of his lover Sara. Rob dies of lung cancer in *The Source of Light* (1981), as did Price's father. In "A Heaven for Elizabeth Rodwell, My Mother," first published in 1984, he has his mother say, as she watches her dying husband, *"This will kill me too. / In a minute I'll flood with cancer."*

More amazing, perhaps, is the route of Price's regaining of creative control in his battle with cancer: he turned back toward the pattern of his childhood. His eighth grade English teacher, in Warrenton, North Carolina, was the first to encourage him in writing and in art, and particularly in the latter. They used to paint, together, everything from wine bottles to dishes, and, as we have seen, he strongly emphasizes the visual among his earliest narrative memories. In his fight to recover from the operation and endure the radium treatments, he returned to painting and drawing those biblical scenes so important to his youth. He also drew a personal vision that he experienced in a strange state between waking and sleeping in which he met Jesus and was assured that he had been cured. This experience and the picture, in turn, became the genesis for "Vision," which seems, like so many of his poems, to enlist the technique of meditation known as "composition of place." He is sleeping with Jesus and his twelve disciples on the east shore of Lake Kinnereth; he has gone not to have his sins forgiven but *to be cured.*

Price's latest work is his second collection of poems, *The Laws of Ice,* in three parts like the first; they seem retrospective and, again, "blindingly lucid," as if the large questions they raise are to be answered by the palpable objects and remembered experiences and people they describe. While their subjects are wide-ranging (e.g., Vivien Leigh, who also figures in *The Source of Light;* Leontyne Price, appearing earlier in the long short story "Walking Lessons" in *Permanent Errors;* Robert Kennedy; places he has visited; relationships; his father; his mother; literary homages; James Dean), the main thrust is summative: again the southerner with his poetic fingers on the pulse of the world and of the experience of the human and the god. The book is prefaced with "Praise," a short, three-stanza invocation of the "Holy flame / By any name" whether "Creator, Terminator, Hand—." The first poem of Part I, "Ambrosia," tries to get inside the godheads and explore the meaning to them of "palpable data," a reminder of *A Palpable God.* He looks again at the Bible stories of Jonathan and David and tells the secrets of Joseph, Mary and Jesus from their individual points of view. As in *Kate Vaiden,* he will prove that a man can empathize with a woman and presents male and female speakers of their stories in "Before the Flood." The blue heron over his pond ("Late Visit") is surely the reincarnation of the one Wesley and Rosacoke are too preoccupied to see in *A Long and Happy Life.* He had described it, too, in "The Annual Heron," a poem published in 1979.

Part II of *The Laws of Ice* is a journal, in thirty-five parts, of the year in his life that unfolded his cancer. It starts on 13 February 1984, before that knowledge, and runs through the aftermath, through 14 February 1985. The Preface, written after the fact, resonates with the sense of coming lucidity: "When I began I had no expectation of the catastrophe that would announce itself on 2 June, but subliminal warnings sound as early as number 21 (3 April)" (35). Nor can the craftsman forbear the link between form and meaning that is another affirmation of the basic order of the universe: "The fact that many of the impulses came in sonnet forms was a surprise and, for me, the confirmation of an old suspicion—that the shape of the sonnet participates in a near-metabolic unity with the western mind's rate of experience and reflection" (35).

As his friend Wallace Kaufman says, "Price is like a funnel through which all memory and . . . material things travel; a funnel which is not only a straight-through narrowing tube but one which is also a blender, which transforms vast quantities of raw material into goblets of clear wine, filled to the brim and a fraction over the brim" (91). Price charges the world he describes—the palpable—with meaning; he knows that the larger world is charged with meaning. The Charger may be left undefined but yet, through Price's descriptions / recognitions of the palpable, becomes somehow palpable. Most important, the ordinary becomes justified, not transcended.

Works Cited

Cockshutt, Rod. "A Conversation with Reynolds Price." *Tar Heel* (May 1981): 28–29, 54–56.

Kaufman, Wallace. "Notice, I'm Still Smiling: REYNOLDS PRICE." *Kite-Flying and Other Irrational Acts: Conversations with Twelve Southern Writers.* Ed. John Carr. Baton Rouge: Louisiana State UP, 1972, 70–95.

Kreyling, Michael. "Reynolds Price." *The History of Southern Literature.* Ed. Louis D. Rubin, Jr., et al. Baton Rouge and London: Louisiana State UP, 1985. 519–22.

Price, Reynolds. "The Annual Heron." *Poetry* (Dec. 1979): 154–60.

———. "A Child's Christmas in North Carolina." *Bazaar* (Dec. 1986): 181, 208, 212.

———. "The Creative Process: The Novel." *North Carolina Historical Review* 56 (Apr. 1979): 206–8.

———. "Dodging Apples." *South Atlantic Quarterly* 71 (Winter 1972): 1–15.

———. "A Form of Thanks." *Eudora Welty: A Form of Thanks.* Ed. Louis Dollarhide and Ann J. Abadie. Jackson: UP of Mississippi, 1979. 123–8.

———. *A Generous Man.* New York: Atheneum, 1966.

———. *Kate Vaiden.* New York: Atheneum, 1986.

———. *The Laws of Ice.* New York: Atheneum, 1986.

———. *A Long and Happy Life.* New York: Atheneum, 1962.

———. *Love and Work.* New York: Atheneum, 1968.

———. *The Names and Faces of Heroes.* New York: Atheneum, 1963.

———. *A Palpable God: Thirty Stories Translated from the Bible with an Essay on the Origins and Life of Narrative.* New York: Atheneum, 1978.

———. *Permanent Errors.* New York: Atheneum, 1970.

———. "Poem Doctrinal and Exemplary to a Nation: A Reading of *Samson Agonistes*." *Shenandoah* 23.1 (1971): 3–36.

———. *Private Contentment.* New York: Atheneum, 1984.

———. "*Pylon:* The Posture of Worship." *Shenandoah* 19.3 (1968): 49–61.

———. *The Source of Light.* New York: Atheneum, 1981.

———. *The Surface of Earth.* New York: Atheneum, 1975.

———. *Things Themselves: Essays and Scenes.* New York: Atheneum, 1972.

Rooke, Constance. "On Women and His Own Work: An Interview with Reynolds Price." *Southern Review* 14 (October 1978): 706–25.

Shapiro, Harriet. "Reynolds Price Defies Cancer to Write His Finest Novel." *People Weekly* 26 (20 Oct. 1986): 69–70.

Solotaroff, Theodore. "The Reynolds Price Who Outgrew the Southern Pastoral." *Saturday Review* (26 Sept. 1970): 27–9, 46.

Tyler, Anne. "Reynolds Price: Duke of Writers." *Vanity Fair* (July 1986): 82–5.

The Collected Stories: A Whole Living World

ALLEN SHEPHERD

Over the past decade Reynolds Price has gradually gained recognition as one of our principal men of letters. Particularly striking are the breadth and vitality of his work: novels, novellas, short stories, poems, memoirs, plays, translations, and essays. His peers among our more prolific polymaths are John Updike and Joyce Carol Oates. It is a curious but engaging fact that although Price has been a published writer for nearly 40 years, it is still difficult, given his increasing multifariousness, to anticipate what will finally constitute his major literary focus or how he will be described in the next century's literary histories. Well into his sixties, with a large body of distinguished work behind him, Price remains a man of perhaps as yet unrealized possibilities.

Price established his considerable reputation with the early Mustian novels, *A Long and Happy Life* (1962) and *A Generous Man* (1966), both of them dark comedies, and with his first two short-story collections: *The Names and Faces of Heroes* (1963), traditionally constructed and readily accessible, and the chillingly titled and more elliptical *Permanent Errors* (1970). Of all Price's work, his first novel and his first short-story collection have been and are likely to remain many readers' favorites.

The Collected Stories (1993), Price's 25th book, evoked mixed but generally appreciative reviews.[1] However, it seems unlikely that the 50 stories collected, half of them new, will in the foreseeable future gain for Price a substantially larger or more various readership, since they are traditionally told, morally earnest, and are neither politically engaged nor sociologically rich. In *The Collected Stories* Price remains determinedly old-fashioned and unfashionable.

Consideration of the substantial differences in subject, structure, theme, and style apparent in Price's three collections of short stories will illustrate the evolution of his art and establish a context for detailed examination of seven stories.

The Names and Faces of Heroes depicts in an open, rather romantic style a semipastoral world in which good country people struggle to enact the

This essay was written specifically for this volume and is published here for the first time by permission of the author.

regional verities of home, family, faith, and historical continuity. There is apparent, even at this early stage in Price's short-story writing, a striking fusion of observation, of detail and revelatory act, with feeling and significance. Price included in this first collection all the stories he had published until that time, and it is not surprising that some are considerably less distinguished than others. Thus, for example, his first published story, "Michael Egerton," is notably derivative, whereas, by marked contrast, "A Chain of Love" offers a uniquely Pricean perspective.

The stories in *The Names and Faces of Heroes* are more varied, more conventional, and more optimistic in tone than those in Price's second collection. *Permanent Errors* is less easy to read or comprehend than its predecessor, as Price has come to prefer the oblique glance and the quick glimpse. Charles Tamplin, a self-conscious, introspective, deracinated, punitive intellectual, is the collection's presiding presence. He devotes himself to what Price describes as the controlling effort of all the collection's stories: "the attempt to isolate in a number of lives the central error of act, will, understanding which, once made, has been permanent, incurable, but whose diagnosis and palliation are the hopes of continuance."[2]

In an uncommonly insightful review, Guy Davenport accurately identified *Permanent Errors* as "a pivotal book in our literary history, as one of the brave steps beyond the fiercely Calvinist pessimism of Southern writing in general, which has consistently presented the only alternative in American thought to charismatic liberalism. Mr. Price's step," he concludes, "is into an even more iron Calvinism."[3] In *Permanent Errors,* the range of human options is much reduced; chaos and moral disorder insistently threaten. The characters are poised at the point where they imagine they can be understood by others—friends, lovers, family—and subsequently discover, their innocence or their egotism smashed, that they are forever opaque and incomprehensible to the world.

For almost 20 years after *Permanent Errors,* from 1969 to 1988, Price attempted no short fiction. "Apparently," he explains, "the narrative and lyric forces that had surfaced in stories moved instead into poems and plays."[4] The 25 new stories, then, that make up half of *The Collected Stories* Price wrote between 1988 and 1992. To construct a generic Price story of this most recent period, one would begin with a white male southerner of approximately the author's age to serve as narrator/protagonist. He is middle class, intelligent, and articulate but has not lived up to his potential. He comes from and is likely to remain in a limited, well-defined world, that of rural and small-town North Carolina. He is moved to reflect on events, often painful or mysterious or both, from his own or his family's past. His reflections focus upon sexual encounters (hetero- or homosexual), love (romantic or familial or both), and death (from childbirth, cancer, suicide, AIDS). In story after story, as Sven Birkerts observed, "the reader confronts illness, betrayal, suicidal impulses, and the seemingly impassable distances that divide people from one another."[5] Things and people pass away, and the options for hope and renewal are few and easily missed.

However, even if his characters usually start in trouble, Price sometimes envisions and celebrates possibilities of resolution or transcendence, or memorializes the glory of their human efforts. Thus in his most recent stories one finds a number of efforts at paternal confession and familial reconciliation. In "The Last News" an institutionalized alcoholic in therapy confesses by letter his "worst trespass" to his son, which was to try to "ruin her [his son's mother] for you" (112). And in "Breath" a self-confessed bad father undertakes to convey his understanding of the cause of his multiple transgressions—that he had had a bad father who in his turn had had a bad mother. In "A Final Account," one of several AIDS stories, another regretful (but not guilty) father tries to explain to his son the power, rewards, and accepted penalties of homosexual love. That we never know how these confessions are received intensifies the poignance of the effort. Another response to the common present-day naturalistic sense of radical human limitation is evident in Price's increasingly overt concern with the existence and influence of a specifically Christian supernatural realm, which figures prominently in "The Enormous Door," "Long Night," "His Final Mother," and "An Early Christmas."

Of the stories chosen for extended consideration here, only one, "A Chain of Love," comes from Price's first collection, *The Names and Faces of Heroes*. That story epitomizes the strengths and limitations of the author's early short fiction. One story, "The Happiness of Others," represents *Permanent Errors*, a volume that some critics (this writer not among them) regard as one of Price's finest works, more significant even than many of his novels. It is apparent that in his most recent work Price develops a number of the same concerns significant in *Permanent Errors*. Both that volume and the author's most recent stories address the failure of love and other losses, illness and death, the importance of work, and the resources of memory. The principal differences lie with the protagonist of Price's most recent work, who is typically a chastened and strengthened survivor, less agonized and more calmly reflective and self-possessed than his predecessors, more willing to discover what life will bring him, and more hopeful of his ability to act purposefully and to good effect. Five stories under examination here derive from Price's most recent work: "Full Day," "Bess Waters," "Nine Hours Alone," "An Early Christmas," and "Endless Mountains." Consideration of these stories focuses attention on the richest and most productive span of the author's career.

The term *stories,* as in *Collected Stories,* needs to be loosely construed, so as to accommodate sketch, memoir, anecdote, and elegy—prose pieces from 2 to 70-odd pages long. The stories are printed as written, Price says (xiii), avoiding what he elsewhere terms "the worst temptation of collectors, the revision of old work in hindsight."[6] The stories are ordered so as to "offer an alternation of voices, echoes, lengths, and concerns" (xiii). Individual stories are unfortunately not dated, which would have been a welcome courtesy to the interested reader.

The principal heroine of Price's early work is Rosacoke Mustian, who appears in "A Chain of Love," *A Long and Happy Life, A Generous Man,* and later, in *Good Hearts* (1988). Almost all readers agree that what is most striking about Rosacoke is that she is likable, virtuous, and attractive—all in all, a generally admirable person. That Rosa is in fact too good has been the suspicion of some readers, and it is a criticism that merits consideration. Price himself has argued, somewhat tendentiously perhaps, that particularly in her relation with her boyfriend, Wesley Beavers, "Rosacoke is very self-congratulatory. I like her a lot; I admire many things about her—but she does have a very typical kind of young Protestant self-righteousness and a very ready willingness to find anyone else's values lacking."[7]

The scene of "A Chain of Love" is a Raleigh hospital to which all of the Mustians accompany the family patriarch, Papa, who receives treatment but will not long survive. The cast includes Papa, the grandfather; Mama, his widowed daughter-in-law; her four children; and other extended-family members and friends, old and recently made, who pass in and out. The title refers to the effort by Rosacoke, the story's protagonist, to extend the "chain of love" to strangers in need, such as the Ledwell family, across the hall, whose father is dying of cancer.

To pursue further the issue of Rosacoke's virtue, we may consider a phrase that Price coined to describe her motivation, "the ethic of the freely given gesture." Rosacoke's "greatness as a woman" is her desire to make the "kind gesture" that "she thought [would] make somebody else happy."[8] Yet Rosa is not an angel of mercy, as is evident in her disinclination to include the elderly "Praise my Jesus" patient in the circle of those owed a duty. "And anyhow (Rosa) didn't like the lady" (492). Such statements tend to humanize Rosa. From the very beginning of the story Price takes seriously the writer's responsibility to *show* us why Rosa merits our affection as he displays links in the chain of love through allusions to family, marriages, deaths, generations, home, church, and food—all of this on the first page.

Familial connections extend even to Snowball Mason, the black orderly, who "turned out to be from Warren County too, . . . which made Papa feel at home right away" (487). Contrasted with Mason is an anonymous nurse of whom Rosa strongly disapproves; she has stumpy legs and dyed black hair and "called Papa 'darling' as if she had known him all her life" (487). Along with the "Praise my Jesus" patient, the nurse is beyond the pale: no freely given gestures to them. What principally inhibits performance of the ethic, however, is Rosa's own ignorance or innocence, her mixed motives, and the unhappy fact that other people often don't understand or can't respond.

Still, the question is how (well) Price depicts goodness, and whether we are prepared to value Rosa as he would have us do. We may well conclude that Price's situating a white statue of Jesus directly in front of the hospital window for Rosa's observation is too contrived, particularly because we are told that "Rosacoke couldn't see his face too well, but she knew it, clear from the day they brought Papa in. It was the kindest face she had ever seen" (490). A number of allusions to Christ appear in the story, intimating the hope of peace after suffering; few are as insistent as this one, however, and Rosa's loving-kindness doesn't need this kind of reinforcement. Price, it seems, tells us what we already know, planting a symbol in her path. The kindest face in the world is followed, five pages later, by "the saddest eyes in the world" (495), those belonging to Mr. Ledwell's grieving son. Despite the parallel superlative, this depiction seems more assured and less insistent, given the merely human agency involved and the fact that Rosa had earlier mistaken young Ledwell for Wesley Beavers, the boyfriend she loves to distraction but in whom she searches in vain for such depth of response.[9]

In "The Happiness of Others," the first story in *Permanent Errors*, we witness the end of another difficult love affair. The scene is Oxford, and a young man, a writer, Charles Tamplin, is spending a last day with a young woman, Sara, before she takes a boat from Southampton and out of his life. They are killing time and each other. Charles Tamplin is always given his full name; he is never Charles, never Tamplin. Thus a certain measure of formality, dignity, and distance is provided him. This is in fact the kind of man he is, something of an aesthete and a prig who tends to view his experience from a self-protective, often literary attitude. He is quick, incisive, and articulate, as is Sara. The tone of the story reflects their mental state—one of heartsick anxiety, frayed nerves, and strained tempers about to snap.

Sara, by her own choice or through Tamplin's default, has become the aggressor, with Tamplin usually drawing back or in flight. Sara doubtless, and justifiably, feels that she has been badly used. Both characters, however, possess a residual awareness of what they have had together, which intensifies their pain and the story's effect. They are united now principally in their recognition of their relation's falseness. They sit eating lunch together, "chewing each bite as long and mercilessly as though their stomachs held ravenous babies, open-mouthed to suck in the stream of tepid pap" (333). Here is an image, that of hungrily feeding babies, that becomes a refrain; it will reiterate the unfruitful quality of their relation. The child—never to be theirs—has become almost an incubus. Tamplin and Sara are eating, but they are simultaneously being eaten.

As they walk out of the inn into the sun, Tamplin notes that it gilds Sara—"it made Sara's body seem gold, warm and workable. Even the black hair transmuting quickly, through bronze to gold. They stood a moment—Charles Tamplin seeing that, she knowing he saw it, both knowing its deceit" (333). The sun "gilds" Sara, transforms her, for a moment at least, and in the eyes of Charles Tamplin, into a precious work of art; and he is a man who sees life in terms of art, thereby often devitalizing life. Sara in the sun seems "gold, warm and workable," a distinctly sensuous figure. They "know" too much, however, know each other and their failures together too well for either to be able to respond. Walking desultorily through the town, they continue their civil war; in the church they end up trading epitaphs on the tombs, each thereby formulating his or her own view of the world and of each other. Sara's memorial verses speak of relatedness; Tamplin's display his essential solitariness, a life lived almost vicariously.

Before this bleak story of parting lovers ends, Tamplin reflects on what is left, what the day now means. The prospects are ambiguous at best. One is that he will achieve a kind of altruistic abnegation, will become one of love's selfless saints. The other is that he has converted the artist's undeniable need for self-sufficiency into a cover for vanity, timidity, selfishness, and other modes of assault and withdrawal. Love and freedom appear to be irreconcilable.

Love and freedom, differently construed, are once again major issues in "Full Day," the more recent story with which Price opens *The Collected Stories.* Again the author depicts a male perspective, or two in this case, Buck's and his elder son's. The setting, rural North Carolina, and the time, 1953, are common in the canon, as is the cast of characters, who are composed of two classes—family and others, or, one might say, two families, since the story poses the question of whether Buck will remain with his own family or shift his allegiance to another. Buck's ambiguous situation may reflect the author's belief that "Marriage basically doesn't work very well,"[10] or it may exemplify the dream of a new beginning, a second chance, which nourishes or betrays a number of Price's characters, male and female.

"Full Day" reflects most directly both Price's "bond with his father and his more general fascination with relationships between fathers and sons,"[11] the focus of a number of Price's stories, most notably "The Names and Faces of Heroes." Yet if one will look outside Price's biography and canon, another likely interpretive perspective suggests itself. At some point early in the reading of "Full Day," one may well be reminded of another analogous narrative, such intertextual intimation consistent with Price's declaration that his honored mentor and dear friend Eudora Welty has "written no story better than 'Death of a Traveling Salesman.'"[12] Without slipping into an influence study of the sort to which Price fiercely objects, it may be helpful to construct a brief composite plot summary to begin to see more clearly, finally by contrast, what Price has made of "Full Day."

Both stories recount the experience of a middle-aged traveling salesman who, driving in the country, has lost his way. Disoriented by the press of affairs, his uncertain health, and the strange hot sun, he is rescued and given shelter in a home, where he then becomes attracted to the woman of the house who seems, briefly, almost accessible to him. Finally, as Welty writes, he "must get back to where he had been before" and so departs.[13] R. J. Bowman, Welty's salesman, shivers in his spiritual malaise and covers his heart at the end of his story. "Having earned his vision," Price writes of Bowman, "the salesman flees the scene of care and continuance and dies of heart failure, literally felled by his knowledge."[14]

Price's salesman, Buck, who had been feeling odd, is discovered late in the afternoon slumped over the wheel of his car at the edge of a country road by a passing schoolchild, whose mother, Nell Abernathy, volunteers her aid—lunch, a nap if he needs it. Once at the house Buck blacks out, in the process wetting his trousers, and on regaining consciousness he finds himself stripped, in Nell's bed, she herself close at hand. During the interval Nell, having examined his wallet for help, has telephoned Buck's wife, Lib, from whom, we discover, he has become increasingly strained and distant. "She'd [Lib] yet to welcome him truly back. And even if she did, the harm was done now and might never heal" (8). That Buck has a family and that Bowman does not is significant, but it is clear that Buck is unhappy with his wife and—if the text is any warrant—gives little thought to his two sons.

It is unsurprising, then, that Buck should feel "this time-out, here under this roof, some high-water mark in all his life" (11), though one is somewhat taken aback that he should actually ask to be allowed to stay, indefinitely. One does, however, see Nell's attractions—she is young, vital, nurturing, sexual, solvent, without a visible husband but with an admirable son—and by happy accident her deceased father's starched trousers almost fit Buck. She declines, however, to accept him as a long-term resident, saying, "We had this time, here now. Your own supper's cooking, up the road, this minute" (10). "This time" is figured in a striking and ominous climactic simile: it was "like a splendid volunteer, the giant flower that suddenly blooms at the edge of the yard, where you least expect, from a secret hybrid in last year's seed that has bided its time" (12).

This account of the blossoming of Buck's "happy day" soon turns fatal in an italicized coda.

> *In four months Buck will die from a growth that reached decisive weight in his body this full afternoon and threw him down.*
> *His elder son made this unreal gift for his father on the eighty-ninth passing of Buck's birthday, though he died these thirty-five years ago.* (12)

The narrator's concluding address to the reader substantially alters his or her sense of the preceding narrative, as the protagonist, last seen grinning at himself in Nell's peeling mirror, is suddenly cut down, moving the reader to think perhaps of the awful fragility of human life or, more prosaically, that it was just as well that Buck went home to die.

Unlike Welty, who announces Bowman's death in her title, Price reserves Buck's death for last-minute disclosure. Price's strategy is climactically to focus the reader's attention on Buck's son, the just-revealed first-person narrator, to establish the importance of *his* invention of scenes of final felicity in his father's life. For the reader to assimilate the meaning of the coda, then, is to reconceive the story. In his generous though "unreal gift," the narrator wishes for the possibility of happiness and fulfillment for his father, at the cost of imagining his own greatest unhappiness—the early disintegration of his family, the end of care and continuance.

We should consider, finally, the nature of the narrator's gift. When Buck awakes in Nell's bed, separated from her by only a few layers of material, she has become a prospective lover, and like R. J. Bowman he may wish that her child were his. By the time Buck has put on Nell's father's trousers, however, he has reason to imagine himself in yet another role. By story's end, in fact, Buck has had the tour, imagining himself as son, lover, husband, and (incorporating Nell's son) grandfather. No wonder he grins at himself in the mirror! That the tour ends just four months later (out of our sight, reported as if by messenger) need not altogether destroy our pleasure in Buck's one happy day, or our appreciation of his son's invention.

Although Price has long known, much admired, and perceptively written about "Death of a Traveling Salesman," it is not the case, despite the existence of striking parallels between the stories, that he has simply rewritten Welty's masterpiece in "Full Day." It is the case, however, that careful attention to their tellings of similar yet distinct stories will demonstrate that it is only at the very end of "Full Day," for reasons earlier stated, that the reader becomes wholly aware of how different Price's story is from Welty's. What essentially distinguishes Price's story from Welty's, as finally becomes apparent, is less his development of setting, character, and subject matter than of structure, thematic concerns, and point of view.

In "Bess Waters" Price offers up another "unreal gift" as partial payment of a long-standing debt in his account of the travails of an ancient black woman. "Bess Waters" is an 8-part, 11-page succession of sharply etched vignettes from the century-long life (1863–1963) of a former slave, beginning when she is still "the property of Mr. Cobb Coleman . . . , the last child born to his slave Nancy before the Freedom" (568), and ending as she sits with a character named Reynolds Price, trying, at his urging, to tell him her life's story, to go back to his grandparents' time, to confirm what he thinks he already knows. Bess emerges as a strong, determined, independent woman: self-possessed, unsentimental, a teetotaler, a believer, who devotes her working life to four generations of two white families.

Men—black, brown, and white—have been of little help in her life, and often have been a danger or hindrance. Her father was "a long-gone runaway" (569), whose name she heard but forgot, and as a young woman she fought "three strong men . . . (she cut one bad)" (569) to preserve her independence unviolated. She will not tell her daughter Em the name of *her* father, though he may be the man with whom she finds Em in bed—both are drunk—before Bess kills him by driving a pitchfork into his back. And when Mr. Buckeye, Reynolds's father, brings her home at 10 P.M. after a long day's and night's work, "old as she is, . . . [she] prays a barely audible sentence, 'Let this white man be tired as me' " (572). Finally, Em's fatherless son, June, later kills a girl and is himself electrocuted.

Like "Full Day," "Bess Waters" is a posthumous tribute, a combination of free invention, informed surmise, and personal recollection. Compared to "Full Day," "Bess Waters" is an ancillary tale of another family's history. We see the writer at work, interviewing his subject, directing and even on occasion correcting her, but also uneasy about what he may discover, as the previously quoted passage of Bess Waters's reflections on Mr. Buckeye suggests.

"Bess Waters" works wonderfully well, the reader's sole unhappy moment coming at the discovery that after only 11 pages there is no more. But in fact in *The Collected Stories* there is much more, since this story is preceded by 567 pages of remarkably coherent text in which, from "Full Day" on, we have met and come to know, on this same ground in all the circumstances of their lives, many of the characters. We have come to know Reynolds Price and his mother, Elizabeth, and his father, Buckeye (also Buck, Will), who—recently married to Elizabeth (who will become Lib, the estranged wife in "Full Day")—is described in "Bess Waters" as "a drunk out of work but pitiful and funny" (572). Such a description makes it the more gratifying to recollect, in the volume's opening story, his "one happy day" with Nell Abernathy before he was struck down.

As narrator, protagonist, or supporting character in his stories, Price claims a number of roles. How he casts himself in "Bess Waters" is suggested by his belief that she "is his hope of understanding what he can't pardon and passing that much on to others" (579). Yet in addition to being a prospective truth teller, he is also a professional storyteller, and on what turns out to be his final visit with Bess Waters, what he wants to hear from her is what he can use. "Start from the first, when you worked for Miss Liz," he says. But Bess demurs. "Her eyes shut now. 'That won't the first,' " she says. Price, however, *knows* what he wants to hear. "But start there please; they were my grandparents," he says to her. As if she didn't know that already. However, if he wants to hear the story from the beginning, she'll give it to him. "The start," she says, "was when my lips came open in Mama's belly and axed for light." But Price doesn't want to hear a hundred-year-long story. More accurately, he aims to produce his *own* version of that story, much as he had done with (for) his father in "Full Day." Thus he says to her, "I've got womb memories too"—which elicits from her the reproof direct: "You want this story or you want to talk? I'm near bout ninety." But he knows better—that she's 100 this month; he found it in a ledger from the Coleman farm, but he keeps it from her, allowing only that "I want that story; tell on" (579). Her mind, however, is only partially attentive to this world, to this insistent 30-year-old white man who writes books and knows everything. She starts, falters, but

what comes out is dark shine and power from her banked old heart and the quick of her bones, dark but hot as a furnace blast with a high blue roar. It burns the boy first [her grandson June, who died in the electric chair]. Bess sees him blown back and starting to scorch; then it whips round and folds her into the light till both of them sit in a grate of embers, purified by the tale itself, the visible trace of one long life too hard to tell. (580)

"Full Day" and "Bess Waters" share characters, subject matter, and thematic concerns, but—most significantly—they share the felt intensity of the narrator's personal involvement.

In marked contrast is the detached, impersonal minimalism of "Nine Hours Alone," about whose characters we are allowed to know and hence can care very little. "Nine Hours Alone" reads like a creative-writing class exercise: In no more than two pages, compose a suicide note, providing context with narrative and expository supplements. Price in fact offers *two* brief letters, from Frances Barnes, a 38-year-old high school teacher, to her husband and young lover, prospective survivors of her soon-to-be-accomplished suicide. There is no letter for her daughter. Mrs. Barnes's motives—a compound of shame, regret and anger—seem generic. Her daughter exists only as a name; her husband and teenage lover are, respectively, stereotypically dominant and insensitive. The latter two she means to assail; irony is her chosen weapon.

Price opens with a domestic scene from a housewife's life: Saturday morning, husband and daughter safely off the premises, Frances (doing her impression of Lady Macbeth) having washed "every spotted object in the kitchen, dried each gently and laid it in place with a loathing indistinguishable from fondness" (470). As if to deny the consequences of her act, she composes a grocery list, setting "each item in the order in which they'd [her husband and daughter] come across it if they took a cart and worked the aisles from left to right—Leah [her daughter] would know" (470). After these preliminaries the rest flows easily.

The first (easier? harder?) letter is to Davis, her husband, prospective widower. Of the two letters, this is likely to be the more public statement, to be preserved as an apologia and read by people other than the addressee. Within the family it may help to define who she was. She writes of her husband's not being to blame, of her having squandered all she promised him, of the thanks she owes him for past effort, of her "utter shame and regret" (470), of their shared "tragic fate," and of her trust in his forbearance regarding her student, who will be, she writes, "as baffled as we at where these two years have ended." Only in the last paragraph does she come to the point.

> *I understand that, with your faith, you will think I now forfeit salvation and the chance to meet you two again and comprehend how strong you are to urge, as you have, that I remain. I hope you are wrong. I hope we all will sleep forever, no glimpse of dream.* (470)

However else he may take her second letter, Frances's student Tom is unlikely to be merely "baffled." Seemingly intent in her first paragraph on exculpating him (much as in the opening of her "Dear Davis" letter), she turns in her second paragraph to her "only regret—in all the world—that you had less to give than I dreamed and, though you are three long years from manhood, will never have more." While he is pondering that terminal prediction, Tom gets to read one more paragraph in which Mrs. Barnes alleges that none of the foregoing prevents her wishing "you now a useful life, with courage to take what you turned back from me, the harmless gifts that your face earns" (471). This letter she seals, stamps, and leaves for her husband to mail. Will he, or will he open and read it?

Shortly she takes the sleeping pills, counting carefully, and looks into the mirror, where she is "smiling mildly." Arranging herself on her side of the bed under an afghan (letter to Davis propped on *his* pillow), she reflects that she has nine hours (or eternity?) alone. The final sentence records that "As her eyes shut down, the muscles along her lean jaw pulled again at her lips, reclaiming the smile from light-years back" (472) and preparing the rictus that will greet her husband and daughter on their return.

In "Nine Hours Alone" we discover—in utero, as it were—familiar Pricean characters and situation (a nuclear family and their relationship with a single outsider), subject matter (profound marital discord), and thematic concerns (the killing force of repressed anger), yet what Price offers is less a fully achieved story than a clever character sketch.

We leave Mrs. Barnes on this side of the Great Divide, uncertain as to her after-death prospects. Increasingly in his most recent fiction, however, Price, a convinced supernaturalist, has posited the integration of the natural and supernatural spheres. He describes himself as a traditional Christian, "shaped in childhood," he says, "by experiences that I took to be direct and graceful contacts from God and his messengers (trees, rocks, animals, angels, angelic humans)."[15] Because Price's perspective distinguishes his fictional practice from that of the vast majority of his American contemporaries and because it substantially affects reader response, it is worth some further attention.

It seems apparent, for instance, that to the true believing rationalist or skeptic of today, the supernaturalist perspective of Price's fiction is both exotic and suspect, perhaps even ominous, somewhat as remains the case with reader response to the work of Flannery O'Connor, whom Price identifies as "an interesting and eccentric but not very large writer."[16]

Supernatural presences in Price's work are numerous, real, and above all perfectly natural; they impinge on characters' daily lives, however undisposed many are to recognize or credit them. Thus, most simply, in "A New Stretch of Woods," a dog, a bird, and a snake, none of the sort the narrator has ever seen before, anticipate his mother's loss of a baby about to be born. Definitive news comes from a thick, out-of-season black snake: *The baby your mother wants to make is a boy. It would be your brother, but it will not live* (196).

In more elaborate fashion, in "The Enormous Door," the 60-year-old narrator recounts how, at age 12, eager to escape the "powerless trap of dumb childhood" (21) and to achieve a man's power and understanding, he discovers in Simon Fentriss, a local high school teacher, his longed-for hero and guide. He watches Fentriss through a hole drilled in the door of an adjoining hotel room, where at last, with exotic musical accompaniment, he witnesses his hero, in company with a naked woman, shift shape from his naked self to a beautiful bird to what is, more clearly, an angel. He knows that "Something huge, far past any power I knew, had done this for me" (36).

To continue this discussion, we must consider a story in which Price's Christian beliefs and his deployment of supernatural messengers and events constitute a central concern. In "An Early Christmas" Bridge Boatner—a middle-aged American landscape painter of some reputation, who is tired, lonely, at loose ends, and not very pleased with himself or his career—ventures on Christmas Eve 1980 into what Price calls "the compact thudding heart of a place [Bethlehem] as near to being *Homo sapiens'* ultimate socket as anywhere else" (591). In "The Enormous Door" an impressionable boy sees, he thinks, an angel, in a small-town southern hotel room. In "An Early Christmas," we may say, Price has upped the ante.

In the furtherance of Boatner's quest he is assisted and directed by a succession of guides, messengers, presiding presences. First in line, doling out tickets for midnight mass, is a French Franciscan monk, housed near Pilate's old headquarters, whose "predatory profile sliced the air like a Grand Inquisitor's" (582). Boatner is finally revulsed by the monk's aggressively sectarian interrogation, thereby gaining for himself, after four more painstakingly delineated stages, the possibility of that radical spiritual and artistic renovation that is the story's major thematic concern.

Once out of the monk's domain, Boatner's course along the Via Dolorosa is superintended for a time by an 11-year-old Arab boy, Jabril, with whose large family he partakes of a stupefyingly bountiful feast. They part after an exchange of gifts, Boatner offering a just-completed drawing of his young host. He is next taken up by George, a beggar and shoe shiner, who says the magic words: "You come with me" (592). As George fades into the background, Boatner finds himself in the first of a series of dark holy places, listening to a succession of seemingly interchangeable old men saying such things as "Jesus—Christ—crucified—here" (596) and "Now Golgotha—here" (597). As he kneels, putting his hand into deep holes, he experiences heat and cold, and comes "as near to prayer as [he]'d come in years" (597).

Principal evidence of his spiritual progress is his seeing, for the first time in his life, "the shape of all my crimes" (599), each of his genuine victims passing in review. The old self here under scrutiny is familiar in its features: self-possessed, introspective, clear eyed, ungenerous. We may recall Charles Tamplin of "The Happiness of Others." Shortly after Boatner is shown the "[a]ctual stone of Jesus' tomb" (603) and told "Your life commences now" (603), he experiences "a jolt in my right thigh—not pain so much as a muffled spasm, a doubling-up deep in the bone, the certain knowledge that something had broke and would never mend" (603).

There remains the longest and most extended of Boatner's educative encounters as he meets again Samir, a servant in Jabril's household (there lame, no longer so), and recklessly volunteers to drive him deep into West Bank country. This he characterizes as "a first small payment on the debts laid out before (his) eyes on Calvary" (605). It is not unusual for the author's more generous characters to offer gifts of their own free will or to recognize and attempt to pay their debts. So it is with Rosacoke Mustian in "A Chain of Love," and with Price in both "Full Day" and "Bess Waters." None of them, however, does so in Israel or cites Calvary as a precedent.

Before the story ends, Price incorporates more uncanniness as well as local danger and hospitality, pledges of mutual regard, a newborn male child, and at last a safe early-morning return to his hotel. Finally a coda brings us up to date: Boatner, now in a wheelchair, has survived that ultimately therapeutic jolt in his right thigh suffered back in Bethlehem and clearly constituting a happy fall.

After thanks to "that band of messengers" (625) who led him where he needed to go, Boatner delivers the artist's credo, speaking of his "driving will to show this world its visible likeness, front and back, crown to toe from where I've stood, in the clean new mirrors of honest pictures that mean to be guide lights usably placed in the frequent, sometimes permanent, dark" (625). What Boatner offers is not unlike what Price elsewhere identifies as Ernest Hemingway's lifelong subject—a "search . . . not for survival and the techniques of survival but for goodness, thus victory."[17]

Price writes well of foreign parts, in a rather high- toned Jamesian way; the socio-historical context of the tale is secure. But what Boatner learns, how his life is altered, his Christian faith apparently renewed—Price's design on the reader—is less persuasively articulated. It is not of course necessary to share Price's Christian faith, which he calls "maybe *the* central fact" about all his work,[18] to appreciate his stories, but "An Early Christmas" suggests that it would be a considerable help.

Without the Holy Land backdrop, without the guides, messengers, and presences, and without the apparently supernaturally derived injury to the protagonist, Price returns in "Endless Mountains" to the delineation of the process of physical and spiritual renewal. The first page or two of the story seems promising and an interesting departure, since it is a Civil War tale, told in the first person by a man in trouble, a recently wounded Confederate soldier. Nowhere else in *The Collected Stories* does Price attempt this sort of historical fiction, though in such stories as "Uncle Grant" and "Bess Waters," both among his best, he shows himself master of a nineteenth-century milieu, as perceived and rendered by a twentieth-century sensibility.

The story's opening line, "The shot went through the white inside of my right thigh on Wednesday near noon" (150), calls to mind the locus of Bridge Boatner's ultimately therapeutic jolt and suggests further that our narrator will be attentive to commonplace facts. One imagines that the protagonist's education is about to begin; thus Melville's line, in "Shiloh": "What like a bullet can undeceive!"[19] Trump Ferrell (an idiosyncratically Pricean name), carried to a bloody hospital tent, is much afraid of losing his leg to the resident butcher, and thus undertakes to escape, to declare a separate peace, though he doesn't at first think of himself as a deserter. One is encouraged, thinking of two excellent Civil War narratives, Crane's "An Episode of War" and Bierce's "One of the Missing."

In great pain, Ferrell walks and walks, en route offering up a number of problematic pronouncements, for instance "What I call *time,* most people call *God*" (151). He also has dark ruminations on his habit of failing those who depend on him, though we never discover just what he's done or hasn't done, only that he's burdened with sins and secrets. His family's absence induces joy, excitement at his new opportunities, guilt at feeling joy; it all seems very familiar, but no particulars are forthcoming. Evidently he is (or was) a dedicated womanizer, performer of "sins of faithless greed" (162), yet the one fleshly encounter he recalls involves his wife-to-be, a distant cousin, who came uninvited to his bed. When she announced her pregnancy four months later, he dutifully married her.

Ferrell, who has left his wife and children, with whom he was unhappy and to whom he gives very little thought, is suddenly struck down. He takes refuge with a substitute family, whom he finds very attractive. It is a recognizable circumstance in the Price canon and will remind the reader of "Full Day." This time, however, the fable does not work as well, for reasons that need to be examined.

Up in the foothills Ferrell is taken in by a very odd teenage pair, Ruth and Autry, who may be sister and brother, wife and husband, wholly unrelated, two orphans who met by chance, residents of the area, refugees, or none of the above; but all such possibilities are intimated. Such unprofitable ambiguity, portentous mysteriousness, is characteristic of the story. Ferrell spends much of his time sleeping and dreaming, and several dreams are transcribed at length; while awake, he is operated upon by the girl who with a knife does what she can for his gangrenous leg, and he is treated, in extremis, by the boy, who performs some sort of homoerotic folk medicine cure, lying naked full length on top of him for hours at a time. About this practice Ferrell says, "It seemed he [Autry] was certain that honest pressure by one careful soul could turn death back from another live body far gone as me and friendless to boot" (160).

Halfway through the story, after almost four months, Ferrell, beginning to recover, thanks his caregivers and proposes a New Year's feast. They shortly exchange unqualified declarations of love, of the sort rather more

common in Price's fiction than in life outside it. Soon after, a new character—
one Margaret Jane, six or seven, deaf and dumb, angelically beautiful—
appears for the first time. Viewing her, Ferrell remarks, "[A] tall clear forehead, the sign of calm" (175) and says, "Her spirit was in one close strong
piece" (176). Who she is, where she came from, what she is doing there, how
she is related to anyone else (if at all), is never revealed, any more than
whether she in fact speaks to Ferrell, as he believes, saying "no" and "now
rest." Very likely she is an angel. When last seen, Ferrell has left his substitute
family behind and is pushing on, up into "[e]ndless mountains, utter freedom, lasting peace—a healed strong man now, done with war" (183). If he
carries a banner, it probably reads "Excelsior!"

In "Endless Mountains" we encounter Price the quasi-allegorist. Both
narrative and dialogue are set down in prose that is notably mannered. For
pages and pages very little happens, and much of what happens seems both
overtly meaningful and only marginally credible. Only infrequently does the
historicity of the account seem of authorial concern, as the occasional period
detail appears. Ferrell shares with many other characters in Price's fiction
what Ron Carlson, in an excellent review of *The Collected Stories*, terms "an
urgent need to testify."[20] Ferrell, however, cannot get beyond swallowed
hints and oblique intimations, cannot bring himself to make a good (even
comprehensible) confession, though by story's end the reader is unlikely still
to be waiting.

"From the start," Price writes, "my stories were driven by heat—passion
and mystery, often passion for the mystery I've found in particular rooms and
spaces and the people they threaten or shelter—and my general aim is the
transfer of a spell of keen witness, perceived by the reader as warranted in
character and act" (xii). The mystery attended to in Price's short stories ultimately concerns the nature of both human and divine reality, usually as construed in traditional Christian fashion. We see, for instance, that the fates of
Price's characters are not predetermined, even in *Permanent Errors*. A number
of characters (women more than men) are likely to impress the reader as
notably virtuous, but none is wholly depraved. A surprising number appear
to subscribe to the notion of redemptive or sacrificial suffering assumed by
the virtuous to spare the sinner. Each of the characters is incomplete in himself or herself, seeking fulfillment, often balked, in the love of others. All are
radically imperfect, prone to evil, but redeemable when their efforts are
assisted by grace. Intimations from the Great World, to which a substantial
minority of the characters (younger rather than older) are responsive, work
through nature yet entirely transcend it. All of this is to say that reading
these stories is serious business, for they confront the reader with consequential choices of belief and behavior.

To read extensively in *The Collected Stories* is, finally, rather like sitting
down of an afternoon with a trusted and congenial family member, your

grandmother perhaps, looking through old photograph albums, you of course as "Exhibit A" growing younger and younger and smaller and smaller, before at last disappearing altogether, itself a salutary learning experience that Price's fiction (rich in photographs) regularly provides. In the process of turning pages you observe houses and dogs and trees and lawns and cars and playmates and schools and the ocean and your parents impossibly young but perfectly recognizable before whichever war and then, or simultaneously, *their* parents, and hearing all the while who these people were (are) and how related to each other and to you and where they came from and the things (funny, heroic, mysterious, terrible) they said and did. To read all 50 of the stories, preferably no more than three or four at a time, is to witness a whole living world—the author's little postage stamp of native soil, R. Price owner and sole proprietor.

Notes

1. Among the most insightful reviews are those of Sven Birkerts, "Reynolds Price: A Lifetime of Stories," *Washington Post Book World* (30 May 1993): 1, 7; Shelby Hearon, "Reynolds Price's Life of Leavetaking," *Chicago Tribune Books* (16 May 1993): 1, 9; and Ron Carlson, "The Collected Stories of Reynolds Price," *Southern Review* 30.2 (April 1994): 371–78.
2. Reynolds Price, *Permanent Errors* (New York: Atheneum, 1970), vii.
3. Guy Davenport, "Doomed, Damned—and Unaware: *Permanent Errors,*" *New York Times Book Review* (11 October 1970): 4.
4. Reynolds Price, "To the Reader," in *The Collected Stories* (New York: Atheneum, 1993), xi. Subsequent quotations from this edition will be identified parenthetically in the text.
5. Birkerts, 7.
6. Reynolds Price, "Answerable Calls," *A Common Room/Essays 1954–1987* (New York: Atheneum, 1987), 73.
7. Reynolds Price, "*A Long and Happy Life:* Fragments of Groundwork," *Virginia Quarterly Review* 41 (1965): 241.
8. Price, "*A Long and Happy Life:* Fragments of Groundwork," 238.
9. The origins of the statue and many of the circumstances of the story are discoverable in Reynolds Price, "A Final Secret: Will Price," *Clear Pictures/First Loves, First Guides* (New York: Atheneum, 1989), 265–99.
10. Constance Rooke, "On Women and His Own Work," in *Conversations with Reynolds Price,* ed. Jefferson Humphries (Jackson: University Press of Mississippi, 1991), 214.
11. James Schiff, *Understanding Reynolds Price* (Columbia: University of South Carolina Press, 1996), 1.
12. Paul Sincing, *The Still Moment: Eudora Welty/Portrait of a Writer* (London: Virago, 1994), 72.
13. Eudora Welty, "Death of a Traveling Salesman," *Selected Stories of Eudora Welty* (New York: Modern Library, 1966), 252.
14. Price, "Answerable Calls," in *A Common Room,* 76.
15. Price, "At the Heart," in *A Common Room,* 403.
16. Jefferson Humphries, "Feast Thy Heart: An Interview," in *Conversations with Reynolds Price,* 221.

17.   Price, "For Ernest Hemingway," in *A Common Room,* 140.

18.   Georges Gary, " 'A Great Deal More': Une Interview de Reynolds Price," *Recherches Anglaises et Americaines* 9 (1976): 154.

19.   Herman Melville, "Shiloh," in *Poems of Herman Melville: A Reader's Edition,* ed. Robert Penn Warren (New York: Random House, 1970), 122.

20.   Carlson, 371.

Fathers and Sons in the Fiction of Reynolds Price: "A Sense of Crucial Ambiguity"

JAMES A. SCHIFF

Since the 1962 publication of his first novel, *A Long and Happy Life*, which won not only the Faulkner Award but was printed in its entirety in *Harper's*, Reynolds Price has been a visible presence in contemporary American letters, yet for some critics the promise of his career has never been fully realized. Though this attitude has changed in recent years, particularly since the publication of *Kate Vaiden* in 1986, Price still has not received a great deal of critical attention—certainly less than other members of his literary generation, such as John Updike, Philip Roth, Thomas Pynchon, Toni Morrison, and Don DeLillo.

Price's prose style explains the neglect in part. Not only is his style, in the words of Constance Rooke, "highly pronounced, unusual, and quite often difficult,"[1] but in an age and environment that favors more idiomatic, casual, and realistic prose, Price's writing strives for an impressive sound that reminds one, more than any other example from contemporary American literature, of the Bible or even *Paradise Lost*. Related to this is the fact that one does not find a detailed sense of the contemporary world in Price's writing, as one does in, say, Updike's Rabbit novels or DeLillo's *White Noise*. Those writers are expert at incorporating sociology into their narratives, utilizing, often in a metaphorical sense, a wealth of information from newspaper headlines, television programs, and social trends. Relatively speaking, Price's fiction relies little upon sociological details; there is a chiseled bareness to his vision, and his characters are depicted at the emotional core, with little regard for the trappings of contemporary life. Thus for readers eager to find detailed sociology in fiction, Price may be something of a disappointment.

In addition, Price's sensibility is, perhaps, too compassionate and tender for contemporary critics who prefer a more ironic and playfully grim authorial presence. As George Garrett writes, "[A]t a time when most American writers are cultivating the ways and means of cynicism, Price continues to write stories of great sweetness . . . without being silly or sentimental."[2] And

This essay is an updated and revised version of an essay that first appeared in *Southern Review* 29.1 (Winter 1993): 16–29. Reprinted by permission of the author.

Jonathan Keates, who tells us in the *Observer* that Price "ought to be as well known and admired among us [the British] as Updike or Bellow," explains, "That he isn't may have something to do with the gentleness and detachment of his authorial voice."[3]

One final explanation for the neglect of Price's work stems from his early and mistaken casting in the role of a "minor Faulkner" (mistaken because Milton, Tolstoy, Welty, and the Bible are far greater influences). Without careful scrutiny of his work, critics placed Price under the enormous shadow of the Mississippian simply because both are southerners. Geographically, Price's home and the area about which he writes are closer to New York City than to Oxford, Mississippi, yet from the perspective of a northeastern literary establishment, North Carolina and Mississippi are joined, just as Colombia and Peru are combined and then called "Latin America" (note that the suburbs of Boston and New York, as depicted in the work of Updike and Roth, are viewed as separate entities; the same should hold true for the fiction of North Carolinians and Mississippians). My point, however, is not to denounce the literary establishment but rather to point out that hasty decisions and generalizations are sometimes made about writers whose geographical status is unfamiliar.

I wish to demonstrate, by focusing upon a central mystery that recurs in his fiction, that Price's vision is indeed unique and bold, and that more attention needs to be paid. My inquiry in these pages concerns the relationship between fathers and sons, the bond of kin that appears to interest Price most. Though all novels are to some degree about family life, Price's work focuses upon the family with an intensity that reminds one of Greek drama and biblical narrative, and at the center of familial relations is what I find to be one of the central mysteries in his fiction: the charged eroticism that exists between fathers and sons. I say "mystery" because Price is intentionally ambiguous about the nature of such an Eros, particularly as it pertains to physical contact.

"The Names and Faces of Heroes" (1963), a story from a collection of the same title, was Price's initial attempt at understanding an intimate relationship between father and son. Years after it was written, Price said of the largely autobiographical story, which is one of his finest:

> I'm certainly aware that it's a very complicated and in many ways a difficult story, perhaps a little more than it ought to be. It's certainly a love story. It's certainly a story containing an enormous amount of Eros. And I may say that I think it's one of those very rare stories in English which deals with the reality that English and American writers have found almost impossible to face or talk about, which is the degree of Eros, the overwhelming amount of Eros, that exists between many fathers and sons.[4]

The story, delivered in the first-person present by a nine-year-old boy nicknamed Preacher (the same name Price's father bestowed on a young

Reynolds), documents a nighttime car ride in which he and his father are returning home from Raleigh after having heard a sermon by a man who claims to have seen Christ. The opening line, in which Preacher says, "We are people in love," leads the reader, not yet aware that the "lovers" are a father and son, to presume some sort of more common adult heterosexual relationship.[5] The reader then is mildly surprised when he learns who the lovers actually are, yet simultaneously he is forced to consider whether it is not indeed natural for fathers and sons to be "lovers" of some sort. One envisions a fraternal love or agape between father and son, but there is actually Eros here as we learn that Preacher is lying with his head in his father's lap: "I the thin fork of flesh thrust out of his groin on the seat beside him, my dark head the burden in his lap" ("NFH," 441). The physical nature of their love is continually stressed as Preacher's father, while driving, explores his son's body: "[H]e drops a hand . . . slipping between two buttons of the coat to brush one breast then out again and down to rest on my hip. His thumb and fingers ride the high saddle bone, the fat of his hand in the hollow I have, heavy but still on the dry knots of boyish equipment waiting for life to start" (442). There is, however, no sexual molestation or abuse here, and no action is taken that is not desired; Preacher and his father are as comfortable and familiar to one another, physically and emotionally, as old lovers.

Though an unusually precocious and perceptive nine-year-old, Preacher is nevertheless a typical child in his anxiety over his father's mortality and in his fear of abandonment and separation; both, of course, are also common fears of lovers. Preacher worries his father will leave him and "take up his life in secret," a worry that is not completely without reason since his father has a history of being "drunk and wild" ("NFH," 463, 459). Riding beside his father through the winter night and remembering the words of a camp minister who urged him to find a hero and "chin [himself] on his example," Preacher considers his father, Christ, and others as possibilities (443). Though it is never resolved whether his father fits the role, Preacher links his father mystically to Christ and views him as a flesh-and-blood representation of divinity.

Near the end of the story, his head buried in his father's lap, Preacher falls asleep, only to wake and realize his greatest nightmare: "my father is gone" ("NFH," 463). Fearing some enemy has succeeded in separating them, or that his father has abandoned him, Preacher searches through the car window, then prays for his father's return. Soon a man appears out of the snow, his "head wrapped in black, a black robe bound close about him" (464), and Preacher, still not fully awake, mistakes him for the hero about whom they just finished speaking, Jesus (recall that they are returning from hearing a minister who claims he has *seen* Christ). The man, of course, is only Preacher's father, who has just returned from urinating.

At this point the strangest part of the story occurs, which links father and son physically and mystically. With his hand cupping his groin, Preacher again falls asleep and this time dreams of his hand, which has been transformed into its adult form while still wrapped about his groin. The hand, which at one moment appears to be his own and at the next seems to be his father's, is molding the "kernels" of life, or more literally, the genitalia. It is the hand that appears to generate creation, and in this part of the dream Preacher is able not only to anticipate his adult self and future powers of creation but also to experience vicariously his own creation as generated by his father. The dream then transports him into a room in which his adult self examines the body and holds "the core" of what appears to be his dead father (he also recognizes himself and his own mortality in his father). In attempting to bring his father back to life and "set him free," Preacher and his father are joined in a sexual sense: "A shudder begins beneath my hand in his core our core that floods through his belly" ("NFH," 467).

Just as Preacher emerges from his father's groin, he attempts to bring life back to his father by stimulating that groin. Though he appears temporarily successful, his father again goes "cold" like "hard ice, final as any trapped in the Pole" ("NFH," 467). Faced with the terror of his father's mortality, Preacher makes a promise that he "will change [his] life," an utterance that mirrors and answers an identical promise his father made during Preacher's difficult birth: "I . . . told Jesus, 'If you take Rhew [my wife] or take that baby, then take me too. But if You can, save her and save that baby, and I make You this promise—I will change my life' " (467, 460). Through this mystical dream sequence Price demonstrates the intense bond between father and son, and he links the two physically through the groin or "core" that produces the seed that becomes the son. Though mothers are often linked to their offspring through the womb, connections of this sort are seldom made between fathers and their children.

"The Names and Faces of Heroes" concludes with father and son arriving home. Freshly awake from the dream of his father's death, Preacher is "flooded" with "sudden need": "to rise, board him, cherish with my hands, my arms while there still is time this huge gentle body I know like my own, which made my own" ("NFH," 469). Because the ground is covered in snow, Preacher is then carried from car to house by his father: "I go . . . into arms that circle, enfold me, lift me, bear me these last steps home over ice" (469). With his face pressed against his father's heart, Preacher, despite the knowledge of his father's future death, experiences triumph: on this night they have arrived home, "alive, together, whole" (469).

Though family relationships remained at the center of Price's fiction during the 1960s and early 1970s, he waited until *The Surface of Earth* (1975) to return to Preacher and his father, with the largely autobiographical pair now renamed and reconceived as Hutch and Rob Mayfield. By placing his characters not only in a large and ambitious novel but ultimately in a trilogy of novels titled *A Great Circle—The Surface of Earth, The Source of Light* (1981), and *The Promise of Rest* (1995)—Price intensifies and expands his study of fathers and sons, leading us through multiple generations of Mayfield men. Interestingly, *The Surface of Earth* began in Price's mind as a story of a father and son together in a car and on the road, traveling through eastern North Carolina[6]—a scene that is archetypal in his fiction, turning up in "The Names and Faces of Heroes," *The Surface of Earth,* and *Private Contentment.*

Though its individual novels found a polarized reception, *A Great Circle* may stand ultimately as Price's grand achievement, and it is certainly one of the finest extended works ever written about fathers and sons. In its sweep, which extends from 1903 until 1993, the family saga follows six generations of Mayfield fathers and sons: Robinson, a needy and sometimes cruel man who abandons his family for the pursuit of flesh; Forrest, a sensitive Latin teacher who elopes with his prize student, quickly loses her, then spends much of his life feeling abandoned; Rob, a teacher who suffers, like his grandfather, from his passionate appetite for flesh and alcohol; Hutch, an ambitious, self-conscious poet who struggles with his sexual identity as well as with his conflicting need for solitude and community; Wade, the first Mayfield to follow and acknowledge openly his erotic desire for other men and for blacks; and Raven Patterson Bondurant, the mulatto child from New York who, as a mixed vessel of black/white, gay/straight, city/country, represents the future of the Mayfield line (in addition, Grainger Walters, the illegitimate mulatto son of Robinson, stands as a male kinsman who in spite of racial segregation participates in and observes the lives of all six generations of Mayfield men).

Though there are many points at which to begin a discussion of the Mayfield men, the most telling and mysterious moment in *The Surface of Earth* occurs early in the novel when Forrest Mayfield recounts his "main memory" of his father, Robinson, who abandoned the family when Forrest was five:

> I remember. . . . that one Sunday . . . I was laid out on my little narrow bed. . . . He came in silent in a cotton nightshirt with plumcolored stripes and lay down on me; I was stretched on my back. Laid his whole weight on me. . . . and when I looked up . . . there were my father's eyes staring down at me. . . . the neediest eyes I've seen, asking me.[7]

For Forrest, and the reader, the scene remains a mystery. What precisely did Robinson want from his young son: sexual contact? human warmth? love? Whatever it was, Forrest is burdened with guilt because of his failure to provide for his father: "That has been the hard thing in my life—thinking of that: that after coming to me and begging for God knows what as food and getting no gift, then he wanted to go. Go away from us" (*SE,* 25). This initial failure to satisfy and hold on to his father leads to other failures, most notably with his wife, Eva.

Variations on this scene are played out on several occasions in the novel. For instance, two generations later Rob Mayfield repeats this act with Hutch:

"So Rob slowly took off his jacket and tie, unbuttoned his collar, stepped out of his shoes, and took the last steps till his legs touched the bed. Then he laid himself—full-length, dead-weight—on Hutch's body" (*SE,* 347). In fact, Hutch's "strongest, strangest memory," which engendered both "fear and happiness," is of his father's enacting this same ritual when Hutch was just four or five; though Hutch experienced "pleasure" during this act, there was also a fear of suffocation, a "joy that also threatened to kill him" (347). Another variation upon this act occurs in the dreams of Eva Kendal, who imagines her father as an incubus bent upon destroying the entire family during a single night:

> [her father] rolled his huge body leftward till he lay full-length on her sleeping mother—who remained asleep as he fastened his open mouth over hers and drew up each shallow breath she exhaled till she lay empty, dead. . . . performed the same smothering theft on Kennerly. . . . Then up the stairs to Rena. (10)

Eva, who at this moment has escaped her father by eloping, then imagines him coming to devour her, thus ending the dream.

Despite variations, one can distinguish a common pattern in Price's depiction of the scene of the incubus: a father enters the bed of his son or daughter, lies on top of him or her, and either seeks or awaits some form of nourishment. Sometimes this scene occurs in a dream, at other times it is recalled as a childhood memory, and in still other instances it occurs in the present. Mostly though the scene is one that transpires between Mayfield men and their sons, and the reader most often experiences it through the sensibility of the son or passive recipient. The scene also resonates with ambiguity and mystery, since the son is usually unaware of what precisely is happening and being asked of him.

Though the incubus traditionally suggests an evil spirit or demon in male form that desires sexual intercourse with sleeping women, the term in modern psychological usage is less demonic and more inclusive, suggesting a nightmare of a sexual nature that gives one the feeling of being burdened with a heavy weight on the chest (the Latin *incubare* means "to lie upon"). For Ernest Jones, a student of Freud and also his biographer, the incubus, which is virtually a synonym for the term *nightmare,* is "an expression of intense mental conflict centreing [*sic*] about some form of 'repressed' sexual desire . . . an expression of a mental conflict over an incestuous desire."[8] Jones's observation that "the normal incest wishes of infancy" are at the center of the incubus sheds light on Price's fiction, particularly since Price follows Freud in suggesting there is "an innate bi- or polysexuality in all creatures" that for social reasons is repressed.[9] According to Price, we have become blinded to the "goodness of the intimacy" between parents and children because any degree of intimacy is quickly transformed into anxiety and obsession with incest.

To return then to Forrest's memory of his father's lying upon him, one questions what Robinson wants from his young son and in what manner he touches the boy. It may be useful to consider how a similar scene was staged in a production of Price's television drama, *Private Contentment* (1984), which also deals centrally with a father-son relationship. Lee Yopp, the adaptor (for the stage) and director of Price's play, explained that Price had told him during a conversation that he wanted a sense of sexual ambiguity in the play's final scene between half brother and half sister:

> We were talking about the climax. Mr. Price said that what took place between the boy and the girl was more than just a kiss. He wasn't trying to be "cutesy" or anything. Mr. Price said that his own guess was that they don't have complete intercourse; on the other hand, they don't just embrace and walk back to the house. There must be, he said, a sense of crucial ambiguity.[10]

Perhaps "crucial ambiguity" best describes the nature of the physical intimacy between fathers and sons in Price's fiction. Though one never senses that anything approaching intercourse occurs, one cannot be absolutely sure of the nature of the contact. Robinson Mayfield does not appear to be attempting coitus with his son, nor does he give any indication of being a pedophile, yet it is suggested that he wants more than merely simple and socially acceptable affection. Typical of the Mayfield men, Robinson possesses a strong appetite for flesh, which is not being satisfied in his marriage, and so he turns to his son for nourishment. What is unfortunate about this particular scene is that Forrest is emotionally harmed because he does not understand what his father wants.

What is perhaps most interesting about the incubus is how it passes between individuals: father to son, husband to wife. Eva—who, like Forrest, finds that her closest bond is not with a spouse or lover but with her father—is also visited by a dream, as was previously described, in which her father appears as an incubus. The dream no doubt expresses her guilt over having abandoned her family, particularly her father, and it also answers to her fear that her father would smother and devour her if she stayed. Yet Eva, who returns to her family within a year, has a tremendous desire to be with her father, and one could interpret her dream as an expression of her desire to be "smothered" or loved by him. Eva's incubus dream occurs on her wedding night, and immediately after the dream, in which she imagines her father "fasten[ing] his open mouth" over the mouths of everyone in her immediate family, Eva turns to Forrest and assumes the role of the succubus: "[H]er hand strained out and took his shoulder and with more strength, even than before, drew him down and over her body . . . and quickly in. Then with her hands on the back of his head, she fastened his mouth over hers and endured in silence the gift she required" (*SE*, 11). Eva utilizes Forrest as a surrogate father and experiences the sexual relationship with her husband that she cannot have with her father. Forrest offers a vehicle through which Eva can bond physically with her greatest love, her father, and at the same time punish her father by abandoning him and eloping with Forrest. Again Price demonstrates how an intense relationship between a parent and child makes it difficult if not impossible for that child to bond with others.

One of the criticisms of Price's fiction, which applies particularly to *The Surface of Earth,* is that his characters are too similar in voice and in range of experience. That so many characters in the novel have at the center of their emotional lives their relationships with their fathers, and that Eva, Forrest, and Hutch all have experiences, whether real or dreamed, in which their fathers appear as incubi is enough to fuel such criticism. How likely is it, after all, for each of these characters to have the same prominent memory or dream? Perhaps it is unrealistic and forced on Price's part, yet it answers to a greater aim in his fiction: to demonstrate how dreams, emotions, and needs are transmitted—unconsciously, genetically—between family members and through generations, and how certain dreams and sensations emerge as archetypal.

Certainly the dominant father-son bond in the trilogy as well as the deepest and healthiest attachment between parent and child is between Rob Mayfield and Hutchins Raven Mayfield (Hutch). As mentioned earlier, this "couple" most resembles Preacher and his father from "The Names and Faces of Heroes," and their story comprises the final third of *The Surface of Earth,* then dominates *The Source of Light.* Though older than Preacher (Hutch is 14 in *The Surface of Earth,* 25 in *The Source of Light*), he shares the younger boy's perceptiveness and sensitivity, and both fathers appear amiable despite histories of alcohol abuse and wildness. Much like the other Mayfield men, Rob is a "runner," a bolter who left his son to be raised by a variety of women (Hutch's mother died in childbirth, so Hutch is raised by aunts, grandparents, and hired help). Rob, however, played a primary role in Hutch's early years, before he was five, and their attachment, as he explains, was intimate: "You slept in my bed from the time you could walk; and I'd lie down beside you in some dim light and watch you for minutes. . . . I loved you till it drew great tears down my cheeks. . . . I would lie some nights after you were deep asleep and whisper you questions up against your ear" (*SE,* 394). Though separated for more than eight years, the reunited Rob and Hutch appear like lovers, sharing a bed, talking, sleeping, and touching. There is a distinct physical component to their companionship that begins at Hutch's conception; as Rob explains to his son in *The Source of Light,* "Rachel [Hutch's mother] pulled you out of me by main force."[11] As they lie together in bed, the 14-year-old Hutch ponders his conception in the body of his father: "He tried to imagine his own life starting in that groin there, yearning out into Rachel fifteen years ago" (485). Once again Price emphasizes how the boy is of his father's body.

Though there does not appear to be genital contact of any sort between the two, there is an erotic attraction: much kissing, touching, and bodily contact. There is also an underlying eroticism to their dialogue:

So Hutch said, "Why don't you sleep with the master?"
Rob said, "Where is that?"
"Isn't this the master bedroom?"
"Yes."
"Well, here's the master bed." Hutch slid to the right half, a cold plain of cloth.
Rob came to join him.
They did not touch at first, of their own volition; but quickly slept in the warming depths of Raven Hutchins' [Hutch's grandfather's] bed, not thinking of his death. (*SE*, 486)

To a degree, one finds similarities between Rob and Hutch's companionship and other buddy relationships in American literature, such as Ishmael and Queequeg in *Moby-Dick* and Huck and Jim in *Huckleberry Finn*. When a teenage Hutch suggests to his father that they change their names, flee to the mountains, and "never go back home," there are indeed echoes of other male buddies who have left civilization for a life of adventure (402). However, Hutch and Rob's relationship possesses a conspicuous physical attraction, and Hutch has been created literally from the genitals of Rob. In addition, the two share an intimacy and trust that surpasses that of even the most constant lovers, leading Hutch's girlfriend to say in *The Source of Light*, "You love your father more than anything else" (184).

In *The Source of Light* the relationship between Hutch and Rob remains central, though the two are 11 years older and a split is imminent: Hutch is headed to Europe for graduate study, Rob will remain in North Carolina and (though Hutch is unaware) prepare to die. In this novel, which takes place in 1955–1956, Price depicts father and son as two orbiting bodies who have together circled some core: the center of earth? the source of rest? However, their mutual orbit, as Hutch later writes in a poem for his deceased father, is ending:

What we had was years
Of circling a spot, mules at a mill.
The figure was rings, concentric rings
Round an unseen center (what were we grinding?)
Till I fled and you quit.

(*SL*, 260)

Rob's inoperable cancer, along with Hutch's departure for Europe, are the perturbations that have upset their normal movement and rotation. Sharing a curative bath in the womblike waters at Warm Springs before Hutch departs, father and son enact a birth and death ritual. In this scene of farewell, Hutch is given the rite of baptism, and with his father's death he will be reborn into a new life. As he writes in that same poem to Rob,

> . . . nine months ago, you and I in
> Warm Springs; the circular pool of fuming
> Water (female essence of the heart of the
> Ground) accepting your hard white limbs and
> Head in farewell grip more total than
> Any you'd known in air with prior
> Partners.
>
> (*SL*, 261)

In this opening scene Hutch is depicted as ascending and assuming his father's place. As Rob baptizes his son in the water, Hutch suddenly "jerks[s] to life and thrust[s] toward the surface," breaking through and rising while saying "Holy Ghost" (5). Having long borne Rob's weight, both literally when his father would lie upon him and figuratively through his father's troubles, Hutch now experiences a lightening of the load.

To some degree the relationship between Rob and Hutch is a reverse or inverse oedipal attachment: instead of killing his father to be with his mother, Hutch has unknowingly "killed" his mother to be with his father (Rachel Hutchins Mayfield died giving birth to Hutch). Yet in spite of their mutual love and devotion, Hutch and Rob have also made life more difficult for one another: Hutch has been a source of responsibility for Rob; Rob stands as the only obstacle in Hutch's path toward freedom. One of the true achievements of *The Source of Light* is how Price frames the paradoxical nature of this father-son union, which resembles the "hard paradox" inherent in the death of Price's own father: though Will Price's death was devastating for the 21-year-old Reynolds, it simultaneously enabled him "to move into that grown life I'd suddenly won."[12]

Although the most crucial and central love relationship in *The Source of Light* is between Rob and Hutch, they are precluded, at the very least by the boundaries of civilization, from any type of genital contact. Directly out of this prohibition arises one of the most interesting features of the novel: Hutch seeks in young men a surrogate for his father. In other words, he experiences his father sexually through the bodies and faces of young men whom he encounters in his European travels. An active bisexual (though later he will express dissatisfaction with that term), Hutch seeks physical love not only in the body of his longtime lover, confidante, and apparent fiancée, Ann Gatlin, but also in attractive young men such as Strawson Stuart, Lew Davis, and James Nichols. These homosexual encounters, as Joyce Carol Oates points out, are of greater import and interest: "Hutch doesn't seem to grasp what the reader so quickly grasps—that his homosexual liaisons are much more meaningful to him."[13] Even 40 years later in *The Promise of Rest,* Hutch does not appear to understand himself sexually, failing to see that it is young men to whom he is primarily drawn.

The young men answer to Hutch's need to know his father as a young man: "Hutch longed to see his father—not the Rob he had left three weeks ago but the grand lost boy who had lain beside him in infancy" (*SL,* 108). As Hutch sleeps with Strawson Stuart, a former student of his at the Episcopal Virginia boys' school, he is drawn closer to his father: "What [Hutch had] honored in this boy for nearly two years was the clear sight of life, a flood of cheerful animal life that had pressed Straw's body and face from within into one more mask of the thing Hutch hunted and worshiped in the world—the same strong grace that still moved the pictures of Rob through his memory" (144). And Hutch's attraction to James Nichols, the mason's helper and ex-convict, is directly linked to his father, who has since died: "something in the boy seemed identical with Rob, of the same good essence. Nothing ghostly or urgent but a gentle palpable return of the oldest presence he'd known and needed—the vulnerable potent needy youth who'd stood at the rim of Hutch's own childhood and asked for help" (309). Every lover who is of any value to Hutch is a mask of his father, an image that first appeared in "The Names and Faces of Heroes." Through the relationship between Rob and Hutch, the reader encounters a significant truth: that love between a parent and child is often more stable, meaningful, and enduring than any other type of love, and it is natural for such a love to generate erotic desire.

As already stated, the relationship between Rob and Hutch closely resembles Price's own bond with his father. Referring to himself, his father (Will), and his mother (Elizabeth) as a "triad" and as "one thing," Price has written in his memoir *Clear Pictures* of their affection for one another: "We constituted not simply a marriage but a romance. I took no share of their sexual bodies, but each of us cherished the others' flesh."[14] And as his recollections of climbing in bed with his parents illustrate, Price felt closest to his father: "Will Price welcomed me beside him; and it was mainly him I joined, him I needed to tame and know."[15] In addition, Price's actual birth engendered a pact between his father and God that parallels the one made between Rob Mayfield and God. In both cases a difficult and potentially fatal birth leads the father to "seal a bargain with God, as stark and unbreakable as any blood pact in Genesis"[16]: if the mother and child live, the father promises never again to drink. Because of Price's own "mythic" birth, it is not surprising he associates his entry into this world less with his mother, the traditional birth giver, and more with the two figures who bargained him into existence, his father and God. The event also helps to explain Price's fascination with the story of Abraham and Isaac, in which Price, like Isaac, is gift and hostage in a divine pact.

Yet as is true in both *A Great Circle* and Price's life, the Isaac figure (Hutch, Price) grows up and must eventually endure what is perhaps *the* central Pricean event: the death of the father (Rob, Will Price). In *The Source of Light,* Rob is in the hospital dying of cancer while Hutch attends to him, holding his wrist and feeling the final pulse as Rob climbs into "his own free flight" and then sees himself entering an old dark house (*SL,* 209). Proceeding through its rooms, Rob is led to a light at the center of the house, where he finds an adolescent girl on a bed delivering a child. Rob, it appears, has arrived at his center of rest and "source of light": "His mother, himself, the room he is born in. Feasible center, discovered in time, revised now and right" (210). With Rob's death comes birth, not only for himself (his literal birth from Eva's womb) but also for Hutch: "The same dense wave that had drowned his father spread up through his hand and raised him higher than he'd been this whole day of hope" (210).

Again for Hutch, Rob's death is paradoxical: there is "a deep relief that Rob was going and yielding him room" and yet "a deeper fear that the room would be vacant, containing no center round which he could move in the confident swings he'd learned from birth" (199). Once Rob is gone, Hutch feels "lighter" than ever, yet he also experiences "Rob's absence fully for the first time" and realizes that there cannot be another center, another single fixed point for him to revolve around (241). Though Rob's ghost makes a return visit, Hutch will be forced to draw upon some other form of motion in his life ahead. The man who created him and planted the seed that resulted in his life is gone. Hutch, though, is alive and happy at the novel's conclusion. Free of familial entanglements, he is on the verge of a new life as an artist, and he has been initiated into a variety of fulfilling erotic encounters.

The next time we see Hutch he is 37 years older, a man of 62, with a son seven years older than he himself was at the end of *The Source of Light.* In this concluding novel to the trilogy, *The Promise of Rest,* Price again focuses on how a father and son negotiate a difficult passage, and again death figures as the central event with which they must cope. The only difference this time is that Hutch must deal with the loss of his son, Wade Mayfield, who is "dying [of AIDS] in upper Manhattan, refusing phone calls or visits from home."[17]

The Promise of Rest moves the family saga forward into the 1990s, where we witness the fourth, fifth, and sixth generations of Mayfield men (Hutch, Wade Mayfield, Raven Bondurant) facing many of the same unresolved questions from the earlier novels—questions concerning sexuality, race, and genetic heritage. In this novel, as in *The Source of Light,* Hutch is the central figure, now a well-known poet teaching at Duke University. Despite the almost 40-year leap forward in time, Hutch continues to be unsure of his relationship with Ann Gatlin: though they have been married more than 35 years, the marriage is a dreadful failure and they have recently separated. In addition, Hutch's sexuality remains a mystery: one wonders whether he has deceived himself his entire life by having chosen a woman over a man. One also wonders whether Hutch has been able to depart from the behavior of his male ancestors, to avoid their wasteful patterns, and whether he, or any Mayfield, will be able to realize, finally, a sense of rest.

Bitterly separated from his wife and dying son at the beginning of the novel, Hutch is alone, shut off from the world. Like the earlier two novels of the trilogy, *The Promise of Rest* then moves father and son toward a final reunion, in which Hutch and Wade are given a last chance at mutual understanding, and with it renewal and healing. What is so strange about this novel, however, is Hutch's attitude toward his son's imminent death. Though painfully grieved by Wade's hopeless condition, Hutch also, as revealed in this conversation with Ann, experiences a growing sense of elation:

> "I love this, Ann."
> "You *love* it?"
> Hutch said "You know I do."
> "Our son's pain and death?"
> In some huge way the answer was Yes, but Hutch didn't say it. (*PR*, 119)

Hutch's attitude, at least initially, does not make sense, particularly since Wade is "the only human [Hutch]'d loved with no real reservation since his own father died" (31).

Again, Price maintains a sense of mystery in depicting the relationship between father and son. Though one can come up with numerous explanations as to why Hutch might feel elated in light of his son's imminent death, none is fully satisfactory. One of the best approaches toward understanding Hutch's attitude is again through the unusual circumstances of his birth. Because his mother died in giving him life, Hutch sees an inextricable connection between birth and death. As horrible as Wade's death is for his father, it also signals resuscitation: from the opening scene forward, Hutch is waking up, returning to life. Thus one finds one of the strangest, most original messages in all of Price's fiction: from the devastating death of a loved child can come rebirth, even elation. Price's epigraph from Eliot's "Little Gidding" may help to explain:

> We die with the dying:
> See, they depart, and we go with them.
> We are born with the dead:
> See, they return, and bring us with them.

Throughout the novel and the entire trilogy there is both loss and gain in death. Hutch loses part of himself literally and figuratively with Wade's death, yet he also realizes significant gains: renewed contact, after eight years of separation, with his son; news of a grandson, Raven Bondurant, whose body and soul have been shaped by Wade; continued hope of an afterlife, "the promise of rest"; reactivation of his creative and sexual energy; and the birth of a new poem.

The relationship between Hutch and Wade is Pricean in that the author again posits a strong eroticism between father and son. Hutch views his son as "one of the three great stunners he'd known, among men at least—that handsomely formed and carefully tended and moved by an open generous heart" (*PR*, 94), and in a conversation Hutch and Wade admit their mutual attraction and desire:

> [Says Wade,] "I *wanted* you to touch me more ways than one, but you were a gentleman round the clock always and a knockout to boot."
> "I'm a blighted cabbage leaf to what I was. You're pretty grand yourself."
> (112)

This strong mutual pull has been destroyed, however, by Wade's decision to take Wyatt Bondurant as his lover, a man who despised Hutch and who Hutch believed "shanghaied Wade Mayfield from his home" and family (48). Wade's defection and betrayal eight years earlier—another mystery to be unraveled—must have been devastating for Hutch, as he lost his son to a man who viewed him and Ann as *Murder Incorporated,* deserving of a horrible "Judgment Day": *"your two progenitors are rushed up against a concrete wall by blazing archangels and mowed to a pulp with whatever brand of automatic weapon the angels are issued for simple justice"* (158, 157).

Much of the strange elation Hutch is experiencing then stems from the fact that he is getting his son back. With Wyatt out of the picture, having opted for suicide as the terminative act to his bout with AIDS, Hutch can reclaim his son and rid himself of the anger and bitterness he has long felt. Yet in bringing Wade back from New York City to his Durham home, Hutch is extraordinarily territorial, striving to have Wade to himself, as if his son is all *his.* Straw even explains to Hutch, "You want to have all his death for yourself," and Ann tells her husband, "[Y]ou're walling me out of all this" (*PR*, 44, 120).

What seems to have precipitated the father-son split is Hutch's instinct toward distance, "his oldest instinct" (*PR*, 148). Hutch has not been frank with his son, at least about himself. Though Wade sensed his father had had homosexual relationships, Hutch was never forthcoming. As Hutch tells his student Maitland, "[Wade] knows next to nothing about his father" (104). Wyatt, on the other hand, is a truth bearer (though his version of reality is sometimes ludicrous); in a letter he tells Wade, *"At least I love you and tell you the truth"* (158). Wade left his father then, in part because Hutch had been so miserly in his offerings and unable to give his son the truth—the great irony being that Hutch, as a poet, is one who seeks truth and beauty.

The split between Hutch and Wade is due also to the two major thematic issues of the novel: sexuality and race. Wade Mayfield has chosen as his partner an African-American homosexual. Wade is the first Mayfield to acknowledge and pursue openly, without guilt, shame, or fear, the two desires that so many of his male ancestors have repressed or experienced only furtively: an attraction to blacks and an attraction to men. By committing himself for life (and death) to a black man, Wade breaks the racial and sexual barriers that confused and stymied his forebears. Rob's love for kinsman Grainger Walters and Hutch's for Strawson Stuart, both of which were repressed, find expression in Wade's love for Wyatt.

Wade becomes what his father could not. In many respects, Wade is Hutch's counterlife, revealing where the father's life could have gone had he followed his desires. Hutch's refusal to continue to seek in male faces the masks of his father accounts for his failed marriage and bone-dry life. Hutch and Straw, it appears, missed a great opportunity nearly 40 years earlier because of Hutch's timidity, confusion, and stinginess. According to Wade, stinginess (with one's body and soul) is Hutch's primary failing, "as mean a failing as anything else but strangling children" (*PR*, 196). Though Hutch argues he and Straw would have destroyed each other, Straw counters, "What would have been worse than you killing me or vice versa?" (54). Straw's question sets up a parallel with Wade and Wyatt, who actually do "kill" one another.

As becomes clear in *The Promise of Rest,* father and son require mutual pardon of one another; Wade tells his father, "Just say the word *pardon*" (*PR*, 98). Wade needs Hutch's forgiveness for loving a man who hated Hutch—did Wyatt's hatred of Hutch somehow attract Wade?—and Hutch needs Wade's pardon for his emotional detachment as well as his refusal to explain himself adequately to his son. By taking care of Wade during the final months of his illness, Hutch hopes "to finish their lives and ease them out with a clear-eyed dignity" (116). And though Hutch is able to repair much of the damage between them, he realizes that his son's love is ultimately with another man. As Wade says, "Pardon me for choosing and loving forever—you've got to know I'll love Wyatt Bondurant forever: a man that flat-out hated you" (98). Even after the moment of Wade's death, when Hutch tells Jimmy Boat, "I've given Wade up to him [Wyatt]," Jimmy replies, "Excuse me, Mr. Mayfield, but maybe you still need to know—Wade hasn't been yours to give for long years" (280).

The pairing of Wade and Wyatt is tragic in that the trilogy's most passionate and mutually satisfying love affair ends in early death, yet it also represents the triumph of love: Wade is strong enough to follow the desires that have fueled his male forebears, and he is willing to love another in spite of what his family or society say. In *A Great Circle* love demands huge risk and sacrifice, and both Eva Mayfield in 1903 and Wade Mayfield in the contemporary era sacrifice their relationships with their fathers, the most important people in their lives to that point, in order to be with their lovers. Yet whereas Eva leaves her husband and returns to her father after just a year, Wade opts permanently for his lover, with whom he will remain "forever." Wade may suggest an end to the Mayfield demon or curse that has prevented these men from creating fulfilling relationships outside of their own family. Wade has broken free of his father and has chosen an outsider to be his own.

The Promise of Rest is also triumphant in that the anticipated death of the Mayfield line does not occur. Instead the Mayfield genes continue through the newest son, the "secret child," whose identity does not become fully clear until late in the novel. Price's narrator reveals that Raven Patterson Bondurant is Wade's son and that Wade's traits will seep into Raven through the Stuart cavalier doll that Hutch gives the young man. A mixture of Mayfield, Patterson, and Bondurant blood, Raven is the culmination of nearly a century of kindness between the Mayfields and Pattersons (see *SE,* 68–71; *SL,* 278–79). A vessel of mixed races and an amalgamation of the trilogy's major bipolar entities—black and white, north and south, country and city, straight and gay—Raven represents the Mayfield (now Bondurant) future. He is the son who can travel beyond the racial, sexual, and familial barriers that have destroyed so many Mayfield men; and he is, for Hutch, the embodiment and resurrection of Wade, offering Hutch a second chance as a father (Hutch also assumes fatherly roles with Maitland Moses, Hart Salter, and Jimmy Boat). In the novel's final scene, Hutch and Raven, walking "hand in hand," return from scattering Wade's ashes and find themselves in "blinding clean sunlight," which suggests a future of "promise," as do Price's concluding words, "they looked on forward and took the first steps" (*PR,* 353).

As we see in Price's work, homosexual desire often arises from, responds to, and acts as a fulfillment of father-son desire: Hutch's desire for young men is a projection of his desire for his father; Wade's desire for Wyatt is fueled in contrasting ways by his love for and rejection of Hutch. Price's young male protagonists, not only in the trilogy but in other stories and novels, often fall in love with a nearby father figure, whom they use as a guide to realize their own sexuality. The older male, whether biological father or simply father figure, becomes a crucial force in the life of the younger male, particularly in regard to the younger's emerging sexual identity. Ultimately Price's most satisfied characters are those who follow their desires, such as Wade, and even Hutch during that brief period in his mid-twenties. Wade is the breakthrough character, the son who is no longer under the spell of the father, the son who finds what his father could not (and still fathers a son in the process). Wade is the embodiment of confident, unapologetic male eroticism, and his example provides both a lesson for his father and a survivor, Raven, whose hopeful presence suggests the possibility, between blood kin, of understanding and love.

In these pages, I have merely scratched the surface in attempting to explain a single mystery in the work of Reynolds Price: the erotic nature of father-son relations. Not only are there other writings in Price's oeuvre that could be included in this discussion—*Private Contentment,* "The Enormous Door," "Deeds of Lights"—but there are other familial relationships (mother-son, mother-daughter, father-daughter, aunt-nephew) as well as other mysteries waiting to be explored. By the word *mystery,* I suggest Price endeavors to limn for his readers moments and sensations that, though beyond our powers of full understanding, can nevertheless be explored and partially grasped. Price plunges into the most primitive aspects of family life and love, allowing us to observe the dangers and joys of intimacy between parents and children. Resistant to those popular tendencies that sensationalize incestuous relations, Price strives to normalize family eroticism and place it within a more natural framework, yet simultaneously he demonstrates that men and women can become paralyzed and suffer immensely because of excessive familial intimacy.

Notes

1. Constance Rooke, *Reynolds Price* (Boston: Twayne, 1983), 12.

2. George Garrett, "Portrait of an Artist," review of *The Tongues of Angels, World & I* 5 (August 1990): 433. Rpt. in *My Silk Purse and Yours* (Columbia: University of Missouri Press, 1992), 199.

3. Jonathan Keates, "Southern Discomfort," review of *Kate Vaiden, Observer* (22 February 1987): 29.

4. William Ray, "Conversations: Reynolds Price and William Ray/1976," in *Conversations with Reynolds Price,* ed. Jefferson Humphries (Jackson: University Press of Mississippi, 1991), 105–6.

5. Reynolds Price, "The Names and Faces of Heroes," *The Collected Stories* (New York: Atheneum, 1993), 441. Subsequent references are to this edition and are cited in the text as "NFH."

6. Reynolds Price, "Given Time: Beginning *The Surface of Earth,*" *Antaeus* 21/22 (Spring/Summer 1976): 57–58.

7. Reynolds Price, *The Surface of Earth* (New York: Atheneum, 1975), 24. Subsequent references are to this edition and are cited in the text as *SE.*

8. Ernest Jones, *On the Nightmare* (London: Hogarth, 1931), 44. Though other psychologists since Jones—for instance, J. A. Hadfield, Roger Broughton, Henri Gastaut, and John Mack—have expanded upon and pushed the study of the incubus further, Jones's work, as David Hufford points out, "has had a great and lasting influence" and is still significant. See Hufford, *The Terror That Comes in the Night* (Philadelphia: University of Pennsylvania Press, 1982), 135.

9. Jones, 75–76; Reynolds Price, "A Vast Common Room," in *A Common Room: Essays 1954–1987* (New York: Atheneum, 1987), 374.

10. Lee Yopp, "Panel Discussion," in *Reynolds Price: From "A Long and Happy Life" to "Good Hearts,"* ed. Sue Laslie Kimball and Lynn Veach Sadler (Fayetteville, N.C.: Methodist College Press, 1989), 105.

11. Reynolds Price, *The Source of Light* (New York: Atheneum, 1981), 6. Subsequent references are to this edition and are cited in the text as *SL.*

12. Reynolds Price, *Clear Pictures* (New York: Atheneum, 1989), 298–99.

13.   Joyce Carol Oates, "Portrait of the Artist As Son, Lover, Elegist," review of *The Source of Light, New York Times Book Review* (26 April 1981): 30.

14.   Price, *Clear Pictures,* 62.

15.   Ibid., 39.

16.   Ibid., 29.

17.   Reynolds Price, *The Promise of Rest* (New York: Scribner, 1995), 16. Subsequent references are to this edition and are cited in the text as *PR*.

Men without Women:
Communities of Desire and Race
in *A Great Circle*

MICHAEL KREYLING

He needed to see women and they were welcome for a while. He liked having them there, sometimes for quite a long time. But in the end he was always glad when they were gone. . . .

Ernest Hemingway, *Islands in the Stream.*

More than 20 years ago, in his essay "For Ernest Hemingway," Reynolds Price judged himself as apprentice writer under a debt to Hemingway. What Price wrote then about the fading heavyweight champ of American literature—acute technical admiration, one artist to another, but touching on Hemingway's central subject too—is an entryway into Price's major achievement, *A Great Circle,* the trilogy of novels working out the Mayfield fate on the broad plain of public event and in the narrow ravine of private desire in the twentieth century. *The Surface of Earth* (1975) concentrates on three generations of Mayfields, from 1903 to World War II; *The Source of Light* (1981) focuses on Rob Mayfield and his only son, Hutch, for one crucial year in the mid-1950s; and *The Promise of Rest* (1995) completes the trilogy with the story of Hutch (in his early sixties) and his son Wade, who is dying of AIDS in the early 1990s.

Price's understanding of Hemingway's themes, locating the intersection of the public and the private, concerns me more in this essay than his pinpoint craftsman's tribute to an elder writer, almost 10 years dead at the time, whose critical reputation was in a free fall that the posthumous publication of *Islands in the Stream* (1970) did little to arrest. Hemingway's hero Thomas Hudson, Price sees, knew one big fact without which all of his craft would have been null and void: love and work are equally important, and if you could touch but not hold the world in acts of love, you could hold it in your work if it was good enough.

This essay was written specifically for this volume and is published here for the first time by permission of the author.

In the story of painter Thomas Hudson and his three sons, Price finds Hemingway grappling "with the only one of the four possible human relations which he [Hemingway] had previously avoided—parental devotion, filial return. (The other three relations—with God, with the earth, with a female or male lover or friend—he had worked from the start, failing almost always with the first, puzzlingly often with the third, succeeding as richly as anyone with the second.)"[1] *A Great Circle,* if it can be said to have a single theme vaulting through the three novels, is about the great theme Hemingway took from the Judaeo-Christian epic, "parental devotion, filial return." Price has seen more acutely than Hemingway how communities of men *and* women close the circle with more difficulty than either sex does on its own. Whereas Hemingway, through a mixture of denial and strategic style, evaded one part of the challenge while dispatching another, Price accepts the fullness of the complication. Blunted in several generations by women and their "puzzling" desires, the Mayfield men nevertheless circle home for fulfillment in *The Promise of Rest,* in which gulfs of age, race, and sexuality are abolished in a resonant, elegiac final ceremony of fatherly acknowledgment and love.

A few years before the publication of *The Surface of Earth,* then, Price found reassuring affinities with his own work in a writer about whom he had not thought seriously in several years. The old man surprised him. "Wasn't his [Hemingway's] lifelong subject *saintliness?* Wasn't it generally as secret from him (a lapsing but never quite lost Christian) as from his readers?" Price asks.[2] It was the possession of virtue through lifelong discipline to work, according to Price, that Hemingway desired, as artist and man: "the love of creation in its witnesses and thereby to confirm an approach by the worker toward goodness, literal virtue, the manly performance of the will of God. *Saintliness,* I've called it. . . ."[3] It is as if Price pledged himself to the same stripped-down, ascetic order to which Hemingway belonged: an order of self-conscious artists modeling themselves on desert anchorites and devoted to the purification of acts of attention (witnessing) rigorously aimed at the world. Price's linking of himself as artist with Hemingway ran against the grain of contemporary critical reception, the overwhelming weight of which paired Price father-and-son with Faulkner—a priest of another sort, whose liturgy emphasized ornamentation, syntactical arabesques, the complication of acts of attention by wave upon wave of qualification. Price acknowledges in Hemingway a "secret" though tougher bond. The challenge of faith, which he detected in Hemingway, outshone the blaze of unbelief in Faulkner.

The men who had performed "literal virtue" most canonically, in Price's view, were the Desert Fathers, the Christian anchorites and writers of the late classical/early Christian West who mapped the terrain of "saintliness" that he and Hemingway traversed. Price's essay on Hemingway takes him, by its conclusion, to the original voices of the Desert Fathers. The writings of one of these, Augustine of Hippo, supplies the epigraph to the first novel and a richly developed articulation of tropes and language to the trilogy as a whole.

From the codes of the Desert Fathers to the contemporary public world of AIDS, Price puts together the language of the Mayfield trilogy. Hemingway is a flawed but powerful father: a lapsing but not lost Christian; a writer whose work left-handedly affirms God; a man who found virtue, work, and women an incompatible mixture but a necessary reality.

That Price has seen his own work, in subject and technique, so closely related to Hemingway's tempts me to suggest a baggy interpretive paradigm by way of Hemingway's durable theme of "men without women": Price's insistence that his precursor in the American novel is a lapsed descendant of the Desert Fathers. Further, his consistent depiction in the trilogy of the superiority of the "manly performance" of desire, friendship, community, and renunciation over whatever might be accomplished with women in similar relationships sets up in the trilogy a progression of idealized male communities inchoate in the mixed communities of men and women "normal" to Western images of society. This emergent ideal articulates Price's pursuit of Hemingway's "secret."

Each of the novels in the Mayfield trilogy concludes with an affirmation of a family unit from which women have been excused. In *The Surface of Earth,* Rob Mayfield, his adolescent son Hutch, and their "kin person" Grainger Walters solemnize a nuclear family of men without women by the exchange of the Mayfield wedding ring, a potent symbol of durable, masculine force associated in the trilogy with the bark man of the heavy phallus, Old Rob's totemic figure. In *The Source of Light,* Hutch (now in his mid-twenties), knowing that Ann Gatlin, his doubtful fiancée, has seen to the abortion of their child, builds a mostly imagined family relationship with an Oxford (England) stonemason, James Nichols, whose daughter Nan has been all but abandoned by her biological mother and her (Nan's) aunt. As the second novel in the trilogy closes, Hutch imagines a family in which he and James parent Nan in a successful social unit that "normal" heterosexual marriage fails to achieve. The deeply moving, psalmic rhythms and imagery of the final scene of *The Promise of Rest* close the "Great Circle" as Hutch, now in his early sixties, departs the spot where he has strewn the ashes of his dead son, Wade, accompanied by his acknowledged (by Hutch, if not by Ann) grandson, Raven Bondurant. The Mayfield ring continues its strong symbolic duty as Hutch slips it on Raven's thumb, thus reaffirming the cords of male tribute and homosocial bonding, the "saintliness" that men can achieve in a community without women.

The simultaneity of the social and the erotic in Price's trilogy is essential to its meaning. For Price's Mayfield men, as for Hemingway's heroes from Jake Barnes on, as for Augustine in his autobiographical *Confessions,* desire does not exist apart from the sexed, physical body in its network of social entanglement. This linkage torments Jake in *The Sun Also Rises* and brings Pedro Romero down from the ecstatic male community of *afición.* Augustine

is likewise tormented until, at Ostia, he hits upon renunciation as the anti-
dote to concupiscence—a drastic solution Price's trilogy only marginally supports. That desired bodies, and desires themselves, have been coded by society as normal and abnormal, good and evil, is a thematic knot the trilogy
tries to unsnarl. Over the coincident spans of the trilogy's two time frames
(nearly a century from the beginning of *The Surface of Earth,* 1903, to the
death of Wade Mayfield in 1993 in *The Promise of Rest;* the two decades
[1975–1995] spanned by the publication of the three novels, two decades of
great significance to human sexuality with the appearance of AIDS and the
public response to it in the West), desire and the body, and the nature of family as a social/private hybrid have loomed large in our cultural conversation.
Nothing less than this entire conversation is Price's subject matter in the trilogy. Because of Price's native ground in the southern United States, race complicates his field. Hemingway attempted nothing of such scope; Faulkner's
Snopes trilogy hits its peak early and collapses into self-parody and artistic
recycling in *The Town* and *The Mansion.*

No languages objectify the body more immediately and combustibly
than race and sex. *A Great Circle* speaks both, in historically resonant accents
pulled up from the subsoil of Christianity in the West and refined, off-site as
it were, by the intervention of Hemingway.

The best point for beginning the interpretation of these languages as basic for
a coherent view of the trilogy is the intertextual exchange with which Price
himself launches the first volume. The quotation from Augustine's *Confessions,*
which functions as epigraph to *The Surface of Earth,* opens more widely to
admit the entire text of Augustine's quest for saintliness within a cultural and
religious context that Price adapts as a kind of master blueprint. Augustine
negotiates a tortuous route from the miasma of simple lust to a promise of
rest in the will of God; his guides are alternatively male and female, paternal
and maternal.

According to Augustine's narrative of his life, his youth, adolescence,
and early manhood were spent in a dank swamp of fleshly desire:

> Bodily desire, like a morass, and adolescent sex welling up within me exuded
> mists which clouded over and obscured my heart, so that I could not distin-
> guish the clear light of true love from the murk of lust. Love and lust together
> seethed within me.[4]

A life in the murk of the purely physical body seems not to have troubled
Augustine's father. "The brambles of lust grew high above my head," the son
writes ruefully, "and there was no one to root them out, certainly not my father."

> One day at the public baths he saw the signs of active virility coming to life in
> me and this was enough to make him relish the thought of having grandchil-

dren. He was happy to tell my mother about it, for his happiness was due to the intoxication which causes the world to forget you, its Creator, and to love the things you have created instead of loving you, because the world is drunk with the invisible wine of its own perverted, earthbound will. But in my mother's heart you had already begun to build your temple and laid the foundations of your holy dwelling, while my father was still a catechumen and a new one at that.[5]

Augustine is up to building the more complicated "foundations," a base of belief about the world that Price does not wholly share. Two things about Augustine's predicament Price sets out to heal: the mutual exclusion of loving the things of creation but not the Creator, and the distance Augustine seeks to make between self and body. Augustine's world is divided into paternal and maternal sides too; on the former is the intoxication of the physical, on the latter a more authentic approach to what Augustine anticipates as saintliness. When, in Ostia, he feels his breakthrough, it is the chaste figure of Continence as a woman who calls him and it is to his mother he breaks the news.[6]

Price's trilogy is similarly Manichean, but not so easily divided between maternal and paternal (male and female) spheres. As "For Ernest Hemingway" makes clear, saintliness (for the artist especially) can be won only through works that themselves approximate the "creation" of which they are witness. Holiness is achieved not by escaping *from* the world but by escaping *into* the surfaces of the earth. Since created things include the body, there is no salvation without desire. Even work, for all its intercourse with a palpable earth, is not enough in itself. This is what Hemingway did not know, and his confusion prevented him, in turn, from knowing that "saintliness" was the grail of his quest.

Price's interweaving of themes is immediately apparent in *The Promise of Rest*. Wade Mayfield, fifth generation in the family line, dying of AIDS in 1993, instructs Maitland Moses, one of his father's undergraduates, who has volunteered to nurse Wade during his final days, on the seemingly irreconcilable "languages" of desire, male and female, queer and straight:

> "If straight men weren't hardwired for women, with all women's training and doubts and plumbing problems, they'd fuck as many times a day as the most crazed queer on the south side of Eighth Street. No, what's wrong with queers—the only wrong thing they don't share with straights—is nothing but children. Queers don't make children, not as a rule. I figured you'd noticed."[7]

Mait had noticed. His desire for men (as murky physically as Augustine's for women, but psychologically running counter to what Mait feels are "normal" desires) and his subsequent role in the "working plans" of the social universe trouble him. In Mait's eyes the Mayfield men, Hutch and Wade, have the puzzle worked out. Mait had approached Hutch as a role model but had won for his pains only some hackneyed pseudopaternal instruction on the distinction between "painted queens" and Hutch's own sexual self—neither gay nor bisexual, "no one pigeonhole" (PR, 101). It is Wade, though, who comes through with declarative but enigmatic instruction. " 'Someway. Have children. One child anyhow' " (PR, 183). Mait is, understandably, stumped; begetting offspring seems incontestably the province of heterosexual couples. Even by the end of the novel there is no indication that Maitland has decided whether or not to enter the furnace of gay sex and the danger of death by AIDS.

This three-way conference of father, son, surrogate son in The Promise of Rest is less a dramatic conversation than an interior monologue, or even a soliloquy that shifts the genre of the trilogy from novel to something akin to confession. In The Promise of Rest Price reduces, like a stock, several differentiated male "characters" to phases of one emerging male identity desiring both love and work but confused as to right objects in each. Clues to the nature of this composite character come from various sources. Maitland, for example, is a name Hutch himself has used: in The Source of Light he signed the Taft Hotel register in New York "Mr. Maitland" when he and Ann Gatlin spent a few hours there before his departure for England. In New York, Hutch was not a stable, single person, as the souvenir photomontage of his several faces indicates.[8] More than simple coincidence, this recurrence of the name (not to mention its abbreviated form, Mait, which suggests the secret sharing of identities) adumbrates a bond between Hutch and his student in which "selves" change places more or less freely: Mait is a double for Hutch himself at a similar life crossroads (his departure to Oxford and work; subterranean reservations in his relationship with Ann). Mait in the sexual free-fire zone of the 1990s is the young man Hutch might have been if the historical conditions he faced at Mait's age had been different, enabling Hutch to "think" his multiple desires in the 1950s. Hutch must see himself when young when he sees Mait.

The relationship between Hutch and Wade, biological father and son, is more concrete than the relationship of Hutch and Maitland. Conversations between the two pairs disclose a deeply conflicted yet shared persona. Unlike Augustine, who saw his father as the enforcer of a life of mere biological reproduction, Price propels Hutch and Wade centripetally upon each other. After Hutch's poetry-writing students have departed their annual supper meeting, Wade, restless, invites Hutch to recite a poem or story. As father and son, this ritual had stitched their lives together. Now, Hutch fears he can't participate, for the poem that comes to his mind is Keats's final poem, "written in the unflinching knowledge of the fact that [he] was dying of TB at twenty-six" (PR, 109). The same poem comes independently to Wade's plagued mind and he begins to say it. The voices of father and son finish it together (110).

The telling of the Keats poem, however, only begins the fusing of father and son. Wade implores his father to confess his secret life—a son's birthright of sexual identity, erotic cravings, and desires—that Hutch protects and Wade has openly lived. Hutch haltingly circles around his "confession," but his son, short on time, interrupts with corrections. " 'Am I telling this story or you?' " Hutch queries. " 'I'm starting to wonder,' " is the son's quick reply (*PR*, 111).

The bond between father and son is so intimate as to cross the realistic/biological frontier, even the Hemingway frontier of "parental devotion, filial return." No two separate bodies are, under normal conditions, as close as those Price presents in intimacy. But the male/male, father/son bond is freighted with so much importance, in *The Promise of Rest* and the two earlier legs of the trilogy, that Price pushes it boldly. Father and son not only loved within the socially "normal" boundaries of filial affection but were honed on each other as erotically charged bodies. Wade was, for his father, "one of the three great stunners he'd known, among men at least" (*PR*, 94), and Wade reciprocated paternal worship: " 'I *wanted* you to touch me more ways than one, but you were a gentleman round the clock always and a knockout to boot' " (112). Wade also remembers youthful intimations of homosexual community in the murmuring talk of Hutch and his lifetime friend Strawson Stuart on summer evenings at the Kendal farm (137). Eroticizing the father-son relationship risks criminalizing it, or turning it into grist for a talk show mill. But Price insists on deeper levels of love and work attainable only in male communities of desire.

Doubling father and son as *eromenos* and *erastes* (desiring subject and object of desire), Price locates same-sex Eros in the three Mayfield novels within the ample paradigm of Attic sexuality and desire. K. J. Dover's *Greek Homosexuality* (1978) begins with a dispassionate disclaimer crucial for distinguishing representations of desire in the trilogy from *mere* concupiscence (Augustine's or anyone else's):

> For the purpose of this enquiry, homosexuality is defined as the disposition to seek sensory pleasure through bodily contact with persons of one's own sex in preference to contact with the other sex. There may well be other purposes for which this definition would be superficial and inadequate; but Greek culture differed from ours in its readiness to recognise the alternation of homosexual and heterosexual preferences in the same individual, its implicit denial that such alternation or coexistence created peculiar problems for the individual or for society, its sympathetic response to the open expression of homosexual desire in words and behaviour, and its taste for the uninhibited treatment of homosexual subjects in literature and the visual arts.[9]

Both Wade and Hutch, and all the Mayfield men back to Old Rob, have lived the high-pitched sexual (and "alternately" bisexual) lives covered in Dover's statement. If Augustine alone were the only patron voice, their history would be futile. The "carved-bark man with the workable penis" that Ann numbers among Hutch's "billion souvenirs from a rich strong life" (*PR*, 176) passes along the generations of the Mayfield men's lives, reminding each that desire is not to be avoided this side of the grave but also that its by-products are not necessarily always within the zone of love. To understand only one end in sexuality is the *mere* sexuality applauded by Augustine's father.

The phallic totem not only symbolically links the generations; it also significantly marks the progress of Mayfield desire from predatory heterosexuality to an ideal of unproblematic, pure, unsurpassable community in male sexual exclusivity. Implicitly disputing Augustine, Hutch interprets his way through the bark man code. For Old Rob and his grandson, Hutch's father, women were more or less sexual fodder. Forrest had found, with Polly—not with Eva—a mutually satisfactory separation of rights and functions. Polly was willing to find comfort in a narrow channel of identity: food preparation and allied domestic work, sexual worship of and service to the male. Eva had found the tacit contract unacceptable; the difficult birth of Rob made further sexual relations with Forrest beyond her scope of love. Eva broke communal agreements; in reneging she bequeathed to her son, grandson, and great-grandson a certain suspicion of the female. In *The Promise of Rest,* for example, Hutch corrects graduate student Hart Salter in the usage of "gender-sensitive language" (*PR,* 14), but his advice is archly ironic, based as it is on a complicated family history.

The trilogy is shaped, for better or worse, by a tidally developing gender hierarchy that originates in historical circumstance and ends, in *The Promise of Rest,* in overt hostility. Signaling authorial consent to this division, each Mayfield male begets to the next generation one son. Wives die (Rachel), decline further procreative relations (Eva), or become deeply cellar locked in rejection of male privilege and suspicion of same-sex community and desire (Ann). As the ample arch of the trilogy's plot completes its reach, only women content to be watchers, servers, attendants at male shows of life and talent (Polly Drewry, Rena Kendal, Alice Matthews, Emily Stuart) emerge with honors. Heterosexual white women (Marleen Pickett or the unnamed prostitute who "starts" Rob on his insatiable sexual quest in *The Source of Light*) lend ease or release in crucial switchbacks in the male Mayfield journey. They do not, however, stay on as full partners in the quest for saintliness.

The place for the sexual female in the Mayfield trilogy evolves only to second best, for she cannot (or does not) add to the community of love and work. Wade discloses part of the imaginary (de)construction of the (white) female in his brief lecture to Mait. "[W]omen's training and doubts and plumbing problems" is a stenographic entry for a vast and ancient text that relegates the sex to a constricted identity (*PR,* 182). Peter Brown, synopsizing classical and early Christian thinking on the biologies of the two sexes in *The Body and Society: Men, Women, and Sexual Renunciation in Early Christianity* (1988), provides a handy gloss for reading the sexual text of the Mayfield trilogy:

Biologically, the doctors said, males were those fetuses who had realized their full potential. They had amassed a decisive surplus of "heat" and fervent "vital spirit" in the early stages of their coagulation in the womb. The hot ejaculation of male seed proved this: "For it is the semen, when possessed of vitality, which makes us men, hot, well-braced in limbs, heavy, well-voiced, spirited, strong to think and act." [Brown quoting Aretaeus the Cappodocian, *Causes and Symptoms of Chronic Diseases*]

Women, by contrast, were failed males. The precious vital heat had not come to them in sufficient quantities in the womb. Their lack of heat made them soft, more liquid, more clammy-cold, altogether more formless than were men. Periodic menstruation showed that their bodies could not burn up the heavy surpluses that coagulated within them. Yet precisely such surpluses were needed to nurture and contain the hot male seed, thus producing children. Were this not so, the doctor Galen added, men might think that "the Creator had purposely made one half of the whole race imperfect, and, as it were, mutilated."[10]

Brown further describes thinking on procreation during Augustine's lifetime in terms clearly adaptable to an understanding of similar motives in the trilogy. Procreation of offspring was not a problematic by-product of personal sexuality. To beget offspring was, in its outcome (and outcome was its chief purpose), a public act, even a duty in piety to state and family, not a personal rush of romantic self-duplication. Heterosexual relationships had, in the epoch Brown has studied, pragmatic rather than expressive parameters of meaning. Wade echoes this tenet in his advice to Mait to have a child.

Patterns of imagery and allusion in the novels argue the aptness of this classical/early Christian code. Forrest Mayfield is a teacher of Roman poetry and Cicero; he quotes Augustine.[11] Distraught over Eva's refusal to resume her conjugal life with him, Forrest translates Catullus's lines describing the self-emasculation of Attis in the service of Cybele (*SE*, 58–59). In *The Source of Light*, Hutch and Ann have a brittle exchange on the same ground (155–56). Hutch's possessions are few when he goes off to England, but when he packs them up in Virginia we find a classical marble torso of a boy and a postcard picture of the maid of Chios (12). Male beauty presents itself in the classical posture of the Greek athlete (imported into the Italian Renaissance with Michelangelo's *David*): Rachel drinks in the sight of Rob in this pose the night Hutch, fatal son, is conceived (*SE*, 310–11); Hutch's desire for Straw is ignited by the latter in a similar pose (*SL*, 226); Hart Salter, stripping for Wade's failing eyesight, unconsciously strikes the Attic pose (*PR*, 87).

The imagery of erotic desire that circulates throughout the Mayfield trilogy is unapologetically antimodern, as is the division of cultural prestige between male and female. As Hutch toils to make clear to Mait when the young man comes out to him, Hutch feels encumbered by the terms *queer* and *bisexual,* and he clearly draws back from the performative parody of sex and gender carried on by the Joan Crawford-ish "Poufs," "a couple of near-transvestites" Mait threatens to join (104). Unlike, for example, theorist and critic of scriptings of sexuality David M. Halperin, who extends but narrows Michel Foucault's investigations of pleasure and sexuality, Price presents sexuality as essential rather than performative, ignited by desire for beautiful forms in particular bodies rather than socially constructed under quasi-political conditioning. Halperin argues that "Unlike sex, which is a natural fact, sexuality is a cultural production; it represents the *appropriation* of the human body and of its erogenous zones by an ideological discourse."[12] Hutch tries to persuade Mait out of such a stance when the young man threatens fatalistically to throw himself into the either/or of outright gay or outright straight life.

Hutch walks a fine line. He agrees with Straw that their mutual, erotic desires do not make them "sissies" (*PR,* 53–54). Yet Hutch will not concede that his decision to marry a woman betrayed either straight society *or* his essentially homoerotic desires. He argues, at least to himself, that in renouncing what would have been a gay life with Straw, he served a higher good: the "normal" family. The modern politics of sexual desire will not permit split allegiance—even if one side is kept in the closet. The paradigm for which Hutch reaches is, then, neither Augustinian nor modern but "Greek" bisexuality, discussed by K. J. Dover and quoted earlier. Objects of erotic desire answer not to majority social norms but to absolutes of beauty. Price "Christianizes" the equation: God put beauty in the world to be like braille guides to Himself. Acts of attention to the world are, therefore, both erotic and prayerful. Reading back through "For Ernest Hemingway" we can see a possible answer to Price's question as to why Hemingway failed to write well of "relations . . . with a female or male lover or friend."[13] Social norms barricaded him; he could behold the world as beautiful but could not include the male body within that world.

The "institution" precipitated into the historical/social sphere by these unfettered desires is not heterosexual marriage (although the trilogy does not utterly deny the efficacy of this "behavior") but male friendship-based community. Halperin summarizes this community in a useful historical (Greek) context:

> Friendship, it seems, is something that only males can have, and they can have it only in couples. . . . The male couple constitutes a world apart from society at large, and yet it does not merely embody a "private" relation, of the sort that might be transacted appropriately in a "home." On the contrary, friendship helps to structure—and, possibly, to privatize—the social space; it takes shape in the world that lies beyond the horizon of the domestic sphere, and it requires for its expression a military or political staging-ground. This type of friendship cannot generate its own *raison d'être,* evidently; it depends for its meaning on the meaningfulness of social action.[14]

Taking place beyond the domestic enclave, then, dyadic male friendship, Halperin argues, is also hierarchical, or it succeeds by virtue of the culturally enforced prestige of the male in configuring the social practices in or near its orbit into a hierarchy of which it is the apex.[15] Insofar as it is extradomestic and hierarchical, women suffer if they aspire to a different role and status than those available in the hierarchy.

In *The Promise of Rest* the supportive and abject character of woman is easier to read than earlier in the trilogy, where it is embedded in historical and regional context. Emily Stuart, Straw's wife, has, for example, accepted her place in the pack of many bodies that have been more (or as) important to Straw as she is herself. She has never read a serious poem in her life and serves mostly as cook and cautioner of Ann, who seems more resentful of the Straw-son-Hutch relationship than she (or woman) should rightly be (*PR*, 129, 142). Emily is low on the "vital heat" Peter Brown finds to be exclusive to the male in antiquity. Emily has seen the primacy of male friendship and bowed to it. She and Straw have one daughter, "pleasant to see and *cold* as a bottle" (34; my italics). Hart Salter's wife, likewise kept offstage, is "still hungry for far more than Hart had to give—he or any man he'd yet known" (87). Mentioned but granted no further recourse, these women only drive the female deeper into a corner. Hutch's assorted female students do not relieve the portrait. Dr. Margaret Ives, the physician who tends Wade with angelic intuition, provides some ballast, but it is not sufficient to offset the great disapproval placed upon (white) women in the single character of Ann Gatlin.

Woman's "training," then (to return to Wade's formula), seems to allude to her aligning individual behavior along "classical" lines of gender hierarchy privileging white males. Wade's words to Mait seem to warn the younger male to watch out for women who assume eye-to-eye parity, a right or power to determine their own status and fate in any given set of circumstances. Ann unforgivably did so in *The Source of Light* when she aborted the child she and Hutch had begun in Rome. Symbolically, Hutch repossesses this child and erases Ann's claims of motherhood when he single-handedly delivers Wade without professional help. The initiative Ann seized (however complicated morally) still rankles in their 40-year relationship. However doggedly Ann survives, ultimately she loses by persisting. When she consigns her son to hell for his homosexual life (and, to her mind, death), Hutch levies the sentence of "pure human sadism" on her (*PR*, 281). Not even Eva, cold as she was, was the glacier Ann becomes.

What Wade might intend by listing women's "doubts" second among the sex's demerits is difficult to ascertain. It is possible that he alludes to the habit of timidity or recessiveness that Price assigns to many of his female characters—a psychologized analog to the "formlessness" Brown describes. *The Promise of Rest* opens with the throes of one of Hutch's female students, who can hardly bring herself to speak in his seventeenth-century poetry seminar. One of Ann's letters to her son—the one and only letter of the several between them that Hutch reads—bears her confession to a habitual state of self-doubt in her marriage to Hutch. "If I'd had a real mind (a strong imagination as opposed to a dedicated homemaking robot inside my skull), I'd have sure-God never let my private soul just die down to nothing but a warm coal or two the way I did" (PR, 176). To her son, Ann laments the consequences of what, in *The Source of Light,* she had in earlier years seen as her great positive offering to Hutch: "What I want is to work inside at home, making life easy (or easier) for two-to-four people in whom I'm involved and who want me to be" (SL, 62). A more significant woman-presence in Hutch's life, Alice Matthews, never entertained the housewifely role nor entered herself in the child-bearing sweepstakes. Her one significant physical relationship was with Rachel Hutchins before Rachel's marriage to Rob (SL, 28). The lesson of that relationship, Alice imparts to the young Hutch with thinly veiled circumlocution, is to follow your desires even when—should they be same-sex desires—they cross the "normal" lines of public society.

Blunted (white) women are the rule in the Mayfield trilogy. The condition is no more vividly dramatized than in the scene in which Rena rubs down her adolescent nephew Rob with cold witch hazel in their hotel room. Usually she just rubs his legs and back, but on this stolen occasion she bids him roll over on his back. In the presence of the phallus, Rena seems to realize and accept her subordinate position in the "natural" hierarchy (SL, 87).

The ancient, classical understanding of the hierarchy of the sexes on which Price builds the trilogy is most readily apparent in Wade's allusion to women's "plumbing problems." Periodic flow has been for men immemorial an obstacle. In *The Source of Light,* for example, Rob tries to initiate his son into the "pleasures" of heterosexuality (and the horrors of same-sex desire) with the story of Little Hubert, who had been schooled by his mother to see the vagina as fanged like a shark when he showed a precocious desire for what was concealed under the dresses of little girls (SL, 8). The punchline not only paints Rob into a corner with Augustine's father, it also adds to the quarantine around the female body. Later in *The Source of Light* another anecdote, Lew Davis's story about an army buddy who sprouts venereal sores around his mouth after visiting a prostitute, carries the stigmatizing of the (white) female body perilously close to misogyny (92–93). Hutch's mutual favors with the prostitute Marleen Pickett redress the balance, but Vivien Leigh as Lady Macbeth, Archie Gibbons's widowed mother, and the doctor's wife who conscripts her own husband to perform the abortion that rids her of a child implanted by Straw flag the female as dangerous to community. Even in moments of apparent apotheosis, there is negative mitigation. When Hutch remembers making love with Ann for the first time, the luminosity of and delight in her body are shadowed by his image for her pubic hair: a "masterly crown of thorns" (PR, 51).

Resistance to the female body is not without precedent in Western culture, and the Mayfield trilogy abounds in traces and clear-cut invocations of the main meanings. In *The Source of Light* Hutch's desire for beauty is given an unmistakable homoerotic and classical character. Strawson Stuart, then a graduating senior at the prep school where Hutch teaches, appears to Hutch just before they physically consummate their mutual attraction in the aspect of the classical male nude of Greece via the Italian Renaissance (*SL,* 146). The classical image, and Hutch's desire, recur back at home after Rob's funeral (226–27). Homage to the virile nude, and the concomitant disparaging of the female body, runs like DNA in the Mayfield plot.

In *The Source of Light,* Price makes the point with comparatively more discussion than he expends in the other two novels, for the middle novel of the three concerns Hutch's transactions with several kinds of love and work. Just after Hutch beholds the apotheosis of the (white) male in Strawson, his emerging ethics and aesthetics of sexuality are explained:

> But here now he [Strawson] seemed a satisfactory image of one of the three kinds of beauty Hutch loved—man, woman, nature. He also recalled Ann in May at her sink, scraping potatoes. Why couldn't both stand still here always—sky and trees beyond them—for him to watch and serve, serve *by* watching? (*SL,* 227)

Ann's apotheosis as "this living Vermeer" (16) captures woman in her essence as adjunct. Food and sex are her services; each bestows on the male a nourishment he craves: fuel for the physical body, offspring for the genealogical "body." Only Forrest and Polly seem to reach mutual stasis in this negotiation. After sex with Forrest, Polly springs from the bed with the unresentful words "I'll cook" (*SE,* 220). Forrest and Polly are, however, a kind of Adam and Eve of an earlier time and place; Hutch and Ann cannot live by their rules in the second half of the century.

The woman's credentials as lifelong erotic partner are doubtful in *The Source of Light,* but Hutch is willing to accept them. He tells Straw, after their ecstatic sex in the hours after Rob's burial, that if he returns to the Mayfield house it will be as a publicly heterosexual, procreative male (*SL,* 230). In the midst of the sorrow of *The Promise of Rest*—the single son of that pledge dying so visibly of a "plague" seen as the consequence of his own homosexual love—Hutch's decisiveness is retroactively shaken. Straw is the one who rattles Hutch with the cry that " 'The two of us together had something a whole lot better than we've ever had since' " (*PR,* 54). What they have had since is marriage to women. Straw's lament is all the more resonant when it connects—serendipitously—with the "queer" but clearly fulfilling and happy marriage of Straw and Ochello in Tennessee Williams's *Cat on a Hot Tin Roof.*

Hutch finds a stealthy image of his self-sacrifice on the altar of procreative heterosexuality in Rome. That image, emasculation, brings along with it the implication that the male body's desires and the imperatives of family might sometimes be mutually exclusive. Hutch is troubled by these intimations but is foreclosed from acting upon them by "the times." After hearing from Grainger the news that Rob is dying of lung cancer, an end Rob knew was coming when he said farewell to his son on his departure for study at Oxford, Hutch wanders Roman streets without Ann—his wish. "He landed at one of his few planned targets—or had he been led?" The target: a church housing Michelangelo's statue of the risen Christ. Whatever the power that brought him to this emblem, the emblem itself is clearly readable in Hutch's situation:

> He entered brown dark and went straight forward past chapels and tombs through a haze of incense to the steps of the choir where Risen Christ stood bare, the pants gone. An inch was broken from the end of the penis, but the balls were intact, and their thin-skinned availability measured more terribly than wounds the day of agony He'd borne to stand here, unquestionably risen, His thick hips and haunches an adequate promise He'd suffered for all and would not fail again. (*SL*, 176)

From the early scene in which Hutch beholds himself "unquestionably risen" with an erection (*SL*, 22), his uncurbed virility and indomitable personality have been intertwined with the principle that his desire (unlike Augustine's) shall be guiltless (rather, in fact, prayerful) in the attainment of its objects— and in the discarding of recommended objects that do not ignite. *The Surface of Earth* concludes, narratively and thematically, with adolescent Hutch cross-examining his father about his failure to ignite with heterosexual desire. He has watched a man and woman making love on the beach and wonders if such behavior and desire are to be his future. He feels no intimations.

At the moment he visits the *Risen Christ* in Rome, Hutch has had sexual relations with two men, a female prostitute, and Ann. Exclusive commitment to Ann, though, is sacrifice (or *seems* so) of such magnitude that the sacrifice of Christ is sufficient analogy. What the Christ tells him in this visitation is at least twofold: exclusive heterosexual commitment mutilates desire, and desire honed on images of classical (male) beauty promises the only ecstasy one is likely to get. Sir Kenneth Clark describes a finished study for this sculpture as "perhaps the most beautiful nude of ecstasy in the whole of art."[16] Hutch cannot have failed to register this braid of meanings and promises; it is, however, the tension of *The Source of Light* that its hero fails or refuses to see the light.

A few days earlier, this confusion was prefigured. On the Palatine Hill, Christmas Day 1955, with Ann, Hutch is surprised in the ruins of the Temple of the Magna Mater. He at first mistakes his actual and symbolic location but at last finds the correct page in his guidebook and reads the pertinent passage. Priests of the Magna Mater customarily emasculated themselves in service to the goddess. Ann unerringly but unwittingly reflects the same message. Finding a shard of marble, she tosses it to Hutch. "Then she gave her best imitation of Mae West—'Keep this in your shaving kit, big boy, and remember me when your razor slips' " (SL, 166). The subtext of castration anxiety and Mae West's engulfing body could scarcely be more closely linked. Nevertheless, a child is conceived when Ann and Hutch make love a few hours before he leaves, alone, for Rob's deathbed.

The conclusion of The Source of Light leaves the issue of Hutch's sexual choices in an ambiguous condition, if you believe, with Mait the Byronic modern, that such choices are terminally either/or. But building around the issue of choosing erotic objects in the "Attic" paradigm, Hutch can at least nominally claim freedom from bipolar restrictions. His ideal, in erotic desire, is not so much a postromantic self-expression as a classical reunification of divided halves of an originally unified self—the restoration of the dream of somatic oneness that is the theme of Aristophanes' explanation of sexual difference in Plato's Symposium.[17] Hutch, at least temporarily, merges with Ann in sexual unity and urges her to accept the Mayfield ring as a pledge that they can continue shared ecstasy (SL, 163). She is noncommittal, and in the aftermath of Rob's funeral, Hutch tells Straw that he (not Ann, who also makes the pilgrimage) is the one person he is gladdest to see. In a sense Hutch is "outed" and the pledge to Ann is undercut before their marriage: a letter from Straw discloses that Rob, according to Straw's laserlike intuition, had known the two young men were lovers (SL, 282).

Not much later in the text, however, at a pub with his Oxford tutor, Hutch, intoxicated perhaps by the freedom Rob's death has bestowed on the field of his desires, by a break in the dreary English weather, and by the rosy sensuality of the innkeeper's daughter, feels a welling up of polymorphous desire—pure concupiscence. He is confident that the girl would "lend him all her competent body" if he were merely to ask (SL, 290). The fantasized Leda-Swan ravishing does not take place, but the tide of desire flows into Hutch's connection with a young English stonemason. Sex with the stonemason is not merely physical, for James Nichols (the mason) has a daughter and Hutch fantasizes that he and James can become de facto parents to the girl. Neither the girl's mother nor her aunt can or will function as viable parent. In Hutch's imagination, as The Source of Light concludes, a queer union can achieve the social ends of procreation—the nourishing and educating of children—even though the biological means are null.

Nothing comes of the imagined union with James Nichols. In The Promise of Rest Hutch tersely reveals that Nichols died. In Wade, though, the uncompleted negotiations of The Source of Light, settling as if in a diplomatic border dispute the claims of socially condoned heterosexuality and privately fuelled homosexuality, present themselves in the figure of Hutch's son and secret sharer. Wade's Christ credentials must not be overlooked in this respect; he is the living return of the tidings but thinly repressed when Hutch viewed the Risen Christ of Michelangelo. After Hutch's writing students depart and one, Mait, returns for more confessional talk, Wade appears. Emaciated, blind, he does not know that his diaper has slipped to the floor:

> For eyes trained like Hutch's and Maitland's, Wade seemed to be two things— a young man suffering intolerably, far past their reach, and also a likeness of hundreds of images in Western art. All of them were young men tortured toward death—the lynched dying Jesus, starved desert saints, impaled rebels in Goya's *Disasters:* all long past help and as pure as new light in their unearned agony. (*PR*, 106)

The mangled Christ in Rome and his pagan counterparts, the emasculated priests of Magna Mater, find their clear meaning in Wade. What has tortured Wade to death is his commitment to ecstasy rather than longevity. He has heeded Alice Matthews's advice to live in his desire, the "eye of this fearful storm" (187). Hutch must know this. With or without eyes trained in the intellectual discipline of identifying emblems and figures, he knows that Wade is the self he did not become when he married Ann and tried to digest the contraries of a public community with women and the private, undis- closed (perhaps undisclosable) ideal of homoerotic community.

One person knows this betrayal as well as Hutch, in the final novel of the tril- ogy at least, and that person is a black man, Wade's lover Wyatt Bondurant, a suicide before *The Promise of Rest* opens. " 'Wyatt told me,' " Wade informs his father, " 'the first night he met you, that you'd cut your heart off from the world the day you got married' " (*PR*, 114). Hutch at first understands this charge to mean that he, Hutch, is racist. This he denies. There seem to be sparse grounds in *The Promise of Rest* for taking either side of the question— pro or con: is Hutchins Mayfield a racist? The heart of the matter is sexuality, relations of desire, usage, and possession in a realm of physical bodies. The theme of racial relations in the small-town South, however, does have a lot to do in shaping the presentation of desire in the Mayfield trilogy. The resolu- tion to the problem of race is offered in one desirable human body—Raven Bondurant.

In a particularly acrimonious exchange with Ann, Hutch accuses his estranged wife (and all white women) of the residual hatred that has erupted in Wyatt's implacable loathing of white people, especially southern whites. " 'Everybody with eyes in the past three centuries knows that white women were the engines of slavery.' " Adequately primed, Hutch continues:

> "White men shanghaied slaves to America, bought and sold them, worked them to death in sugarcane fields or treated them like pet minstrel dolls you can slam up against the wall anytime you're tense or a little discouraged with your day; but unless the perpetual-virgin white wives and daughters had stood on the porch or at the field edge, broadcasting hate and fear and attraction, the worn-out men would have given up such a costly burden long years sooner— the whole monster business—and done their own work, just killing each other and occasional Indians." (*PR*, 173)

" 'That's appropriately weird,' " Ann replies.

"Weird" it might be, but not unheard of. A fellow North Carolinian of Hutch's, Wilbur J. Cash, gave the sex-race thesis credibility in *The Mind of the South* (1941). And yet another North Carolina writer, Thomas Dixon, made it the thematic keel of his turn-of-the-century reconstruction novels, an amalgam of which became D. W. Griffith's *Birth of a Nation* (1915). Ann hints that she knows more about her husband than she usually says in the novel: from her point of view, it would be "appropriate" to the laureate of the Mayfield men to accuse white women of all the racial misery in the South, and frigidity in the conjugal bed to boot. If Ann knows that Hutch, at this moment, is something of hysteric, she is not vouchsafed a retributive stroke at male ascendancy.

Purely from within the ample bounds of the trilogy, Hutch could absorb enough Mayfield and racial memory to substantiate, in his mind, the theory he espouses. Beginning with *The Surface of Earth*, black and white women have presented several generations of male Mayfields stark alternatives for their sexual lives. Old Robinson, born in 1839, took black women as his rightful fodder. Rover Walters, Grainger's father, is Old Rob's son by a female slave of his wife's family, Elvira. Like the slave woman ancestor Ike McCaslin discovers in Faulkner's *Go Down, Moses*, Elvira committed suicide and Old Rob, telling the tale to Forrest, seems hardly to register his complicity in her death (*SE*, 111–12). White men "niggering" on black women's bodies was, to Old Rob, a fact of white male hygiene as "natural" as trimming hangnails. Forrest seems to take his father's guilt to heart; his exchange of vows and ring with Grainger functions in the plot of *The Surface of Earth* as one of a few successful, durable, and all-male nuptial rituals (*SE*, 122) that offset failed heterosexual marriages (Bedford Kendal and Charlotte Watson [Eva's parents], Kennerly Kendal and his wife, Grainger and Gracie).

Charter to the bodies of black women continues in Forrest's son Rob, born in 1904. Rob's heterosexuality, and his innate yet "innocent" sense of racial superiority, are as comfortable to him as they are rasping to Hutch, his son. On the evening of his graduation from high school, his hoped-for severing of the moorings to family, Rob capers before Sylvie with the tail of his white shirt pulled through the fly of his pants. *He* thinks the prank is just a clever joke; *she* sees it as an unthinking reminder of the bondage she—sexually and racially—lives as her identity (*SE*, 127–28). Before dawn the next morning, the graduate, having failed to obtain Min Tharrington's body on terms satisfactory to him, crawls to Sylvie's house and finds comfort with Flora, another black woman who seems more equable than Sylvie about her status as natural body sans individuality (135).

Rob's heterosexual craving is one of the central motive forces in *The Surface of Earth*. He inherits it from his grandfather. At Goshen, unknowingly under the sharp night eyes of Rachel Hutchins, Rob fucks Della, stocking up on the "staples" while he keeps his daylight eyes on Rachel as a possible wife (*SE,* 179–80). To Grainger, he calls this sex "rubbing on black," reinforcing the unabashed impression that his sexual imperialism over black women is less than interpersonal meeting. He is even a little miffed at his wedding supper when Della expresses resentment for having to do so much hard work. "You're paid," he says; "Shit *on* you," Della responds (260). As far as Rob's outlook or insight can go, that is the ultimate stalemate in racial/sexual relations and shared identities. Twenty-five years seem not to make much difference. When Rob revisits Della in 1944, he leans on her for her body again and she consents. Sex with her is not like sex with a white woman but is more mythic—like being borne up on an oceanic tide (477–78).

Rob's physical and emotional relations with women, black and white, are inscribed within certain limits; even from the early stage of *The Surface of Earth* Price must have had something like the end of the trilogy in his mind's eye. Price undercuts Rob's vaunting with the text's narration. Writing to Hutch of his life's top moments, Rob remembers the unique vacation with Rena (the one during which she rubbed his whole body with witch hazel) when he was not much more than an adolescent. On this stolen holiday, Rena has brought along a novel called *My Poor Dick.* " 'It [the novel] was set in England,' " Rob recalls, " 'and it put me under—a hero named Dick that everybody loved' " (*SL,* 87).

Rob's relations with men, although never genital, are nevertheless superior to any he has with the (white) women in his life: Eva, Rachel, Min. Grainger expands his nuptial commitment to Forrest to include Forrest's son, even though Rob takes Grainger's loyalty for granted (*SE,* 122, 250). In a crucial passage, Grainger, feeling his racial identity stirring, renews his decision to sacrifice his life to the hierarchy controlled by the Mayfield men:

> And now at thirty-six, his older knowledge—what he'd heard from Miss Veenie, Mr. Forrest, Miss Hatt, his captain in France—began to seem in danger, not so much of being lies but of having been always a grinning cheat, the meanest joke. What had they ever told him but this?—*If you mind your step, stay clean and pretty, stay well and on-time, you can be our pet; we will see you through.* (*SE,* 313; italics in text)

Grainger is on the brink of rebelling, a kind of latter-day Nat Turner, when he is stalled by the conviction that no one (black) he knows has had a better life. The buildup of black male self-expression and determination, and rage against the "rubbing" of white on black, waits for Wyatt Bondurant in *The Promise of Rest.*

Price does not, however, leave Grainger in a cul-de-sac. His blood kinship with the Mayfields, by virtue of his being Old Rob's grandson, is metamorphosed into communal male friendship at the end of *The Surface of Earth.* The key image is the wedding ring that comes down, along with the bark man with his heavy phallus, from Old Rob. Forrest had "wed" the boy Grainger by bestowing the ring. Then Grainger and Gracie, for a time, had sealed their vows with it. The ring circles further to bind Grainger, Rob, and Hutch into a three-way, intergenerational, interracial, same-sex "marriage" at the climax of *The Surface of Earth*. This complex episode is a powerful engine that runs the two novels that follow.

Toward the close of the novel, during Rob and Hutch's excursion to Virginia Beach, father and son tread difficult, separate paths through performances of sexual identity. The live peep show that follows the film *Young Mr. Pitt* and, more significant, the lovemaking Hutch watches on the beach earlier fail to ignite in Hutch either the shame or the desire Rob, presumably, expects. The naked girl onstage only leaves Hutch with questions; the biggest one is the meaning of heterosexual curiosity and desire:

> To the loudest music yet, she spread her arms straight like wings and faced them quickly. At the fork of her clamped legs, the short fold of flesh—as hairless as her mouth—was lined with bright stones that glistened three seconds. Then every light blackened.
>
> Rob clapped with the others. (*SE*, 387)

Explaining this "initiation" moment to Hutch later that evening, Rob assures his son that the meaning and impact of what he has seen will dawn upon him in time. Hutch will, presumably, focus on the woman's body, will become, as Wade lectures Mait in *The Promise of Rest*, "hipped . . . on cunt" (*PR*, 182). A strong thematic hawser running from the end of the first volume of the trilogy to its elegiac conclusion is Hutch's working through competing imperatives of cunt and cock. He confronts each choice not as simple lust but always as desire that achieves, at its end, a type of Augustinian "rest" in wholeness reclaimed.

The nuptial ritual that concludes *The Surface of Earth* sums up these concerns in that novel and propels them into the two following works. Returning like a flock of homing pigeons to the Hutchins place in Goshen, Rob, Grainger, and Hutch solemnize their extraordinary male community. The master's bed is the only place to sleep. Hutch triggers the nuptial scene by inviting his father to sleep in the bed with him. Rob's mainly failed life spools across his memory as he tries but fails to sleep, but he "spoons" closer into the sleeping body of his son. When all of the events of his recorded life prove dead-ends, Rob kisses his sleeping son's shoulder and promises again to be faithful to what is left of Mayfield flesh. The novelist has a crucial say here, for Price times this consummation to occur on the 41st anniversary of Rob's own conception by Forrest's seed in Eva's womb. The vows are confirmed in the morning by Grainger, who slides the Mayfield ring onto Hutch's finger (*SE*, 489–91). What is certified here is not only the transgenerational claim of the Mayfield saga. By virtue of the fact that Grainger bestows the ring, misce-

genation is shorn of its taboo and admitted to the sanctuary of Mayfield identity. Mixed-race identity is, moreover, coupled with same-sex identity, for
Hutch's rite of passage at the conclusion of *The Surface of Earth* sets him into
deep but not frictionless grooves of same-sex desire.

The Source of Light, as I have tried to argue, follows Hutch's uneasy and
eventually inconclusive negotiations of the diverging paths of desire for bodies of both sexes and of a successful answer to the imperative of offspring.
Many of the characters in the intermediate novel of the trilogy comment,
mostly caustically, on the racial politics of the American South in the 1950s,
but their commentary fails to mix with the fictional medium as subtly as the
subtext of desire does. It remains mostly editorial. An exception occurs in the
first subdivision of the novel, when Rob and Grainger are hunting for Hatt
Shorter's place, one stop on Rob's farewell tour. Grainger crosses the fairly
obvious lines legislating what a black man can say to a white (boy or man)
and still escape lynching. Rob cautions him, but Grainger refuses to express
contrition (*SL,* 66).

Grainger survives into *The Promise of Rest,* but he passes on his function
as monitor of the racial-sexual relations localized in the Mayfield clan. At 101
years of age, Grainger is more icon than viable character. To his students,
Hutch acknowledges him as a cousin; late in the novel, after Wade's death,
Grainger reminds Hutch that he is "kin people" (*PR,* 9, 290). For most of the
novel, though, Wyatt Bondurant, kin to the Bankey Patterson whom Forrest
meets in *The Surface of Earth* (*SE,* 69ff; *PR,*124) functions as the torrid angel
of racial/sexual retribution in the Mayfield narrative and as the strand of narrative continuity.

Wyatt as figure rather than character fuses Eros and race in the final
novel of the trilogy. He is dead before the action begins, but his literal ghost
stalks the plot. Wyatt is not simply "race." To Ivory, Wyatt's sister, Hutch
confesses the obvious: " 'all three of us [Hutch, Wade, Wyatt] badly lost our
heads on the subject of race and sex and all else' " (*PR,* 65). The sharp wedge
Wyatt thrusts between Wade and his father is not only that Wyatt is
quadroon and the Mayfields are white (and have, in the not-too-distant past,
engendered mixed-race persons) but also that Hutch had betrayed his sexuality in marrying a woman (*PR,* 114). When, therefore, *The Promise of Rest*
strives to close the thematic circle of sexuality, it also addresses race.

Price puts both large subjects directly before the reader. As professor,
Hutch teaches his literature class that race is the immense but scarcely
uttered verb in American literature, and that its intersection with sexual
desire (miscegenation) has been taken up by no American writer since the
death of William Faulkner. Understandably, Hutch's literary opinions
rebound instantaneously upon *The Promise of Rest,* coaxing readers to follow
the trail of miscegenation toward meaning: saving grace or damnation. Ann,
deviled by Calvinist fixations of right and wrong, is prepared to accept

Wyatt's blanket indictment, but Hutch resists, convinced that as Wade nears death he too relinquishes Wyatt's fierce hatred of whites (*PR,* 120). Hutch's way has always been to accept Grainger as his kin and to alleviate the damage of racism by consistent, "trim," and "decorous" acts of acceptance and courtesy (159). At times his solid ground seems to slip, as when in conversation with Grainger on the occasion of Wade's final visit to the Kendal place Hutch suddenly understands Grainger's life from the racial other's point of view:

> Grainger's eyes were crouched and gleaming with the helpless need to do a duty he'd felt all his life to a few white men that were his blood kin, though they'd let him live like a whole different creature in a parallel world that ran— when it moved at all—beneath their feet, never higher than their knees: a world that was generally either ice-cold or blistering hot, furnished with big-eyed hungry children and men and women as old as Grainger, harder than ironwood and wild in their minds. (133–34)

At other times, as in the meetings with the angelic Jimmy Boat, both Hutch and Straw seem flawlessly in tune with the black man and a detoxed system of racist communication (69). Not surprisingly, the women do not share facility in communication. When Ann arrives at Hutch's house on a visit to Wade, Jimmy Boat immediately recognizes not just a rival for service to Wade but an enemy; he goes "a little cold" and drops below radar level into a scullery role (258).

If there is redemption for an American South implicated in racial guilt in the trilogy, it comes in the physical body of Raven Bondurant. The child represents the Mayfield diaspora reattached to the main, male trunk. Raven bears Hutch's christened name (Hutch was born Raven Hutchins Mayfield) and a family racial heritage that genetically acknowledges the earlier generations of Old Rob and Forrest. The child is also suprahistorical. His face, as striking as a "bronze head from Benin or Delphi" (*PR,* 307), fuses the ideals of the Western tradition (valorized in imagery consistently throughout the trilogy but especially in *The Source of Light*) with a late recognition of something like Afrocentrism. He is an object to be honored and loved, to be passionately desired, to be "wed." After the somber scattering of the fistsful of Wade's ashes, Hutch rescues the Mayfield ring (again a gift from Grainger) and slips it onto the thumb of his grandson. The ceremony proclaims, as its precursor in *The Surface of Earth* did, and as the miscarryings of the ring in *The Source of Light* did not, the reconciliation of race and sex, the powerfully redemptive character of the male friendship community, the retrieval of "stunning" beauty from random acts of lust.

As epigraph to the first novel in the trilogy, Price chose a few lines from Augustine of Hippo's *Confessions.* Augustine's lifelong torment, the grain of sand that irritated his life into saintliness and honor, was an irreconcilable struggle between his desire for rest in the omnipotent peace and truth of God and the restless, unquenchable desires of his flesh. Peter Brown, whose writings on Augustine and the late classical and early Christian era are rightly honored, puts the Augustinian agony into sharp focus for readers of Price's trilogy:

> Such a way of seeing things placed a far greater weight than hitherto on sexuality. In the ascetic literature that we have met so far, the heats of young love and the cares of the married household, the itch of sexual temptation and the dull ache of the belly tended to mingle indiscriminately. They all formed part and parcel of the great aboriginal catastrophe of physical existence. If anything, physical greed—the most sinister inversion of all of Adam's primal hunger for the Wisdom of God, and the most blatant curse of human suffering in a famine-ridden society—stood out in slightly higher relief, above the generalized blur of sensuality and aching care associated with man's loss of the angelic state.[18]

A version of the Augustinian vision arcs through *The Great Circle*. From Old Rob's phallic talisman we are reminded of human life's origin in the ache of the belly and the itch of sex, the physical greed that builds up both guilt and capital in the possession of others' bodies. But life in the body, "the great aboriginal catastrophe of physical existence," is not abandoned to Augustine's Manichean splitting. As early as the sketching trip with Alice Matthews in *The Surface of Earth,* Hutch had seen "primal hunger" as primal joy: there is no life but in the body, no desire except the desire to touch, no relief to famine except in devouring the physical world. It is therefore not improbable that, at the moment of his death, Wade should meet (not God himself or a deputized disembodied angel) but his own grandfather Rob in a glorified body, poised to embrace his grandson in a fusing of divided sexual personae. If there is, as Hutch believes, a giant asleep in a cave who is dreaming human life, then that giant is dreaming bodies: hungers, thirsts, sucklings, couplings, immersions, socketings, kisses, all the ways that bodies can touch. The fed in the trilogy know this; the hungry don't.

Over two decades and more than one thousand pages of prose fiction, Price sustains a human universe comparable to the one dreamed by his imagined giant. Trilogies produced by American novelists in this century can scarcely match *A Great Circle*'s sweep and finesse. After *The Hamlet,* Faulkner was hard pressed to finish *The Town* and *The Mansion;* most of his readers and critics think he rather misspent his creative time on the latter two novels. Dreiser's "Trilogy of Desire" does have weight but poetic inertia to match. Price's achievement with the Mayfield trilogy is to adapt the finesse exemplified in Hemingway and make it bear the weight of nearly a century's complement of character, theme, and circumstance.

Notes

1. Reynolds Price, "For Ernest Hemingway," in *Things Themselves: Essays and Scenes* (New York: Atheneum, 1972), 179. Parentheses in original. This essay is reprinted in Price's *A Common Room: Essays 1954–1987* (New York: Atheneum, 1987), 136–59.

2. Price, "Hemingway," 183.

3. Ibid., 188.

4. Augustine of Hippo, *Confessions,* trans. R. S. Pine-Coffin (Harmondsworth, England: Penguin, 1961), 43.

5. Augustine, 45.

6. Augustine, 176–78.

7. Reynolds Price, *The Promise of Rest* (New York: Scribner, 1995), 182. Subsequent references are cited in the text as *PR.*

8. Reynolds Price, *The Source of Light* (New York: Atheneum, 1981), 35–36. Subsequent references are cited in the text as *SL.*

9. K. J. Dover, *Greek Homosexuality* (London: Duckworth, 1978) [1].

10. Peter Brown, *The Body and Society: Men, Women, and Sexual Renunciation in Early Christianity* (New York: Columbia University Press, 1988), 9–10.

11. Reynolds Price, *The Surface of Earth* (New York: Atheneum, 1975), 21. Subsequent references are cited in the text as *SE.*

12. David M. Halperin, *One Hundred Years of Homosexuality and Other Essays on Greek Love* (New York: Routledge, 1990), 25.

13. Price, "Hemingway," 184, 179.

14. Halperin, 77.

15. Ibid., 78.

16. Kenneth Clark, *The Nude: A Study in Ideal Form* (1956; rpt. Princeton: Princeton University Press, 1972), 307.

17. Plato, *Symposium,* trans. W. H. D. Rouse (New York: New American Library, 1956), 85–89. For other translations: see Aristophanes's tale, 187C–194B.

18. Brown, 406.

From the Virgin Mary to Rosacoke

DORIS BETTS

One night in the mid-seventies I was asked to emcee a panel featuring Alice Walker and Reynolds Price at the high school auditorium in Sanford, North Carolina, on the subject of the southern family. Walker had already been in town for several days on one of those grants intended to bring artists and humanists down to the grass roots; Price would drive the 40-odd miles from Duke; onstage would be several historians from nearby predominantly black colleges; and my job was to preside and then field questions from the audience.

The occasion seemed auspicious. I'd served on the local school board during recent tense years when Sanford-Lee County schools had merged and integrated; the community was calmer now. Ms. Walker had spoken earlier at UNC–Chapel Hill, to which I commuted to teach, and had been a lively speaker, generous with students. Sanford was the town where I'd first met Price 20 years before; he used to do readings from his work, with much grace, for a local ladies' afternoon book club whose gray-haired officers had ties to his own women kin in Warren County. (I always said we were first introduced in a gathering where he and I were the only ones who still had our own teeth.)

Now this evening promised to bring together two writers who would be genial and articulate; the topic of "southern family" promised to cross racial lines onto common ground. I foresaw synthesis.

So I boned up slightly on Price's Mustians, Walker's Copelands; I could fall back on quilt making (*In Love and Trouble*) and maybe Mrs. Hill in *Meridian* (or maybe not), and also, Price's first novel on the Mayfield and Kendal families had recently appeared and bore some likenesses to what I knew of Price's own family history.

That evening I arrived early to check the mike and water pitchers, but Walker was already there, pacing, and asked rather urgently where the women's toilet was. We found it. But her real urgency lay in the question she wanted to ask in its privacy: "Is Reynolds Price a racist?"

"Reynolds? Oh. Mercy. No, I don't think so. Reynolds?"

"You've read his new book, *The Surface of Earth?*"

This essay was written specifically for this volume and is published here for the first time by permission of the author.

I dimly heard her question over the flapping wings as Synthesis tried to fly out the window.

To my nod she said, "And you noticed in that novel how every black person *smells?*"

I hadn't. Did they? Really? Grainger? Sylvie? Della? And did my blank mind mean I was a worse racist myself?

In the hot summertime around here we *all* smell, I thought but decided not to say; and I also decided not to bring up who used to have hot and cold running water vs. who did not. Walker's own family had lacked the indoor plumbing her neighbor Flannery O'Connor took for granted.

Instead I did talk a little about what I knew of Reynolds Price, whose good manners alone would have prevented overt racism, who had also never to me betrayed covert racism. He often wrote about a time and place where attitudes toward race were stylized and circumscribed, but to insert Black Panther rhetoric back into pretelevision Macon, North Carolina, would have been a literal and aesthetic falsehood. She heard me in silence.

All too quickly it became time to move into the auditorium. From the stage I saw only a scattering of women from that afternoon literary club. Instead, as I looked over a largely African-American audience, all of whom already loved Alice Walker after her three friendly days visiting their churches and socials, I foresaw the awful moment when pale and dark armpits might become everybody's subject of discussion.

Walker and Price shook hands. I shook inwardly.

Yet from the first, both speakers, their interaction, the historians' questions, all flowed smoothly. Here were two professionals, professional speakers as well as writers, and they both spoke well on the assigned subject. I braced myself for Ms. Walker to bring up body odor; she did not. Only once did I even wince when one scholar made clear that she had read none of Price's work but went on to quiz him sharply about race in his fiction anyway.

His answers were not at all defensive—they were patient, good humored, well chosen. But what leapt out at me was a subordinate clause, his taken-for-granted aside: "since I'm a Christian . . ."

His casual words were as much a jolt to me as any charge about separate but unequal odors would have been, since during that decade I was in my Ms. Alberta Camus phase, an upscale Stoic.

So that night there was no confrontation except inside myself, nor did I have then these later words to offer Alice Walker, which open Price's chapter "Black Help" in *Clear Pictures* (1989).

From near the first, I remember thinking that their skin was beautiful, especially the smooth two-toned hands. I remember their clean but different odor, as if they were made of a powerful metal—something finer-grained than our fragile skin. I remember their gentle voices and the rub of their stiff starched clothes.[1]

Nor could I quote then from another chapter, "Credible Light," in which Christianity and civil rights do fuse, and Price's social and personal ethic expands from that almost parenthetical statement that evening, "since I'm a Christian."

In *Clear Pictures* he singles out among his "guides" in life the black household servants Flora Rushing and Grant Terry and calls segregation a "brute and tragic machine."[2] He even accuses himself and his household for their complicity in the southern status quo; in *The Promise of Rest* he further writes of a militant black activist hostile to the remnants of that Jim Crow society. Price is harsher in his judgment of Price than Alice Walker would have been.

In the years since that panel, Price's subordinate clause about religion has enlarged via many compound and complex sentences in his own writing and experience; and I—undernourished by French existentialism—have returned to the Presbyterians. For Price, an increasing emphasis on what the New Testament says, the language—both Greek and English—in which it gets said, and why the good news matters, have figured not only in his fiction and poetry but especially in his translations and essays (*A Palpable God, Three Gospels*) and his memoirs. Religious themes coalesced in his own mystical vision captured in the poem "Vision" and more fully in *A Whole New Life,* his account of surviving the spinal cancer that struck at age 51 and left him paraplegic.

Price, as well as some of his characters, such as Kate Vaiden, resemble his parents, who were "religious but not churchly."[3] The maternal half of my own parents was *very* churchly—yet we both (like many southern children in the thirties) were given as preschoolers Hurlbut's *Story of the Bible,* our imaginations marked thereafter by what Price calls its "surprisingly unlaundered" content.[4]

In a 1996 collection of essays by 27 North Carolina writers on books that affected their lives,[5] I chose to remember Hurlbut, but after Price listed childhood favorites (*Little People Who Became Great, King Arthur, Wigwam and Warpath, Treasure Island*) he instead wrote vividly of his discovery, at age 15, of *Madame Bovary.* As he rushed through its final 50 pages in a "powerless, unbroken trance," he glimpsed "the fiery lure of the work I knew I'd follow for the rest of my life."[6] Yet even that term, "the fiery lure," seems to arrive on first bounce off those pillars of cloud and fire via Hurlbut that we and the Israelites pursued through the Book of Exodus.

Price has traced connections between the influence of Bible stories on his own early writing and indeed on all Western storytelling in his essay "The Origins and Life of Narrative," which opens *A Palpable God* (1978). And here begin most clearly the examples of how Price's mode of thought brings together the way most oral family stories bear a heavy significance for those who hear and inherit them, with a similar aggrandizement of, for instance, shepherd boys to kings, ordinary people lifted to myth. Price writes that the first—and final—aim of narrative is "compulsion of belief in an ordered world"[7] and believes Adam invented narrative in Genesis.

Northrop Frye in *The Great Code* notes that "Bible stories were charged with a special seriousness and importance" and that typology assumes "there is some meaning and point to history."[8] Typological thinking that causes St. Paul to quote Habakuk also functions in oral family narrative. As soon as Uncle Joe sets out to assemble a full family tree, holiday anecdotes turn into saga; traits get inherited; the dead find ways to get part of themselves repeated.

Price is a typological (but not allegorical) thinker and writer, so much so that some contemporary critics have found him outdated, and others have found him just puzzling. Typology has a vision of history in which individual lives and family patterns take on larger purpose and meaning, though dimly perceived; there is also a faith that eventually this meaning will be made clear. In *The Source of Light* Rob writes in a letter to Hutch, "[We] would be grateful if anyone looked back on us (not down) and saw that we'd made anything like a diagram in these fifty years. . . . that's the hope, Son—that we make some figure. If we do you'd be the one to know (though it may take awhile to know you know)."[9]

Not only is such typological thinking scattered through his fiction but it occurs in the way Price "looks back" on the "diagram" of his own and his family's life. Here, too, Price exhibits the same forward-moving typological thinking Christians bring to the two large divisions of their Bible. Just as believers look back to the Old Testament for inadvertent (though divinely planted) clues to the New (Luke 24:44), Price reexamines his family photo album and finds their futures implicit in those unaware faces of his kin, already prophesied, already moving toward fulfillment of pattern.

In *Clear Pictures* even his captions under family snapshots carry this element of foreshadowing. Under one of his father, Will, at 18, Price writes: "He thinks he will soon be shipped away to the trenches of France and cannot know that the armistice of November 11th will save him. Unclouded yet by drink or care, his gray eyes burn with the hopeful fervor he'll fight to reclaim, fifteen years from now."[10]

The habit of reading-in meaning by hindsight, as when in 1Peter a link is drawn between being baptized in Christ and being saved like Noah after the flood, occurs in secular thought as well. Paul Harvey's radio broadcasts, "The Rest of the Story," trade on typology; those children's stories of boys with unsuspected gifts who later grew up to be Beethoven and Lincoln (early favorites of Price), Marxism, evolution, millennialist cults, psychics with selective memory, are always finding past clues that explain how life is now or will be. The logic here is one of pattern, gestalt, some template larger than cause and effect that may even stand outside time.

Unlike Christianity, the typology of the Messiah is—in Judaism—still awaiting fulfillment. But many of Hurlbut's Old Testament stories end by emphasizing typology. In the account of the near-sacrifice of Isaac by Abraham, a story that has long fascinated Price, Hurlbut writes: "And it looked onward to a time when, just as Abraham gave his son as an offering, God should give his Son Jesus Christ to die for the sins of the world. All this was taught in this act of worship on Mount Moriah."[11]

For centuries after the printing press brought Bibles into every home and also used them as the repository of family births, deaths, marriages, and anti-alcohol pledges, this Christian habit of seeing tomorrow's tree already implicit in today's seed was standard in the Western world. Christ as the Passover sacrifice and the Eucharist were said to be prefigured in the Paschal Lamb of the Exodus. Naturally what Jesus cried out on the cross was the first verse of Psalm 22, and so on.

Likewise, what was said and done on the day a child was born would be later repeated and made fraught with implication. Price, for example, has often written of his own difficult breech birth and how his father made a vow to quit drinking if mother and child would live. Will Price "sealed a bargain with God, as stark and unbreakable as any blood pact in Genesis," writes Price.[12] From 1936 on, this vow was kept, and of course this family story was told Price over and over and gave to his infant survival an overarching meaning that transformed him into a hostage or emblem to surrounding adults whose lives he had changed. Price explores this vow in his story "The Names and Faces of Heroes" and in his poem "A Tomb for Will Price."

Nor do I find it a bit unusual that he grew up among people who would bargain with Heaven for his life and then expect him to feel divinely spared. Though I was born a year earlier than Price, at age 11 my own mother, herself born with a cleft palate and always shy about the nasal speech it produced, made God a vow that if she ever had a child whose speech was normal she would, like Hannah, dedicate that child to God's service. Alas, she got me; but her promise bears down on me still. There must be thousands of us—especially in the South—who carry lifelong the weight of predictions, deathbed sayings, vows and bargains, significant birthmarks and scars, planting by moonsigns, strange coincidences, and family curses—with the Bible much more the underlying cause of regional attitudes than the Civil War.

Aside, but in fairness, too, that imposition of meaning on what may only be coincidence—more like Jung's synchronicity than Freud's theories—may also ascribe AIDS to God's wrath, a view Price never even considers in *The Promise of Rest*. A straining for typology—while thinning the veil between natural and supernatural—can also degenerate into its superstitious cousins, from astrology to Ouija boards. (In his fiction, Price sometimes introduces ghosts or angels and has never chosen to explain them away.) But Price is too intellectual to descend to the level of crystal balls and Barbie-doll guardian angels, as the tabloids do. He simply remains alert, in autobiography as well as in his fiction, to that "intricate figure woven at the heart of my life, and the world's, by what I've called the *unseen power.*"[13]

He grew up in Macon, a North Carolina village of 200 people on the Seaboard rail line, a town in "the shape of a Jerusalem cross."[14] From those years he recalls memories as if they were revelations. Scenes in his ostensibly realistic fiction have a similar effect; few readers forget the sight of Rosacoke Mustian portraying Mary in the Christmas pageant, or Wesley up a tree like Zacchaeus, in *A Long and Happy Life*. As a Rhodes scholar at Oxford his thesis was on Milton (*Samson Agonistes*), who certainly saw human life *sub specie aeternitatis*. Price still regularly teaches Milton at Duke. His books bear epigraphs from Dante, St. Augustine, Scripture itself; one of my students meant it as no compliment when she said, "Mr. Price takes himself so seriously!" Like Rosacoke Mustian, Price is always reading his own life for signs, discovering later in his early 1984 poems portents of the spinal cancer he did not then know was already twining like a serpent up his backbone; and of course he takes note that when he went to the hospital for surgery on 31 May 1984, there was a total eclipse of the sun. Looking very far back, Price even thinks that his illnesses as a baby were the "first signs of the often congenital type of spinal tumor" that smoldered for half a century before it began to consume him.[15] In interviews he has spoken of a number of mystical events, though none is as vivid as his encounter with Jesus while suffering with unremitting pain from that cancer. In his life as well as in his novels, stories, and poems, events for Price push against that natural/supernatural veil and occasionally break through, so families seem fated, their interactions epic in size, their short earthly stories growing into trilogies. Even a memoir subtitle ("First Loves, First Guides") suggests Virgil and Dante.

Unlike his aside to Alice Walker—casual to her, startling to me—Price's Christian beliefs have become steadily clearer to his readers and perhaps to him as well. In *A Palpable God* Price offered as his credential "twenty-one years of work as a narrator of human encounters with the sacred," but even that long ago his Yaweh prefigures the benevolent Abba of Jesus rather than the stern judge; Price chose for 26 of his 30 Bible translations those that would "affirm the active presence of divine care and vindication in the lives of God's loyal servants."[16] In this book, too, he makes his first translation of Mark from the Koine Greek, a preparation for *Three Gospels* in 1996. In *Things Themselves* (1972) he writes about Rembrandt's four treatments of the near-sacrifice of Isaac by Abraham, a story that seems associated with the way God spared Price's infant self in childbirth, and Price's version sent many of us back to read Kierkegaard. That story and Jephthah's daughter affect *The Surface of Earth*. His essay "At the Heart" made clear his belief in what he called "bedrock along the seismic narrative line of the Apostles' Creed."[17] In this essay, too, he sees the history of our universe as an infinite story God tells himself and, in part but with mystery, tells humans as well.

Price's general theology seems to have escaped Calvinist sin and determinism, not only because his parents were not very "churchly" but perhaps because in his teens, when he moved from his "trees-and-rocks mysticism into my years of church religion,"[18] he began attending Edenton St. Methodist Church in Raleigh instead of some rural fundamentalist church where he might have soaked up hellfire sermons. I did not escape quite so well, and write more often than he of violence, cruelty, willful evil; but Price's characters—at worst—are no more than misguided, blind, weak, prone to error. In his recent *Three Gospels,* in which he revised the earlier translation he made of Mark, he even changes the word *sin* to *wrong* or *error,* noting that *hamartia* means no worse than "a failure of aim, a missing of the mark."[19] If he views himself and family in typological terms, it is with a far gentler predestination than John Calvin had in mind.

Even his criticisms of others do not become attacks. In *A Whole New Life,* though he was critical of the cool distance shown him by certain medical personnel, these people remain anonymous; Price names only the people he can praise. Unlike me, he seems to have eluded the temptation toward malice and harsh judgments and to have understood the heart of the verse Tolstoy loved, "Judge not, that ye be not judged."

In this regard he differs from another southern Christian writer, Flannery O'Connor, whose characters gain their enlightenments on the horns of bulls, at the point of a convict's gun; or from the one who shares his fascination with Kierkegaard, Walker Percy, who still found a lot to judge harshly in satirizing American life and angst. Eudora Welty, who discovered him young and whom Price much admires, has also avoided the tag of southern gothic, perhaps less from Christian principles than from the Aristotelian precept of keeping most violence offstage; and Price's former student Anne Tyler (another Welty fan) reviews only books she's sure to like and exhibits so much avoidance of villainy in her novels, with such a hopeful view of human nature, that the *New York Times Book Review* called her vision "Quakerish."[20] (It is.) Welty and Tyler were two on Price's list of six modern writers he admired.[21]

But readers with a preference for strong action, quarrels that produce murders depicted with maximum gore, interior monologues of psychopaths, detailed sex, and so on may find the absence of wickedness and violence in Price's novels to be a flaw. Some students of mine, indoctrinated by instant conflict and nearly instant copulation in a thousand television programs, will predictably throw up their hands when Price's characters keep sitting one another down to relate yet one more long family recollection, write one more rather literary letter, dream the same dream a previous character has already told, stare off into space and reflect on themselves as if each one were a Hamlet or a Karamazov. Women students, too, may read the author's repressed male hostility into so many deaths of Price's women in childbed. Having grown up in widely scattered families, many of today's students do not find plausible those southern families in which the third-generation father repeats the same mistakes as fathers in the first and second. Such students want less pattern, typological or not, and more exciting events.

One might as well complain of Hemingway's lack of lush descriptive passages, or Hardy's failure to use more jokes. Critics as well as students often complain (though in loftier language) simply because writer A is not writer B, whom they prefer; in fact, Richard Gilman's review of *The Surface of Earth* essentially complained that Price was not John Barth nor Donald Barthelme.[22] Even when Price does use what is presumably a violent act in his fiction (the rape of Rosa, for example, in *Good Hearts*), it does not resemble the cruel rapes made prurient in technicolor at the local cineplex. This one, in the long run, leads to improvement in Rosa's life.

The fact is that Price is typological even in his apparent philosophy, alert to the hope that good will be brought out of evil. He sees the Old Testament not only fulfilled in but even repaired by the New; and he is never going to make modern characters as evil as King Ahab, Queen Jezebel, Absalom, or even Judas. To Price, their bad news has already been redeemed by the Good News.

It seems consistent, then, that after a cancer that nearly killed him and did, indeed, kill one life and replace it with a second and different one, Price should translate no more Old Testament stories, often themselves judgmental, but move to the larger, more redemptive one that they prefigured. In the preface to *Three Gospels* he acknowledges what his other work has more and more affirmed, that the message of the New Testament Gospels is *"Your life is willed and watched by a god who once lived here."*[23] He makes some revisions of his 1978 translation of Mark (the earliest) and starts from scratch translating John (the strangest), then he adds his own apocryphal "honest account of a memorable life," making use of all known sources. This third gospel is Price's fulfillment of an assignment he gave Duke undergraduates in a New Testament seminar.

Price is aware of Northrop Frye's warning that translations more easily get the sense but miss the rhymes, puns, and assonances between words of similar reference—such as *God* and *Good* in English.[24] In Matthew 16:18, for example, in the verse that still divides Catholic from Protestant ("thou art Peter and upon this rock *petra*"), the Greek pun also works in the Aramaic Jesus would have spoken. But Price has given such succinct and modest notes about his choices and their reasons that they should satisfy most lay readers, except for that woman who once said flatly with a sharp snap of her head, "If the King James was good enough for Jesus, it's good enough for me."

Reviews of *Three Gospels* have been highly favorable, Larry Woiwode pointing out that one "great beauty" of the book is its ability to view the Gospel narratives as stories encountered for the first time.[25] Price here reiterates in introductory notes what all his work has been saying, that he shares with the Gospel writers a wish to "transform speech and act into story with the purpose of discovering both the path of a life and that life's meaning."[26]

If these translations echo Price's general beliefs, they also help explain some changes in his prose style in the prolific work he has done since his cancer.

James Schiff has noted that 18 years ago Price called his style "paradoxically baroque plain."[27] The prose has grown less baroque in the memoirs, perhaps affected by Price's steady contact with what he calls Mark's "rude but functional language and structure," his "blunt air of no-nonsense reportage, his bat-out-of-hell commitment to vivid action over slowed-down speech"; and also by Price's immersion in the urgent but condensed message of John the eyewitness, whose few thousand words can be read through in an hour.[28] *The Promise of Rest,* though not especially short, is—being contemporary—written in plainer prose, and this novel also deals with subjects of concern to my college students: sex, both hetero- and homosexual; race; the scourge of AIDS. It is instructive to think of Price's early and late work in the light of Eric Auerbach's well-known chapter "Odysseus' Scar," contrasting the Homeric and Biblical prose styles.[29]

Nowhere is Price's pared down but still poetic style more noticeable than in the third of the gospels—the one he wrote himself, "An Honest Account of a Memorable Life." He adheres to Mark's chronology, shuffles some other sources, even invents a few speeches (but none is attributed to Jesus himself). All these minor changes he makes for the same reason he believes the Gospel writers varied their own accounts, "with the purpose of discovering both the path of a life and that life's meaning."[30]

Part of that life's meaning reverberates at the end of Price's apocryphal gospel, in which he notes how the apostles have never lost hope that they would see Jesus come again on clouds to claim them. Price writes:

> One of their cries in their own language was *"Maranatha"*—"Lord, come now!" They thought he had promised that.
> In other lives their cry has lasted near two thousand years.[31]

But to read Price's personal gospel after having just read through much of his previous work is to pause longest over the words with which he begins it. Here is his first sentence: "It began with a girl who was loved by God."[32]

She could have been Rosacoke, such readers will think. The Father-God Price believes in so loves this ordinary world that He functions in minor villages like Nazareth and Bethlehem, even Macon, North Carolina, in the lives of carpenters and fishermen or a salesman of electric appliances, like Will Price. Price believes that kind of covenant-God was willing to strike a local bargain on 1 February 1933, the night his father sealed a vow and he was finally born.

As in the parable of the talents, there's been quite a payback on that original investment.

Notes

1. Reynolds Price, *Clear Pictures* (New York: Atheneum, 1989), 83.
2. Price, *Clear Pictures,* 77.

3. Reynolds Price, *A Palpable God* (New York: Atheneum, 1978), 11.

4. Price, *A Palpable God,* 11.

5. David Perkins, ed., *Books of Passage* (Asheboro, N.C.: Down Home Press, 1996).

6. Reynolds Price, "Gustave Flaubert's *Madame Bovary,*" in *Books of Passage,* Perkins, ed., 157.

7. Price, *A Palpable God,* 34.

8. Northrop Frye, *The Great Code* (New York: Harcourt Brace Jovanovich, 1982, 1983), 33.

9. Reynolds Price, *The Source of Light* (New York: Atheneum, 1981), 56.

10. Price, *Clear Pictures,* 22.

11. Jesse Lyman Hurlbut, *Hurlbut's Story of the Bible for Young and Old* (Grand Rapids: Zondervan, 1904, 1982), 71.

12. Price, *Clear Pictures,* 29.

13. Ibid., 14.

14. Ibid., 18.

15. Ibid., 33.

16. Price, *A Palpable God,* 49, 22.

17. Reynolds Price, "At the Heart," in *A Common Room, Essays 1954–1987* (New York: Atheneum, 1987), 402.

18. Price, *Clear Pictures,* 255.

19. Reynolds Price, *Three Gospels* (New York: Scribner, 1996), 18.

20. Edward Hoagland, "About Maggie, Who Tried Too Hard," review of *Breathing Lessons,* by Anne Tyler, *New York Times Book Review* (11 September 1988): 44.

21. Ashby Bland Crowder, "Reynolds Price on Writing," in *Conversations with Reynolds Price,* ed. Jefferson Humphries (Jackson: University of Mississippi Press, 1991), 198.

22. Richard Gilman, "A Mastodon of a Novel, by Reynolds Price," review of *The Surface of Earth,* by Reynolds Price, *New York Times Book Review* (29 June 1975): 1–2.

23. Price, *Three Gospels,* 13.

24. Frye, 4.

25. Larry Woiwode, "And the Word Was Made Flesh," review of *Three Gospels,* by Reynolds Price, *Washington Post Book World* (5 May 1996): 5.

26. Price, *Three Gospels,* 239.

27. James Schiff quoting Price, *Understanding Reynolds Price* (Columbia: University of South Carolina Press, 1996), 76.

28. Price, *Three Gospels,* 25.

29. Eric Auerbach, *Mimesis* (Princeton: Princeton University Press, 1968), 3–23.

30. Price, *Three Gospels,* 239.

31. Ibid., 287.

32. Ibid., 243.

Index

The Volume Editor

◆

James Schiff is the author of several books, including *Understanding Reynolds Price, Updike's Version: Rewriting "The Scarlet Letter,"* and the forthcoming *John Updike*. His essays on contemporary American literature have appeared in *Southern Review, American Literature, Studies in American Fiction, South Atlantic Review,* and *Critique*. With degrees from Duke University and New York University, he currently teaches at the University of Cincinnati.

The General Editor

◆

Dr. James Nagel, J. O. Eidson Distinguished Professor of American Literature at the University of Georgia, founded the scholarly journal *Studies in American Fiction* and edited it for 20 years. He is the general editor of the Critical Essays on American Literature series published by Macmillan, a program that now contains over 130 volumes. He was one of the founders of the American Literature Association and serves as its Executive Coordinator. He is also a past president of the Ernest Hemingway Society. Among his 17 books are *Stephen Crane and Literary Impressionism, Critical Essays on* The Sun Also Rises, *Ernest Hemingway: The Writer in Context, Ernest Hemingway: The Oak Park Legacy,* and *Hemingway in Love and War,* which was selected by the *New York Times* as one of the outstanding books of 1989 and which has been made into a major motion picture. Dr. Nagel has published over 50 articles in scholarly journals and has lectured on American literature in 15 countries. His current project is a book on the contemporary short-story cycle.